These Bones Shall Rise Again

A volume in the SUNY series in Chinese Philosophy and Culture

Roger T. Ames, editor

These Bones Shall Rise Again

Selected Writings on Early China

David N. Keightley

Edited and with an Introduction
by
Henry Rosemont Jr.

Dong,
Where books are concerned,
I'm behind in any exchange
we have. Hope you'll enjoy
this — even if Keightley insists
on using W-G!
Ed
October '17

SUNY
PRESS

Cover image courtesy of David N. Keightley

Published by State University of New York Press, Albany

© 2014 State University of New York

For information, address State University of New York Press, Albany, NY
www.sunypress.edu

Production by Diane Ganeles
Marketing by Kate Seburyamo

Library of Congress Cataloging-in-Publication Data

Keightley, David N. and Rosemont, Henry Jr.

These bones shall rise again: selected writings on early china

ISBN 978-1-4384-4747-6 (hardcover : alk. paper)

ISBN 978-1-4384-4746-9 (pbk.: alk. paper)

Library of Congress Control Number: 2014934475

10 9 8 7 6 5 4 3 2 1

CONTENTS

David N. Keightley

ACKNOWLEDGMENTS

My first thanks for assistance in putting this volume of David Keightley's writings together go to David himself, who assisted me in gathering materials for it and for assistance in going through the galley proofs. I am pleased to have brought this collection of his papers together for two reasons, first as a small but not, I hope, insignificant service to the field of Chinese studies, and second as small recompense for the pleasure of having had David as a friend for a third of a century. Amanda Buster, Ph.D. student in history at Berkeley, saw to securing all necessary permissions to reprint the articles included here, and I am grateful for her efforts. Professor Emeritus Ken-ichi Takashima of the University of British Columbia was of major assistance in making and copying fresh images of many of the illustrations in this volume, for which I, electronically challenged to an extreme, am particularly thankful. My greatest debt for helping me with this volume goes to Professor Michael Nylan, cherished friend of mine, David's successor at Berkeley, Amanda's mentor, and Professor Takashima's friend. Her efforts with all three of them on the West Coast, and with me in Newport, Rhode Island, were crucial for getting this book into its present form, completed and published, and she did it all efficiently, with grace and warmth to boot. I am deeply grateful to her, disappointed only by her declining my entreaties to join me formally as co-editor of it. At SUNY Press, I enjoyed working with Nancy Ellegate and Diane Ganeles, both highly efficient, graceful and warm; I am especially indebted to them (and SUNY Press) for accepting this work for publication without my having to redo every one of the papers herein to conform to the stylesheet of the Press. Every editor should be so fortunate to work with such a professional editor and production manager.

Finally, but without which not, I am pleased to acknowledge the original publishers of these articles of David's here listed *seriatim* in the order in which they appear:

Photo of David Keightley by Grant Ward; courtesy of the San Francisco Chronicle, 1986 (on the announcement of his MacArthur award).

"Archaeology and Mentality: The Making of China," *Representations* 18, Spring 1987.

"Early Civilization in China: Reflections on How It Became Chinese," in *Heritage of China*, edited by Paul S. Ropp. Berkeley: University of California Press, 1990.

"What Did Make the Chinese 'Chinese?': Musings of a Would-be Geographical Determinist" first appeared in *Lotus Leaves* 3.2, Summer 2000, and was reprinted in *Education About Asia* 9.2, Fall 2004.

"The Religious Commitment: Shang Theology and the Genesis of Chinese Political Culture." *History of Religions* 17, 1978.

"Late Shang Divination: The Magico-Religious Legacy," in *Explorations in Early Chinese Cosmology*, edited by Henry Rosemont Jr. Chico, CA: Scholars Press, 1984.

"Shang Divination and Metaphysics," *Philosophy East & West*, 38.4, October 1988.

"The Making of the Ancestors: Late Shang Religion and Its Legacy," in *Chinese Religion & Society: The Transformation of a Field*, vol. 1, edited by John Lagerway. Hong Kong: Ecole Francaise d'Extreme-orient and the Chinese University of Hong Kong Press, 2004.

"Theology and the Writing of History: Truth and the Ancestors in the Wu Ding Divination Records," *Journal of East Asian Archaeology* 1.1–4, 1999.

"Marks and Labels: Early Writing in Neolithic and Shang China," in *Archaeology of Asia*, edited by Miriam T. Stark. London: Blackwell, 2006.

"Clean Hands and Shining Helmets: Heroic Action in Early Chinese and Greek Culture," in *Religion and the Authority of the Past*, edited by Tobin Siebers. Ann Arbor: University of Michigan Press, 1993.

"Epistemology in Cultural Context: Disguise and Deception in Early China and Early Greece," in *Early China, Ancient Greece: Thinking Through Comparisons*, edited by Steven Shankman and Stephen Durrant. Albany: State University of New York Press, 2001.

" 'There Was an Old Man of Changan…' Limericks and the Teaching of Early Chinese History," *The History Teacher* 22.3, May 1989.

PREFACE

Professor David N. Keightley was born in London in 1932 and spent the World War II years there, coming to the United States in 1947. A graduate of Amherst College (an English major and biochemistry minor) in 1953, he studied medieval French at the University of Lille in northern France as a Fulbright student and received his M.A. in modern European history at New York University in 1956. After a number of years working as a fiction and nonfiction editor and freelance writer in New York City, he entered Columbia University's graduate school in 1962 and received his Ph.D. in East Asian history in 1969. During that time, he spent two years in Taiwan and Japan in language training and research.

Convinced, when a freelance writer, that China was one of the frontiers of our time, Keightley decided to learn Chinese in order to write about contemporary Chinese society and culture. After three years of study, however, he realized that some of the most fundamental issues that help explain the many differences between Chinese and other societies lay far back in the past. Resisting both the theories of Karl Wittfogel about "oriental despotism" and of Marxism about "slave society," Keightley's Ph.D. dissertation, "Public Work in Ancient China: A Study of Forced Labor in the Shang and Western Chou," attempted to place the mobilization and control of labor in its religious and social context.

A member of the faculty at the University of California at Berkeley from 1969 to 1998, and a specialist in China's earliest historical documents, Professor Keightley was the author of *Sources of Shang History: The Oracle Bone Inscriptions of Bronze Age China* (1978) and *The Ancestral Landscape: Time, Space, and Community in Late Shang China*, ca. 1200–1045 B.C. (2000), and the editor of *The Origins of Chinese Civilization* (1983). One of the founders and editors of the journal, *Early China*, he published over seventy articles dealing with the religion and history of the Chinese Neolithic and Bronze Ages. His work paid particular attention to the cultural significance of early Chinese religion and divination (as seen in the Shang dynasty oracle-bone inscriptions), to the Neolithic roots of China's bronze-age culture, and to comparative studies of "classical" literature and "classical" role-models in bronze-age China and bronze-age Greece.

Keightley authored the articles on Chinese "Prehistory" and "The First Historical Dynasty: The Shang" in *The New Encyclopedia Britannica: Macropaedie* (1987), a chapter, "The Shang: China's First Historical Dynasty," for the *Cambridge History of Ancient China*, edited by Michael Loewe and Edward L. Shaughnessy (1999), and the entry for the "Shang Dynasty" in the *Microsoft Encarta Reference Library* 2002. Given the difficulty of the oracle-bone inscriptions, he also reviewed books—particularly in the *Harvard Journal of Asiatic*

Studies in 1977 and 1982 and the *Journal of the American Oriental Society* in 1900 and 1997—that served as new to the field.

Professor Keightley visited the People's Republic of China seven times and was a visiting scholar at Peking University in the spring of 1981. He helped organize two international conferences with Chinese scholars, one on "Shang Civilization" in 1982, the other on "Ancient China and Social Science Generalizations" in 1986. Professor Keightley received ACLS Fellowships in 1972 and 1975, a Guggenheim Fellowship in 1978, a Wang Fellowship in 1984, and a MacArthur Fellowship in 1986; he was elected to the American Academy of Arts and Sciences in 2000. He has also served on various national committees involved in Chinese academic exchanges and scholarship, including the American Council of Learned Societies and the Committee for Scholarly Communication with the People's Republic of China. He served as Chair of Berkeley's Center for Chinese Studies from 1988 to 1990, as Chair of Berkeley's History Department from 1992 to 1994, and as Interim Director of the East Asian Library from 1999–2000.

Professor Keightley has just published another book, *Working For His Majesty*, a study of public work in the Shang dynasty. It includes extensive notes, a glossary of Shang terms, and a glossary of over 340 oracle-bone inscriptions, placing them in a full political and cultural context.

INTRODUCTION

Although the field of sinological studies in the West might well be said to have begun very shortly after the Jesuit Father Matteo Ricci settled in China in 1583 to begin the conversion of the Chinese[1]—remaining there until his death twenty-seven years later—it was over 300 years before anyone in Europe or the United States began to learn anything of substance about the Shang (Yin) Dynasty of ancient China, or even that such a dynasty had actually existed outside of myth and legend. A few articles were published in French at the turn of the 19th Century, and the first work in English came out only in 1917, when James M. Menzies published his *Oracle Records from the Waste of Yin*.[2]

The next significant work dealing with the Shang—whose traditional dates were 1766–1122 or 1056 BCE—accessible to the intelligent layperson was H. G. Creel's *The Birth of China*,[3] published in 1936. Based on his own research, and extensively employing contemporary Chinese sources, Creel put together pictures of the life, times, and artifacts of the Shang that were emerging from the great burst of archaeological activity that was going on in China, now made more sophisticated by the introduction of modern scientific archaeological methods, introduced in part by Menzies. This archaeological activity was so extensive and intensive that Creel noted in the Preface to his book[4] (which he wrote in 1935) that:

> The discoveries of the last year have been so revolutionary, and have made necessary such a complete re-orientation of our conception of Shang culture, that all previous publications in Western languages, including my own, are rendered more or less obsolete.

But then the activity stopped. The full-scale invasion of China by Japan in 1937 halted all archaeological efforts, not to be significantly resumed until the 1950s, after Liberation and the early years of reconstruction in China. The work proceeded apace, but publication of results was slow to appear, all in Chinese, and not easily accessible even to scholars in the West as China had pretty well closed itself off from (and was closed off by) the outside world for several decades.

Thus much about the Shang Dynasty and its people were still a mystery when David Keightley began his Ph.D. studies, and a great deal of what we have come to know of them is due to his efforts. Before World War II and the Anti-Japanese War, many, perhaps most Western scholars of Chinese history believed the Shang Dynasty to be basically mythological, even though the Chinese sources attributed to it a lengthy reign time, and to an even an earlier, more shadowy dynasty, the Xia (2205–1766 BCE), supposedly founded by the Sage-king Yu, associated with

China's flood myth. Even after early archaeological work confirmed the Chinese sources, Western scholarly skepticism lessened only slowly largely because of the difficulties of extrapolating from the material unearthed to a description of what the Shang Dynasty might have been like.

Combining a keen interest and appreciation for anthropology as well as archaeology with his original work as a historian deciphering oracle bone inscriptions, Keightley has provided many such descriptions of Shang life, and he has asked and answered scholarly questions in his field(s) that have ramifications far beyond the Shang, in part due to the specific scholarly approach he has always taken to his studies.

That approach has not been uncontroversial to some. First, while always closely attentive to his sources, Keightley has written relatively few articles that have not contained more speculation than some other historians (and many archaeologists) would deem proper. Such speculations are sprinkled liberally throughout the essays in the present book. For example, Keightley believes we may make intelligent generalizations about Chinese civilization as a civilization, whereas a number of his peers today believe that China has always been sufficiently pluralistic and changing as to preclude there being any "Chineseness" for anyone to write about. But as the 2nd and 3rd articles in this volume show clearly, Keightley believes there are a number of things to be said on this score, chief among them being that many of the distinctive features of Chinese civilization were already in evidence in the Shang Dynasty, 3200 years ago, or even before.

This claim is in many respects astonishing. In the first place, unlike the agricultural patterns of later China that employed large-scale systems of irrigation, Shang agriculture—what there was of it—was rainfall dependent, hence with social patterns that should have differed from those of the later Chinese. Second, the Shang were masters of working with bronze, but the iron age began later, in the mid-Zhou, again generating many changes, not least in warfare. The sheer size of China after the Qin dwarfs the area of Shang domination, another seeming difference of consequence. Yet David Keightley has argued long and rigorously that the continuities are there to be seen, and are deserving of our attention and reflection today.

Another speculative aspect of his approach to his subject matter is Keightley's consistent efforts to recapture the thoughts of those many miles and centuries distant from him. Although our academic disciplines are different, and the historical period of his focus (ca. 13th–10th centuries BCE) ends where mine begins, I have personally learned a great deal that is of professional as well as general value from this dimension of Keightley's approach to his materials, just as I am similarly indebted to another distinguished scholar and friend, Nathan Sivin, for the same reason: on the basis of very close examinations of their materials, both of them were willing to interrogate those materials yet again to speculate about the mental activities of the people responsible for their manufacture. Thus, as a philosopher I have cited one or both of them in well over twenty of my own published papers,[5] in part because they both asked pretty much the same fundamental question in conducting their research, a question which, in my opinion, was and is of philosophical no less than historical importance, and significantly responsible for the originality and illuminating nature of their historical work. Sivin framed it as ". . . a large question I find boundlessly interesting: How did Chinese scientists in traditional times explain to themselves what they were doing?"[6] Similarly for David Keightley: "The simple question 'What did the Shang diviner think he was doing?' is well worth asking."[7]

To appreciate the importance of asking this question we may turn to the oracle bones, the area in which Keightley has perhaps done his most detailed work. These bones—cattle scapula and tortoise plastrons—were supposedly fortune-telling devices: A query was written on the bone, it was heated until it cracked, and the diviner interpreted the pattern of the crack to obtain an "answer" to the question asked.

But Keightley has shown clearly and repeatedly that much more was going on, both with respect to what was actually written on the bones, and what the function(s) of the divination ritual were. A typical one might read something like the following: "Crack-making on Day X by Diviner Y: 'It will rain tomorrow.'" Then, usually parallel to this line would be another: 'Perhaps it will not rain.' Elsewhere, and later, it would be written that it did (or did not) actually rain the next day. Moreover, the cracks made in the bones were not very different from each other: a vertical line 1–2 inches in length, with a horizontal (more or less) line roughly half that length on one side. When it is now kept in mind that the "writing" on the bones were actually and literally incisions thereon, we must wonder why such lengths were taken to prognosticate the weather, why the oracle was given both options as possible answer, why the results were recorded, and how the cracks were interpreted. (The front cover of this volume is an example).

Thanks to his curiosity about what the Shang diviners thought they were doing, Keightley has provided answers to these and related questions about not only the bones themselves, but about court life and thought during the later Shang as well; although there is much yet to learn about it, the dynasty is no longer merely in the shadows of Chinese history.

The penetrating answers both Keightley and Sivin have given to their methodological question (and of course to many others) have been transformative for their respective fields, but they do much more than that, for they illuminate a Chinese world distant from us in both time and space that simultaneously illuminates *our* present as well; the contrasts they have drawn both implicitly and explicitly between "them" and "us" show clearly that the course of development of modern Western civilization in science, the arts, government, religion, philosophy and much else was not—is not—the only viable or inevitable road that could have been taken. In the same way, when Keightley asks "What makes China Chinese?"[8] he obliges us to raise the closely related question of ourselves: "What makes us 'us'?"

The potentially far-reaching implications of his work, however, and his commitment to measured speculations, should not lead anyone to think that Keightley (or Sivin) have not stayed *very* close to their source materials before extrapolating to matters less directly empirical and more general. As already noted, many contemporary archaeologists, as Keightley well knows,[9] are loath to speculate about the mental and/or psychological states of the manufacturers of the artifacts they have unearthed. Thus, while he has examined, analyzed and evaluated many archaeological materials ranging from ornamental jade artifacts to bronze ritual drinking vessels, he remains an historian and not an archaeologist, shown clearly in the bulk of his work, which is devoted significantly to the divination charges recorded on the "oracle bones" of the later Shang Dynasty of the 12th and 11th centuries BCE—the earliest form of Chinese writing extant.

It is, moreover, at all times a careful historian we see at work. An attentiveness to detail has always been a characteristic of Keightley's work, for as he remarked in the Preface to his *Sources of Shang History*,[10]

> … [T]he line between a study of historical sources and the writing of history using those sources is exceedingly fine, especially in the field of ancient history where the comparative paucity of documents gives great significance to each one. We can never fully understand Shang history or any other as it really was, but we must, as a first step in our study of the Shang, understand the documents as they really are.

The same might be said for the study of unearthed artifacts as well. What readers of this book will find singular, however, is the extent to which Keightley is able to attend to both the documents and the artifacts with great care and attentiveness to minute detail, and yet be able to make consistently original and illuminating speculations about the producers of them. He is certainly correct to insist that we can never fully understand Shang (or any other) history as it "really was," but he has provided numerous intelligent hints about what that history may have been like in his writings, some of which are gathered together in this volume.

The selection of papers for inclusion herein were based on several criteria, first among them being originality and contributory to Keightley's stature in the profession (and undoubtedly responsible in part for his having been awarded a MacArthur "genius" 5-year fellowship in 1986). Equally important was accessibility of the papers to the interested non-specialist.[11] And the selection process also included consideration of the disparate venues in which Keightley's papers first appeared. I have little doubt that some other scholars of early China might have made different choices, especially with respect to the exclusion of the more technical pieces; which could, of course, be gathered together and published as another, more specialized volume of his writings, a project I commend to any of David's colleagues more competent then myself in the Shang materials. In any event, a complete Bibliography of all of his writings is appended at the end of the present volume.

The twelve papers thus selected have been grouped in four areas, to each of which the author has made signal contributions. In the first, we read David Keightley addressing the general question of what made the Chinese Chinese in three papers published over a period of seventeen years. In the first, "Archaeology and Mentality: The Making of China," he closely examines tools, ritual and other artifacts from two distinct areas of Neolithic North China, and by comparing and contrasting them, speculates on the mental life of their manufacturers. The word "Making" in the title signals Keightley's stance toward his subject matter. With reference to this first article, (and the seventh and ninth), he wrote to me:[12]

> It was an attempt to demonstrate how ceramic and jade technologies of the East Coast Neolithic, which involved model-use, an "airborne" esthetic, componential construction, mensuration, and constrained usage, contributed to the rise of Shang culture. This relates to my conception of culture as the product of particular choices. I was not so interested in "The Birth of China" or "The Cradle of the East," but in the "Making"—as, e.g., in many other papers of mine as well, including "The Making of the Ancestors: Late Shang Religion and Its Legacy," and "Marks and Labels: Early Writing in Neolithic and Shang China."

"Early Civilization in China: Reflections on How it Became Chinese" was written for a general audience, and in this paper Keightley develops his ideas more fully, adding to them his considerations of a related but very different theme, namely, how the later Chinese themselves came to see how they became who they were. The third essay in this section was written especially for scholar/teachers at all levels who teach things Chinese. In "What Did Make the Chinese 'Chinese'?" Keightley addresses a number of issues in brief compass, from environmental influences to the great significance the Chinese attached to filial piety and ancestor veneration, unique among ancient cultures (and modern ones as well).

The second section of the book is the most philosophically oriented of them, dealing with issues of what *we* would be inclined to classify as metaphysics, religion, and theology. What the four papers in this section suggest, however, is that these categories are indeed ours, and that almost certainly the conceptual world of the early Chinese was not demarcated in this way. Readers will learn much in these essays on how religion and politics cannot be easily distinguished in Shang China, nor the deceased ancestors from deities, nor magic from cosmology; many other distinctions we are inclined to draw are similarly absent in these accounts of Shang "metaphysics." To say this is not at all to belittle the Shang, or later Chinese for that matter—the classical philosophers like Confucius did not use our Western philosophical categories either—but rather to draw our attention to the fact that the world can be made sense of intellectually by slicing it in ways other than the one(s) we now employ in the modern West,[13] which Keightley does with great skill in all four essays, published between 1978 and 2004.

With the third section the book the focus shifts specifically to the early forms of Chinese writing as found in the oracle bone inscriptions. In "Theology and the Writing of History: Truth and The Ancestors in the Wu Ding Divination Records," Keightley shows how the records of divinatory activities by and for the Shang king Wu Ding provide much evidence not only for establishing continuities between early and later forms of Chinese writing, they equally tell the careful reader of them much about Shang "cosmology" (again, as we would call it), the role of the king's ancestors in religious matters, early Chinese efforts at record-keeping, and much more. In the second article, "Marks and Labels:

Early Writing in Neolithic and Shang China," Keightley proffers his considered opinions (the article was published in 2006) on patterns of symbols found on very early pots and other artifacts, the use and function of the oracle bone inscriptions, their relation to more perishable written records and to the symbols which preceded them, the relation of the oracle bone inscriptions to later writing patterns, and the significance of the growth of literacy as it was tied to power and authority. Again, we see him focusing on the "making" of Chinese culture.

The two papers in the fourth section of this volume are explicitly and altogether comparative in nature between early China and ancient Greece. In the first, "Clean Hands and Shining Helmets," Keightley compares and contrasts (more the latter) the idea of the hero as found in the *Iliad* and *Odyssey* of Homer, and Hesiod's *Theogony*, with the Chinese hero as depicted in three of the early Classics: the books of *Documents* (or *History*), the *Odes* (or *Poetry*) and a commentary on another written document of early Chinese history, the *Zuozhuan*. He also considers the significance of these portrayals for Greek and Chinese art and other literature, and society more generally. I firmly believe that after going through this and the following article, "Epistemology in Cultural Context: Disguise and Deception in Early China and Early Greece," Western readers will see the heritage of the ancient Greeks in a very different light, both on its own terms, and for the influence of that heritage for modern Western civilization. In the best Chinese tradition of scholarship, in these two articles David Keightley is being didactic no less than academic, for as he concludes the first of these pieces,[14]

> ... [I]f Westerners would more fully understand themselves, understand the authority of their own past and how its religious conceptions have shaped their views of the individual protagonist and his responsibilities, an understanding of China and its cultural imperatives provides a valuable perspective.

One brief piece that is no less characteristic of how David Keightley thinks than the eleven articles just sketched did not fit into any of the four categories of the book, but seemed obligatory to include nevertheless: "'There Was an Old Man of Chang'an...': Limericks and the Teaching of Chinese History." It is embarrassing to admit that I didn't know of this little piece much earlier, else I certainly would have used Keightley's method in my courses, as I suspect readers who are also teachers will do after reading it themselves. And I know of no other of his papers that displays his wry sense of humor so well, the better to appreciate him as the wide-ranging intellect he has always been to everyone who knows him.

Two closing technical notes to the reader.

1. The twelve essays that follow span a period of almost three decades, over the course of which the *pinyin* form of transliterating Chinese terms employed in the Peoples' Republic has become standard in virtually all Western scholarly writing, slowly replacing the older Wade-Giles system common throughout the first half of the 20th Century. David Keightley made the transition once for all in the early 1990s, and consequently the reader will find both systems of transliteration in these essays, depending on when he published them. To reduce confusion a brief transcription conversion table immediately follows this Introduction.

2. Because these essays appeared in a wide variety of original venues, the reader will find some small differences between them in the method of citation of sources. In no cases, however, is the source of the citation unclear, hence there did not seem to be a genuine need, given the expenditure of time and money involved, to undertake their standardization.

References

1. See, for example, *The Memory Palace of Matteo Ricci,* by Jonathan Spence. Yale Univ. Press, 1986.
2. London: Kelly and Walsh.
3. London: Jonathan Cape.
4. Ibid., p. 13.
5. In Keightley's case, beginning in 1974 before he had published any of his major findings, I cited two of his mimeographed papers in my "On Representing Abstractions in Archaic Chinese," in *Philosophy East & West,* vol. 24, no. 1. For Sivin in this context, see my "Nathan Sivin: A Man for All Seasons," which was the introductory essay in the *Festschrift* for him which appeared as a special issue of *Asia Major,* Third Series, vol. XXI, Part I, 2008.
6. "Why the Scientific Revolution Did Not Take Place in China – Or Didn't It?" in Li Guihao, Zhang Mengwen, and Cao Tianqin, eds., *Explorations in the History of Science and Technology in China.* Shanghai Chinese Classics Pub. House, 1982, p. 91.
7. See also the "Preamble" to his *Sources of Shang History.* It should be noted that in answering this question as he does, Keightley challenges and significantly undermines another answer given by Karl Wittfogel, who characterized China (as well as ancient Egypt and the Indus Valley civilization of early India) as a "hydraulic society." Wittfogel, an ex-communist turned arch-conservative, claimed to answer the question raised by the references in the writings of Karl Marx to "The Asiatic mode of production," an ostensible set of important counterexamples to the thesis, central to dialectical materialism, that those who had power in society owned the means of production, whereas in China (India, Egypt) they did not. Wittfogel said the power stemmed from the state monopoly on water control, necessary for the irrigation of crops in areas of inadequate rainfall. Wittfogel's arguments are found in his major work, the

title of which well described his answer to the question of Chinese distinctiveness: *Oriental Despotism* (Yale University Press, 1963). Keightley's work has been a major contribution to the scholarship that has put paid to Wittfogel's account.

8. A consistent theme in a numbers of the essays in this volume.

9. See, for example, "Archaeology and Mentality" below, p. 2.

10. Berkeley: University of California Press, 1978, p. xiii.

11. Even so, there are over 400 notes to the selected papers collectively.

12. Personal communication.

13. This is a major theme of an anthology I edited, in which Keightley's "Late Shang Divination" first appeared: *Explorations in Early Chinese Cosmology*. Chico, CA: Scholars Press, 1984.

14. See below, p. 276.

TRANSCRIPTION CONVERSION TABLE

Pinyin	Wade-Giles
b	p
c	ts', tz'
ch	ch'
d	t
g	k
ian	ien
j	ch
k	k'
ong	ung
p	p'
q	ch
r	j
si	ssu, szu
t	t'
x	hs
yi	i
yu	u, yu
you	yu
z	ts, tz
zh	ch
-i (zhi)	-ih (chih)
-ie (lie)	-ieh (lieh)
zi	tzu

1

ARCHAEOLOGY AND MENTALITY: THE MAKING OF CHINA (1987)

DAVID N. KEIGHTLEY

The great problem for a science of man is how to get from the objective world of materiality, with its infinite variability, to the subjective world of form as it exists in what, for lack of a better term, we must call the minds of our fellow men.

—Ward H. Goodenough[1]

COMPARATIVE STUDY of the differing ways in which major civilizations made the transition from the Neolithic to the Bronze Age has, in recent times, generally emphasized such common factors as developing social stratification, emergence of complementary hierarchies in the political and religious spheres, and complex division of labor.[2] In China, the transition from a kin-based, Neolithic society to an Early State, Bronze Age civilization—represented by the Late Shang cult center (ca. 1200–1045 B.C.E.) at Yinxu in northern Henan (see fig. 1)—may be characterized in such universal terms. Increasing sophistication in tool production in particular, and in lithic, ceramic, and construction technology in general, may be associated with increasingly sharp distinctions in economic and social status, concentration of wealth, declining status of women, development of human sacrifice, and the religious validation of exploitation and dependency. By the Late Shang an elite minority of administrators, warriors, and religious figures was controlling, and benefiting from, the labors of the rest of the population.[3]

Such analyses show us how Chinese civilization followed certain general patterns of social development, how the early Chinese were the same as other peoples. But if we are to understand more deeply the development of the Shang, and of the classical Chinese civilization that followed, we also need to consider the features that made the Shang different.

The features which characterize early Chinese civilization include millet and rice agriculture, piece-mold bronze casting, jade working, centralized, proto-bureaucratic control of large-scale labor resources, the strategic role of divination, a logographic writing system, a highly developed mortuary cult, and the development of social values, such as *xiao* (filiality), and of institutions, such as ancestor worship and the custom of accompanying-in-death, that stressed the hierarchical dependency of young on old, female on male, ruled upon ruler. The complex

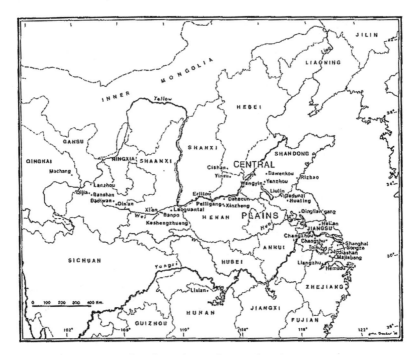

Figure 1 The major archaeological sites discussed in this essay.

manner in which these elements coalesced, fed upon, and encouraged one another lies at the heart of our understanding of Shang civilization.

All these and, no doubt, other features of early Chinese culture need to be studied comparatively and explained, that is, related genetically and structurally, to the other features of the natural and man-made environment if we are to understand what made China Chinese. The more modest intent of this article, however, is not to address such comparative questions directly but to suggest new ways of approaching the Chinese archaeological evidence as a preliminary to such comparative analysis.[4] In what follows, I shall limit myself to the pre-Shang evidence, attempting to identify the particular features that reveal prehistoric habits of thought and behavior that were to play, I believe, a strategic role in the genesis of Shang culture.

I am aware that I occupy disputed ground in attempting to link artifacts to mentality. "New" archaeologists have declined to explain the past in mental terms, on the grounds that neither the thoughts nor the activities of individual actors are available to us.[5] My own position is more traditional, in that I wish, so far as possible, to ask historical and cultural questions of the material data, directed to particular events and the meaning they had for their participants. This places me among the ranks of the cognitive anthropologists, as indicated, for example, by the epigraph at the head of this essay. As Ian Hodder has written:

> All daily activities, from eating to the removal of refuse, are not the result of some absolute adaptive expedience. These various functions take place within a cultural framework, a set of ideas or norms, and we cannot adequately understand the various activities by denying any role to culture....
>
> Behind functioning and doing there is a structure and content which has partly to be understood in its own terms, with its own logic and coherence.[6]

I believe that material culture expresses and also influences, often in complicated, idealized, and by no means exact ways, social activity and ways of thinking, and that the goal of archaeology must be *comprendre* as well as *connaître*. I do not use the word *ideas* in what follows, but I do attempt to infer, from pots and other artifacts, some of the structure and content of the mental activities that underlay the behavior of China's Neolithic inhabitants. Readers must judge for themselves whether the risks taken in this exploratory essay are worth the insights gained.

The essence of my argument is twofold. First, I assume that the way people act influences the way people think and that habits of thought manifested in one area of life encourage similar mental approaches in others. I assume in particular that there is a relationship between the technology of a culture and its conception of the world and of man himself, that "artefacts are products of human categorization processes,"[7] and that style and social process are linked.[8] It is this assumed linkage that encourages me to think in terms of mentality, whose manifestations may be seen in various kinds of systematic activity. If it is true that "the philosophies of Plato and Aristotle [strongly] bear the imprint of the crafts of weaving and pottery, the imposition of form on matter, which flourished in ancient Greece,"[9] and if pottery manufacture, in particular, can, in other cultures, be found to reflect social structure and cultural expectations,[10] then we are justified in attempting to discern similar connections in the crafts of prehistoric China. Artifacts provide clues, incomplete and distorted by material constraints though they must be,[11] to both the social structure and the mentality of those who made and appreciated them. To quote Hodder again, "the artefact is an active force in social change. The daily use of material items within different contexts recreates from moment to moment the framework of meaning within which people act."[12]

Second, I assume that one of the essential features that distinguished Bronze Age from Neolithic mentality, in China as elsewhere, was the ability to differentiate customs that had hitherto been relatively undifferentiated, to articulate distinct values and institutional arrangements, to consciously manipulate both artifacts and human beings. This is not to claim that prehistoric man did not make distinctions or that he was not conscious of what he was doing. The difference is one of degree. In the prehistoric evidence, accordingly, I shall be looking for signs of enhanced differentiation, for signs of increasing order in both the material and mental realms, for signs of what Marcel Mauss called the "domination of the conscious over emotion and unconsciousness."[13]

Two Cultural Complexes

With regard to the purposes of this paper, I believe that we can make considerable sense of the Chinese Neolithic without having to reconstruct, prematurely, the entire picture of its cultural development, desirable though the attainment of such a goal eventually will be. If we are not yet able to map the development of every Chinese cultural trait with assurance, and if, in particular, we are not yet able to determine whether similarity of traits in various Chinese sites and regions is *homologous*, implying genetic connection, or merely *analogous*, implying independent invention but convergent development, I nevertheless hope that this paper will demonstrate the importance of mapping certain, strategic traits by both space and time.

Even though it is important to think, both first and last, in terms of a mosaic of Neolithic cultures whose edges blur and overlap (see fig. 1),[14] I believe that, for analytical purposes, one can—with all due allowance being taken for the crudity of the generalizations involved—still conceive of the Chinese Neolithic in terms of at least two major cultural complexes: that of Northwest China and the western part of the Central Plains, on the one hand, and that of the East Coast and the eastern part of the Central Plains, on the other.[15] I shall, for simplicity, refer to these two complexes, which should be regarded as ideal types, as those of the Northwest and the East Coast (or, more simply, East). There were numerous regional cultures within these two complexes. In the sixth and fifth millennia, for example, cultures like Laoguantai, Dadiwan, and Banpo flourished in the Northwest; cultures like Hemudu, Qinglian'gang, and Majiabang arose in the area of the East Coast. The interaction between the two larger complexes is of great significance. By the fourth and third millennia, one sees East Coast traits beginning to intrude in both North China and the Northwest, so that the true Northwest tradition reaches its fruition during the third millennium in Gansu and Qinghai while fading away in the region of the Central Plains and even in the Wei River valley.[16] As we shall see, the emergence of Shang culture in the Central Plains (ca. 2000 B.C.E.) owes much, though not all, to this infusion of elements from the East.

With assumptions and terminology thus established, I should now like to turn to the two central questions of this essay: what did the peoples of prehistoric China do? And what significant cultural conclusions can we draw from their activities?

Pottery Manufacture

Broadly considered, the essential characteristics of the East Coast ceramic tradition (figs. 2–13) include the following features: 1) pots were unpainted; 2) angular, segmented, carinated profiles were common; 3) pots were frequently constructed componentially; and 4) pots were frequently elevated in some way.[17] The ceramic tradition of the Northwest (figs. 14–15), by contrast, was characterized by a more limited repertoire of jars, amphoras, and round-bottomed

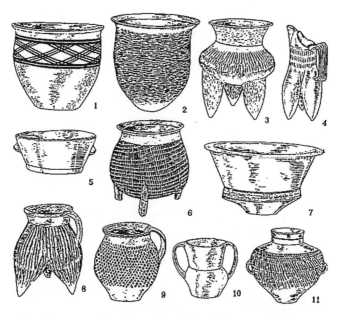

Figure 2 East Coast pots, Longshan. Reproduced from Feng Xianming, et al., *Zhong-guo laoci shi* (A history of Chinese ceramics; Beijing, 1982), 15.

bowls and basins, only a certain proportion of which were painted.[18] What can these two ceramic traditions tell us about the mentality of, as well as the material constraints imposed upon, the potters who made the vessels and the people who used them?

From the viewpoint of manufacture, the tectonic formality of sharp, angular silhouettes and the absence of rapidly painted surface decoration in the East (figs. 2–13) suggest deliberation and control, a taking of time to plan the shapes, to measure the parts, and to join them together. The interest in silhouette, frequently articulated or "unnaturally" straight-edged, rather than in surface decor, further suggests a willingness to do more than simply accept the natural, rounded contours of a pot.[19] It suggests a willingness to impose design rather than merely accept it as given by the natural qualities of the clay. It suggests, as we shall see, that Eastern pots, by contrast with the "all-purpose" pots of the Northwest, were designed with specific functions in mind.

The existence of an East Coast disposition to manipulate and constrain is confirmed by a closer look at pot construction. Unlike the more practically shaped Northwest pots, most of which would have been built up *holistically* by coiling and shaping at one time, many of the characteristic East Coast pots— like the tall-stemmed *bei* drinking goblets (fig. 3, no. 6; fig. 6, nos. 1–6; fig. 10, nos. 12, 16, 17; figs. 11–13), the *ding* cauldrons (usually tripods; fig. 2, no. 6; fig. 4, nos. 1, 2; fig. 5, no. 2; fig. 6, nos. 10–20; figs. 8–9; fig. 10, no. 6), the *dou*

Figures 3–5 East Coast pots. *Top*: Dawenkou; *center*: Longshan; *bottom*: Majiabang. From ibid., 21, 22, 28.

offering stands (fig. 3, no. 1; fig. 5, no. 1; fig. 7, no. 4; fig. 10, nos. 3–5), and the hollow-legged *gui* pouring jugs (fig. 3, no. 7; fig. 4, no. 3; fig. 7, nos. 8–19; fig. 13) and *xian* steamers (fig. 6, nos. 7–9)—would have required the separate molding and piecing together of several elements—feet, stand, legs, spout, neck, handle, and so on, in a *prescriptive* method of manufacture. This distinction between holistic and prescriptive is of fundamental importance to my attempt to link artifacts to mentality.[20]

The prescriptive, and thus componential, construction of pots[21]—which was inevitably involved whenever feet were prefabricated and added on to a vessel such as a *ding* cauldron, or whenever vessels were built up sectionally—appears to have developed as a significant method of manufacture in the Yangzi delta around the year 4000 B.C.E. In the fourth and third millennia, componential construction was frequently used in the Daxi and Liangzhu cultures of the Middle and Lower Yangzi and also in the Dawenkou culture area of Shandong and northern Anhui. It was present in the Late Neolithic Middle Yangzi culture of the third millennium, where, although the potter's wheel was in use, most pots were still handmade, and where large ones were frequently built up by coiling, being produced in sections with appliqué bands being added where the parts were joined.[22] It was also present, of course, in the Central Plains and Northwest as East Coast pot forms became more prevalent (see note 16).

A simple but elegant tripod from Songze (ca. 4000 B.C.E.) illustrates the nature of East Coast componential construction (fig. 8): 1) the bottom was shaped first; 2) the sides were then built up on a slow wheel; 3) the rim was luted on; 4) legs were fabricated separately and 5) appended to the body. It should

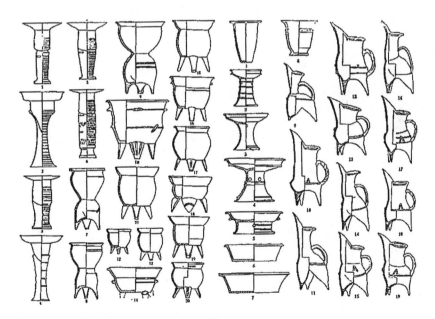

Figures 6 and 7 East Coast pots from Shizihang. *Left*: Longshan; *right*: Dawenkou, Longshan. From "Shandong Wei xian Shizihang yizhi fajue jianbao" (Preliminary report of the excavation of the Shizihang site in Wei xian, Shandong), *KG* 1984, no. 8:678–79, figs. 7–8.

be noted that whenever tripod legs or ring feet, which were both characteristic Eastern features, were added to a bowl, the body of the vessel would presumably have been turned upside down at that stage of manufacture. Such inversion would have involved what may be seen as more deliberate manipulation than the potters of the Chinese Northwest, who generally made legless vessels, would have had to employ.[23] The procedure may be seen as more artificial, as well as more deliberate, because it reversed the orientation of normal use.

A certain amount of componential building certainly was used by the Northwest potters. The rims of at least some *ping* amphoras and *guan* jars at Banpo (fig. 15, no. 7), for example, were added on.[24] The flaring, wide-girthed Banshan pots were made by constructing the bottom and top of the pot separately by ring coiling and then luting the two parts together.[25] Painted pottery vessels with tall or collared necks would also have been made in two or three pieces. The rare three-footed *bo* bowls from Dadiwan I would have had their legs pieced on.[26] Similarly, the Northwest potters were certainly capable of making "impractical" shapes that were componentially constructed.[27] But such forms were not common in the Northwest. As with most studies of the Chinese Neolithic, comprehensive statistics would greatly increase the reliability of conclusions that are frequently subjective in nature. But there is little doubt, in this case, that tripods and other legged vessels, vessels constructed by section, ring feet, handles, spouts, fitted lids—all the elements that require prescriptive, componential construction—were far more prevalent in, much more characteristic of, far more valued by the cultures of the East Coast.

The point, in any event, is not merely one of numbers but of style. In the Northwest, such joinings were generally not integral to the design and visual impact of the pot; potters sought to conceal such joins so as to produce soft-cornered, harmonious, unified, globular shapes. The potters of the East, by contrast, tended to accentuate, to emphasize the discontinuities of silhouette and shape, so that their pots explicitly revealed the process by which they were made. The intentional "failure" of the slab legs to completely join with the body of the *ding* tripod (fig. 10, no. 2) found in a Huating burial at Dadunzi, for example, explicitly reveals the componential nature of its construction. The same aesthetic disjointure is found on Songze tripods where the shape, decor, and surface texture of the legs is at deliberate variance with that of the vessel body (fie 9, nos. 4, 8, 9, 10).[28]

It was not hard, in short, to discover, as the Northwest potters had also done from an early stage, the technique of sticking one pot part to another. But the practice became significant when it was emphasized, when it became integral, as in the cultures of the East, to the design and manufacture of major vessel types, and when it permitted the consistent and prevalent construction of vessel forms and shapes, such as the *ding, dou*, and *gui*, which the mere coiling or throwing of pots could not produce. The Northwest potters used the technique to continue making essentially holistic forms; the East Coast potters used it to make radically different, prescriptive ones that both required and emphasized the joining together of parts made separately but for each other.

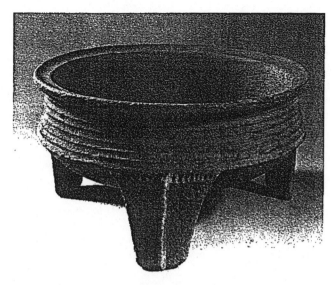

Figure 8 East Coast *ding* tripod from Songze. From René-Yvon Lefebvre d'Argence, ed., *Treasures from the Shanghai Museum: 6,000 Years of Chinese Art* (Shanghai and San Francisco, 1983), no. 3; reprinted by permission.

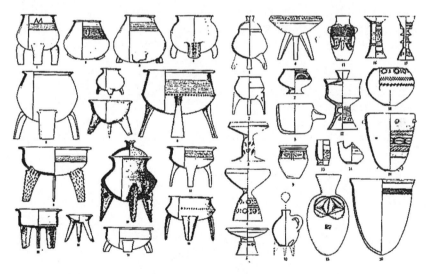

Figure 9 (*left*). East Coast *ding* tripod from Songze. From "Shanghai shi Qingpu xian Songze yizhi di shijue" (Trial dig at the site of Songze in Qingpu xian, Shanghai city), *KX* 1962, no. 2: 13, figs. 10.4, 10.8–10.

Figure 10 (*right*). East Coast pots from Dadunzi (Huating style). From "Jiangsu Pi xian Dadunzi yizhi dierci fajue" (The second excavation at the site of Dadunzi in Pi xian, Jiangsu), *Kaoguxue jikan* 1 (1984): 44, fig. 19.2.

Componential construction, furthermore, suggests the need for temporal coordination and scheduling in manufacture, for it requires that the bowl, legs, spouts, necks, handles, and so on be of the right, leathery consistency at the time they are joined together. The making of prescriptive, componential pots is, therefore, by its nature more rigorously scheduled than the making of holistic ones; it requires greater coordination on the part of the craftsman.[29] As the activities being coordinated become more complex, coordination is likely to have assumed increasing qualities of control. Such control in the Neolithic, to the extent that it existed at all, would probably have been personal and ad hoc, but it would have contained the seeds of the later "technical" and "bureaucratic" forms of control required by the prescriptive piece-mold bronze casting of the Shang.[30]

One may note two final consequences of such construction techniques. First, Ursula Franklin has proposed that, in the sequential stages of prescriptive construction, "a considerable degree of abstraction and a thorough technical understanding is required to perceive a division of the process into unit processes dictated by the technical requirements of construction."[31] Prescriptive construction, in short, implies the ability to think more abstractly than does holistic construction. Second, the prescriptive nature of componential construction implies not only the allocation of time, and the planning and measurement of the component elements (see below), but it also implies talking. To the extent that certain potters might have specialized in the making of spouts, handles, legs, and so on (see note 29), the greater coordination of activities required to make a componential, prescriptive, East Coast pot implies more verbal communication, more articulation about final goals and immediate methods, than would have been required for the construction of a pot that could be coiled at one time and by one person, working in comparative independence, isolation, and silence about the task at hand. One cannot easily tell from the archaeological evidence if such Neolithic specialists did exist; it seems unlikely, however, that the tall, thin-walled, black ware of the classical Longshan (the four *bei* in fig. 11), for example, could have been turned on a fast wheel, constructed, and fired by amateurs (see too note 43 below). The East Coast articulation of pot components, in any event, admits the possibility of verbal as well as technical articulation. The greater variety of vessel types in the East further implies the existence of a larger vocabulary of vessel names.

Model Emulation

Still more is implied when we move from the solid-legged vessels to the hollow-legged ones like the mammiform *gui* tripod jug (fig. 3, no. 7; fig. 4, no. 3; fig. 7, nos. 9–19), the *xian* steamer (fig. 6, nos. 7–9), and the *li* tripod (fig. 2, no. 8), all associated in their origin or development with either the cultures of the East or the Central Plains. These vessels imply more than the technical skill to standardize lengths and shapes, to successfully coordinate the separate elements. To produce such bulbous-legged vessels, identity of leg size and shape was essential; it required, in some cases, the use of a central core about which the three legs could be individually molded.[32] This is of significance technically, since it is from such procedures and conceptions that the piece-mold casting of the Shang bronze makers, who used a central core model and outer ceramic molds, developed.[33] But it is also of significance socially and conceptually, since it implies a vision of creation as one of molding, of conformation to a model, of standardization—of "engineering" in short. It is no surprise that the emulation of moral exemplars was to play such a central role in later Chinese social and political thinking.[34]

Analogous conceptions lie behind the technique of rammed-earth construction, associated with the Late Neolithic cultures of Shandong and northern Henan, in which moist earth was rammed hard between the molding boards.[35] The same inspiration may also be related to the East Coast customs of skull deformation and tooth extraction—further instances of "engineering," now applied directly to the human body.[36] It is plausible to think that such techniques for molding and modeling, whether applied to the human body, to clay, or to earth, must, by analogy, have reinforced, and been reinforced by, social and religious conceptions of discipline, order, and obedience to prescribed pattern.

Upward and Onward

Elevation—through the use of ring feet, legs, and stands of various sorts—was another characteristic feature of the East Coast pots, the elevation frequently being emphasized through the aspiring, upward-reaching shapes of the vessels themselves (e.g., fig. 2, nos. 3, 4; fig. 3, nos. 1, 6, 7; fig. 4, no. 3; fig. 6, nos. 1–6; fig. 7, nos. 9–19; fig. 9, nos. 8, 9; fig. 10, no. 6; figs. 11–13). The "legginess" and lightness of many of the East Coast *bei, dou, ding,* and *gui* lends them a certain perky, rapid, birdlike quality. The judgment is subjective, but the bird motifs carved on certain Eastern jades and bone implements, together with later legends of bird ministers and bird tribes in the region,[37] encourage us to view the cultures of the East as more "airborne" than those of the Northwest, whose more earthbound disposition can be discerned in their "semi-subterranean" pots (see below) and houses, and even in the construction of the querns used for grinding grain. At Banpo sites in the Wei River valley, for example, the querns were not footed and were presumably set directly on the ground;[38] in Peiligang sites in the Central Plains, by contrast, they were uniformly provided with four feet.[39] These querns from the sixth millennium, incidentally, may be some of the oldest four-footed objects in China. Since the legs were carved out of the grinding stone, the querns would have taken considerable effort to manufacture. The preference for feet, and generally for four feet rather than three (which were rarely found),[40] implies that, in the Central Plains, the users of these grinding stones had a level surface on which to place them, an implication that may also be drawn from the precarious,

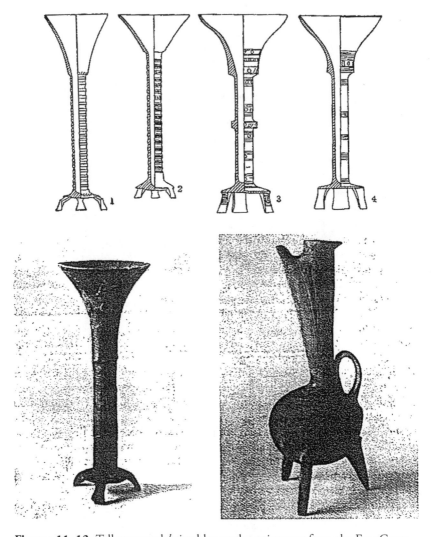

Figures 11–13 Tall-stemmed *bei* goblets and a *gui* pourer from the East Coast.
Top: four *bei* from Dadunzi, Jiangsu. From "Jiangsu Pi xian Sihu zhen Dadunzi
yizhi tanjue baogao" (Trial diggings at Dadunzi in Sihu zhen, Pi xian, Jiangsu),
KX 1964, no. 2:37, fig. 30. *Bottom left*: *bei* from Liulin, Jiangsu. From *Jiangsu
shen chutu wenwu xuanji* (Selection of cultural relics excavated in Jiangsu
province; Beijing, 1963), no. 43. *Bottom right*: *gui* from Taigansi, Xishanqiao,
Jiangsu; from ibid., no. 18.

footed or tall-stemmed *bei* of the East (figs. 11–12). Once again, one is struck by
the implied neatness and regularity in the lives of those who made and used these
objects, and by the implied absence of such traits among those who did not.

The motivations for what may be seen as this upward-reaching aesthetic of the East were undoubtedly complex and, quite possibly, not fully articulated by its practitioners. On the technical level, the construction of tall, thin ceramic objects is an indication both of technological skill (involving in particular the development of the fast wheel) and of an interest in shaping materials in new and artificial ways.[41] It also provides additional clues to the mentality of the potters.

First, the throwing of pots on a fast wheel indicates the greater care with which the clays involved would have had to have been selected and washed.[42] This provides one example of the greater precision required by the potters of the East compared to those of the Northwest. It also suggests the emergence of specialized craftsmen.[43]

Second, to the extent that elevated pots might have saved kiln space,[44] one may detect a possible concern with efficiency on the part of the East Coast potters that may not have been present in the Northwest; the greater the height and smaller the girth, the greater the number of vessels that could be fired with the same amount of fuel. The development of oxygen-poor, reduction firing, which produced the characteristic grey and black ware of the East and classical Longshan (e.g., the *bei* from Liulin in fig. 12), may have been stimulated by the desire to economize on fuel; it indicates that, once again, the potters of the East were more willing to experiment than the "natural" potters of the Northwest, who were still firing their pots in open kilns.[45] Any efficiency of fuel use, however, must have been balanced against the evident inefficiency of the Eastern pot shapes themselves, which, by contrast with the globular, holistic pots of the Northwest, would have generally provided less capacity for the amount of clay used. The contradiction suggests that the potters of the East may have been willing to give aesthetic concerns priority over economic ones and that fuel may have been in shorter supply than fine clay.

Third, elevation may also have been connected to a more general desire to get off the ground, to distinguish and separate oneself and one's possessions from the earth. This impulse was evidently present in the pile dwellings built at Hemudu, for example,[46] and it may indeed have been originally a response to the dampness of the low-lying lands and house floors of the Yangzi delta. Whatever the origins of this upward-reaching feature of the East Coast cultures, it stands in contrast to the more "down to earth" aesthetic of the Northwest potters, whose houses, as well as pots, tended to be semi-subterranean or seated in the ground (see the narrow, unpainted pot bottoms in figs. 14–15) rather than placed above it.

Fourth, one may note that the upward vision of the East Coast peoples appears to have been maintained even in death. My preliminary research suggests that, in the cultures of the Northwest, there was a tendency for grave goods to be placed near the legs and feet of the deceased. Most painted Northwest pots, being decorated only on their upper surface, were designed to be viewed from the top;[47] the dead maintained that same vantage point. By contrast, grave goods and tools in the Eastern cultures were more likely to be placed all around the deceased or near the hands, waist, or upper abdomen.[48]

Fifth, one may speculate that the willingness to think in vertical terms and to value height may also have been connected to emerging social stratification

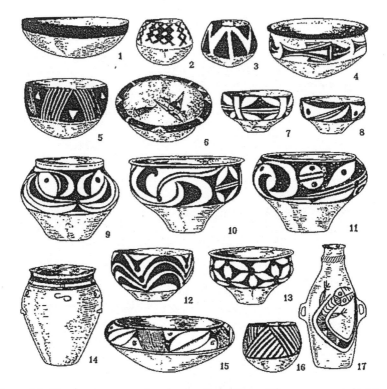

Figure 14 Northwest pots, painted ware. From Feng, *Zhong-guo taoci shi*, 10.

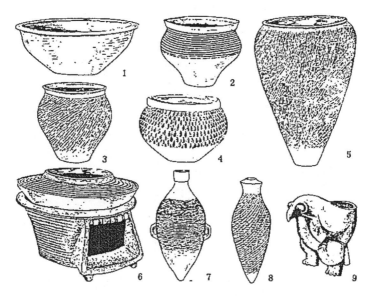

Figure 15 Northwest pots, unpainted ware. From ibid., 11.

in the East, and thus to the way in which Eastern-derived culture traits, such as upwardly aspiring pot forms and rammed-earth housing platforms, together with the culture bearers of those traits, eventually dominated, became ascendant over and superior to, the Northwest cultures of the Central Plains and beyond. The connection between elevation and dominance, which may be a human universal, was certainly appreciated by the Shang and Zhou Chinese.[49]

Pottery Use

Now that we have considered pot shape, pot manufacture, and mentality, I should like to turn to pot shape and usage, with a view to discovering what further clues the functions of these vessels can provide about the mentality of not just their makers but their users.

The first and most obvious point is that the East Coast peoples and the later cultures that derived from them made and used a far greater variety of shapes (figs. 2–13) than did the peoples of the Northwest, whose repertoire consisted essentially of round-bottomed bowls, jars, and amphoras (figs. 14–15), used, so far as we can tell, rather indiscriminately. Apart from the broad and by no means rigorous or consistent distinction posited by modern scholars between pots used for cooking, eating, and storing, the Northwest vessels seem in general to have been vessels of general purpose. There is no way, for example, to tell, on the basis of shape, what might or might not have been a ritual vessel. Pot usage, and presumably other aspects of life, was not yet differentiated in this way.

In the East, by contrast, in addition to the bowl and jar shapes, one also finds *ding* tripods, *dou* serving stands, *bei* drinking goblets, *gui* pouring jugs (see figs. given at p. 14 above), *he* spouted kettles (fig. 3, no. 8), and, in the Late Neolithic, Eastern-derived cultures of Henan, Shaanxi, and, rarely, Shandong, the mammiform, three-legged, *li* cooking tripod (fig. 2, no. 8).[50]

This greater variety of pot forms implies, in the first place, a greater willingness to experiment, to devise new solutions. Franklin has argued that an "essential predictability" is inherent in the prescriptive process; "there is no room for surprise."[51] This is undoubtedly true at the level of the craftsman who works on only one part of the manufacturing process. But there is no reason why the overseers could not, within the limits of invention permitted by the technology, plan for new shapes. Certain of the componential forms did indeed manifest a considerable degree of variability.[52] As Friedrich Engels is said to have noted, "The separation of planning for labor from the labor itself ... contributed to the rise of an idealistic world outlook, one that explains people's actions 'as arising out of thoughts instead of their needs.'"[53] To the extent that supervision of componential construction implied divorce from the actual labor, one may detect the seeds of such labor-free "idealism," so potent for the development of civilization, in the ceramic technology of the East Coast Neolithic.

In the second place the greater variety of pot forms suggests greater practicability in such basic activities as pouring accurately or in cooking, where a *ding* tripod, placed over a fire, would presumably have been more efficient and easier to use—in terms both of heat transfer (when the legs were hollow) and stability—than a round-bottomed pot. Globular Heartland pots, presumably placed directly in the ashes, might have been more susceptible to thermal shock and would certainly have been less stable than the tri-legged vessels of the East.[54] I suspect that the peoples of the East particularly valued the stability that legs gave to steamer vessels. These *zeng* and *xian* (fig. 6, nos. 7–9), popular in the East,[55] necessarily involved a certain tallness of design, for the grill on which the food was steamed had to be placed above the boiling liquid below; globular-based steamers would have been prone to tipping over. Some of the Northwest pots were certainly marvelously well designed for their function—one thinks in particular of the *ping* amphoras for drawing water from rivers (fig. 14, no. 17; fig. 15, nos. 7, 8)—but the larger, more varied repertoire of East Coast vessels indicates a greater willingness to innovate and specialize.

When routinized and standardized, the separate fabrication of the various elements suggests, as we have seen, specialization of manufacture. It also suggests specialization of use, for some of the vessels that resulted were so thin and fragile (figs. 11–13) that they imply special, and probably ritual, function. Not only did such vessels require a compartmentalization of manufacture, therefore; their specialized shapes also imply an analogous compartmentalization of experience, with some pots being reserved for nonroutine, perhaps nonsecular, functions.[56] In accordance with Louis Sullivan's dictum that form follows function, the variety of Eastern forms suggests a greater variety of functions.

One may suppose that if Eastern pots were being assigned special functions, so were human beings—and not just in the ceramic workshops but in other social and political activities. It must be noted that the relationship is not merely analogical. Specialized pots would have been made to satisfy specialized functions; greater differentiation in pottery would have resulted from a more socially differentiated society.[57] Once again, it is worth stressing that we are dealing with matters of degree. There would have been no reason for a hypothetical Northwest conservative, looking at the ceramic technology of the East, to lament, as Thomas Carlyle was to do the impact of the Industrial Revolution, that "men have grown mechanical in head and in heart, as well as in hand."[58] Nevertheless, Carlyle's protostructuralist assertion that "the same habit regulates not our modes of action alone, but our modes of thought and feeling" is relevant. The "sprouts" of such compartmentalization, of a social, political, and above all intellectual, revolution in human organization, were certainly present in the making, and in the using, of the pots of the Neolithic East Coast.

Channels of Constraint

Vessel shapes and vessel use affect one another in a variety of miniscule yet cumulative ways. This is well demonstrated if we consider such seemingly insignificant innovations as pouring lips, pouring spouts, single handles, lids, and legs.[59]

These were rarely present on Northwest vessels of the sixth to fourth millennia, whose makers evidently found no special virtue or pleasure in such refinements. Spouts, handles, lids, and legs variously appeared in the Yangzi delta area starting in the fourth millennium and continued to figure prominently in the developing cultures of the Middle Yangzi and the East, frequently serving as characteristic horizon markers for the regional Late Neolithic cultures.[60] (The degree to which such features appear in the bronze and ceramic vessels of the Shang needs no emphasis here.)[61]

Lips, spouts, handles, and legs constrain the way in which pots can be used. Pots so furnished are designed for, and indeed they require, a particular kind of use. Unlike the Northwest peoples, who could, in general, pour from or pick up their all-purpose bowls and vases in a variety of ways—and presumably did so, for safety's sake, with two hands[62]—the East Coast peoples would have been likely to pick up a single-handled *gui* pitcher, *he* pourer, or handled *bei* cup, for example, in a certain way, usually with their right hands, and would have poured from a lip or spout in a certain direction. Handles give man a better grip on, a better control over, his creations.[63] Like spouts, they standardize the way vessels are to be used.

This channeling of options implies greater efficiency. It also implies greater care for the handling of vessels. Given the design of their vessels, there would

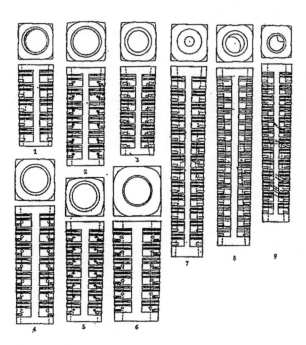

Figure 16 Jade *cong* tubes excavated at Sidun. From "1982 nian Jiangsu Changzhou Wujing Sidun yizhi di fajue" (The 1982 excavation of the site at Sidun in Wujing, Changzhou, Jiangsu), *KG* 1984, no. 2:119.

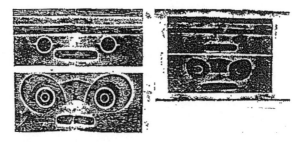

Figure 17 Animal face designs on the corners of *cong* excavated at Sidun.
From ibid., 120.

now have been, for the peoples of the East Coast, *a right way* and *a wrong way* to
do things, a rightness and wrongness that would have been less likely to confront
the users of typical, handleless, spoutless Northwest pots that lacked orienting
appendages. It may be noted, incidentally, that this concern with correct placement is also revealed by the jade *cong* tubes so characteristic of the Lower Yangzi
cultures of the fourth and third millennia (see below). Recent archaeological
discoveries have revealed that the *cong* were placed with the slightly narrower end
at the bottom so that the highly abstract, "animal mask" designs carved onto the
corners of the registers were suitably oriented (figs. 16–17).[64] Once again, there
was a right way and a wrong way to do something, that rightness and wrongness
being designed into the artifact itself. Similarly, the bird profiles carved onto
the surface of certain East Coast jade *bi* disks[65] required that they be oriented
in one correct direction. These "unipositional" pots and jades stand in contrast
to the multipositional pots of the Northwest cultures, whose flowing, abstract
designs, even when divided by cartouches into a "four quarters" pattern, did not
require, or even provide, an indication that one orientation was to be preferred
to another.

    In the same way, well-made lids, especially fitted ones that were more
characteristic of the East Coast and descendant cultures,[66] imply a concern with
careful storage, with cleanliness, even with that ultimate indicator of civilized
man, delayed gratification. And they imply the willingness to design and construct permanent containers to satisfy those concerns. The Northwest potters
(who may have used stoppers made of perishable materials) were more casual
about lids, generally preferring to invert a bowl over the mouth of another vessel.[67]
The issue, in this case, is not one of efficiency—such makeshift lids can provide
an excellent seal—but of the Northwestern potters' indifference to making objects
for precise functions and to precise specifications. Such indifference is entirely
consonant with the awkwardness of their early, and generally abortive, experi-
ments with legged or footed vessels.[68]

    The users of the East Coast pots, in short, were faced with a series of mini-
constraints that would have produced greater convenience and efficiency—there

is less spilling when spouts are used, for example, less risk of dropping a pouring vessel when there is a handle by which to hold it—but which also standardized and structured the routines of daily life: vessels were expected to be picked up in a certain way, and even to be placed in a certain position, with the handle oriented so that they could be picked up easily again. Vessels with legs, and cups and pedestals with high feet or stems, had to be set down with care, lest they tip over (figs. 11–13). Similarly, fitted lids were not only troublesome to make, but they had to be replaced with some precision.

Each one of these mini-constraints—involving legs, feet, spouts, handles—would, taken individually, have had minimal impact on the mental habits of the users, but the cumulative effect, of both using these prescriptive vessels and of designing and making them, would, I suggest, have been sufficiently significant to distinguish, in terms of both material and mental culture, the inhabitants of the East Coast from those who lived in the Northwest. People who make their pots differently live their lives differently and, it goes without saying, vice versa.

Fit and Mensuration

The prescriptive style of their ceramic technology provides further indication that the peoples of the East Coast were more concerned than those of the Northwest with precise measurement and fit. This is seen in the identical size required of the legs on *ding* tripods, *gui* pitchers, and *he* kettles. It is seen in the way the separately formed elements of any of the componentially constructed vessels had to be planned and shaped with precision. It is seen in the way close-fitting lids had to be shaped and fired so that they would fit their parent vessels.

Turning from clay to wood, we find an equal concern with mensuration in the Southeast. This is seen in the exactitude of the mortise and tenon construction used in the pile dwellings at Hemudu (stratum 4, ca. 5000 B.C.E.).[69] It is seen in the remarkable regularity—remarkable, given the stone axes, adzes, and chisels available to the carpenters—with which the planks used in house construction in Majiabang sites of the fourth millennium had been trimmed.[70] It is seen in the exact measurements used to construct a late Liangzhu well (ca. 2000 B.C.E.?) with the boards of the shaft braced by cross struts fitting into measured holes.[71]

The most striking precision, however—striking both for the difficulties involved and for the early date of the evidence—is surely that manifested by the craftsmen working in jade. The sawing, drilling, grinding, and polishing of ritual and ornamental jade and jadelike hard stones (nephrite, tremolite, and actinolite) is perhaps the most characteristic and most revealing of all the horizon markers of the East Coast cultures from Qinglian'gang and Hemudu onwards.[72] The *bi* rings and *cong* tubes were crafted with remarkable precision. At Sidun, in Jiangsu, for example, in Liangzhu strata of the third millennium, the diameters of the individual *bi* did not vary by more than about 1 millimeter in any direction, and the differences in the sizes of the registers found on individual *cong* were even smaller.[73] These multiregistered *cong*—which resemble rulers in appearance, though not perhaps in function—represent the essence of prescriptive, standardized, design, each register being identical to the rest (fig.16).[74] The central hole in both the *bi* and *cong* was bored from both sides of the object, resulting in a hole that was slightly wider at its opening than at the center where the two bores met. In a fair number of instances, especially in the case of the *cong*, which might be as tall as 36.1 centimeters (fig. 16, no. 7, with thirteen registers), the two boreholes did not meet exactly in the middle, so that a small ridge was left inside the jade (e.g., fig. 16, nos. 1 and 8). But these ridges are remarkably small—only 0.05–0.1 millimeters wide—and occur in less than half of the *cong* found at Sidun,[75] and in only one of the four *bi* found in the Liangzhu site at Jialingdang, near Changshu in Jiangsu.[76] In at least half of the *cong*, therefore, the drilling from one side through some 10 to 15 centimeters of jade was so skillful that it could meet with great accuracy a bore drilled the same distance from the other side with no ridge being left at all. Such results could only have been achieved by the most persistent attention to precise measurement.[77]

In the pot making, carpentry, and jade working of the East Coast, therefore, measurement was vital and may well have been associated with—to the extent that numbers must have been used—a more mathematical view of the natural world than the peoples of the Northwest would have found necessary or congenial. These were workers who followed a prescribed plan, who conformed to molds or models (either real or conceived), who employed their sophisticated tools with care and precision, who manifested a comprehensive competence in designing and building structures of various sorts.

I would note, finally, that, in the Aegean, writing seems to have developed as an aid to overcoming problems of mensuration and reckoning.[78] Such a connection is not out of the question in the East Coast cultures of China, especially when we recall that the componential construction of vessels required some form of scheduling, that is, the mensuration of time. And one might even see a significant correlation in the nature of the subsequent written script which, at least by Late Shang (ca. 1200 B.C.E.) was as "componential" in its construction, with graphs being composed of both phonetic and semantic elements, as were the vessels of the East Coast tradition and their piece-mold, cast-bronze descendants. The "componential" protograph designs found on certain Liangzhu jades[79] and Huating pots[80] are predictable products of the componential cast of mind I detect in the cultures of the East; the origins of the writing system of the Shang, which is characterized by its combination of semantic and phonetic symbols, may well have been associated with these mental dispositions. Few if any of the marks scratched on Northwest pots are similarly componential in character.

One cannot, in conclusion, assign particular meaning to the shapes of the pots or jades of the East Coast. But the shapes of these East Coast artifacts, and the planning and technology involved in their manufacture, suggest a world view that was more fundamentally controlled, precise, measured, standardized, mathematical, componential, articulated, and differentiated. And the special, fragile quality of some of the East Coast vessels, together with the impressive amounts of labor required to produce the jades, further suggests a world that was more hierarchical, a world in which certain finely made objects were reserved for special functions and, presumably, for special people. Craftsmen were not only working to prescribed plan. They were working for others.

The Mentality of the East

Man in the Northwest was the surface designer, the embellisher of globular, holistic forms. Man in the East Coast was the maker of shapes, the manipulator, the "handler," the coordinator, the measurer, the one who was more likely to be buried with his tools at hand. Of the products of the two culture areas, those of the East Coast potters, carpenters, and jade craftsmen represent the greater triumph, not necessarily of mind over matter—though that would be a fair judgment insofar as the working of jade (and also, it may be remarked, of lacquer)[81] is concerned—but, in the realm of handicrafts and in the social organization associated with those handicrafts, of articulation over inarticulation. Their technological achievements imply an increasing differentiation in craft, in society, and in spiritual conceptions.[82] The degree to which the eventual technological and political domination of the Eastern traditions may have involved the movement of peoples from the East Coast into the Central Plains and beyond is not yet clear.[83] It may be supposed, however, that the demographic and political successes of the Late Neolithic, Eastern-influenced if not Eastern-derived, regional cultures, sprang ultimately from intellectual pressure, applied to the environment—natural, material, and social.

On the basis of the archaeological evidence, one also has reason to think that it would have been in the cultures of the East that theological and social justifications for the rituals involved in the strategic mortuary cult would have begun to be articulated and isolated. I call the cult "strategic" because the early Chinese treatment of the dead, in both the Northwest and the East, was so remarkably rich and assiduous that it must be regarded as one of the defining features of early Chinese culture.[84] The Neolithic mortuary evidence in Greece is trivial by comparison and provides little or no evidence of ritual concerns.[85] Such strong mortuary concerns had the potential for significant cultural consequences, depending upon the way they intersected with other activities.

Significant regional differences in early Chinese religious belief are reflected in such mortuary practices as secondary burial, placement and quality of grave goods, display of those grave goods on ledges, use of coffins and coffin chambers, construction of ramps to permit access to tombs, and offering of animal victims. Here again, firm conclusions must await the publication of more archaeological data and its comprehensive mapping. Several suggestive features, however, bear on the argument of this essay. First, the sex ratios so far reported for the skeletons in large Neolithic cemeteries indicate, down to the third millennium, a higher ratio (frequently of the order of two to one) of males to females in East Coast, as opposed to Northwest, cemeteries. At least two inferences may be drawn. Either—if we assume that female infanticide or preferential feeding explains these disparities—the cultures of the East treated their female children in a more "Spartan" manner than did those of the Northwest. Or, the women of the East were less likely to receive formal, cemetery burial than men.[86] One may also note that infants may have received special mortuary treatment earlier and more consistently in the Northwest than in the East. Both these findings, if confirmed by subsequent reports, suggest that the inhabitants of the Northwest were more tender with their children, less disposed to regard them, before adulthood, as expendable,[87] and that the inhabitants of the East, by contrast, paid greater attention to "social engineering."[88]

This mortuary evidence suggests that Eastern religious practices—particularly those involving the burial of highly crafted mortuary jades, the display of grave goods, and the construction of coffin chambers—would have served to validate and articulate the expressions of order and control that I have discerned in the realms of technology and social organization among the various East Coast cultures and among their Late Neolithic regional descendants in the Middle and Lower Yangzi, Shandong, and the Central Plains.[89] If more recent finds confirm an Eastern origin for the scapulimancy and plastromancy by which the peoples of the Late Neolithic communicated with the spirits, presumably their ancestors, in an attempt to divine and influence the future, this would be a further instance of the way in which the peoples of the region were able to devise new, differentiated methods for religious communication.[90]

What the peoples of the Northwest or Central Plains invented or discovered, the peoples of the regional Late Neolithic cultures, influenced to greater or lesser degree by the technologies and work habits of the East, frequently elaborated and put to more extensive use.[91] I would include the introduction of metal working into China in this category; the holistic, wrought-metal working of copper may well have been discovered in Northwest China,[92] but in the earliest cast bronzes of the Central Plains it appears to have been adapted to the prescriptive, precisely measured, proto-piece-mold techniques of the East Coast peoples, who saw how they could "translate" metal from wrought to cast and who already had the prescriptive, quasi-industrial ceramic technology and mental dispositions, and perhaps the social organization, to do so.[93]

To sum up, these East Coast inhabitants were the fabricators of sharply shaped and sharply differentiated vessels, some modeled on ceramic cores, some constructed componentially. The specialized designs of their pots required coordination and constraint in both manufacture and usage. They were supremely successful in the drilling, grinding, and perforation of hard-stone artifacts such as axes, spades, and beads, and the jade *bi* and *cong* that were evidently reserved for burial with the dead. They carved and incised their designs on jade, stone, and pottery. They practiced tooth extraction and skull deformation, the application of molding and ramming techniques to the human form. Their treatment of children, particularly of girls, seems to have been more severe than that in the Northwest. They appear to have pioneered the practice of scapulimantic communication with the spirits. They may have accompanied their rituals with millet wine;[94] if intoxication were involved, this may be seen as another form of manipulation, this time of consciousness itself, that permitted a cathartic release, perhaps, from the strictly ordered patterns of their daily experience as well as from the rigid order imposed by death.[95]

These cultures, in short, were the elaborators and beneficiaries of a tradition that believed in shaping, reshaping, and manipulating, and in making deep, permanent, marks on pots, on jades, and, perhaps, on the world itself; they emphasized neither two-dimensional, surface decoration nor "natural," globular form. These Easterners were, one is tempted to say, the ectomorphs, the proto-Confucians (at least in their ritualizing and ordering mode), of the Chinese Neolithic, by comparison with the endomorphs, the dreamers, the surface decorators, the "proto-Taoists" of the Northwest tradition. The delicate and precarious nature of the ritual pots of the East suggests a concern that, in particular contexts of importance, things should be in their right places. And it is worth recalling that the prescriptive process by which some of their most characteristic pot forms were made was, in Franklin's view, characterized by its "essential predictability," its lack of surprise.[96] One may detect, indeed, in the peoples of the East that quality which Marcel Mauss has referred to as "education in composure." This is not quietism but "a mechanism inhibiting disorderly movements ... [which] subsequently allows a co-ordinated response of co-ordinated movements setting off in the direction of a chosen goal." And he concludes with a passage that appositely sums up the distinctions I have been attempting to make about the East Coast and the Northwest of the Chinese Neolithic. "This resistance to emotional seizure is something fundamental in social and mental life. It separates out, it even classifies the so-called primitive societies; according to whether they display more ... unreflected, unconscious reactions or on the contrary more isolated, precise actions governed by a clear consciousness."[97]

It is important to repeat that we are dealing only with differences of degree. The various painted-pot traditions of the Chinese Northwest certainly give evidence of considerable experimentation with the possibilities of abstract surface design. Many of these pots, despite their all-purpose shapes, would have required great care to plan, to shape, and to paint. They may even have been used in differentiated ways, even in rituals, that have left no archaeological trace. But the fact remains that the pots were not greatly differentiated, one from the other, in shape or function. Neither, one suspects, were the people. The Northwest potters did one thing and they did it very well. They were more the "hedgehogs" of the Chinese Neolithic; the peoples of the East were more the "foxes." The Easterners were, metaphorically speaking, Neolithic "Marxists"—their goal was not simply to understand, or even to depict and imitate the world, but to change it.

What I am proposing, in short, is that certain features of Neolithic Chinese culture, recoverable from the archaeological record, mattered very much and that if we merely content ourselves with cataloging pot shapes and artifact types we risk reducing archaeology to antiquarianism. These certain features would include: sedentary agriculture (a necessary source of stability for most if not all the other features);[98] decent, well-provided burials; mortuary rituals; male dominance; a particular theology of the afterlife that validated status distinctions and obligations in this one; sacrifices, both animal and human, that would have served the same function; houses raised off the ground; vessels raised off the ground; vessels specialized by design and function; prescriptive, componential ceramic technology; prescriptive jade working; the use of molds and models; careful attention to mensuration and planning; and, eventually, some system of notation, of proto-writing.

These features would have been present to a greater or lesser degree in various parts of China during the Neolithic. I would not argue that in every instance the peoples of the East Coast did something first or did it exclusively. But it was in the cultures of the East that these traits were sufficiently strong and became sufficiently concentrated to work on one another in what Colin Renfrew, writing of the Aegean, has termed the "multiplier effect."[99] These traits eventually produced in combination what none would have produced in isolation—a new, more highly differentiated society that was more competent, both technologically and socially, and more explicit, both theologically and intellectually.

Most of these strategic Eastern features serve to define Shang culture: the articulated shapes of the footed and legged ritual vessels in both bronze or clay; lips, spouts, handles, and fitted lids; highly worked jades; lacquer wares; monster masks (as in fig. 17) carved into the precisely measured piece molds used in prescriptive bronze casting; the use of clay cores; impressive burials with animal and human accompaniers-in-death and ledges for the display of burial goods; lavish animal and human sacrifices; use of rammed earth to fill graves and to raise house foundations above the soil surface; elaborate forms of pyromantic divination with permanent records carved into the bone; male domination; extensive social control directed by a central elite.

Strong filiations, which link the Shang culturally to their East Coast antecedents, confirm the degree to which certain roots of later Chinese culture, to say nothing of social and political organization and technical skills, are to be found in the religion, craft, and mentality of the prehistoric cultures of the East Coast where, as we have seen, the archaeological record indicates a developing emphasis on models, mensuration, control, planning, manipulation, specialization, efficiency, and ritual, all of which served to enhance and concentrate, as they ordered and constrained, the productive and organizational capacities of the society.

The characteristic role played by the potter's, carpenter's, and jade worker's metaphors of molding, bending, grinding, and measuring in Eastern Zhou writings on human nature and good government (mainly from the sixth to the third centuries B.C.E.), and the degree to which such metaphors appear in writings of men whose cultural roots were in the East, supports the argument that many of the techniques described in this essay were of fundamental and ancient importance. Just as Neolithic craft techniques had shaped and been shaped by the mentality of their practitioners, so did the metaphors and analogies of Eastern

Zhou shape, as they expressed, the way in which social reality was conceived and structured. The Confucian philosopher Xunzi (298–238 B.C.E.), to cite but one example, wrote:

> All rules of decorum and righteousness are the products of the acquired virtue of the sage and not the products of the nature of man. Thus, the potter pounds and molds the clay and makes the vessel—but the vessel is the product of the potter's acquired skill and not the product of his original nature. Or again, the craftsman hews pieces of wood and makes utensils—but the utensils are the product of the carpenter's acquired skill and not the product of his original nature…. So then the rules of decorum and righteousness and laws and institutions are similarly the products of the acquired virtue of the sage and not the products of his original nature.[100]

It is not surprising, given the antiquity and power of these cultural features, that Zhou thinkers found it congenial to argue about morality and human nature in terms of the manufacture of artifacts.[101]

One obvious caveat needs to be stated. For all the weight I attach to the mentality and social organization of the peoples of the East, the fact remains that the early Bronze Age culture of the Shang—or possibly of the pre-Shang, which some archaeologists now identify as Xia—did not arise in the East but in the Central Plains, particularly in the sites associated with Erlitou in north central Henan.[102] This Early State culture evidently developed at the end of the Late Neolithic as a result of Eastern stimulation, but also as a result of local predispositions to accept and develop whatever innovations arrived from outside. The precise nature of the cultural mixing involved still remains to be explored, but there was, apparently, insufficient "multiplication" in the East to produce Shang culture in that region.[103] Craftsmanship and material evidence cannot explain everything about a culture's noncraft, nonmaterial aspects. For all its Eastern qualities, Shang culture was not merely the product of the East.[104]

When Engels stressed the centrality of labor—as expressed in toolmaking—he referred only to the way in which tools elevated *Homo faber* above the animals.[105] But particular kinds of tools and products make a particular kind of man. In the case of China, where the contrast between the material remains of the Northwest and East Coast cultures is, in certain technological and aesthetic features, so striking, we may, I suggest, use the material culture, in the ways adumbrated above, as a vital clue to the mental life, the tacit knowledge, the sensibility of the tool makers. Even if one does not accept, in the deliberately broad terms employed in this essay, the primacy of East Coast traits in the eventual Bronze Age synthesis of the Central Plains, one can still appreciate the importance of asking how artifacts were made, how they were used, and what social habits and mental dispositions the answers to such questions imply. For not all artifacts are created equal. We need to ask in each case how their making and their using—whether in different parts of Neolithic China, or in different cradles of civilization elsewhere—may be related to the cultures that made them, used them, and were made by them.

Notes

An initial version of this paper was delivered at La Civilita Cinese Antica, Venice, April 1985. I am grateful for, and have done my best to take advantage of, the critical comments offered by Derk Bodde, George Dales, David Goodrich, Jonathan Haas, Louisa Huber, Thomas Laqueur, Brian Moeran, Richard Pearson, Nancy Price, Henry Rosemont, Jr., Randolph Starn, Norman Yoffee, and Richard Webster. Funding for the initial research was provided by the Wang Institute of Graduate Studies.

1. Ward H. Goodenough, "Cultural Anthropology and Linguistics," in Paul Garvin, ed., *Report of the Seventh Annual Roundtable Meeting on Linguistics and Language Study* (Washington, D.C., 1957), 173.
2. For the origins of the state, see, e.g., Elman R. Service, *Origins of the State and Civilization: The Process of Cultural Evolution* (New York, 1975); Jonathan Haas, *The Evolution of the Prehistoric State* (New York, 1982).
3. Paul Wheatley, *The Pivot of the Four Quarters: A Preliminary Enquiry into the Origins and Character of the Ancient Chinese City* (Chicago, 1971), 3–106; Kwang-chih Chang, *Shang Civilization* (New Haven, 1980), 361–67; Richard Pearson, "Social Complexity in Chinese Coastal Neolithic Sites," *Science* 213 (4 September 1981): 1078–86.
4. For my initial explorations of this topic, see David N. Keightley, "Early Civilization in China: Reflections on How It Became Chinese" (included in this volume).
5. See, e.g., Colin Renfrew, *The Emergence of Civilisation: The Cyclades and the Aegean in the Third Millennium B.C.* (London, 1972), 16.
6. Ian Hodder, "Theoretical Archaeology: A Reactionary View," in Hodder, ed., *Symbolic and Structural Archaeology* (Cambridge, 1982), 4. Goodenough's earlier formulation is equally apposite. Culture, he wrote in 1957, "does not consist of things, people, behavior, or emotions. It is rather an organization of these things. It is the forms of things that people have in mind, their models for perceiving, relating, and otherwise integrating them"; "Cultural Anthropology and Linguistics," 167.
7. Daniel Miller, "Artefacts as Products of Human Categorization Processes," in Hodder, *Symbolic and Structural Archaeology*, 17–25. Such an awareness may have been in Confucius' mind when he declared, "The *junzi* [noble man] is not to be treated as a vessel" (*Analects* 2.12); the moral man was not to be shaped by the conventional categories that produced either pots or people. For further discussion of this passage, and the links between Neolithic craft and conceptions of society, see David N. Keightley, "Craft and Culture: Metaphors of Governance in Early China" (Paper delivered at the Second International Conference on Sinology, Taibei, December 1986), 33. I shall be glad to supply, upon request, copies of my various unpublished papers cited in this essay.
8. Daniel Miller, *Artifacts as Categories: A Study of Ceramic Variability in Central India* (Cambridge, 1985).
9. A.J. Ayer, review of J. David Bolton, *Turing's Man*, in *New York Review of Books*, 1 March 1984, p. 16. See too Friedrich Solmsen, "Nature as Craftsman in Greek Thought, *Journal of the History of Ideas* 24, no. 4 (1963): 473–96, who documents how "many of the verbs employed by Plato suggest a carpenter's or builder's work" (481) and how, in Aristotle, "nature acts like a modeller, a painter, a cook, a carpenter, a housebuilder, or a channelbuilder" (489).

10. Brian Moeran, *Lost Innocence: Folk Craft Potters of Onta, Japan* (Berkeley, 1984), esp. 174, 217, demonstrates the relationship, in one area of twentieth-century Japan, between pottery manufacture, social change, and aesthetic ideals. His conclusion that "so-called aesthetic *mingei* [folk craft] ideals are in fact no more and no less than prescriptions for the organization of Japanese society" (217) is particularly suggestive for the argument of this essay.

11. On the inadequacy of the archaeological record to recover many of the simple techniques, such as pounding and binding, that people employ, see Marie Jeanne Adams, "Style in Southeast Asian Materials Processing: Some Implications for Ritual and Art," in Heather Lechtman and Robert Merill, eds., *Material Culture: Styles, Organization, and Dynamics of Technology*, 1975 Proceedings of the American Ethnological Society (St. Paul, Minn., 1977), 25–26.

12. Hodder, "Theoretical Archaeology," 10.

13. Marcel Mauss, "Techniques of the Body," *Economy and Society* 2, no. 1 (February 1973): 76, 86; this article was originally published in *Journal de psychologie normale et pathologique* 32 (1935): 271–93.

14. An Zhimin, "Tanshisi duandai he Zhong'guo xinshiqi shidai" (Carbon-14 dating and the Chinese Neolithic), *Kaogu* (Archaeology; hereafter abbreviated as *KG*) 1984, no. 3:273, fig. 2, presents a recent table of cultures arranged by period and region but based, however, upon uncalibrated carbon-14 dates (271).

15. This division corresponds, superficially, to the old dichotomy between painted-pottery, Yangshao culture in the west and black-pottery, Longshan culture in the east. For an account of this two-culture theory, which dates back to the work of Li Chi in the 1930s, see Kwang-chih Chang, *The Archaeology of Ancient China* (3rd ed., revised and enlarged; New Haven, 1977), 146–47. I prefer to avoid the use of Yangshao and Longshan as general designations. Yangshao village was, in fact, a Miaodigou II site much influenced from the East; Longshan was a Late Neolithic culture whose manifestations were generally limited to Shandong.

16. The degree to which the cultures of the East penetrated the Central Plains and beyond, and the precise dating and nature of that penetration, require further study. Initial discussions of the emergence of Eastern traits in the Northwest may be found in William Watson, *Cultural Frontiers in Ancient East Asia* (Edinburgh, 1971), 35; Barbara Stephens, "Technology and Change in Shang China" (Paper delivered at the Association for Asian Studies Annual Meeting, Chicago, 31 March 1973); Jessica Rawson, *Ancient China: Its Art and Archaeology* (London, 1980), 27, 33, 35; Louisa G. Fitzgerald Huber, "The Traditions of Chinese Neolithic Pottery," *Bulletin of the Museum of Far Eastern Antiquities* 53 (1981): 120; Huber, "The Relationship of the Painted Pottery and Lung-shan Cultures," in David N. Keightley, ed., *The Origins of Chinese Civilization* (Berkeley, 1983), 204.

17. For much of this characterization of the cultures of the East, though she does not unify them as broadly as I do here, I am indebted to Huber, "Painted Pottery and Lung-shan Cultures," 187–202. Margaret Medley, *The Chinese Potter: A Practical History of Chinese Ceramics* (Oxford, 1976), 28, also argues for the existence of two distinct ceramic traditions "in terms of technique, form and decoration."

18. Data bearing on the question of proportion have not been consistently reported. It has been estimated that only 2–3 percent of the Banpo phase pots (fifth millennium B.C.E.) in Gansu were painted; Yan Wenming, "Gansu caitao di yuanliu" (The origins of Gansu painted pottery), *Wenwu* (Cultural Relics; hereafter abbreviated as

WW) 1978, no. 10:63. In the Miaodigou remains (first half of fourth millennium), we are told either that 10–15 percent or 14.02 percent of the pots were painted; in the 1964 excavations at Majiayao (late fourth to early third millennium) the proportion was said to be 30 percent; "Cong Majiayao leixing bo Waxiliyefu di 'Zhong'guo wenhua xilai shuo' "(A refutation, on the basis of the Majiayao type, of Vasiliev's 'Theory that Chinese culture came from the west'), *WW* 1976, no. 3:27; Yan, "Gansu caitao di yuanliu," 63. Over 64 percent of the 4,705 Machang-style pots (last half of third millennium) excavated in the burial area at Ledu were decorated; "Qinghai Ledu Liuwan yuanshi shehui mudi fanyingchu di zhuyao wenti" (The main issues posed by the primitive-society cemetery at Liuwan, Ledu, in Qinghai), *KG* 1976, no. 6:366.

19. Whether vessel shapes were related to types of clay needs study. It is possible, for example, that Eastern potters adopted componential construction (see text below) because the body of their clays was too weak to bear the full weight of large, holistically constructed pots (suggestion of Brian Moeran, 19 September 1986). Systematic studies of the temper and type of clay used in the various culture areas have not yet been undertaken, however, and I do not address such questions below.

20. Ursula Martius Franklin, "The Beginnings of Metallurgy in China: A Comparative Approach," in George Kuwayama, ed., *The Great Bronze Age of China: A Symposium* (Los Angeles, 1983), 96, defines these terms as follows: "A holistic process ... involves basically a single, step-wise approximation toward the final object. The craftsman, starting with a selection of suitable raw material, must know intimately the whole sequence of steps necessary to produce the object." Prescriptive processes, on the other hand, represented quintessentially by bronze casting, involve the making of a model and "a sequence of unit processes." She calls "this type of subdivided or subdividable process 'prescriptive' in order to indicate the characteristic external pre-ordering and normalizing inherent in it."

21. The term *componential construction* has been applied to the Chinese case by Clarence F. Shangraw, *Origins of Chinese Ceramics* (New York, 1978), 39, 40. My use of the phrase includes the meaning of two distinct Chinese terms: *fenduan shengchan* (production by sections) and *fenbie zuohao hou zai jiehe qilai di* (made separately and then joined together).

22. He Jiejun, "Changjiang zhongyou yuanshi wenhua chulun" (A preliminary discussion of primitive culture in the middle reaches of the Yangzi), *Hunan kaogu jikan* (Papers on Hunan Archaeology) 1 (1982): 50–51.

23. This inversion represents an interesting antecedent to the analogous, if not homologous, Shang bronze-casting practice in which container vessels were frequendy cast in the upside-down position.

24. See too, *Xi'an Banpo* (Banpo village at Xi'an; Beijing, 1963), pls. 122.1–2, 123.3–4, 135.6, 137.1–6. I am grateful to Shi Xingbang (conversation of 25 October 1984) for calling these examples to my attention.

25. Shangraw, *Origins of Chinese Ceramics*, 28.

26. E.g., "Gansu Qin'an Dadiwan yizhi 1978 zhi 1982 nian fajueh di juyao shouhuo" (Main results of the 1978 to 1982 excavations at the site of Dadiwan in Qin'an, Gansu), *WW* 1983, no. 11:22, fig. 4.

27. E.g., a narrow-waisted, painted *guan* jar excavated from Yongdeng and a *ping* amphora, with a trumpet-shaped neck, from Yuzhong—both on display in the Gansu Provincial Museum in late October 1984.

28. See too, the *fu*-shaped *ding* from early period graves at Wangyin; "Shandong Yanzhou Wangyin xinshiqi shidai yizhi fajue jianbao" (Preliminary report of the excavation of the Neolithic remains at Wangyin in Yanzhou, Shandong), *KG* 1979, no. 1:8, figs. 3.4, 3.7–8; p. 9, figs. 5.1–3.

29. Moeran, *Lost Innocence*, 50, 203, notes that in Onta it was the women who put on the handles and spouts and that teacup handles were thought too troublesome to attach.

30. For the various types of control that may develop from the coordination of manufacturing activities, see Richard Edwards, *Contested Terrain: The Transformation of the Workplace in the Twentieth Century* (New York, 1979), 16–22.

31. Franklin, "Beginnings of Metallurgy in China," 96.

32. It has been suggested that Henan was the original home of molded ceramic ware; Noel Barnard and Sat Tamotsu, *Metallurgical Remains of Ancient China* (Tokyo, 1975), 53, citing the work of G. D. Wu, Cheng Te-k'un, and Li Chi. I suspect, however, that the inspiration derived from the hollow-legged *gui* forms of the East. The legs of some *li* were apparently made on a wheel and were then patted and shaped, using a core as interior support; conversation with Zheng Guang, 22 October 1984, referring to 59AHG H2/H14 on display at the Xiaotun research station. Other *li* legs were made not by molding but by forming tubes and then pinching them at the bottom; conversation with Lin Yun, 23 June 1986. In this case, it would still have been necessary to make the tubes of equal diameter and length (see the discussion of mensuration in the text below).

33. See, e.g., Cheng Te-kun, "Metallurgy in Shang China," *Toung Pao* 60 (1974): 223–24.

34. For a discussion of "model emulation" in the philosophical sphere, see Donald J. Munro, *The Concept of Man in Early China* (Stanford, Calif., 1969), esp. 96–102; Keightley, "Craft and Culture," 28–31.

35. Chang, *Archaeology of Ancient China*, 280.

36. *Dawenkou: Xinshiqi shidai muzang fajue baogao* (Dawenkou: Excavation report of the Neolithic burials; Beijing, 1974), p. 12, pl. 2; Han Kangxin and Pan Qifeng, "Wo guo baya fengsu di yuanliu ji qi yiyi" (The origin and significance of the custom of tooth extraction in our country), *KG* 1981, no. 1:64–76.

37. E.g., "Hemudu yizhi diyiqi fajue baogao" (Report on the first season of excavation at the site of Hemudu), *Kaogu xuebao* (Acta Archaeologica Sinica; hereafter abbreviated as *KX*) 1978, no. 1:60, fig. 14.4, pl. 8.11; Julia K. Murray, "Neolithic Chinese Jades in the Freer Gallery of Art," *Orientations* 14, no. 11 (November 1983): p. 16, fig. 4; p. 17, figs. 6, 7; Wu Hong, "Yizu zaoqi di yushi diaoke" (A group of early jade carvings), *Meishu yanjiu* (Fine Arts) 1979, no. 1:67; Wu, "Bird Motifs in Eastern Yi Art," *Orientations* 16, no. 10 (October 1985): 36. On the basis of both the archaeological and legendary evidence, Wu Hong argues in his two articles for the existence of bird totemism in the Shandong region; see, too, David N. Keightley, "The Eastern Yi: Archaeological and Textual Evidence" (Paper delivered at the Association for Asian Studies Annual Meeting, Chicago, 21 March 1986).

38. E.g., *Xi'an Banpo*, pp. 70–73, pl. 86.2; "Yijiuqiqi nian Baoji Beishouling yizhi fajue jianbao" (Preliminary report of the 1977 excavations at the site of Beishouling in Baoji), *KG* 1979, no. 2:105.

39. E.g., "Henan Xinzheng Shawoli xinshiqi shidai yizhi" (The Neolithic site at Shawoli in Xinzheng, Henan), *KG* 1983, no. 12, pl. 1.2; "1979 nian Peiligang yizhi fajue baogao" (Report on the 1979 excavations at the Peiligang site), KX 1984, no. 1, pls. 2.1, 2.3. Many other four-footed querns have been reported from Peiligang sites. I know of no querns, footed or unfooted, from the East Coast.

40. Cishan querns with three feet have been reported; see An Zhimin, "Peiligang, Cishan he Yangshao" (Peiligang, Cishan, and Yangshao), *KG* 1979, no. 4:336; Yan Wenming, "Huanghe liuyu xinshiqi shidai zaoqi wenhua" (Early Neolithic culture in the Yellow River basin), *KG* 1979, no. 1:46.

41. The slow wheel or turntable was used in many areas of Neolithic China. The general development of the fast wheel has not yet been comprehensively studied, but it is likely that it was developed first and more extensively by the cultures of the East. Richard Pearson, "The Neolithic Cultures of the Lower Yangtze River and Coastal China" (Paper delivered at the Symposium on the Origin of Agriculture and Technology: West or East Asia, Moesgard, Denmark, 1978), documents the gradual appearance of the potter's wheel at Dawenkou. Wheel-made (fast?) pottery was common in the Liangzhu culture of the Yangzi delta (third millennium); An Zhimin, "Luelun sanshi nian lai wo guo di xinshiqi shidai kaogu" (A brief account of the last thirty years of Neolithic archaeology in our country), *KG* 1979, no. 5:400. Traces of the fast wheel have been detected on pots from Late Neolithic Middle Yangzi sites, though most of the pots were still handmade; He, "Changjiang zhongyou," 50. The eggshell blackware of the Late Neolithic in Shandong (e.g., fig. 11) was turned on a fast wheel. The development of the fast wheel may have been associated with or stimulated by the rotary saws that the Liangzhu jade cutters are thought to have used; Wang Zunguo, "Liangzhu wenhua 'yu lian zang' shulue" (A brief account of 'shrouding and burying in jade' in Liangzhu culture), *WW* 1984, no. 2:33.

42. Medley, *Chinese Potter*, 26. She notes that "the use of the wheel for throwing was confined to the production of the dark grey and black ware [characteristic of the East— D. N. K.]. This is because it was not possible to throw satisfactory shapes with clays that had a variable or very coarse particle size; a relatively fine and even particle size is a prerequisite for this method of construction."

43. Medley, ibid., 26–27, argues that the use of the wheel "inevitably led to a greater degree of specialization in social terms, since those good at making pottery by the older coiling method, or by using the pad and beater, might not be sufficiently skilled in the use of well prepared clay to throw well on the wheel, while the skilled thrower might not have the patience to engage in coiling and using the pad and beater."

44. Moeran, *Lost Innocence*, 199, 202. Unfortunately, I know virtually nothing about kiln-loading techniques in the Chinese Neolithic.

45. For an introduction to the evolution of Neolithic kilns and reduction firing, see Watson, *Cultural Frontiers*, 67–70; Clarence F. Shangraw, "Early Chinese Ceramics and Kilns," *Archaeology* 30, no. 6 (November 1977): 382–93.

46. "Hemudu faxian yuanshi shehui zhongyao yizhi" (Important remains of the primitive society excavated at Hemudu), *WW* 1976, no. 8:12, fig. 27; "Hemudu yizhi," pp. 42–48, fig. 5.

47. Gu Wen, "Mantan xinshiqi shidai di caitao tu'an huawen dai zhuangshi buwei" (Informal discussion of the decorative location of pictures and design bands on Neolithic painted pottery), *WW* 1977, no. 6:67–69.

48. For particular burials that support this view, see David N. Keightley, "Truth Is in Details: Archaeological Methods and Historical Questions in the Chinese Neolithic" (Paper delivered at the Conference on Ancient China and Social Science Generalizations, Airlie, Va., 22–26 June 1986), p. 39, n. 74.

49. The assumption that good is up and bad is down is certainly central to many expressions in English; see the examples in George Lakoff and Mark Johnson, *Metaphors We Live By* (Chicago, 1980), 16. The Shang oracle-bone inscriptions referred to the more senior ancestors as *gao*, "high." The early Zhou referred to Shang Ti, "the Lord on High," As a statesman in the "Chu yu" section of the *Guo yu* (probably compiled in the third century B.C.E.) is reported to have said: "On earth there is high and low; in heaven there is dark and bright. Among people there are lords and servitors; among states there are capitals and appanages. This is the ancient system"; *Guoyu Wei Zhao zhu* (Discourses of the States with commentary by Wei Zhao; 1800 ed.; reprint ed., Taibei, n.d.), *juan* 17, p. 9b. Numerous Eastern Zhou philosophical texts refer to elites and subordinates as "upper" and "lower," *shang* and *hsia;* as Han Fei Tzu (d. 233 B.C.E.), for example, wrote, "If the ruler [*shang*] loses an inch, his subordinates [*hsia*] gain a yard"; *Han Fei Tzu*, trans. Burton Watson (New York, 1964), 40.

50. For further illustrations of these shapes, see "Tantan Dawenkou wenhua" (A discussion of Dawenkou culture), *WW* 1978, no. 4:62–63. The *li* was probably a vessel form developed in the Central Plains, though its antecedents were presumably the hollow-legged forms of the East Coast; Shangraw, *Origins of Chinese Ceramics*, 22; Rawson, *Ancient China*, 30.

51. Franklin, "Beginnings of Metallurgy in China," 96.

52. See, e.g., the variety of *gui* shapes listed at p. 14 above. Barnard and Sato, *Metallurgical Remains*, 7, contrast "the remarkable variety of shapes and structures" of the ceramic *li* tripods and solid-legged vessels toward the close of the Longshan period (i.e., the Late Neolithic) and particularly during the early phases of Early Shang, with the "comparatively sluggish development continuing in flat-base and rim-base types."

53. Eleanor Burke Leacock, paraphrasing and quoting Engels in her editor's introduction to Friedrich Engels, "The Part Played by Labor in the Transition from Ape to Man," in *The Origins of the Family, Private Property and the State* (New York, 1972), 245.

54. A nonglazed pot, its exterior fairly damp, would be subject to fracture if placed in the fire too quickly (conversation with Brian Moeran, 19 September 1986). Experiment would be needed to determine if the shape of *ding* tripods or hollow-legged vessels protects against thermal shock.

55. David N. Keightley, "Pot Makers and Users in the Central Plains: Cultural Interaction in the Chinese Neolithic" (Paper delivered at the American Historical Association Annual Meeting, New York City, 28 December 1985), appendix 4, "Steamer Vessels: Origins and Distribution."

56. The correctness of this interpretation is suggested by the clusters of drinking goblets found in the earth fill of certain Dawenkou burials. Their placement above the corpse, at the edge of the pit, suggests they were not grave goods belonging to the deceased but had been used by the mourners in some final rite of farewell as the grave was filled in. For a discussion of these and other "ritual" vessels found in burials, see David N. Keightley, "Dead But Not Gone: The Role of Mortuary Practices in the Formation of Neolithic and Early Bronze Age Chinese Culture, ca. 8000 to

1000 B.C." (Paper delivered at the Conference on Ritual and the Social Significance of Death in Chinese Society, Oracle, Ariz., 2–7 January 1985), 44–46.

57. As W. David Kingery has proposed, "the development of ceramic techniques and materials is always a consequence of societal change rather than a cause"; "Interactions of Ceramic Technology with Society," in Prudence M. Rice, ed., *Pots and Potters: Current Approaches in Ceramic Archaeology*, Monograph 24, Institute of Archaeology, University of California (Los Angeles, 1984), 171–72.

58. Thomas Carlyle, *Signs of the Times*, quoted by Moeran, *Lost Innocence*, 10, 11.

59. For *spouts*, see, e.g., fig. 2, no. 4; fig. 3, nos. 2, 7, 8; fig. 7, nos. 9–19; fig. 13; for *single handles*: fig. 2, no. 4; fig. 3, no. 4; fig. 7, nos. 9–19; fig. 10, nos. 8, 10; fig. 13; for *lids*: fig. 2, no. 11; fig. 4, nos. 2, 3, 5; fig. 9, no. 10; fig. 10, nos. 1, 12; for *legs*: fig. 6, nos. 7–20; fig. 7, nos. 9–19; fig. 9; fig. 10, no. 6; figs. 11–13.

60. For spouts and lips, see, e.g., *Dawenkou*, p. 86, fig. 69; p. 91, fig. 74.3; p. 92, fig. 76; "Jiangsu Pi xian Dadunzi yizhi dierci fajueh" (Second excavation of the Dadunzi site in Pi county, Jiangsu), *Kaoguxue jikan* (Journal of Archaeology) 1 (1981): p. 44, fig. 19.14, pls. 12.2, 12.7. Handles are, of course, a feature of the East Coast *gui* (see p. 14). For teacup-like handles of East Coast *bei*, see, e.g., "Zhejiang Jiaxing Majiabang xinshiqi shidai yizhi di fajue" (Excavation of the Neolithic site at Majiabang in Jiaxing, Zhejiang), *KG* 1961, no. 7:350–51, figs. 8, 9; "Hemudu faxian," p. 13, figs. 20, 21.

61. See, e.g., Barnard and Satō, *Metallurgical Remains*, p. 4, fig. 1.

62. In the Northwest, two small loop handles were frequendy found on opposite sides of painted-pottery *hu* vases of the third millennium; they were presumably for the passage of supporting ropes or rods. Small "finger" handles sometimes appear at the necks of these vessels, for either the passage of a rope or, perhaps, for lifting them off the ground with two hands. Examples of these various handle types can be seen in "Gansu Lanzhou Jiaojiazhuang he Shelidian di Banshan taoqi" (Banshan pottery from Jiaojiazhuang and Shelidian in Lanzhou, Gansu), *KG* 1980, no. 1, pl. 1. In general, however, the Northwest handles were not sufficiently large or correctly placed to be held or manipulated by one hand.

63. One may note in this connection that stone hand axes with hand grips were a special feature of Liangzhu sites; *jiangsu sheng chutu wenwu xuanji* (Selection of cultural relics excavated in jiangsu province; Beijing, 1963), no. 44; this was a culture that liked to grasp and grip.

64. Murray, "Neolithic Chinese Jades," 19 (note, however, that the *cong* in her figs. 1.7 and 1.8 are reproduced upside down); Wang, "Liangzhu wenhua," 28.

65. Murray, "Neolithic Chinese Jades," p. 16, fig. 4; p. 17, fig. 6.

66. E.g., "Li xian Dongtian Dingjiagang xinshiqi shidai yizhi" (The Neolithic site of Dingjiagang in Dongdan, Li county), *Hunan kaogu jikan* 1 (1982); p. 11, fig. 13.2; *Shanghai gudai lishi wenwu tulu* (A pictorial record of ancient historical relics from Shanghai; Shanghai, 1981), 18, 23; René-Yvon Lefebvre d'Argencé, ed., *Treasures from the Shanghai Museum: 6,000 Years of Chinese Art* (Shanghai and San Francisco, 1983), no. 6; "jiangsu Hai'an Qingdun yizhi" (The site of Qingdun in Hai'an, jiangsu), *KX* 1983, no. 2:175, figs. 27.25–27. In the Keshengzhuang II culture the lids of *weng* urns were apparently made as one with the vessel and were then cut away before firing, being scored to make a tight fit; "Shilun Qijia wenhua yu Shaanxi Longshan wenhua di guanxi" (Exploratory discussion of the relations between Qijia culture and the Longshan culture of Shaanxi), *WW* 1979, no. 10:61.

67. E.g., the urn-burial containers depicted in *Xi'an Banpo*, pl. 145.

68. E.g., the stubby-footed vessels from Dadiwan I; "Gansu Qin'an Dadiwan xinshiqi shidai zaoqi yicun" (Remains from the early Neolithic at Dadiwan in Qin'an, Gansu), *WW* 1981, no. 4:8, figs. 13–16.

69. "Hemudu faxian," p. 12, fig. 27; "Hemudu yizhi," pp. 42–48, fig. 5.

70. Wu Shanjing, "Luelun Qinglian'gang wenhua" (Preliminary discussion of Qinglian' gang culture), *WW* 1973, no. 6:58.

71. "Zhejiang Jiashan Xin'gang faxian Liangzhu wenhua mu tong shuijing" (A wooden-tube water well of Liangzhu culture discovered at Xin'gang in Jiashan, Zhejiang), *WW* 1984, no. 2:94–95.

72. Wu, "Luelun Qinglian'gang wenhua," 58; "Hemudu yizhi," p. 72, fig. 25.3–5.

73. "1982 nian Jiangsu Changzhou Wujing Sidun yizhi di fajue" (The 1982 excavation of the site at Sidun in Wujing, Changzhou, Jiangsu), *KG* 1984, no. 2:118–19, fig. 9; p. 123, pl. 41.

74. My measurement of the registers carved into the *cong* in the Freer Gallery did not reveal a standard "Neolithic inch," though a wider sample should be studied with this question in mind; on three of the *cong* (Freer 16.157, 16.410, 16.500A) the registers were all ca. 24 mm high. The registers of two of the nine *cong* illustrated at fig. 16 were also approximately 24 mm high (my measurements are approximate since I derive them from the figure itself, which is drawn to scale). The registers on no. 4 were 25 mm high; on no. 6 they were 23 mm; the other registers ranged between 18 and 21 mm in height.

75. According to "1982 nian Sidun yizhi," 118, the tubular saws did not quite meet in fourteen out of thirty-three cases; Wang, "Liangzhu wenhua 'yu lian zang' shulue," 31, refers to fourteen out of thirty-two.

76. "Jiangsu Changshu Liangzhu wenhua yizhi" (The Liangzhu culture site at Changshu, Jiangsu), *WW* 1984, no. 2:14.

77. Further noting that the circles, which formed the eyes of the animal masks that decorated the *cong* registers, were only 2 mm in diameter, Wang, "Liangzhu wenhua 'yu lian zang' shulue," 33, has suggested that metal, tubular drills, presumably of bronze, must already have been in use. Clarence Shangraw has suggested to me that some of the grid designs painted on Northwestern pots filled their spaces so neatly that he believes a jig might have been used (conversation of 9 July 1984); this may well be so, but the distinction remains that in the Chinese Northwest such measurement would have been applied to surface decoration rather than to the construction and shaping of the pot or jade itself.

78. Renfrew, *Emergence of Civilisation*, 407.

79. E.g., the "sun and moon" within the cartouche carved on the jade *bi*, Freer 17.348A; or on the small bracelet, Freer 17.385A. See Wu, "Yizu zaoqi di yushi diaoke," 64–70; Murray, "Neolithic Chinese Jades," p. 16, fig. 4; p. 17, fig. 6.

80. Chang, *Archaeology of Ancient China*, p. 163, fig. 72, gives three componential examples involving sun, moon, and fire-or-mountain shapes.

81. Evidence for the early use of lacquer among the cultures of the East Coast is only beginning to appear. Primitive lacquer objects have been reported from the Majia-bang culture site of Weidun in Changzhou, southern Jiangsu (first half of the fourth millennium?); see Wang Zunguo, "Taihu diqu yuanshi wenhua di fenxi" (Analysis of the primitive culture of the Taihu region), *Zhong'guo kaogu xuehui diyici nianhui lunwenji* (Collected papers of the first annual meeting of the Chinese archaeological society; Beijing, 1979), 119. The Zhejiang Provincial Museum was displaying (November 1984) wooden bowls and barrels painted with lacquer from Hemudu

(first quarter of the fifth millennium B.C.E.). Since lacquer is a poison, its use provides one further example of "unnatural" Eastern manipulation of raw materials. Lacquer was another Eastern feature that characterized the Shang.

82. On the development of differentiated religious symbol systems, see Robert N. Bellah, *Beyond Belief: Essays on Religion in a Post-Traditional World* (New York, 1970), 16. The humanization of spiritual forces that Wu Hong ("Yizu zaoqi di yushi diaoke," 68) sees in the jade carvings of the East represents precisely the kind of clarifying, defining, and incarnating world view I discern in the technologies of the area. The sharp-toothed savagery of some of the jade masks he discusses—which anticipate in spirit, if not in form, the *taotie* "monster masks" on the Shang bronzes—also suggests a harsher approach to reality than that found in either the pot forms or designs of the Northwest. (On the probable Eastern origins of the *taotie* itself, see, e.g., Rawson, *Ancient China*, 38–40.)

83. My initial study of burial customs, artifact types, and housing patterns at one site, that of Dahe village, suggests no major influx of Eastern populations into that area of northern Henan in the centuries on either side of 3000 B.C.E, the period of greatest Eastern influence at the site; Keightley, "Pot Makers and Users," 83. The site has not yet been fully reported, however, and numerous similar surveys need to be conducted in the Central Plains before any reliable generalizations can be made.

84. Keightley, "Dead But Not Gone," 75–76; "Spirituality in China: The Neolithic Origins," in Charles Long, ed., *World Spirituality: An Encyclopedia of the Religious Quest*, vol. I, *Asian Archaic Spirituality* (in press).

85. Renfrew, *Emergence of Civilisation*, 63–80, esp. p. 79; T W. Jacobsen and Tracey Cullen, "A Consideration of Mortuary Practices in Neolithic Greece: Burials from Franchthi Cave," in S. C. Humphreys and Helen King, eds., *Mortality and Immortality: The Anthropology and Archaeology of Death* (London, 1981), 89, 94, 95. That large numbers of Neolithic cemeteries have been found in China, and relatively few in, say, Greece or Mesopotamia, may be due to the accidents of archaeological discovery, but the consistent divergence in the evidence so far available is striking.

86. The evidence is presented in Keightley, "Truth Is in Details," pp. 32–33, table 1. A third inference, as noted in that paper, would stress the difficulty involved in sexing skeletons accurately. It is possible that the reported variation in sex ratios reflects the bias of the modern archaeologists—some of whom may have assumed more than others, for example, that big skeletons and bones were male, small ones were female—rather than the Neolithic situation.

87. Ibid., 34–36.

88. Such a conclusion may need to be qualified, however, when we consider the custom of accompanying-in-death. Here again, the evidence is scanty and the practice does not seem to have been widespread. My preliminary research suggests that, during the last part of the third millennium, accompanying-in-death was more common in parts of the Northwest—along the network of rivers on the Qinghai-Gansu border to the west of Lanzhou—than in the East. This suggests the degree to which the elites of the Machang and Qijia cultures in this area may occasionally have developed ties of obligation and servitude. The elites of the East, by contrast, may have preferred to take advantage of the skilled labor of the living, as opposed to the post-mortem labor of dead accompaniers; such preference would be indicated by the highly worked jade *bi* disks and *cong* tubes placed in the Eastern burials. On these issues, see ibid., 48–54.

89. For the distribution of these features, see Keightley, "Dead But Not Gone," and "Truth Is in Details," 30–57.

90. Scholars such as Shi Zhangru and It Michiharu have argued for the Eastern origins of such divination; see the sources cited by David N. Keightley, *Sources of Shang History: The Oracle-Bone Inscriptions of Bronze Age China* (Berkeley, 1978), p. 8, n. 26.

91. For the view that a variety of prototypical vessels, such as early forms of the *ding* tripod, the *dou* pedestal bowl, and the *zeng* steamer originated in the Central Plains but were subsequently elaborated in the East and were there given more precise functional definition, greater structural strength, and greater aesthetic coherence, see Keightley, "Pot Makers and Users," 75, 92–114.

92. An Zhimin, "Zhong'guo zaoqi tongqi di chubu yanjiu" (Preliminary study of early bronze artifacts in China), *KX* 1981, no. 3:287–90; Yan Wenming, "Lun Zhong'guo di tong shi bingyong shidai" (On China's chalcolithic age), *Shiqian yanjiu* (Prehistory) 1984, no. 1:36–41.

93. Ursula Martius Franklin, "On Bronze and Other Metals in Early China," in Keightley, ed., *Origins of Chinese Civilization*, 288, stresses the particular kind of social order required by the large-scale bronze production of the Shang.

94. Modern scholars have frequently assumed that the tall-stemmed goblets, which were characteristic East Coast vessels (e.g., figs. 11–12), may have been filled with wine drunk in mortuary rituals. For the probable use of alcohol in the Neolithic East, see Keightley, "Dead But Not Gone," 44–46; "Eastern Yi," 10–13. See too the evidence cited in n. 56 above.

95. An anthropologist's explanation of the "lively, even tumultuous socializing and play" that characterizes the funerals of the Bara of Madagascar is relevant here. "An important aspect of the representation of vitality is the idea that it is chaotic, as opposed to the order of the ancestor cult. ... It is in this regard that rum takes on special significance. Rum is served not merely because intoxication is pleasant, but because disorderly conduct is essential"; Richard Huntington and Peter Metcalf, *Celebrations of Death: The Anthropology of Mortuary Ritual* (Cambridge, 1979), 114.

96. Franklin, "Beginnings of Metallurgy in China," 96.

97. Mauss, "Techniques of the Body," 86.

98. To the extent that any ecological explanation bears on the voluntarist, activist strain proposed for the cultures of the East, one is tempted to suggest that the rice cultivation upon which these cultures, at least in the lower Yangzi drainage, depended was more demanding in terms of scheduling and social discipline than the millet agriculture of the Northwest. One would need to know more than may be archaeologically recoverable, however, about the way in which Neolithic rice was grown, how much attention the paddy fields, if any, required, whether water flow had to be allocated and measured, how frequently the shoots had to be weeded, and so on. If it is true, as Karl A. Wittfogel suggested ("The Foundations and Stages of Chinese Economic History," *Zeitschrift für sozialforschung* 4, no. 1 [1935]: 36), that the danger of flooding made the North China plain difficult for habitation (he, in fact, pronounced it "uninhabitable" before the construction of dikes), then we would have another environmental challenge to which the peoples of the East might have had to respond.

99. Renfrew, *Emergence of Civilisation*, 27–44, 476–504.

100. Wm. Theodore de Bary, Wing-tsit Chan, and Burton Watson, eds., *Sources of Chinese Tradition* (New York, 1960), 121; *Xunzi* (Taibei, 1964; Sibu beiyao), *juan* 17, pp. 2b–3a.

101. Keightley, "Craft and Culture."
102. Chang, *Shang Civilization*, 335–55.
103. For the kind of detailed study needed, see Louisa G. Fitzgerald Huber, "The Role of Art in Questions of Cultural Contact in Neolithic and Early Shang China" (Paper delivered at the Annual Meeting of the American Historical Association, New York City, 28 December 1985); see too the works cited in nn. 16 and 17 above. Any future explanation for the genesis of Shang culture is probably going to have to take account of the contribution made by the Hongshan culture, situated in Liaoning, Jilin, and Heilongjiang, with its amazingly rich jades, and by the Lower Xiajiadian culture, found in northern Hebei, southeastern Inner Mongolia, and western Liaoning, with its striking painted pots and early bronzes. Thougli these cultures, whose importance has only recently been appreciated, may to varying degrees be associated with the cultures of the East Coast, their more northern location and their various affiliations with the Central Plains suggest one of the many ways in which the idealized Northwest-East Coast dichotomy utilized in this essay stands in need of qualification. They also confirm that Neolithic cultures near China's borders by no means observed modern political boundaries. For an introduction to these cultures, see, e.g., for Hongshan: *Xin Zhong'guo di kaogu faxian he yanjiu* (Archaeological Excavation and Research in New China; Beijing, 1984), 172–76; the group of articles in *WW* 1984, nos. 6 and 11; Su Bingqi, "Liaoxi guwenhua gucheng guguo" (Old culture, old city, and old state in western Liaoning), *WW* 1986, no. 4:42–43. For Lower Xiajiadian: An Zhimin, "Some Problems Concerning China's Early Copper and Bronze Artifacts," trans. Julia K. Murray, *Early China* 8 (1982–83): 59–61 (the original article appeared in *KX* 1981, no. 3:269–84); Su, "Liaoxi guwenhua," 43.
104. The contribution that the peoples of the Northwest made to the eventual Shang synthesis needs to be explored, but it seems that the "mental" dimension of their activities has not left the kind of archaeologically recoverable traces that I discern in the East. There may well indeed have been right ways and wrong ways to use the painted pots of the Northwest. Nor can one argue that the relative simplicity of Northwestern pot manufacture and usage necessarily implies noncomplex social or ritual arrangements. What distinguished the cultures of the East, however, was precisely their ability to express their social arrangements in their crafts, doing so to a degree that was not replicated in the Northwest.
105. Leacock, in Engels, *Origins of the Family*, 247.

2

EARLY CIVILIZATION IN CHINA: REFLECTIONS ON HOW IT BECAME CHINESE

(1490)

David N. Keightley

If we are to understand how the culture of China differs from that of other great civilizations, two fundamental and related questions need to be addressed: How did China become Chinese and how do we define "Chineseness"? Answers to these questions not only aid our understanding of the origins of Chinese culture but also, by implication and contrast, throw light on how Western values and social organization developed differently.

Before pursuing these questions, three prefatory comments are in order. First, only in broad, comparative treatments such as this one are generalizations about "Chinese culture" permitted. Even for the early period, we need to remember that there were many versions of Chinese culture that varied with time, place, and social level; I hardly do justice to all of them in this chapter. In particular, I focus less on the explicit philosophical tradition represented by such early thinkers as Confucius and more on the religious, social, aesthetic, and political practices of the Neolithic to the early Bronze Age from which these philosophers drew their assumptions and values.

Second, it must be stressed that my concerns as a historian are explanatory, not judgmental. I emphasize this point because on occasion I describe early China as having "lacked" certain features present in my Mesopotamian and Greek "touchstone cultures." But this negative terminology is contrastive, not pejorative; as we see by the end, it is in no sense meant to imply that such features ought to have been present.

Third, I should like to call attention to the word "reflections" in my subtitle, for it serves a double function. Our visions of early Chinese (or Greek, or Mesopotamian) culture are partly and inevitably a product of the later culture's own conceptions of what its past was or ought to have been. The values of the present, generated by the past, reflect back on that past; fact is seen as value, and value in turn affects what facts are seen. Accordingly, the present chapter does not simply express my reflections on how the Chinese became Chinese. It also in part reflects how the later elite Chinese, on their reflection—represented by the editing and promoting of certain texts and quasi-historical scenarios—thought that they

became Chinese. The discrepancies that arise between these later idealizing reflections and earlier unedited reality are the continuing concern of the professional
historian. It is one of the functions of this chapter to place those concerns in a
wider context.

The Hero and Society

Heroic Action: Its Representation and Consequences

Because cultures are man-made and serve to define man's conception of himself, it is helpful in considering the question of what it means to be "Chinese"
to start by comparing the conception of man as hero in ancient China with
analogous conceptions in Classical Greece (fifth to fourth century B.C.), a culture that has contributed so much to our Western understanding of the human
condition. The legend of Achilles and the Amazon queen, for example, which
was popular in both Greek and Roman cultures, expresses strategic views about
the individual and society that would have been entirely foreign to Chinese
contemporaries.[1]

If we consider the legend of Achilles and the Amazon queen as treated by
the Penthesileia Painter on a kylix vase from ca. 460 B.C. (figure 2.1), we note a
variety of characteristic features. The two protagonists are heroic in size, seeming
to burst the confines of the bowl. Achilles is virtually naked. And the representation is characterized by the particularity of both its subject and its artist: we can
identify the two figures, Achilles and Penthesileia, and we can identify, at least as
an artist if not by name, the individual who made the vase. Most important, there
is the ironic tale itself. At the moment when Achilles plunges his sword into the
breast of his swooning victim, their eyes cross—and he falls in love! That moment
of dramatic and fatal pathos is the one the artist has captured.[2] The painting and
the legend express in powerful, individual, and supposedly historical terms one
of the major assumptions of the classical tradition in the West, namely, that the
human condition is tragic and poignant, that the best and most heroic deeds
may lead to unwished-for consequences, and that even heroic virtue must be its
own reward. People live in a quirky, unpredictable, and ironic world that is by no
means responsive to human values and desires.

The decoration found on an Eastern Chou Chinese bronze *hu* vase from
about the same period (figure 2.2) is strikingly different. Instead of individuals
we are presented with stereotypical silhouettes, all of whom wear the uniform
of their fellows. We do not know the names of any of the people represented.
We do not know the names of any of the people involved in casting the vessel.
We do not even know with any assurance the meaning of the actions depicted
(see figure 2.2 caption). Whatever their precise iconographic coherence—which
may have involved some generalized depiction of rituals and martial skills—the
overwhelming impression conveyed by these tableaux is one of contemporaneous,
regimented, mass activity, whether in peace or war; even the birds appear to be

Figure 2.1 Kylix by the Penthesileia Painter. Munich, Antikensammlung. Photograph: Hirmer Fotoarchiv München.

flying in formation. The individuals portrayed, small and anonymous, have been subordinated by an equally anonymous master designer to a larger order.

This Chinese vase expresses the ideals of organization that were being applied with increasing effectiveness during the period of the Warring States (453–221 B.C.), a period when men fought less for individual honor, as Achilles had done, and more for the survival of the state. Aesthetic concerns were focused on the general, the social, and the non-heroic rather than on the particular, the individual, and the heroic. This stereotyping, this bureaucratization of experience, is implicit not only in the decor of the Chinese bronze—for somebody was presumably overseeing these soldiers and orchestra players—but also in its manufacture—for somebody had surely directed the numerous artisans involved in the industrial-scale casting of the vessel. Once again, this contrasts sharply with the practices of the Greeks, who both admired the individual and who organized their workshops around a series of acts performed by single craftsmen.

The Hands of the Hero: Dirty or Clean?

The role of hero and protagonist was radically different in the two cultures. Achilles acts for himself. He feels the thrust of the blade as it pierces his opponent's breast; he is directly responsible; he has "dirty hands." The analogous Chinese vision of the hero, at least by the time of the Eastern Chou, was radically different.

Figure 2.2 Drawing of the decor on an Eastern Chou (late sixth to fifth century
B.C.) *hu* wine vase from Chengtu, Szechwan. From *Wen-wu* 1977. 11:86.
Moving up the vessel, we see: *bottom register*, a battle by land and sea; *middle
register, clockwise from bottom left*, archers shooting at birds, a banquet scene,
a bell-and-chime orchestra; *top register*, more archery (*in the bottom half*), the
plucking of mulberry branches (perhaps for the making of bows), an archery
contest. At least three examples of bronze *hu* decorated with these kinds of
scenes have been found. See Jenny F. So, "The Inlaid Bronzes of the Warring
States Period," in *The Great Bronze Age of China*, ed. Wen Fong (New York:
Metropolitan Museum and Knopf, 1980), 316, and Esther Jacobson, "The
Structure of Narrative in Early Chinese Pictorial Vessels," *Representations* 8 (Fall
1984): 77–80.

Ssu-ma Ch'ien, for example, the "Herodotus of China," who wrote at the start of the first century B.C., presents five Chou and Ch'in case histories in a chapter entitled "Biographies of the Assassin-Retainers."[3] The leitmotif is that of a statesman who has an enemy he wishes to dispatch. Rather than undertaking the task himself, as Achilles would have done, the Chinese protagonist relies on the charisma of his elevated social and political position to engage an assassin. The assassin, in turn, attempts to perform the deed (with results fatal to himself in four of the five cases), not for monetary gain but to requite the overwhelming social honor the lord had conferred by deigning to entrust him with the task.

The genesis of such characteristic social obligations is a theme to which I return later. Here I simply note that the lord delegates what, in the Greek case, would have been the heroic, the personal, and thus the tragic, task. His hands are clean; they are not on the sword; he is not even near when the deed is undertaken. A bureaucratic chain of command protects the initiator from the shock and consequences of his deeds. The lord is not the hero; he has become an administrator. The hero, in these cases, does not act for himself; he is a delegate. There is a division between the lord's original motivation for the deed and the protagonist's heroic execution of it.

Ambiguity and Optimism

The pedagogical role of the hero (or the heroine—the role of gender in such matters would be worth exploring) in the two cultures also differed. The heroes of the Greeks often served only as tragic, negative examples; few Greeks would wish to imitate Achilles by killing the woman he loved (or imitate Oedipus by killing his father, Orestes by killing his mother, or Antigone by killing herself—the examples are numerous). And when Greeks in their hubris acted in the arbitrary and passionate ways of the gods, they met disaster. Achilles would have loved Penthesileia, but he killed her; he did love Patroclus, but his arrogance as he sulked in his tent led to Patroclus's death.

In early China, by contrast, heroes were heroes precisely because they were models worthy of emulation; the universe of moral action, at least as it was represented in the accounts of myth and history, was untrammeled by ambiguities. The basic, optimistic assumption of the *Tso chuan*, the massive semihistorical chronicle compiled in the fourth century B.C., was that the virtuous man would be rewarded here and now—by promotions, honors, and status. Cause and effect in the universe were rigorously fair; the moral prospered, the wicked did not. The subversive thought that the best intentions might lead to chaos and regret—not, as in the cases of Confucius or Ch'ü Yuan, because those in power were too unenlightened to employ them, but because there was something flawed in the human condition itself—was rarely dramatized (see the discussion of theodicy below).[4]

One could multiply many instances of this early, uncomplicated Chinese view of man as a social being, embedded in and defined by the obligations and rewards of a hierarchical, ethical, bureaucratic system. The large-scale recruitment of labor by a centralized bureaucratic elite (as suggested by figure 2.2), the members of which, as Mencius (ca. 372–289 B.C.) pointed out, labor with their minds rather than their hands, may be discerned in the Chinese record from at least the early Bronze Age, if not earlier (see the discussion of Neolithic burials below). Eastern Chou states were builders of major public works, particularly city walls and the long, defensive walls that eventually culminated in the building of the Great Wall at the end of the third century B.C. The massive recruitment of labor was idealized in semihistorical accounts in which the people, both elites and masses, had cheerfully flocked to serve virtuous rulers, often dynasty founders, who had won their allegiance not by coercion but by exemplary government. Virtue was again rewarded, in this instance by the loyal service of others.

Such optimistic faith in the comprehensibility and benevolence of the universe, which runs through the classical texts and which was explicitly articulated in the view of Mencius that man's nature is basically good, can be related to what Thomas A. Metzger has termed the fundamental "epistemological optimism" of early Chinese philosophy. This optimism may be defined as the willingness to accept large, roughly defined moral ideas—like "benevolence" or "righteousness"—as reliable, universal, and objective; Metzger contrasts this with the kind of pessimistic epistemology represented by Descartes's "clear and distinct ideas."[5] Optimism about man's lot helps to explain the lack of interest in dramatic detail found in early Chinese texts (discussed below). It also helps explain the Chinese distrust of laws and constitutions, the traditional preference for *jen-chih*, "government by men," rather than for *fa-chih*, "government by laws."

Later I consider the sources of this confidence, but it was surely such "radical world optimism,"[6] such trust in one's leader as a moral *chün-tzu*, or "noble man," and the optimistic assumption—by the recruiters, if not always by the recruits— that such voluntary and nonproblematic state service was natural and proper that helps to explain the Chinese readiness to trust great leaders, whether Emperor Wu of the Han or Mao Tse-tung of the People's Republic. This optimism also helps to explain the lack of safeguards against the power of the state that has characterized Chinese government for at least two thousand years. If leaders are good—and if the good is unambiguous—who needs to be protected against them? Achilles, his hand on the sword, his act regretted as it is committed, represents a more somber vision. To the Greeks, the hero might not be bad, but he might be fundamentally and tragically mistaken. To the Chinese, a hero, by definition, was good; his mistakes, if he made any, were likely to be tactical in nature. His intent was free from error and regret.

The Neolithic to Bronze Age Transition

I now turn to the evolution of Chinese culture in the Neolithic and early Bronze Ages, with particular attention to such subjects as individualism (or its absence), ritual and decorum, bureaucratic control, dependency and obligation, and metaphysical optimism. The Neolithic is of fundamental importance because of the remarkable continuity of post-Neolithic cultural development in China. It is probably truer for China than for most parts of the world that as the Neolithic twig was bent the modern tree has inclined.

Neolithic cultures in China flourished during the Postglacial Climatic Optimum, when it is probable that temperatures were some two to four degrees Celsius warmer than they are today and rainfall, in at least the Middle Yangtze and north China, was more abundant. The development of early Chinese culture must be understood in the context of these relatively beneficent natural conditions.

Socially, the transition from the Neolithic to the Bronze Age in China, as elsewhere in the world, witnessed the evolution of urban forms, the genesis of the state, the institutionalization of exploitation and servitude, the validation of characteristic forms of sacrifice, and the systematic articulation of religious beliefs. Spiritually and psychologically, this transition witnessed the development of a temperament and mentality that found certain worldviews and cosmological assumptions natural and comfortable, involving, in particular, the willing acceptance of hierarchy, filiality, and obedience.

In the realm of religion, the Neolithic and Bronze Age cultures of the Near East, Greece, and East Asia—to say nothing of those of Egypt and India—developed belief systems and institutions that dealt in different ways with the one certainty that faces us all: eventual death. Death can, paradoxically, be a lively topic, for from Neolithic times onward the way people have treated death and the dead has been deeply expressive of, and has had a significant impact on, the way they have treated the living.

Neolithic China

Archaeological evidence provides considerable reason for thinking that distinctions between rich and poor, male and female, and the powerful and the weak were emerging in China by the fourth and third millennia B.C. Not only did grave goods become more abundant, but the general egalitarianism of the early Neolithic burials was replaced by marked discrepancies in energy input, wealth, and ritual care in later burials (figure 2.3). Similarly, certain houses and certain village areas begin to reveal differentiation in the goods available to the living. The presence of grave goods—which, although finely made, were generally items of daily life—presumably indicates a belief in some kind of postmortem existence.

The burial, particularly in Eastern sites, of superbly made polished stone and jade tools, such as axes and spades, whose edges reveal no traces of use, also indicates that status differentiation was prolonged beyond the grave. These objects suggest that certain members of the society had been the possessors of symbolic, rather than working, tools—emblems of the owner's power to control the labor of others, both in this life and in the next. There were already by about the mid fourth millennium B.C. some people in China whose hands were not as "dirty" as those of others.

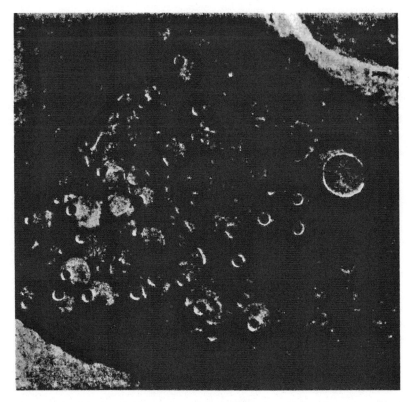

Figure 2.3 A Late Neolithic supine-extended burial with abundant grave goods at Liu-wan, eastern Tsinghai. From *K'ao-ku* 1976.6, plate 2.

The Late Neolithic saw the emergence of scapulimancy and plastromancy, methods of divination in which the scapulas of animals (usually cattle) or the plastrons of turtles were scorched or burnt, the diviner interpreting the resulting cracks to foretell good or ill fortune. The presence of some of these "oracle bones" in cemetery areas suggests that the living, by cracking oracle bones, were attempting to communicate with the dead. One may assume that a consistently successful diviner would have acquired increased political authority, an authority supported by his powerful kin, both living and dead.

The Neolithic Chinese treated their dead with remarkable and characteristic assiduity. Corpses were buried in orderly rows, oriented to certain compass directions depending on the area of China in which they had lived. This orderly layout presumably reflected expectations of social order among the living. The corpses were also generally buried in the supine-extended position (see figure 2.3), a practice that required more labor for the digging of the burial pit than, for instance, a flex burial. The log construction of coffin chambers in certain Eastern burials, particularly at the Ta-wen-k'ou site in

Shantung, or of tomb ramps in the northwest is a further indication of the labor expended on mortuary concerns.

The practice of collective secondary burial, which, although never dominant, flourished in the Central Plains and the Northwest during the fifth millennium, is particularly revealing. The cleaning away of the flesh and the careful reburial of the bones—frequently arranged in the standard supine-extended posture of the primary burials, and with skulls oriented to the prevailing local direction (figure 2.4)—implies the ability to mobilize labor resources for the collective reinterment of up to seventy or eighty skeletons in one pit. It also implies that the dead must have been kept alive in the minds of their survivors during the period of months, if not years, between primary and secondary burial.

Other mortuary rituals were employed. The placement of some of the jars and goblets in Neolithic burials, for example, suggests the existence of farewell libations by mourners as the grave was being filled in (figure 2.5); the precarious, tall-stemmed black goblets of the East (figure 2.6)—whose fine, eggshell-thin construction itself suggests some special ritual function—may have been used for the consumption of millet wine at the time of interment.

One of the most remarkable of all Neolithic burials is M3 at the Liangchu culture site of Ssu-tun in Kiangsu (ca. 2500 B.C.; figure 2.7). which

Figure 2.4 Secondary burials in grave M441 at Yuan-chün-miao, Shensi. From *Yuan-chün-miao Yang-shao mu-ti* (Peking: Wen-wu Ch'u-pan-she, 1983), plate 33.

Figure 2.5 Grave M25 at Ta-wen-k'ou, Shantung. The eight tall *pei* goblets at the bottom of the picture had been placed in the earth fill and had presumably been used in a farewell ritual. From *Ta-wen-k'ou: Hsin-shih-ch'i shih-tai mu-tsang fa-chueh pao-kao* (Peking: Wen-wu Ch'u-pan-she, 1974). plate 13.3.

gives ample evidence of ritual activity: the corpse had been placed atop ten jade *pi* disks that had been burned; the body had then been surrounded by a variety of jade and stone tools and ornaments, including a perimeter of twenty-seven jade *ts'ung* tubes; and five of the twenty-four jade *pi* in the burial had been deliberately broken in two and placed in different parts of the grave. Given the difficulty of working with jade, a material that has been described as "sublimely impractical," the presence of large numbers of finely carved jade *pi* and *ts'ung* in other Lower Yangtze burials of the third millennium—they have never been found in the housing remains—is further indication of the way in which the labors of the living were exploited for the service of the dead.

Some burials also contained victims: animal and, occasionally, human. Human sacrifice was not widespread in the Neolithic, but there is evidence—both in a Yang-shao burial at P'u-yang in northern Honan (end of the fifth millennium?) and in Ma-ch'ang and Chi-chia burials in eastern Tsinghai and western Kansu (toward the end of the third millennium)—that a small number of people were accompanying others in death, further evidence of the kinds of payments

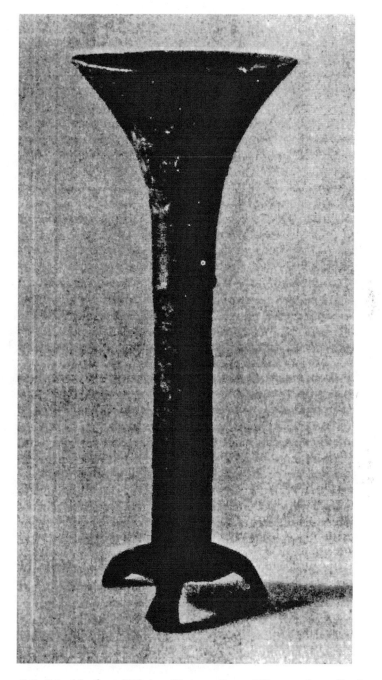

Figure 2.6 *Pei* goblet from P'i hsien, Kiangsu. From *Chiang-su sheng ch'u-t'u wen-wu hsuan-chi* (Peking: Wen-wu Ch'u-pan-she, 1963), no. 43.

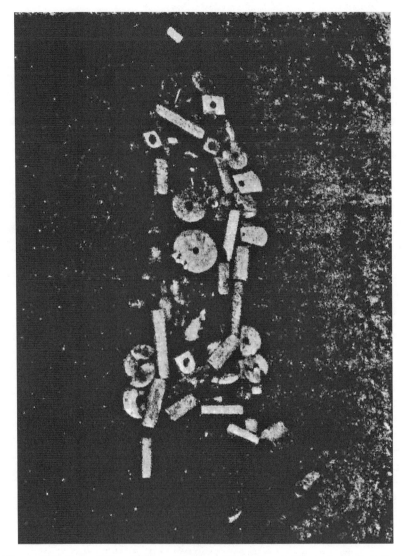

Figure 2.7 Grave M3 at Ssu-tun, Kiangsu. The corpse is "shrouded in jade." From *K'ao-ku* 1984.2, plate 2.

the living were constrained to offer the dead (figure 2.8). The presence of an occasional tool by the side of the victim indicates, at least in the later sites, that a servant in this life was to continue as a servant in the next life. Ties of obligation and servitude were so strong that they persisted after death.

Bronze Age China

By the Late Shang period (ca. 1200–1045 B.C.), represented by the archaeological finds at Hsiao-t'un, near Anyang in the northern Honan panhandle, increasing

Figure 2.8 Grave M327 at Liu-wan, eastern Tsinghai. The central corpse, buried in a flex position, is thought to have accompanied the other two corpses in death. From *Wen-wu* 1976.1: 75, figure 11.

stratification and the institutionalization of power were both represented and reinforced by a highly developed cult of the dead. The oracle-bone inscriptions reveal that the dead were worshiped as ancestors according to an increasingly precise ritual schedule. Neolithic mortuary traditions were amplified but not radically altered.

With regard to grave goods, for example, the unrifled burial known as M5—which has been linked to Fu Hao, a consort or royal woman associated with the powerful king Wu Ting (ca. 1200–1181 B.C.)—contained over sixteen hundred grave goods, including 468 bronzes whose total weight was over one and one-half tons. Extrapolation from this relatively small burial suggests that the contents of the looted tombs in the royal cemetery at Hsi-pei-kang, across the river to the northwest of Hsiao-t'un, would have been even more impressive. The tombs were veritable underground storehouses of the finest products that Shang civilization could create; these great cruciform, ramped pits, up to forty-two feet deep (figure 2.9) and equipped with beamed, room-sized grave chambers up to nine feet high, were monuments to the affection and obligation that linked living descendants to dead parents.

Such tombs are eloquent proof of the intensity with which the mortuary cult both exploited and stimulated the labors of the community. The digging and refilling (with rammed earth) of such a pit alone, quite apart from the labor involved in furnishing it with the wooden chamber, coffin, and costly grave goods like bronzes and jades, would have taken one hundred men well over two hundred days to complete. The continual draining of wealth to provide goods for the dead was the early Chinese equivalent of conspicuous consumption

Figure 2.9 A Late Shang royal tomb at Hsi-pei-kang. From Liang Ssu-yung and Kao Ch'ü-hsun, *Hou-chia-chuang 1002-hao ta mu* (Taipei: Academia Sinica, Institute of History and Philology, 1965), plate 3.

and planned obsolescence; it stimulated the productive powers of craftsmen and laborers by expropriating the fruit of their efforts in a culturally rational manner. A system of exchange was evidently involved. Motivated by spiritualized kinship ties, mortuary taxes on the immediate wealth of the living served to guarantee the future prosperity of their descendants.

The number of human victims associated with the Shang royal burials is impressive, as it was undoubtedly intended to be. It may be estimated that some of the royal four-ramp tombs would have claimed the lives of over three hundred sacrificial victims and accompaniers-in-death and that, over the course of the approximately one hundred and fifty years in which it was in use, some five thousand victims may have been buried in the Hsi-pei-kang burial complex; these figures, which do not include some ten thousand human sacrifices recorded in divinations about the regular ancestral cult, represent a rate of about thirty-three victims a year, or 550 per king. The mortuary victims were drawn from a cross section of Shang society: elite accompaniers-in-death, placed near the king and buried whole, sometimes with their own coffins, grave goods, and even accompaniers-in-death; guards, buried whole with their weapons; and prisoners of war, the most numerous group, generally young males, decapitated or dismembered and buried in the earth fill, in the ramps, or in adjacent sacrificial pits. This last group, the sacrificial victims, outnumbered the accompaniers-in-death by a ratio of about twenty to one.

Similar large-scale immolations were not unknown in Mesopotamia—for example, in the royal cemetery of Ur, where from three to seventy-four attendants accompanied the ruler—but there the custom was short-lived and virtually unrecorded in texts. Human sacrifice was rarely practiced in the Greek Bronze Age.[7] More significantly, there is virtually no evidence of accompanying-in-death. Elite Greeks were not linked to each other by ties of obligation and dependency that bound them in death as they had presumably been bound in life. In China, by contrast, the custom was practiced for a far longer period, continuing to a significant degree in the burials of local rulers and even emperors down to the Ch'in–Han period and beyond, with the number of victims varying from a few to over a hundred.

The oracle-bone inscriptions—with their records of systematic offerings to dead kings, whose own powers and abilities to intercede with Ti, the Lord on High, extended to such fundamental areas as weather, climate, and victory in battle—reveal the central, institutionalized role that ancestor worship played in the workings of the Shang state. This power accorded to dead fathers and grandfathers suggests, accordingly, that Shang lineages were strong and that kinship affiliation, reinforced by religious sanctification, was a powerful force for allegiance and motivation. It may be supposed that Shang ancestor worship, which promoted the dead to higher levels of authority and impersonality with the passage of generations, encouraged the genesis of hierarchical, protobureaucratic conceptions and that it enhanced the value of these conceptions as more secular forms of government replaced the Bronze Age theocracy.

Ancestor Worship and Its Consequences

The Late Shang state emerged by building upon and institutionalizing, rather than opposing, the ties of affection, obligation, and dependency indicated by the mortuary practices of the Neolithic. The close fit between dynastic and religious power that resulted had at least three significant consequences.

First, it meant that there was no independent priesthood that might serve as an alternative locus of power or criticism; the king, as lineage head, was his own priest. The heads of all powerful lineages had access to the independent and friendly religious power of their own ancestors without the mediation of other religious specialists. Second, it meant that the way in which the values of kinship obligation, ancestor worship, and dynastic service reinforced one another led to an enduring unitary conception of the state as a religio-familial-political institution that could embrace, ideally, all aspects of one's allegiance, leaving little ideological ground vacant as a base for dissent. Given the totality of the Chinese state, it is no wonder that the only Eastern Chou "oppositionists" who left much of an intellectual mark, the Taoists of the Chuang Tzu school, had to reject conceptions of service and hierarchy. Confucius and his followers could certainly lament contemporary realities, but they were essentially meliorists working within the value system rather than radical critics of the system itself. It is also no wonder that rebels against the state were frequently to appeal to the vast world of popular nature powers, gods, and Buddhist saviors, who stood outside the normative politico-religious structure of the lineage. Third, it meant that the Chinese humanism of the Eastern Chou, represented by such great social thinkers as Confucius, Mencius, and Hsun Tzu, did not see any opposition between secular and religious values and were able, in Fingarette's striking phrase, to treat "the secular as sacred."[8] The humanism that resulted, therefore, was based on social and kin relations sanctified by religious assumptions. Ritual and hierarchical expectations were applied to all aspects of a monistic cosmos; just as there had been no opposition between king (or lineage head) and priest, so there was no tension between the counterclaims of god and man, between a Zeus and a Prometheus. The optimism of the Chinese tradition, which has already been noted, can be understood as both producing and being reinforced by this fundamental sense of harmonious collaboration. There was, once again, no sense of immanent moral paradox or conflict.

Death and the Birth of Civilization

Next I attempt to integrate early Chinese mortuary practices with other aspects of the culture, considering how the meaning of one set of customs may be more richly understood when seen in the context of others, how one set of assumptions about the human condition was reinforced by, and would have reinforced, others.

Death and Continuity

Shang burial customs helped to define what it was to be a ruler (or a retainer). The wealth, the dependents, and the victims accompanying the king into the next world demonstrated that his superior status (and the inferior status of his retainers) would be unchanged after death. This view of death as a continuity rather than a new beginning had already been implied by the grave goods and mortuary customs of the Chinese Neolithic. Death offered none of the escape, none of the psychic mobility offered by the mystery religions of the Near East or by Christianity itself with its vision of a redemptive death and rebirth as "in Abraham's bosom." In early China death provided an effective opportunity for survivors to validate the central values of the culture. No dead Chinese king would have been permitted the lament made by Achilles in book 11 of the *Iliad*—"Better, I say, to break sod as a farm hand/for some country man, on iron rations,/than lord it over all the exhausted dead"—for such an admission would have undermined the respect and obedience owed to the dead elites and thus to their living descendants. Once a king, always a king; death could not change that.

Death as Unproblematic

One striking feature of the early Chinese written record is its view of death as unproblematic. Death was simply not the issue it was for the ancient Mesopotamians or the ancient Greeks. Nowhere, for example, in the ancient Chinese record does one find the mythical claim, found in Mesopotamian texts, that death existed prior to the creation of both the universe and man. Nowhere does one find the angry and anguished voice of a Gilgamesh, horrified by the death of Enkidu and by Enkidu's depressing account of the life to come:

> the house where one who goes in never comes out again,
> the road that, if one takes it, one never comes back,
> the house that, if one lives there, one never sees light,
> the place where they live on dust, their food is mud.
>
> . . . .
>
> My body, that gave your heart joy to touch.
> vermin eat it up like old clothes.
> My body, that gave your heart joy to touch,
> Is filled with dirt.[9]

There is no ancient Chinese myth, like that of the Garden of Eden, that accounts for the "invention" of death or that treats death as some flaw in the divine plan. There are no visits to, or descriptions of, the realm of the dead that would compare with the descriptions we have of the Netherworld for the Mesopotamians or of Hades for the Greeks. Nowhere do we find the epic concerns of the *Iliad* and *Odyssey*, which focus on the manner of death, the ritual treatment of the dead, and the unhappy fate of the shades after death and which express so powerfully the tragic (once again the word recurs) poignancy that death confers on the human condition. Nowhere do we find a philosophical discourse, like Plato's *Phaedo*, that is devoted to the nature of death and the soul.[10] The very silence of the Chinese texts about such matters suggests a remarkable Chinese ability to emphasize life over death. Ancestor worship and the endurance of the lineage served to render the loss of the individual more palatable. Indeed, these practices would have served to promote, as they were promoted by, a conception of the individual and his role quite different from that held by the Mesopotamians and Greeks.

Morality and the Absence of Theodicy

The great mythic themes in China were not dying and death but social order and social morality; there is no Chinese equivalent to the heroic and adversarial universe of Gilgamesh or Inanna, Achilles or Hector. One is impressed and attracted by the general harmony that pervades the relations of the Chinese to their gods. For example, although there had been a flood, dimly described, its main function was to provide the sage emperor Yü with a sphere for his labors in political geography, delineating the borders for the various regions of China. The famous saying, recorded in the *Tso chuan*, "But for Yü we should have been fishes," pays tribute to his having made the world habitable; the myth does not address the issue of why the flood occurred. There is, in fact, a characteristic lack of theodicy in early Chinese culture, its fundamental optimism seeming to render unnecessary any explanations for the presence of evil.

There was no sense in early Chinese mythology that the gods were malevolent, that they resented human success, that they might conspire to destroy man, or that man was becoming too numerous and too tiresome, themes that are all present in Mesopotamian and Greek myth and in the Old Testament. Just as there was no Prometheus, neither was there any Zeus. Given this lack of divine animus, of immanent man-god hostility, it was natural that death in China should not have been regarded as an affront to mortals to the degree that it was in Mesopotamia and Greece; rather, it was part of the inevitable and harmonious order. In a kin-based society where the royal ancestors were in Heaven, there was little discord between god and men. There was little need, in short, for a Chinese Gilgamesh or a Chinese Job, asking why a man who has done no wrong should die or suffer. The issue, when it did arise, as in the cases of Po Yi and Shu Ch'i (note 4, this chapter) or of Confucius himself, who was shunned by the rulers of his age, was usually conceived in terms of employment, reward, and recognition rather than suffering or destruction. Even in his moving letter to Jen An in which the great historian Ssu-ma Ch'ien, who had been punished by Emperor Wu of the Han, laments his castration, his regrets are characteristically couched not in terms of his own loss but in terms of his having failed to serve the emperor and his colleagues effectively.[11]

Death, the Individual, and the Supernatural

Attitudes toward death depend on cultural conceptions of what has been lost. Just as the bitter reactions to death in the cases of the *Gilgamesh* and the Greek epics, for example, may be related to strong conceptions of personal roles in the two cultures, so may the quieter, more accepting responses of the early Chinese, who were less anguished metaphysically by death, be related to their deemphasis on individual heroic action.

The lack of emphasis on the individual may also be seen in the realm of the supernatural. By contrast with the Mesopotamians and Greeks, for whom misfortune and defeat stemmed from the harassment and disorderly interference of individual gods like Enki and Ishtar or Zeus and Aphrodite, the Shang Chinese presumably would have explained such events in terms of improper sacrifices and dissatisfied ancestors. Those ancestors would have been mollified not by the particularistic pleas of humans or by erratic interventions and divine favoritism but by ordered sacrifices whose efficacy was tested in advance through divination and offered in accordance with the status of the ancestors responsible. Given this protobureaucratic attitude toward the supernatural, it was entirely natural that death itself would also be treated in a more matter-of-fact, more impersonal manner.

The Chinese of the Western Chou, whose Mandate of Heaven doctrine moralized the political culture, explained misfortunes and defeats in terms of immoral behavior; some thinkers of the Eastern Chou, by contrast, adopted the impersonal cycles of *yin-yang* and "five-phase" theory. No matter which of these explanations one turns to, the Shang and Chou elites lived in a more ordered, more "rational" world of large, general forces that implemented the will of hierar-chically ordered ancestors or "Heaven," on the one hand, or that were incarnated in natural cycles, on the other. By contrast to the Mesopotamian or Greek dei-ties, Chinese ancestral spirits were remarkably depersonalized, a point to which I return later.

Origins and Eschatology

The absence of origins myths until relatively late in the Chinese record was also surely related to conceptions of life and death. I would suggest that conceptions of creation ex nihilo are related to and stimulated by a radical, nihilistic view of death itself. Cultures that are less anxious about eschatology, such as that of ancient China, are less likely to be concerned about their origins; cultures that are more worried about final destinations, such as those of Mesopotamia and Greece, are more likely to devote attention to the question of whence they came. The Greek concern with questions of origins, "first causes," and "first principles" is well known. In China, where identity was conceived as biological and social, the question of origins was often one of genealogy and history. A hierarchy of ances-tors leading back to a dimly perceived founding ancestor or ancestress was answer enough because it satisfied the kinds of questions that were being asked.

Critical Distance

The "openness" of Greek society, which was coming into existence during the Archaic period (ca. 760–479 B.C.), has been called "its most precious single legacy," serving to encourage both "the intellectual speculations of the few and individual freedom among the many."[12] The characteristic Greek readiness to question and complain about the human condition—whether that questioning was religious, metaphysical, or political—may be related to the marked differ-ence that distinguished mortals from immortals in Greek legend. This distance allowed the Greeks to take a stance more critical than that permitted a Chinese worshiping his ancestors, who were merely ex-humans, not radically different beings.[13] A strong, hierarchical, lineage system does not encourage children to criticize parents or descendants to criticize spiritualized ancestors; it also does not encourage the pursuit of radical innovations. I would not deny that, as the work of scholars like Nathan Sivin and Joseph Needham has revealed,[14] Chinese craftsmen and technologists have been among the most inventive in the world. The point is, however, that such innovators were generally not rewarded with or stimulated by commensurate social prestige.

For the early Chinese, as for their imperial descendants, it was the past that was normative. The Greeks, like most traditional cultures, certainly revered the past; yet they succeeded in a situation that M. I. Finley has referred to as one of "compulsory originality" in producing a series of unprecedented cultural innovations.[15] The past was accorded greater respect by the Chinese because the past was, through the lineage, the integrated source of biological, religious, and political identity. This great respect helps explain the lesser emphasis placed on individual creativity and innovation; emulation of dead ancestors was all the originality required. Such an environment encouraged what might almost be called a spirit of "compulsory unoriginality." Once again we encounter the strength of the lineage in early Chinese culture—already seen in the mortuary evidence and the cult of ancestor worship—as one of its most distinctive features. It is no accident that the greatest innovations in early statecraft and social theory appeared in the Warring States period (453–221 B.C.) of the "hundred schools," the age when the great aristocratic lineages of the Spring and Autumn period (721–479 B.C.) were disappearing from the scene.

Aesthetics and Style

Ingrainedness

Characteristically, there is no visual image or even textual description of any early Chinese ruler or deity to compare with the images and descriptions of particular rulers, heroes, and gods we have from Mesopotamia and Greece. There is no Chinese equivalent to the bronze head, which may depict King Sargon the Great, no Chinese version of a heroic, life-size, naked bronze Poseidon. In the Neolithic, the Shang, and the Western Chou the iconographic tradition was, with few exceptions, profoundly nonnaturalistic. Gombrich's formula, "making comes before matching,"[16] was not only true of the designs painted on Chinese Neolithic pots but continued to be true until relatively late in the Bronze Age. Whatever the so-called monster masks on the Shang and Chou bronzes (see, for example, Fig. 17 above, p. 18) represented—and it is by no means clear that they were intended to "match" any natural animal—they were primarily magico-aesthetic expressions of design, symmetry, and an almost dictatorial order.

This concern with general order rather than particular description—manifested in the early aesthetics, social rituals, and philosophy of early China—may also be seen, to return to one of our earlier themes, in representations of death. No early Chinese text provides vivid, unflinching details like the worm crawling out of the dead Enkidu's nose in the *Gilgamesh* or the brains bursting from a mortal thrust and running along the spearhead in book 17 of the *Iliad*. The relative unconcern with material details can be seen as a further expression of the "epistemological optimism" referred to earlier, the willingness to embrace ideas that were more dependent on social custom and general category than on rigorous analysis and precise description.

Both aesthetically and socially, the Chinese did not manifest what has been called "the Greeks' personifying instinct," that instinct that rendered Greek myths so rich in personalities and thus so un-Chinese.[17] Indeed, if one word had to be used to describe early Chinese aesthetic, and even philosophical, expression, I would suggest "ingrainedness." By ingrainedness I mean the willingness to concentrate on the symbolic meaning of an´event, usually moral or emotional and frequently expressive of some normative order, rather than to express, or derive comfort or insight from, its existential qualities for their own sake. Such ingrainedness has nothing to do with abstractions or with the ideal forms of Plato's dialogues. It is in the Chinese case entirely immanent. The patterns, symbols, messages, rules, and so on are entirely within reality; they do not transcend reality metaphysically but merely render its existential details of minor importance. As Girardot has written of Chinese myths,

> Mythic materials and themes have entered into Chinese literature as a series of extremely abstract, and essentially static, models for organizing and evaluating human life.
>
> Mythic themes in early Chinese literature, in other words, often seem to be reduced to their inner "logical" code or implicit cosmological structure of binary *yin-yang* classification.[18]

Chinese ingrainedness, then, stands in sharp contrast to the passionate Archaic Greek attention to individual detail for its own existential sake, the recognition of the quirky, ironic, indifferent, nonsymbolic, existential, nonessential nature of reality, the "outgazing bent of mind that sees things exactly, each for itself, and seems innocent of the idea that thought discerps and colors reality." These traits are absent in the early Chinese texts that have come down to us. John H. Finley has referred to this Archaic Greek attitude as that of "the Heroic Mind"; his account is worth quoting in full for the contrasting light it throws on the Chinese evidence.

> When in the sixth book of the *Iliad* Hector briefly returns to Troy ... and meets his wife and infant son at the gate and reaches out to take the boy in his arms, the child draws back frightened at his father's bronze armor and helmet with horsehair crest; whereupon Hector laughs, takes off the helmet, and lays it all-shining on the ground. In so deeply felt a scene surely no one but Homer would have paused to note that helmet still shining beside the human figures. It is as if in whatever circumstances it too keeps its particular being, which does not change because people are sad or happy but remains what it is, one of the innumerable fixed entities that comprise the world. Similarly in the heroic poems ships remain swift, bronze sharp, the sky starry, rivers eddying. Though heroes fight and die, everything in the outflung world keeps its fit and native character.[19]

There are no comparable scenes, no "shining helmets," in early Chinese literature. Even in the *Book of Songs* (*Shih ching*), where early Chinese lyricism is most prominent, the general supersedes the particular, and nature is pregnant with allegorical or symbolic meaning, usually moral. There are love poems but no great lovers. Nature is not independent but participates in man's moral and emotional cosmology; its role is to express human concerns. To put the matter another way, early Chinese texts, like early Chinese bronze designs, reveal marks of what, to a Greek artist, would have seemed like severe editing, in which particular detail had been sacrificed to abstract order. Either there never was a Chinese equivalent of the Heroic Mind or it has left no reflection; in either case the contrast with the Classical Greeks, who were so deeply inspired by the epics of the Archaic period, is significant.

The Heroic Mind is superficially reminiscent of the epistemological optimism of the early Chinese thinkers. Both forms of thinking reveal unquestioning acceptance. The differences, however, are fundamental. First, the Heroic Mind accepts existence without question; the epistemologically optimistic mind, by contrast, accepts ideas and formulations. Second, the Heroic Mind in Finley's analysis yields by the Classical Age, to what he calls the "theoretical mind" and then the "rational mind"; what we may call the "metaphysical optimism" of Homer is replaced by the "epistemological pessimism" of Plato. No such radical evolution was to take place in China, whose thinkers were to remain consistently satisfied with their epistemological optimism, an optimism they would characteristically reassert in the eventual Confucian response to Buddhism's nihilistic metaphysics. This lack of change, this satisfaction with early, and hence ancestral, cultural forms, is a theme to which I return.

Metaphysical and Technological Correlates

Although Plato's concern with ideal forms, which is so radically un-Chinese in its metaphysical assumptions about a separate, nonimmanent realm of perfection, is alien to the Homeric view of reality, one can nevertheless note the way in which it derives from the Homeric emphasis on individual particulars, objects, and persons. When, for example, Plato employs metaphors of the workshop in discussing such matters, it is the shoemaker's inability to make individual and identical shoes each time, his inability to match the ideal conception of a shoe, that concerns him. Bronze-working in classical Greece would have manifested the same troubling variance; each wrought object—such as Achilles' sword—would have been made singly and thus differently by a smith, hammering and beating it into an approximation of the ideal form. Chinese piece-mold bronze casting, by contrast, permitted no such individual variation. The technological process, involving ceramic molds placed around a central core, guaranteed that when molten bronze was poured into the space between the mold and the slightly pared down or shrunken core, the initial clay model would be duplicated virtually exactly (figure 2.10).[20] This duplication of models is analogous, in the technical realm, to the emulation of heroes and ancestors referred to earlier, just as the Greek techniques of smithy bronze production are analogous to the Greek emphasis on the individual hero.

Given this context, it is fitting that the problem of variance, of the failure to match an abstract ideal, did not occur to the early Chinese as a major theoretical problem, as opposed to a practical one. They assumed that individuals were identified and valued in terms of the human roles they played within the kinship group. "There is good government," said Confucius, "when the father is a father and the son a son" (*Analects* 12.11). They also assumed, with characteristic optimism, that people were educable to the good and were capable of performing

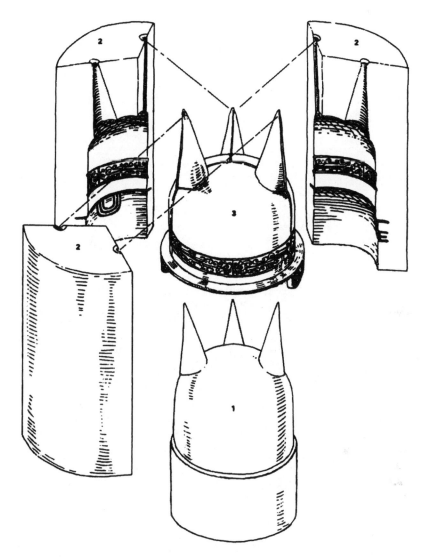

Figure 2.10 Schematic drawing of the piece-mold casting assembly used to cast a Middle Shang tripod: (1) core, (2) mold sections, (3) completed bronze vessel. From Wen Fong, ed., *The Great Bronze Age of China: An Exhibition from the People's Republic of China* (New York: Metropolitan Museum and Knopf, 1980), 72. Drawing by Phyllis Ward.

those roles adequately; their epistemological optimism did not require them to define or analyze those roles, such as that of father and son, with the rigor and precision that a Plato, more pessimistic about the human capacity to know and understand, would have demanded.

The Absence of Drama

The central importance of dramatic performances in the Athens of the fifth century B.C., acted in theatrical competitions before audiences of some fourteen thousand citizens and challenging and lampooning some of the most cherished values of the state while being supported in part by public funds, needs no comment here; the absence of such an artistic and political form in China is another feature that separates the two cultures.

The absence of dramatic confrontation may also be discerned in other areas of Chinese expression. I have already noted, for example, the lack of narrative tension in the pictorial representations on the Eastern Chou *hu* vases (see figure 2.2). In the realm of expository prose one of the striking differences between the writings of the early Chinese philosophers and Plato is the particularism with which Plato incarnates his arguments, describing the time, the place, and the persons to give dramatic force to Socrates' conversations. Confucius's sayings, by contrast, are usually divorced from the emotional hurly-burly of debate with keenly delineated individuals on particular historical occasions. There is little dramatic tension in early Chinese philosophical texts comparable to the "tense liveliness," the "dialectical friction," of Plato's dialogues.[21] This successful incarnation of the general in the particular characterizes Greek art, philosophy, and conceptions of the immortals. In China, by contrast, in art, philosophy, and religion the individual is submerged in more general concerns.

This absence of dramatic tension in both philosophy and art relates to the Chinese concern with ritualized social hierarchy that we see emerging as early as the oracle-bone inscriptions of the Shang and that becomes fully developed in the classical ritual texts of the Eastern Chou and Han. The Chinese *li* were canons of status-based, role-related social decorum, reciprocity, and ethical consideration that operated in the religious, social, and political spheres; they implied by their very nature that basic social questions had already been resolved in favor of a patriarchal status quo. The ideals of social behavior were known: "Let the father be a father, the son a son"; the only point at issue—so well exemplified by the early Han in the esoteric moral catechisms of the *Kung-yang* (late Chou) and *Ku-liang* (early Han?) commentaries to the *Spring and Autumn Annals*, supposedly composed by Confucius—was how to fit particular cases to general rules.

Such a socio-moral taxonomy, eventually articulated in the doctrine of the "rectification of terms" (*cheng-ming*), is both impersonal and undramatic. Assuming that a familial-style commitment to shared values is preferable to a society of adversarial relationships, the promoters of the *li* manifested a cast of mind that was uninterested in logical argument designed to change opinions; they preferred instead to appeal in set-position speeches to the authority of hallowed books and traditions.

Art and Ancestor Worship

Chinese aesthetic and even philosophical uninterest in particular detail may also be related to ancestor worship. As Fortes notes, "The ancient Greeks appear to have had elaborate cults concerned with beliefs about ghosts and shades, but no true ancestor cult." He emphasizes that "ancestor worship is a representation or extension of the authority component in the jural relations of successive genera-tions; it is not a duplication, in a supernatural idiom, of the total complex" of kin or other relationships. Ancestor worship, in short, does not simply involve belief in the dead; it involves belief about the dead, who are conceived in a certain way.[22]

Following this line of thought, I propose that an inverse relationship exists between an emphasis on hierarchical roles of authority, whether for the living or the dead, and the vagueness with which the afterlife is conceived. The cultures that depict the afterworld, or even this one, with some attention to specific detail may not need, or may do so precisely because they do not have, a well-defined social hierarchy or ancestral cult. When the authority of the elders and ancestors func-tions well in this world, there is less need to depict the environs of the next. This suggestion—which may be related to the earlier discussion of the impersonality of the dead—would also help explain the well-known fact that, although there are many mythic personages alluded to in ancient China, there is little evidence of a sustained, anecdotal mythology.[23] In this view there would have been no need in China for the precision of event and personality that we associate with the art and mythology of Mesopotamia and Greece; the "mythological issues," as it were, would have already been resolved by the invention of the ancestors, who were ances-tors precisely because they were not comprehensive or detailed representations of personality and social role. The Mesopotamian and Greek concern in both religion and art with personality, social role, and the chaos of unstructured, adversarial exist-ence was replaced in China, if it had ever been present, by a generalized concern with harmonious order and design and with ingrained and symbolic meanings.

Harmony and Moral Chauvinism

The emphasis on harmony in early Chinese art, literary expression, and philos-ophy—a corollary to the absence of critical and dramatic tension—may also be related to the deep-seated moral and epistemological optimism and confidence already noted. This optimism and confidence could only—and here I speak as a child of the Western tradition—have been achieved by glossing over, frequently by generalizing and classifying, those sharp, awkward, and frequently nonharmo-nious details that caught the attention of the Greek artist or philosopher.

One of the characteristic and non-Chinese features of the *Iliad*, for instance, is that the audience hears, and has its sympathies engaged by, both sides of the story, within the walls of Troy as well as without. Similarly, neither Creon in *Antigone* nor Oedipus in Sophocles' trilogy is presented as an unsympathetic or unremittingly evil figure. This ambiguity about what and who is right lies at the essence of the tragic vision; our sympathies are not, should not, and cannot all be on one side.

Greek epics derive much of their complexity and dramatic tension from the frank recognition that unresolvable conflicts exist in the world, that choices are frequently made not between good and evil but between two goods. By con-trast, no early Chinese writings—with, as is so frequently the case, the possible exception of the *Chuang-tzu*—take a similarly detached and complex view of the human condition. There is no passage in early Chinese literature analogous to Antigones' wrenching cry, "Ah Creon, Creon, / Which of us can say what the gods hold wicked?"; the epistemological optimists of China thought that they could say. The vanquished were simply categorized as "ingrainedly" immoral and their point of view was never presented as worthy of consideration, dramatically or historically. From the *Book of Documents* (*Shu ching*) through *Mencius* and beyond, last rulers of dynasties were by definition bad and those who overthrew them, whom we should unquestioningly trust, were by definition good; there was no sense of a "loyal opposition" as even conceivable, let alone desirable or human. There are few Trojans in early Chinese literature; generally, there are only Achaeans, only victors.[24]

Religion, Lineage, City, and Trade

Ancestor Worship: The Strategic Custom

To the extent that it is possible to speak of one strategic custom or institution in the mix of early China's cultural variables—strategic because of its pervasive ability to sanctify all other aspects of life and to legitimate and reinforce the lineage—it would seem to be ancestor worship and its social and political corollaries involving hierarchy, ritual deference, obedience, and reciprocity. At some point, probably still in the Neolithic, the commemoration of the dead—a feature common to many early cultures, including the Greek and Mesopotamian—probably became more orderly and articulated in China, taking on an ideological and juridical power of its own. The values of this new ancestor worship would have been intimately related to, and could not have been generated without, the existence of strong lineages. The traditional Chinese ideal of the extended family in which several generations were to live under one roof is only practicable when family members are trained to value group harmony above personal independence. Indoctrination in the value of *hsiao* (filiality or obedience), whose roots can be discerned in the sacrifices made by the Shang kings, if not in the offerings placed in Neolithic burials (see figures 2.3 and 2.5), provided just such a training and socialization. Forming part of a rich vocabulary of familial and religious dependence and obligation in which even rulers would refer to themselves as a "small child," presumably still under the eye of their dead parents, *hsiao* was precisely not the kind of lineage virtue that would have been validated by the independence and unpredictability of the Mesopotamian and Greek gods and heroes.

In addition to its impact on mortuary practices and its validation of filiality, ancestor worship had important demographic consequences. To the extent that a cult of the ancestors requires the procreation of cultists to continue the sacrifices, the eschatology of death in early China encouraged population growth in a significant way. This sanctification of posterity, and especially of male progeny, is a constant theme in the bronze inscriptions of the Western Chou, many of which end with a prayer such as, "For a myriad years, may sons of sons, grandsons of grandsons, long treasure and use (this vessel)." The multiplication of progeny recurs as a theme in the *Book of Songs* (*Shih ching*) and is given its most articulate emphasis in Mencius's famous dictum that nothing is more unfilial than to fail to produce descendants. The supreme obligation to one's ancestors was to become an ancestor oneself.

The considerable demands of the ancestral cult, visible in the grave goods of both the Neolithic and the Bronze Ages, also served to stimulate the production of material wealth. In social rather than economic terms, however, the order being "revitalized" by Chinese mortuary cults was the lineage, the power of senior kin over junior kin, and the conservative and ascriptive ties of affection, obligation, and exploitation that were stronger than life itself.

Belief in ancestors had additional consequences. Although there is no doubt that the Shang and Chou Chinese worshiped nature powers or spirits—rivers, mountains, and fertility figures like Hou Chi (Prince Millet), the legendary ancestor of the Chou—the argument that these spirits had originally been local deities, the ancestors of particular tribes, has much to recommend it.[25] Similarly, there is some evidence that Shang Ti, the Lord on High, may have once been a progenitor of the Shang royal lineage. And it is clear that the Chou ruler came to regard himself as the T'ien Tzu, "Son of Heaven." Even though the biological relationships are murky in many of these cases, the general conception of man's relationship to the spirits of the universe was implicitly genealogical. Rulers were thought to have a special, quasi-familial relationship to the supreme deity; man was the offspring of the spirits, ancestral and otherwise. Accordingly, there was no sense of a radical difference between spirits and humans. The spiritual universe was unitary and man's relationship to that universe relied less on personal observation and exploration and more on participation in the social groups that were the primary focus of religious feeling.

The Ancient Chinese City

Despite its ability to focus and accentuate cultural values, religion is not an independent variable. Because religion operates within society and is a product of society, we cannot ignore the environment and the economic context that produced the Chinese form of lineage dominance. The ancient Chinese city is instructive in this regard because it differed significantly from the city found in Mesopotamia or Classical Greece. Not only was it visually and aesthetically different, being built largely of rammed earth, timber, thatch, and tile rather than of stone, but its political composition was different too. Early Chinese cities may be regarded as politico-religious embodiments of lineage and dynastic power, centered on a palace-temple complex and existing primarily to serve the needs of the ruling elites whose ancestors were worshiped there. These settlements were characterized by a regulated layout and unitary power structure in which merchants and artisans, subordinate to the elite lineages, played a relatively minor political role.

In Mesopotamia, by contrast, the sprawling cities grew by accretion and housed large and diverse populations. Secular power and religious power were

clearly distinguished and often in opposition; the palace was confronted by coun-
tervailing sources of authority as represented by the temple, the military, private
wealth, and merchants. Lineages, in particular, do not seem to have played the significant political role they did in China; the character of Mesopotamian urbanism
appears to have "dissolved" the social and religious strength of the kinship units.

Ancient Chinese cities stand in even sharper contrast to those of Classical
Greece. Greek cities were characterized by their variety of changing political forms,
such as tyranny, oligarchy, and democracy, their emphasis on overseas coloniza-
tion and commerce and the consequent exposure to the challenge of other cultural traditions, their reliance on "citizens," who had both rights and duties in the
state, their emerging conception of equality before the law, their dependence on
legal and economic slave-labor and the corollary discovery of personal freedom.
In Athens the lack of any permanent officialdom, the preference for direct citizen
participation in government—once more the reliance on "dirty hands"—rather
than on representation and bureaucracy, is particularly notable. The Eastern Chou
analogues of the Greek citizens, the *kuo-jen*, "people of the state" (the state being
conceived primarily as the walled capital itself), may have had certain privileges,
but they appear to have had no separate corporate or legal existence.

Notable also is the absence in China—so puzzling to Marxists inspired by
the Greek case—of the *stasis*, or social conflict, between "the few" and "the many"
that was a characteristic feature of the Greek city states. The rare urban upheavals
recorded in the *Tso chuan* involved factional struggles among the noble lineages and
their supporters; they did not involve class interests and were not fought over economic issues.[26]

This nonpluralistic Chinese urbanism helps to explain why the shift from
kin-based to class-structured society that is associated with the rise of states in general seems to have taken place less completely in traditional China, where the government at both the dynastic and bureaucratic level continued to be marked by its
familial nature in terms of both ideology and personnel. Despite the remarkable
commercial activity that characterized many cities of post-Sung China—Marco
Polo, for example, was astonished by their size and wealth—merchants in China
did not achieve the kind of political, legal, and economic independence that they
did in the West. This is a distinction of fundamental importance whose deep and
ancient roots are partly to be found in a political system that gave kinship ties and
their political extensions priority over commercial and legal ones.

The Ultimate Question

The ultimate question is, Why did early China develop in these particular ways?
Why did its values and cultural style differ from those of the ancient Near East or
ancient Greece? Speculation is tempting.

First, the great abundance of Neolithic sites in China suggests greater population density than in Mesopotamia and Greece, even at this early date. If this

impression is confirmed by subsequent excavations and by statistical analysis, we may conclude that Chinese experience would have been more "peopled" and that such "peopling" is congruent with a less individualistic, more group-oriented social ethic.

Second, one can speculate that the Chinese environment, which encouraged such population growth, together with the population growth itself, helped to set the basic mood of the culture. If one can relate the trusting and self-confident mood of the ancient Egyptians to the benevolence of the Nile valley, and the pessimism and anxiety of the ancient Mesopotamians or ancient Greeks to the comparative harshness and uncertainty of their environment, then one may argue that the comparatively favorable Neolithic climate in China would have encouraged a characteristic optimism about the human condition. The agrarian nature of the civilization also suggests that the characteristic dependence on superiors was related to the inability to move away from coercive leaders once one's labor had been invested in clearing the land and rendering it fertile.

Third, the nonpluralistic nature of early Chinese culture is a trait of great significance for which we should try to account. I have noted the relatively undifferentiated character of the early cities. We may further note the lack of significant foreign invasions and the absence of any pluralistic national traditions; the challenging linguistic and cultural contrast that the markedly different Sumerian and Akkadian traditions presented to the inhabitants of early Mesopotamia, for example, was simply not present for the early Chinese literati. Also, to the degree that the trading activities of merchants and the value placed on them in Mesopotamia and Greece can be explained by their relatively resource-poor hinterlands, then private merchants would have been less powerful in China because they would have been less needed. in this case geography may have played a role. Because the major rivers in north and central China—the Yellow, the Huai, and the Yangtze—flow from west to east rather than along a north-south axis, trade, to the extent that it followed the river valleys, would have generally been between regions in the same latitude whose crops and other natural products would have been similar; the distinctive ecogeographical zones in China are those of north and south, not east and west.

In this view the market economy would not have had the strategic value in China that it had in other parts of the world. A significant proportion of Chinese trade in early historical times, in fact, seems to have been tribute trade—reciprocal or redistributive in character, political in function, and dealing in high-cost, luxury items reserved for the elites, who controlled the merchants by sumptuary regulations and by co-opting them as necessary into the administrative bureaucracy.[27] The lack of an inland sea like the Mediterranean, the absence of rocky shores and good harbors along much of the north and central China coast, the absence of major trading partners across the China Sea to provide cultural as well as economic stimuli, and the presence of deserts and mountains separating north China from Central Asia, would have further encouraged the noncommercial, agrarian bias of the early Chinese city and state and the self-confidence of its isolated, indigenous culture.

These considerations, which are basically geographic, suggest that characteristically Chinese formulations of property and legal status would have developed in a culture where economic power was primarily agrarian power. Although there is no early evidence to support Karl Wittfogel's view of an agromanagerial despotism running the state's essential water-control works, one can nevertheless see that wealth in the early state would have depended less on control of land—there was probably a surplus—and more on control of a labor force that could clear that land and make it productive. Social control—originally motivated and legitimated by religious and kinship ties—rather than technological or military control, would have been the key to political success. Access to lineage support, ancestral power, and divinatory reassurance would have been more important and more inheritable than mere claims on unpeopled, and thus unworkable, property. The problem, as revealed by King Hui of Liang near the start of the _Mencius_ (1.A.3) in a conversation that is purported to have occurred ca. 320 B.C., was how to attract people to serve a ruler and his state: "I do not find that there is any prince who exerts his mind as I do. And yet the people of the neighboring kingdoms do not decrease, nor do my people increase. How is this?" This problem was one of the major concerns of the Eastern Chou philosophers. It is worth recalling that the kind of bronze-casting industry that the Shang elites patronized and that expressed both their military and their religious power had depended on the ability to mobilize labor on a large industrial scale.[28] These early patterns of behavior and legitimation subsequently made possible the larger water-control projects of imperial times; it was not the projects that created the patterns.

Speculations of this sort encourage us to seek for still earlier, more "ecological," more geopolitical, more material explanations for the origins of Chinese culture. They do not, however, satisfactorily explain why early Chinese culture took the precise forms that it did. That question, in fact, unless we narrow its scope, is unanswerable because cultures are to a large extent self-producing, the products of a virtually infinite combination of interacting factors. Many of these factors are mental and many of them are unidentifiable in the archaeological or early historical record. To put the matter another way, with the exception of the most basic precultural factors, such as climate and geography, which can only provide the most general of answers, there is nothing but dependent variables. It is truer to what we understand of cultural development—and truer, perhaps, to Chinese than to traditional Western approaches to explanation—to think in terms of the gradual coevolution of many factors rather than of a few prime movers.[29]

Because we cannot explain "everything," universal laws of development with a specificity sufficient to explain the genesis of Chinese, or any other, culture must elude us. Nevertheless, we can, as I have attempted to do, suggest some significant and characteristic features of early Chinese culture whose interrelationships were strong and whose subsequent influence on the civilization of imperial China was large.

Conclusion

What then do we mean by "Chinese" from the Neolithic to the early imperial age in the Han? Impressionistic though any attempt to define a worldview or cultural style must be, it may be suggested that "Chinese" referred in part to a cultural tradition permeated by the following features (listed, on the basis of the above discussion, in no order of causal priority):

1. Hierarchical social distinctions—as revealed by opulent Late Neolithic burials (see figures 2.3 and 2.7), by the high status of the Bronze Age elites both in this life and in the next, and by the human sacrifices demanded, both in blood and in obligation, by those elites.
2. Massive mobilization of labor—as revealed by the early Bronze Age city walls, the royal Shang tombs (see figure 2.9), the industrial scale of Shang bronze-casting (see figure 2.10), and the large-scale public works, such as the long walls and tombs of imperial times.
3. An emphasis on the group rather than the individual—expressed in the impersonality and generality of artistic and literary representation (see figure 2.2) and generated and validated by a religion of ancestor worship that stressed the continuity of the lineage and defined the individual in terms of his role and status in the system of sacrifice and descent.
4. An emphasis on ritual in all dimensions of life—seen in Neolithic mortuary cults (see figures 2.5 and 2.7), in the emphasis on ritual practice revealed by the oracle-bone inscriptions of the Shang, and in the classical cult treatises of the Eastern Chou and Han.
5. An emphasis on formal boundaries and models—as revealed by the constraints involved in rammed-earth construction, by the use of molds in Neolithic ceramic technology and in the bronze technology that evolved from it (see figure 2.10), by the dictatorial design system of the bronze decor (see figure 11.3), by the use of models in both bronze technology and social philosophy, and by the great stress on social discipline and order in ethics and cosmology.
6. An ethic of service, obligation, and emulation—consider the burials of accompaniers-in-death and human victims in Neolithic (see figure 2.8) and Shang times, the elevation of sage emperors and culture heroes who were generally administrators rather than actors, the motivations of Ssu-ma Ch'ien's assassin-retainers, and the obligations and unquestioning confidence that the princely man might engender. The endurance of this ethic is dramatically expressed by the army of some seven thousand life-sized terracotta soldiers, buried ca. 210 B.C., proud and confident as they accompanied the First Emperor of China in death (figure 2.11).
7. Little sense of tragedy or irony—witness the evident belief, well developed even in the Neolithic, in the continuity of some form of life after death. Witness, too, the general success and uncomplicated goodness of legendary

heroes and the understanding of human action as straightforward in its consequences. Confucian optimism about the human condition was maintained even in the face of Confucius's own failure to obtain the political successes that he needed to justify his mission. The optimism, both moral and epistemological, was a matter of deep faith rather than of shallow experience.

This list is by no means exhaustive, but I am proposing that particular features such as these, combined in the ways I have described, help to define what we mean by Chinese for the early period. It must be stressed that other scholars could well emphasize different features of the culture—such as the influence of millet and rice agriculture, the acceptance of a monistic cosmology, the influence of a logographic writing system, the nature of early historiography, the role of shamanism, and Confucian conceptions of benevolence and good government. As I indicated at the start, I do not focus on the Eastern Chou philosophers not only because they have already been studied extensively by Western scholars[30] but also because my main concerns are "prephilosophical"; I attempt to relate legend, history, aesthetics, and political practice to the culture of the Neolithic-to-Bronze-Age transition. My analysis, accordingly, is neither definitive nor comprehensive; it does not propose to explain "everything."

Furthermore, in making cultural comparisons, we should generally think in terms of emphasis or nuance, not absolute distinctions. I do not claim that the ancient Chinese had no sense of individual heroism, that no leader ever did things for himself, that death was not a source of terror, that the early Chinese ignored details, or that merchants played no role. But if one imagines a series of axes on which individualism, personal involvement, attention to detail, anguish at the death of loved ones, service to the group, and so on could be plotted, one would find that the Chinese responses differed to a significant degree from those of other seminal civilizations.

Finally—to return to a caution raised at the start of this chapter—I would remark that the very nature of cultural comparison, which involves moving from the familiar culture to the unfamiliar one, results in a rhetoric that seems critical of the "target" culture, which is described as deficient in certain features. But should such features have been present? Is what has been called the Greek "lust to annihilate" attractive?[31] Are gods who masquerade as swans to rape their victims? Are sons who overthrow their fathers? What we may regard as the good and the bad features of any culture are inextricably linked. All great civilizations have their costs as well as their benefits, and it would be instructive—indeed, it is essential if full cultural understanding is to be achieved—to rewrite this chapter from the Chinese point of view, stressing and seeking to explain all the features that early Greek culture, for example, lacked. The most notable of these would surely include the emphasis that many early Chinese thinkers placed on altruism, benevolence, social harmony, and a concern with human relations rather than abstract principles.

Figure 2.11 Part of the seven-thousand-man army of terra-cotta figures buried with the First Emperor of China, ca. 210 B.C. From *Ch'in Shih Huang ling ping-ma yung* (Peking: Wen-wu Ch'u-pan-she, 1983), no. 7.

The cultural traditions established in the Neolithic and the Bronze Ages of China were ancestral to all that followed, continuing to exert their influence down to recent, if not contemporary, times. It could be argued—as the discussion about the extensive ramifications of ancestor worship has suggested—that the Chinese were relatively slow to desacrilize their world. Ancient social practices tied to the lineage continued to be attended with powerful religious qualities throughout imperial times. A major question—in our own case as well as that of the Chinese—is to what degree will the older, deeply seated traditions help or hinder the search for new solutions? Recent claims that "traditional Chinese cultural values may be conducive to the economic life typical of the modern epoch" suggest that the answer is by no means a foregone conclusion.[32] The combative individualism of the West may yet prove more costly than the harmonious social humanism of China. To address a question such as this, surely, is one of the reasons we study history and why it is important to understand the past as clearly as we can. As Ssu-ma Ch'ien wrote some two thousand years ago, "He who does not forget the past is master of the present." When we consider George Santayana's more negative formulation that "those who forget the past are condemned to repeat it," Ssu-ma Ch'ien was the more optimistic. But that would have been characteristic. And how appropriate that his should have been a confidence in the virtues of the past.

Notes

One version of this essay was given at Stanford University on 18 November 1986. I have done my best to take account of the valuable criticism offered by many colleagues, who are not, of course, responsible for my errors. In particular I should like to thank David Johnson, Thomas Metzger, David Nivison, Jeffrey Riegel, Betsey Scheiner, Irwin Scheiner, Raphael Sealey, David Ulansey, Richard Webster, and Yeh Wen-hsin for their careful reading of an earlier draft.

1. For an introduction to the legend, see Emily Vermeule, *Aspects of Death in Early Greek Art and Poetry* (Berkeley: University of California Press, 1979), 158–59.
2. For an introduction to the artistic representations of this story see J. J. Pollitt, *Art and Experience in Classical Greece* (Cambridge: Cambridge University Press, 1972), 20–22.
3. Burton Watson, trans., *Records of the Historian: Chapters from the "Shih Chi" of Ssu-ma Ch'ien* (New York: Columbia University Press, 1969), 45–67.
4. The only direct expression of this subversive thought in early China appears in Ssu-ma Ch'ien's "Biography of Po Yi and Shu Ch'i" (in Watson, *Records*, 11–15), in which the historian is sorely troubled by virtuous actions that are unrewarded and unrecognized. On Confucius's philosophical equanimity in a world where perfection is not possible, see Benjamin I. Schwartz, *The World of Thought in Ancient China* (Cambridge: Harvard University Press, 1985). 80–81.
5. Thomas A. Metzger, "Some Ancient Roots of Ancient Chinese Thought: This-worldliness, Epistemological Optimism, Doctrinality, and the Emergence of Reflexivity in the Eastern Chou," *Early China* 11–12 (1985–1987): 66–72.
6. The phrase is Max Weber's. See Max Weber, *The Religion of China*, trans. Hans H. Gerth, with an introduction by C. K. Yang (New York: Free Press, 1951), xxx, 212, 227–28, 235.
7. That Achilles, in book 23 of the *Iliad*, put "twelve radiant sons of Troy" to the sword at the funeral of Patroclus was more a sign of his fury than common custom. (The quotes

from the *Iliad* and the *Odyssey* in this chapter are taken from the translations of Robert Fitzgerald, which are published by Doubleday.)

8. Herbert Fingarette, *Confucius: The Secular as Sacred* (New York: Harper, 1972). Anyone reading this provocative book should also read the detailed critique provided in Schwartz, *The World of Thought in Ancient China.*

9. John Gardner and John Maier, trans., *Gilgamesh: Translated from the Sin-leqi-unninni Version* (New York: Knopf, 1984), tablet vii, column iv, tablet xii, column iv, 178, 265.

10. The ripostes and anecdotes about death found in the *Chuang Tzu* merely confirm this point. Chuang Tzu is arguing for a nonhuman view of death precisely because he is arguing for a nonhuman view of life. He is, in these passages, less concerned about death itself than with the institutions and values that the civilized Chinese had developed to deal with it. Unlike Plato, he deals with death as a social problem, not a philosophical one, because, in his view, society itself is the problem. His cheerful acceptance of death might well have filled Plato with envy.

11. The letter is translated in Burton Watson, *Ssu-ma Ch'ien: Grand Historian of China* (New York: Columbia University Press, 1958), 57–67.

12. Anthony Snodgrass, *Archaic Greece: The Age of Experiment* (Berkeley: University of California Press, 1980), 161.

13. See Vermeule, *Aspects of Death,* 125, on the way in which the epic permitted the Greeks to laugh at and even despise their gods. Jasper Griffin has made a related point. For the Greeks the "world makes less sense through moral self-examination"— which would have been the Chinese approach—"than through recognition of the gulf that separates mortal men from the serene superiority and shining gaze of the immortal gods" ("From Killer to Thinker," *New York Review of Books* 32, no. 11 [27 June 1985]: 32).

14. Joseph Needham. *Science and Civilisation in China,* 7 vols. projected (Cambridge: Cambridge University Press, 1954–). For Sivin, see his contribution to Paul Ropp, ed., *Heritage of China.* Stanford University Press, 1990.

15. M. I. Finley, *The Ancient Greeks: An Introduction to Their Life and Thought* (New York: Viking, 1964), 23.

16. E. H. Gombrich, *Art and Illusion: A Study in the Psychology of Pictorial Representation* (Oxford: Phaidon, 1977), 99.

17. L. R. Farnell, *Greek Hero Cults and Ideas of Immortality* (Oxford: Oxford University Press, 1921), 359.

18. Norman J. Girardot, "Behaving Cosmogonically in Early Taoism," in *Cosmogony and Ethical Order: New Studies in Comparative Ethics,* ed. Robin W. Lovin and Frank E. Reynolds (Chicago: University of Chicago Press, 1986), 71. Girardot also refers to Sarah Allan's judgment (*The Heir and the Sage: Dynastic Legend in Early China* [San Francisco: Chinese Materials Center, 1981], 18) that "in using myth in political and philosophical argumentation, the Chinese writer operated at a higher level of abstraction and with greater self-consciousness than is normally associated with mythical thought. He did not narrate legend but abstracted from it."

19. John H. Finley, Jr., *Four Stages of Greek Thought* (Stanford: Stanford University Press, 1966), 3, 4, 28. Similar observations about Homer's style in the *Odyssey* may be found in "Odysseus' Scar," the opening chapter of Erich Auerbach's *Mimesis: The Representation of Reality in Western Literature* (Princeton: Princeton University Press. 1953).

20. For a brief introduction to piece-mold casting and its aesthetic consequences see Robert W. Bagley, "The Beginnings of the Bronze Age: The Erlitou Culture Period," in *The Great Bronze Age of China: An Exhibition from the People's Republic of China*, ed. Wen Fong (New York: Metropolitan Museum and Knopf, 1980), 70–73.

21. The phrases are those of Alvin W. Gouldner, *Enter Plato: Classical Greece and the Origins of Social Theory* (New York: Basic Books, 1965), 361, 385. Even in the *Chuang Tzu*, A. C. Graham notes the rarity of "genuine debates" in which "spokesmen of moralism … and of worldliness … are allowed their say before being defeated" (*Chuang-tzu: The Seven Inner Chapters and Other Writings from the Book "Chuang-tzu"* [London: Allen & Unwin, 1981], 234).

22. Meyer Fortes. "Some Reflections on Ancestor Worship in Africa," in *African Systems of Thought*, ed. M. Fortes and G. Dieterlen (London: Oxford University Press, 1965), 125, 133.

23. Derk Bodde, "Myths of Ancient China," in *Mythologies of the Ancient World*, ed. Samuel Noah Kramer (Garden City, N.Y.: Doubleday Anchor, 1961), 369–70; Bodde notes that "the gods of ancient China … appear very rarely or not at all in art, and are commonly described so vaguely or briefly in the texts that their personality, and sometimes even their sex, remains uncertain."

24. Even in Ssu-ma Ch'ien's detailed portrayal of Hsiang Yü—the great antagonist of Liu Pang, who eventually founded the Han dynasty—there was little tragic about his defeat, which, if we take the Grand Historian at his word, was entirely justified: "It was hardly surprising that the feudal lords revolted against him. He boasted and made a show of his own achievements. He was obstinate in his own opinions and did not abide by established ways…. 'It is Heaven,' he declared, 'which has destroyed me….' Was he not indeed deluded!" (Watson, *Records*, 104). Even if Ssu-ma Ch'ien is being ironic here, he in no way portrays Hsiang Yü with the kind of sympathetic and dramatic detail that Homer accords Hector. Although Hsiang Yü's flawed character brings destruction, the destruction is not tragic because his character is not presented as admirable.

25. See David N. Keightley, "Akatsuka Kiyoshi and the Culture of Early China: A Study in Historical Method." *Harvard Journal of Asiatic Studies* 42 (1982): 294–99.

26. See, for example, the struggles in the state of Wei in 470 B.C. (James Legge, trans., *The Chinese Classics*, vol. 5, *The Ch'un Ts'ew with the Tso Chuen* [Oxford: Oxford University Press, 1872], 856–57); the palace workers, of relatively high status themselves, provided the manpower, not the motivation, for the revolt of the great officers. Their role is in some ways analogous to that of the assassin-retainers discussed earlier.

27. These speculations need to be treated with caution for at least two reasons. First, the traditional Confucian bias against trade has meant that commercial activity has not been well recorded in the early texts. Second, the kinds of archaeological techniques that would enable us to "finger-print" the sources of pots and jades, for example, have not yet been applied to the Chinese evidence. For both reasons the commercial role of early cities in China and the kinds of exchange networks that linked them to one another and to other regions of China still remain to be explored.

28. Ursula Martius Franklin, "The Beginnings of Metallurgy in China: A Comparative Approach," in *The Great Bronze Age of China: A Symposium*, ed. George Kuwayama (Los Angeles: Los Angeles County Museum of Art, 1983), 94–99.

29. On the correlative or "organismic" Chinese view of the world in which "conceptions are not subsumed under one another, but placed side by side in a *pattern*, and things

influence one another not by acts of mechanical causation, but by a kind of 'induct-ance,'" see Joseph Needham, with the research assistance of Wang Ling, *Science and Civilisation in China*, vol. 2, *History of Scientific Thought* (Cambridge: Cambridge University Press, 1956), 280–81.

30. The most recent comprehensive study is that of Schwartz, *The World of Thought in Ancient China.*

31. Eli Sagan, *The Lust to Annihilate: A Psychoanalytic Study of Violence in Ancient Greek Culture* (New York: Psychohistory Press, 1979).

32. John C. H. Fei, "The Success of Chinese Culture as Economic Nutrient ...," *Free China Review* 36, no. 7 (July 1986):43.

3

WHAT DID MAKE THE CHINESE "CHINESE"?

SOME GEOGRAPHICAL PERSPECTIVES

DAVID N. KEIGHTLEY

ANY REFLECTION on the origins of civilization in China has to consider both the "whatness" and the "whyness" of the question: what the early culture was and why it assumed the particular forms that it did.[1] I have discussed, in a number of papers, the religious, aesthetic, and stylistic choices that, in my view, helped to define the content of early Chinese culture, that represent its "whatness."[2] Some of these strategic cultural features would include: (1) A stress on hierarchical social distinctions; (2) the ability to mobilize labor on a massive scale; (3) an emphasis on the group rather than the individual—expressed in the impersonality and generality of artistic and literary representation, and generated and validated by a religion of ancestor worship that defined individuals in terms of their role and status in the system of sacrifice and descent; (4) an emphasis on ritual in all dimensions of life; (5) an emphasis on formal boundaries and models, as revealed in part by the great stress on social discipline and order in ethics and cosmology; (6) an ethic of service, obligation, and emulation; (7) little sense of tragedy or irony.[3] The issues addressed here represent some of my speculations on the "whyness" of the issue. They are designed to stimulate enquiry and reflection without necessarily hoping to convince.

And we can ask, what made the ancestors "ancestors"? ... in the sense of what were the factors that led the early Chinese to make their ancestors, and their High God, in the particular ways that they did.

A consideration of the origins of civilization in China is likely to be shaped by what the literate Chinese of the early historical period thought, or claimed, had made them what they were. The kind of selective reshaping of the past, the creation of historicized fiction, that the Zhou (circa 1045–221 BCE) engaged in to justify their own political and cultural situation is, of course, not uncommon. One thinks, for example, of Israelite historiography, which has also reworked, if it did not create, the early history of Israel to tell a particular story of the chosen people.[4] In the case of China, the transmitters of the received texts chose to emphasize the story of a morally-superior, centralizing elite, a story that can certainly be challenged on a variety of historiographical, regional, and class-based lines. Nevertheless, the early texts do much to establish the cultural terminus, at least that reserved for elites, to which early Chinese civilization, under a teleological perspective, may be seen as heading. I am prepared to define the emerging culture of the Eastern Zhou (771–221 BCE), Qin (221–206 BCE), and Han (206 BCE–CE 220) elites—with its respect for the written language, its concern with ritual and filiality, and its creation of a bureaucratic state that was nevertheless permeated with metaphors and practices that derived from kinship ties—as "Chinese," and to treat the significant legacies those cultures inherited from the Shang as proto-Chinese.[5]

Nobody, of course, can fully know why the Chinese became Chinese. Only God, or Shang Di 上帝—the early Chinese name for their High God—knows. But, on Robert Green Ingersoll's principle that "an honest God is the noblest work of man," even Shang Di himself can be understood as a construction of the early Chinese—so that we could still ask, why did the Chinese make Shang Di in the way that they did?[6] And we can ask, what made the ancestors "ancestors"?—not in the sense of what it was to be an ancestor, which I have attempted to address elsewhere,[7] but in the sense of what were the factors that led the early Chinese to make their ancestors, and their High God, in the particular ways that they did.

Speaking broadly, we are faced with at least two approaches to questions of this sort. One approach is represented by the great, cold slabs of social science analysis, involving categories like matriarchy, patriarchy, slave society, and oriental despotism, slapped onto the Chinese evidence. These give their users a gratifying sense that they have pigeonholed and understood what was going on, but, in my view, they squeeze much that was uniquely Chinese out of the scenario, making the Chinese case just one further example of universal laws. The other approach, and here I am certainly exaggerating, argues that all history is local history, that generalizations are difficult and misleading, and that we should simply focus on particular texts and situations in their own right without attempting to develop broader, explanatory meanings. Historians, in this view, should not ask why things happen, but only what happened and how. Consider, for example, David Hackett Fischer's view of the matter. After arguing in favor of "how," "what," and "when" questions, he writes:

> These are urgent questions, and they are empirical questions, which can be put to the test. The reader will note that none of them are "why" questions. In my opinion—and I may be a minority of one—that favorite adverb of historians should be consigned to the semantical rubbish heap. A "why" question tends to become a metaphysical question. It is also an imprecise question, for the adverb "why" is slippery and difficult to define. Sometimes it seeks a cause, sometimes a motive, sometimes a reason, sometimes a description, sometimes a process, sometimes a purpose, sometimes a justification. A "why" question lacks direction and clarity; it dissipates a historian's energies and interests.[8]

I have much sympathy for this view. The problems of causation are so complex, and compounded now by the insights of the chaos theorists, that it would seem almost foolhardy to attempt to explain why anything happened. But a careful consideration of how the Chinese became Chinese, of what factors may have played a strategic causative role in the adoption of particular cultural choices, may throw instructive, if inevitably speculative, light on why they did so.

One can point to at least two directly opposed explanations about the origins of Chinese civilization, both involving, explicitly or not, assumptions about class that many, if not all, of the historical protagonists actually involved in the process might have found entirely foreign. The first, which we might label "Zhou traditional," emphasizes the rise of *the junzi* 君子, "noble man," who constructs an enlightened social hierarchy dominated by the benevolent concern of paternal elites who venerate the ancestors for the blessings they shower upon them and their dependents. The second, let us call it "Marxist," emphasizes the rise of an elite that conceals its violence and exploitations by appealing to a superstitious, self-interested ideology of respect, awe, and obedience rooted in a paternalistic kinship structure that invoked the ancestors to justify the continuing domination of their descendants. The model that one favors will, of course, greatly depend upon one's own point of view and temperament, to say nothing of one's class status.

Most of us, I suspect, without bothering to articulate in detail the methodological issues involved, adopt a middle ground in these matters, avoiding the big, abstract theories and the rigid reliance upon class analysis, but nevertheless seeking to make cultural connections and strong inferences that appear to explain particular features of Chinese civilization in their own terms. My own approach, I hope, has been within this moderate camp. I believe in getting our hands "dirty," in looking carefully at particular texts, particular archaeological sites, particular institutions, attempting to determine how they functioned at the micro level, attempting to recapture some of the realities of early Chinese experience—or, as I should more properly say, of local experiences in various parts of early China.[9] And it is then allowable, I hope, to take the insights that such dirty-handed analysis permits, and use them to propose larger patterns, to posit the existence of synergistic cultural relationships in various parts of early China, and to suggest theories of causation. I am proposing significant linkages rather than final solutions.

> *I believe in getting our hands "dirty," in looking carefully at particular texts, particular archaeological sites, particular institutions, attempting to determine how they functioned at the micro level, attempting to recapture some of the realities of early Chinese experience—or, as I should more properly say, of local experiences in various parts of early China.*

The Impact of Geography

I am not prepared to subscribe to the view of the environmental or geographical determinists, who believe "that social and cultural differences between human groups can ultimately be traced to differences in their physical environments."[10]

Cultural production, is, I believe, more complicated than that, but at the same time it is by no means divorced from geographical considerations.[11] And in the Chinese case, I would urge the importance of considering the influence that a series of local environments may have played in influencing the social and economic and ideological choices that various cultures made during the Neolithic and the Bronze Age.

I most emphatically do not subscribe to Wittfogel's theories of a pan-Chinese agro-managerial despotism that developed to construct and administer the needs of the large-scale water-control works required by the environment;[12] I think that, for the North China Plain at least (see n. 27), he has his history backwards.[13] The disposition and ability to organize Chinese society in the ways Wittfogel proposed antedated by a considerable period the construction of the works he had in mind. But it is, I think, worth considering the degree to which geography—the climates and environments of ancient China, together with their paleo-flora and paleo-fauna—helps to explain the cultural forms that were to develop within its boundaries.

The variations in human biology that distinguish the inhabitants of contemporary north and south China evidently existed in Neolithic times if not earlier.[14] What cultural consequences these variations might have involved, I do not know. But if we turn to environmental factors, I wonder, for example, about the possible cultural impact of water tables and soil chemistry in north and south China. Higher water tables in the south may have made the Liangzhu 良渚 inhabitants bury their dead on the surface (as in the case of the Sidun 寺墩 burial M3), in altar mounds on hillsides (as at Huiguanshan 匯觀山,[15] or in relatively shallow graves, just as the dampness encouraged them to build stilt houses (as at Hemudu 河姆渡).[16] The inhabitants of the drier north, by contrast, buried their dead in increasingly deep pits beneath the surface. Status, in the north, was evidently linked to the size, and hence to the depth, of the grave pit. Denied that means of expression in the south, the Liangzhu inhabitants appear to have invested their labor in high-status grave goods, such as highly-worked jade *cong* 琮 tubes and *bi* 璧 jade disks.[17]

Climate, I would suggest, may also have had a bearing in other ways on mourning, burial practices, and the invention of the ancestors. In modern Bali, we are told, "the conventional time required for putrefaction [of the royal corpse] to be completed" is forty-two days.[18] The relative shortness of this particular time interval may be related to the hotter climate in Bali. Could one, however, establish a link between ancestor worship and climate? Quick putrefaction allows little time for the "translation" of the dead to take place, so that the mourners at the time of the burial would still have been dealing with the "real, unabstracted" personality of the deceased. A longer interval, however, encouraged by the colder climates of north China, would have permitted a long period of decay, more pre-burial ritual activity, and thus a more radical transformation to the ancestral status.[19] The Liangzhu solution—to burn the corpse, as in the Sidun burial M3—would, of course, have been another way of speeding up the translation to ancestor.

Does the regularity of the climate patterns in north China help to account for the regularity of the ancestral cult and the reliability of divine intervention that we find in the early textual evidence?[20] Note that the Mandate of Heaven, the doctrine (usually employed as part of the victor's propaganda) in which Heaven confers rulership on the virtuous and destroys the wicked, provides a simple moral explanation for historical causation. Such a view of history does not encourage, nor is it congruent with, the kind of political and psychological complexity one encounters in either Mesopotamian or Greek mythology. Consider, for example, the account of the Death of Ur-nammu, with its Job-like theme of a life unfairly ended by the gods,[21] or the origins of, and personal rivalries dramatized in, Homer's Trojan War—there is no Mandate here, but personal emotion, dislike, hatted, and disagreement congruent with the harsh and unpredictable environment of the cultures that produced these mythologies. It is consistent with such an ecological view of the cultures concerned that the Greeks, in their mythology and literature, address the hostility of the gods and the quirkiness of fate; the Late Shang and Zhou Chinese address the importance of harmoniously following the rules.

Consider too the cultural reaction to the shifts in the Yellow River during the third millennium BCE. These may have been catastrophic to the Neolithic communities inundated in the North China Plain,[22] but were somehow, optimistically, seen as manageable, not existentially threatening, by the early Chinese legend-makers: the Sage Emperor Yu 禹 had taken care of it and rendered China habitable. This optimism stands in contrast to, say, the treachery and malevolence represented by the Mediterranean sea, for the early Greeks, or by the harsh and unpredictable environment of ancient Mesopotamia.[23] The cultures of Neolilthic China were incomparably richer than those of Neolithic Greece; the early Chinese had—in terms of climate, crops, and other resources—much to be optimistic about. That the early Chinese, unlike Gilgamesh, say, did not quarrel with their gods or ancestors may have been in part because there was less to quarrel about, ecologically and environmentally.

> *Does the regularity of the climate patterns in north China help to account for the regularity of the ancestral cult and the reliability of divine intervention that we find in the early textual evidence?*

Indeed, the relative benevolence of the early Chinese environment may also help to account for the pacific and abstract cosmogonic legends of the Eastern Zhou, which stand in sharp contrast to their Mesopotamian counterparts. The Babylonian epic, *Enuma elish*, for instance, "describes the creation not as a beginning, but as an end, ... the result of a cosmic battle, the fundamental and eternal struggle between those two aspects of nature: Good and Evil, Order and Chaos."[24] Impersonal forces are certainly found in the Chinese cosmogonies—one thinks, in particular, of the alternating forces of *yin* 陰 and *yang* 陽, "inherently complementary, not antagonistic," or the various cycles of the five phases (*wu xing* 五行) with their cycles of "conquest" and "generation";[25] their interactions are disciplined; the texts do not present them as battling in violent and unpredictable ways. And the distinctions are also evident in myths about the creation of man. For the Babylo-nians, Marduk had created man:

> I will establish a savage (*lullu*), 'man' shall be his name.
> Verily, savage-man I will create.
> He shall be charged with the service of the gods
> That they might be at ease!"[26]

Man, in short, was once again at the mercy of hostile or dominant powers, created to serve at their pleasure. In early China, by contrast, man was to be at the service of men—or former men, the ancestors—and most early creation myths involved the genesis of the elite lineages to serve as a charter for such expectations.

Geography and environment may also have played a role in the eventual dominance of north China over south. Gary Pahl, who studied thirteen walled Neolithic settlements in the plain of the Yangzi and Han Rivers, observed that around 2000 BCE the settlements seem suddenly to have been abandoned, with their populations generally diminishing until about 800 CE. Rather than credit external intervention and attacks from the north, he suggests that the populations may have fallen victim to schistosomiasis.[27] This will require further archaeolog-ical testing, but it alerts us to the possibility that south China, for all its fecundity, may not have been as salubrious as the north. And the inhabitants of Neolithic settlements in China, north or south, may well have been susceptible to disease in general. Agriculture, as Jared Diamond explains,

> sustains much higher human population densities than does the hunter-gathering lifestyle—on the average, 10 to 100 times higher. In addition, hunter-gatherers frequently shift camp and leave behind their own piles of feces with accumulated microbes and worm larvae. But farmers are sedentary and live amid their own sewage, thus providing microbes with a short path from one person's body into another's drinking water.
>
> Some farming populations make it even easier for their own fecal bac-teria and worms to infect new victims, by gathering their feces and urine and spreading them as fertilizer on the fields where people work. Irrigation agri-culture and fish farming provide ideal living conditions for the snails carrying schistosomiasis and for flukes that burrow through our skin as we wade through the feces-laden water.[28]

Paleobotany may also help to explain cultural distinctions between north and south China in the prehistoric and early imperial period. The botanist, Li Hui-lin, for instance, concluded that:

> Botanical and phytogeographical evidence of the great differences between the environments of North and South China points to the existence of two separate centers of plant domestication. Each center produced a well-rounded complex of crops independently capable of nurturing human culture.[29]

And once again the cultural impact of these differences may have been mediated by geography.

While China's north-south gradient retarded crop diffusion, the gradient was less of a barrier there than in the Americas or Africa, because China's north-south distances were smaller; and because China's is transected neither by desert, as is Africa and northern Mexico, nor by a narrow isthmus, as is Central America. Instead, China's long east-west rivers (the Yellow River in the north, the Yangtze River in the south) facilitated diffusion of crops and technology between the coast and inland, while its broad east-west expanse and relatively gentle terrain, which eventually permitted those two river systems to be joined by canals, facilitated north-south exchanges.[30]

Environment, I would also suggest, may throw light on the $64 question: Why were the early Chinese so filial, so respectful of seniors, compared, say, to the Classical Greeks whose legendary figures were so ready to challenge authority and the patriarchy. Why did the authority of the kin group remain so strong in China even as the state was emerging? Surely environment plays a role here too: seafarers and traders, people who move around, who are not tied down, who are exposed to other cultures, who are left to their own resources, and who are not under the eye of authority in the way that farmers tied to the land are, are more likely to question or ignore their parents and those who would lord it over them.[31] It is no coincidence that, by the Eastern Zhou, the Qin minister Shang Yang, keen to encourage agriculture, was concerned about merchants, who moved about too easily, and that the *Zhouli* 周禮 were concerned about registering peasants and fixing them in one place.[32] Agriculture fostered hierarchy and stability in a way that seafaring and trading at a distance did not.[33] As G. E. R. Lloyd has remarked, "Agriculture ... had a far higher ideological profile in China than in the Greco-Roman world."[34]

> *Environment, I would also suggest, may throw light on the $64 question: Why were the early Chinese so filial so respectful of seniors, compared, say, to the Classical Greeks whose legendary figures were so ready to challenge authority and the patriarch?*

I would also like to suggest, however, that the "modular" nature of the early Chinese environment with its wide latitudinal bands of common products and similar climates would have conferred a certain freedom on a peasantry disposed to flee from harsh rulers.[35] Such freedom may not have been so readily available, for example, in the Mesopotamian case, where the harshness of the environment would not have held the easy promise that the grass was greener elsewhere. I am struck, for example, by the degree to which all the Mesopotamian rulers of the Early Dynastic period boast of their conquests;[36] they show little of the Mencian or Confucian, or even Legalist, concern for attracting people or providing good government. But Chinese peasants, moving from one state to another, of course, would only have been exchanging, not escaping from, the domination of lords.

The agrarian basis of the culture also bears on what appears to have been the relative unimportance in early China of "the market as a factor in economic and political diversity." Gordon Willey, for example, has suggested "the great importance of the Near Eastern temple markets" as "institutions separate from the palace and the king."[37] And David Tandy has explored the links between the new market economy in Greece and the development of the polis.[38] That there seem to have been no economic institutions that produced a comparable social and political impact in early China is partly explainable in terms of geography. The major rivers in China flowed from west to east. They did not, accordingly, greatly encourage interregional trade—since they flowed through latitudes where the environments were similar. As a result, the riverine routes did not provide sufficient economic incentives and rewards for a strong merchant class to develop that was independent of the trade in luxury goods associated with the court and its dependents. Some of the copper ores that the Late Shang bronze casters used in North China may well have been shipped over considerable distances from the south,[39] but these ores were employed to cast the bronze vessels that the dynastic elites used to serve their ancestors. The lack of extensive, non-dynastic trading networks in early China may also be explained by the widespread distribution of resources needed for daily life. This contrasts with the situation in ancient Mesopotamia, for example, where metal ores (copper, tin), hard stone, and good timber were in short supply. At a very early date, therefore, an extensive network of trade routes was developed within Mesopotamia and with the rest of the Near East.[40] A society in which merchants play a significant role is likely to develop a culture different from that of a society in which they do not. Once again, this is not to say that the environment is all determining—as C. C. Lamberg-Karlovsky, commenting on the Algaze article cited in the previous note, has remarked: "Environments are filtered, transformed, and given their material reality by the beliefs and practices of a society."[41] But the environment certainly helps to shape the cultural choices available.

The archaeological evidence, in fact, has led a recent study to conclude that "the acquisition of vital resources" in early China

> seems to have operated on the state level. The states were able to gain a monopoly on procuring and transporting these resources by moving populations into resource-rich regions, constructing outposts in major junctions along transportation routes in these regions, and managing craft production forces.[42]

Rather than emphasizing the importance of trade—as indicated by the Mesopotamian model—the authors conclude that

> the relationship between urban centers and peripheral regions in early states in China (from the Erlitou to Early Shang) may have been a one-way military and political domination operated by powerful royal lineages in the capital city. The interregional network, which operated the resource flow, may have been kin-based, rather than purely bureaucratic. The religious and political motivations—such as ancestral worship rituals, divinatory ceremonies, royal hunts, and elite feasting and drinking—were the underlying dynamics for the procurement of copper and the manufacture of bronze objects on a massive scale directly controlled by the state.[43]

The dynasty's ability to provide abundant metal ores also appears to have encouraged the development of, as no doubt it was encouraged by, the large-scale dynastic bronze-casting operations of the Late Shang. As Robert Bagley has noted, the *Si Mu Wu fang ding* 司母戊方鼎), a square tripod that weighed 875 kilograms, the largest Shang ritual vessel yet found, reveals

> that Shang workshops were organized on a scale exceedingly large by the standards of the rest of the ancient world. In Shang China there is no trace of the independent artisans who in the West might supply all the metal needs required by a typical Bronze Age community. The number of bronze vessels known from the Shang period implies production on an industrial scale, and the foundry which produced the *Si Mu Wu fang ding* must have been awesome.[44]

Once again, one observes the cultural consequences of geography or, in this case, geology.

Finally, the geographic isolation of China presumably played a role in the genesis of early Chinese culture. No foreign invasions appear to have created major discontinuities in the development of the cultures of early China. In particular, the absence in early China of any experience analogous to that of the Dark Ages in pre-classical Greece is significant;[45] there was no break in cultural development, no rupture, no fresh start. There was, in short, no radical challenge to culture, no "death" of culture, just as there was no flood that had destroyed mankind, no radical "death" of humanity in the theology and the mythology of the Zhou. That kind of major cultural hostility, with invasions striking to the heart, had generally been precluded by the geographical position of China.

Conclusions

I have no global conclusions to offer, save to urge the educational value of attempting to consider, if not answer, some of the questions above, I don't think we will ever fully know what made the Chinese Chinese. But by trying to understand the mechanisms, cross-fertilizations, and cultural and ecological embeddedness of the choices that the early inhabitants of China made, we will come closer to understanding the factors that would have been involved. The Chinese, after all, have probably fed more people, more successfully, than any other culture in world history. How they developed the social capital to do this is well worth our study.

Notes

1. A preliminary and far shorter version of this article originally appeared as "What Did Make the Chinese 'Chinese'?: Musings of a Would-be Geographical Determinist," in the newsletter, *Lotus Leaves* (Society for Asian Art, San Francisco) 3.2 (Summer 2000): 1–3. I am grateful to the anonymous readers for *Education About Asia*, many of whose suggestions I have incorporated in this revised version.

2. See, in particular, David N. Keightley, "The Religious Commitment: Shang Theology and the Genesis of Chinese Political Culture," *History of Religions* 17 (1978):221–22; "Clean Hands and Shining Helmets: Heroic Action in Early Chinese and Greek Culture," in *Religion and Authority*, ed. Tobin Siebers (Ann Arbor: University of Michigan Press, 1993):113–51; "Epistemology in Cultural Context: Disguise and Deception in Early China and Early Greece," in *Early China, Ancient Greece: Thinking Through Comparisons*, eds. Steven Shankman and Stephen Durrant (Albany: State University of New York Press, 2001):119–53. (All three cited papers are included in this volume).

3. I take this list of cultural features, abbreviating it and omitting the illustrative examples given, from David N. Keightley, "Early Civilization in China: Reflections on How It Became Chinese," (p. 68, above).

4. I was struck, with all the hoopla about the release of the 1998 Dream Works movie, "The Prince of Egypt," that nobody, in the popular press at least, raised the question: were the Jews ever in Egypt? For the historiographical uncertainties involved, see, e.g., Nahum M. Sarna, "Israel in Egypt: The Egyptian Sojourn and the Exodus," in *Ancient Israel: A Short History from Abraham to the Roman Destruction of the Temple*, ed. Hershel Shanks (Englewood Cliffs, NJ, and Washington, DC: Prentice-Hall and Biblical Archeological Society, 1988):31–52; Donald Redford, *Egypt, Canaan, and Israel in Ancient Times* (Princeton: Princeton University Press, 1992).

5. On the legacies of Shang culture, see, e.g., Keightley, "Late Shang Divination: The Magico-Religious Legacy," (included in this volume; see below).

6. I would put considerable stock in the view that the idea of Di as supreme deity or Power did not develop until the institution of Shang kingship, involving similar conceptions of centralized power and authority, had developed on earth. See, e.g., C. C. Shih, "A Study of Ancestor Worship in Ancient China," in *The Seed of Wisdom: Essays in Honour of T. J. Meek*, ed. W. S. McCullough (Toronto: 1964), 184–85. There is much more scholarship on this issue.

7. David N. Keightley, "The Making of the Ancestors: Late Shang Religion and Its Legacy," (included in this volume; see below).

8. David Hackett Fischer, *Historians' Fallacies: Toward a Logic of Historical Thought* (New York: Harper & Row, 1970):14.

9. As William G. Boltz noted in his review of the conference volume. *The Origins of Chinese Civilization*, ed. David N. Keightley (Berkeley: University of California Press, 1983), "Consider how different the conference might have been if it had been called "Origins of Civilization in China," instead of "Origins of Chinese Civilization" (*Journal of the American Oriental Society* 15.4 [1985]:763).

10. Martin W. Lewis and Kären E. Wigen, *The Myth of Continents: A Critique of Metageography* (Berkeley: University of California Press, 1997):42; see, too, 195.

11. See, e.g., Lewis and Wigen, *The Myth of Continents*, 102.

12. See, e.g., Karl A. Wittfogel, *Oriental Despotism: A Comparative Study of Total Power* (New Haven: Yale University Press, 1963).

13. David N. Keightley, "Public Work in Ancient China: A Study of Forced Labor in the Shang and Western Chou" (PhD dissertation, Columbia University, 1969):123–25, 134–38, 346–48. See too, Lewis and Wigen, *The Myth of Continents*:93–100.

14. Dennis A. Etler, "Recent Developments in the Study *of Human Biology* in China: A Review," *Human Biology* 64.4 (August 1992):567–85. He discusses, in particular, the distribution of immunoglobulin GM and KM allotpyes, stature, and cranial and facial dimensions.

15. Zhejiang sheng wenwu kaogu yanjiusuo and Yuhang shi wenwu guanli weiyuanhui, "Zhejiang Yuhang Huiguanshan Liangzhu wenhua litan yu mudi fajue jianbao 浙江餘杭匯顧山良緒文化祭壇與墓地發掘簡報 *Wenwu* 文物1997, 7:4–19.

16. Zhejiang sheng wenwu guanli weiyuanhui and Zhejiang sheng bouwuguan. "Hemudu yizhi diyiqi fajue baogao 河姆渡遺址第一期發掘報告," *Kaogu xuebao* 考古學報 1978,1:42 48, fig. 5.

17. For an introduction to and illustrations of these artifacts, see, e.g., *Mysteries of Ancient China: New Discoveries From the Early Dynasties*, ed. Jessica Rawson (London: British Museum Press, 1996):52–55.

18. Richard Huntington and Peter Metcalf, *Celebrations of Death: The Anthropology of Mortuary Ritual* (London: Cambridge University Press, 1979):130.

19. It has been suggested to me by Michael Depew that one reason we Find the skeletons of "slave" victims in Shang burials are well preserved and the skeletons of the grave lords are generally not, is that the corpses of the grave lords at Anyang 安踢, the Late Shang cult center (circa 1200–1045 BCE), have vanished because of the delay between the time they died and the time, already in a state of decay, when they were put in the ground; by contrast, the skeletons of the victims and "slaves" were preserved because they went into the ground relatively quickly and thus "fresh." Whatever the reason, it does seem as if something changed in the treatment of certain elite corpses with the arrival of the Bronze Age. Sacrificial victims and prisoners were still given "Neolithic" treatment and their bones survived. But the "Bronze Age Mortuary Special" evidently led to the bones of the elites not surviving.

20. For the pigeonholing of the Late Shang ancestors by their temple names (based on the names of the ten days of the Shang week), so that each ancestor received rituals and offerings according to an unvarying schedule, see Keightley, "The Making of the Ancestors," (see below, pp. XXX). For the "optimistic rationality of Shang religion, its faith that there was a rule, a divination, a sacrifice, for every occasion." see Keightley, "The Religious Commitment," (see below, p. XXX). For "the metaphysical and epistemological optimism that underlies much early Chinese philosophy," see Keightley, "Epistemology in Cultural Context," (see below, esp. p. XXX).

21. Samuel Noah Kramer, "The Death of Ur-nammu and His Descent to the Netherworld," *Journal of Cuneiform Studies* 21 (1967): 104–22.

22. David N. Keightley, "The Environment of Ancient China," in *The Cambridge History of Ancient China*, 32–33.

23. E.g., Roux, *Ancient Iraq*, 25: "Mesopotamia constantly hovers between desert and swamp. This double threat and the uncertainty it creates as regards the future are believed to be at the root of the 'fundamental pessimism' which, for some authors, characterizes the philosophy of the ancient Mesopotamians." See too Roux, 104.

24. Roux, *Ancient Iraq*, 97.

25. See, e.g., *Sources of Chinese Tradition*, eds. Wm. Theodore de Bary and Irene Bloom (New York: Columbia University Press, 1999, 2nd ed.):238, 347–49.

26. Roux, *Ancient Iraq*, 100.

27. Gary Pahl, "Bovines, Cups, and Miniatures….," Archaeology Brown Bag Lecture, Archaeological Research Facility, University of California at Berkeley, 10 February 1999. Pahl also makes the point that the Neolithic inhabitants of the Yangzi-Han River towns may have built their "walls" (which were piled up, rather than built of rammed earth) as water management devices, rather than as defensive works.

28. Jared Diamond, *Guns, Germs, and Steel: The Fates of Human Societies* (New York: Norton, 1997):205.

29. Hui-lin Li, "The Domestication of Plants in China: Ecogeographical Considerations," in *The Origins of Chinese Civilization*, ed. Keightley, 50.

30. Diamond, *Guns, Germs, and Steel*, 331.

31. Li-jun Ji, Kaiping Peng, and Richard Nisbett ("Culture, Control, and Perception of Relationships in the Environment," *Journal of Personality and Social Psychology* 78.5 [2000]:953) have argued that "sedentary agricultural groups stress interpersonal orientation and conformity in child rearing, and they have a tight social structure in which group members need to accommodate each other and strive to regulate one another's behavior. Alan Cromer (*Uncommon Sense: The Heretical Nature of Science* [Oxford University Press, 1993]:74), in fact, has gone so far as to argue, referring to the *Odyssey*, that "The sea is freedom, adventure, wealth, and knowledge—all factors important to the development of science."

32. For these themes in Zhou political culture, see David N. Keightley, "Peasant Migration, Politics, and Philosophical Response in Chou and Ch'in China," Berkeley Regional Seminar in Confucian Studies, 11 November 1977.

33. Adam T. Smith (*The Political Landscape: Constellations of Authority in Early Complex Polities* [Berkeley: University of California Press, 2003]:84) notes that for Aristotle, the perfection of the polis "depended on an ideal number of citizens distributed across a territory that allowed for self-sufficiency in production, preferably with access to the sea in order to allow for long-distance trade."

34. *The Ambitions of Curiosity: Understanding the World in Ancient Greece and China* (New York: Cambridge University Press, 2002):80.

35. Keightley, "Peasant Migration."

36. Roux, *Ancient Iraq*, 134–39.

37. Gordon Willey, "Ancient Chinese—New World and Near Eastern Ideological Traditions: Some Observations," *Symbols* (Spring 1985):23. He was commenting on the views of K. C. Chang and on C. C. Lamberg-Karlovsky, "The Near Eastern 'Breakout' and the Mesopotamian Social Contract," *Symbols* (Spring 1985):8–11, 23–24.

38. David W. Tandy, *Warriors into Traders: The Power of the Market in Early Greece* (Berkeley: University of California Press, 1997).

39. Li Liu and Xingcan Chen, *State Formation in Early China* (London: Duckworth, 2003):37–44.

40. Georges Roux, *Ancient Iraq* (New York: Viking Penguin, 1980):30. For further discussion of this theme, see Marc Van der Mieroop, *The Ancient Mesopotamian City* (Oxford: Clarendon Press, 1997):30–31, 40; Guillermo Algaze, "Initial Social Complexity in Southwestern Asia," *Current Anthropology* 42.2 (2001):199–233 (which includes the subsequent comment on his arguments); Smith, *The Political Landscape*, 279.

41. *Current Anthropology* 42.2 (2001):220.

42. Li Liu and Xingcan Chen, "Cities and Towns: The Control of Natural Resources in Early States, China," *Bulletin of the Museum of Far Eastern Antiquities* 73 (2001):40.

43. Liu and Chen, "Cities and Towns," 41.

44. Robert W. Bagley, *Shang Ritual Bronzes in the Arthur M. Sackler Collections* (Washington, DC: The Arthur M. Sackler Foundation and Museum; Cambridge, Mass: Harvard University Press, 1987):18.

45. On the Greek Dark Age and its impact, see, e.g., M. I. Finley, *The World of Odysseus* (Harmondsworth: Penguin, 1978; 2nd ed. 1979); Robert Drews, *The End of the Bronze Age: Changes in Warfare and the Catastrophe ca. 1200 BC* (Princeton: Princeton University Press, 1993).

4

THE RELIGIOUS COMMITMENT: SHANG THEOLOGY AND THE GENESIS OF CHINESE POLITICAL CULTURE

DAVID N. KEIGHTLEY

THE TRIUMPHS of Chinese civilization—its ethic of social benevolence, its bureaucracy open to talent, its belles lettres and painting, its major public works—have not generally been regarded as animated by religious impulses. Confucianism and Legalism said little about death, the realm of the spirit, or ultimate values that transcend human society. "The Chinese mood," it has been said, "was essentially secular."[1]

Such a view stresses the great tradition at the expense of the numerous lesser ones, and it ignores the later contributions of Buddhism and Neo-Confucianism. Its accuracy may also be challenged for the early historic period. It is the argument of this exploratory essay that the secular values and institutions representing the great tradition of the Chou and Han dynasties were characterized to a significant extent by habits of thinking and acting that had been sanctified, at least a millennium earlier, by the religious logic of Shang theology and cult.

To speak of religious logic as a separate category of Shang thought is an analytical convenience. Such an approach obscures the fact that all aspects of Shang life could be impregnated, as the occasion arose, with religious significance. But the homogeneity of the Shang world view that this implies reinforces the assumption that Shang religious conceptions were the conceptions of Shang life as a whole.[2] A study of the essential nature of Shang religion will tell us much about the ethos and world view of the ancient Chinese, and it will suggest the ways in which their conceptions, both religious and secular, shaped later developments.

I derive my understanding of Shang religion and political organization from the pyromantic inscriptions carved on cattle scapulas and turtle shells during the reigns of the last eight or nine Shang kings who ruled in the area of An-yang, northern Honan, during the last centuries of the second millennium B.C.[3] Any attempt to assess the mentality of the Chinese bronze-age elite some 3,000 years ago will be speculative at many points. With regard to religion, for example, the inscriptions provide a flat and abbreviated view telling us more of the notes of Shang cult than of the music of Shang belief. Nevertheless, there is no reason to doubt that the structure of Shang religion recorded by the oracle inscriptions is, so far as it goes, accurate.[4]

Religion and the Shang State

Shang religion was inextricably involved in the genesis and legitimation of the Shang state.[5] It was believed that Ti, the high god, conferred fruitful harvest and divine assistance in battle, that the king's ancestors were able to intercede with Ti, and that the king could communicate with his ancestors. Worship of the Shang ancestors, therefore, provided powerful psychological and ideological support for the political dominance of the Shang kings. The king's ability to determine through divination, and influence through prayer and sacrifice, the will of the ancestral spirits legitimized the concentration of political power in his person. All power emanated from the theocrat because he was the channel, "the one man,"[6] who could appeal for the ancestral blessings, or dissipate the ancestral curses, which affected the commonality. It was the king who made fruitful harvest and victories possible by the sacrifices he offered, the rituals he performed, and the divinations he made. If, as seems likely, the divinations involved some degree of magic making, of spell casting, the king's ability to actually create a good harvest or a victory by divining about it rendered him still more potent politically.[7]

The king depended upon his ancestors. But the ancestors depended for their strength upon the grain offerings, the flesh and blood of animal and human sacrifices, and the millet-wine libations that the king offered to them.[8] The magnificence of the royal sacrifices—which could involve several hundred head of cattle[9]—served to impress all concerned with the awesome power of the ancestors who received them. The more state wealth that was devoted to sacrificial cult, the stronger the powers of the ancestral spirits and their descendants below appeared. The belief that the maintenance of the dynasty and the maintenance of the royal cult were inseparable provided a strong motive for the Shang to increase both their material prosperity and their military power. Technical innovations such as writing, bronze making, and the chariot may have first permitted the Shang to conquer their neighbors. But it was the belief in the strength of the Shang ancestors, the central value of the state, which legitimized the Shang dominion.[10]

The Bureaucratic Logic
of Shang Religion

There is nothing uniquely Chinese in this account so far. Religious belief has played similar roles in the genesis of other states.[11] Significant in the Chinese case, however, were the modes of conceptualization central to the theology. For it is in the logical relationships that Shang theology postulated as basic, and in the emotions associated with those relationships, that we find the characteristic elements which influenced the development of political culture in Chou and later times. We find, in fact, a paradoxical situation: a Shang state permeated with a commitment to the ancestors, strongly religious in the totality of its demands; and yet we find that the commitment can be characterized as nonreligious, nonmysterious, and—because so explicitly goal directed—rational, in its logic. The logic may be characterized, in fact, with appropriate cautions to which I shall return, as "bureaucratic" in Max Weber's sense of the term.[12] I do not mean to imply, incidentally, by the use of this term, that the Chinese, then or later, were pure, Weberian bureaucrats. For all its bureaucratic logic, Shang ancestor worship and Shang political culture stressed the lineage as a source of authority. Such considerations of kinship continued to influence if not sabotage the operations of bureaucratic administration throughout imperial times; their role in Shang religion does not need reiterating here.

Shang religious practice rested upon the *do ut des* ("I give, in order that thou shouldst give") belief that correct ritual procedure by the Shang kings would result in favors conferred by Ti.[13] Ti stood at the apex of the spiritual hierarchy. Beneath him were the royal ancestors, who were to intercede with Ti as the result of sacrificial payments offered to them, often as a promise or contract, by the living kings at a still lower rank.[14] So far as we can tell, the relationships between the members of the hierarchy were, in Weber's terms, "ordered systematically"; that is, the right sacrifices ensured the right responses, and the right responses by the spirits led, in turn, to appropriate thank-offerings by the kings.[15] Offerings, presumably provision offerings made to provide the ancestors with sustenance and strength, were frequently made, not in connection with a particular request, but in accordance with a rigid sacrificial schedule.[16] It may not be too farfetched to see here the origins of the conception of a routine salary system designed to keep the ancestors at their posts by contrast with a more primitive, or at least less bureaucratic, method of unsystematic bribery according to need.

The logic of the sacrificial offerings and divinations was itself frequently bureaucratic: the nature of the offering was inscribed on the oracular bone or shell (Weber's "stipulated, written criteria"); the success of the offering depended upon the correct fulfillment of "defined duties," that is, the right number of cattle, to the right ancestor, on the right day. The concern with ritual number and ratios manifested in the sacrificial divinations—two sheep or three sheep? five human victims or ten? what ratio of male to female animals?[17]—anticipated, as it may help explain, the commitment to numbers, both real (as in census figures) and idealized (as in the symmetries of *Chou-li*), of later bureaucrats and thinkers. The mind of the Shang diviner was a quantifying mind.

These sacrifice-offerings were required in order to keep all areas of life "strong, fertile and fortunate,"[18] and they were conceived of in these contractual, numerical, bureaucratic, terms. Furthermore, all the areas of experience that the offerings were designed to influence were seen by the Shang theocrats as a series of ritual jurisdictions, each falling within the domain of particular ancestors and their particular sacrifices.[19] In the oracle bones experience was compartmentalized into a series of discrete and tentative statements, testing and examining pro and con the approval of the spirits. This readiness to divide experience into manageable units again suggests the workings of a bureaucratic mentality.

The optimistic rationality of Shang religion, its faith that there was a rule, a divination, a sacrifice, for every occasion, should also be noted. The faith that the world is manageable in stipulated, negotiable, discoverable terms is a necessary corollary of bureaucratic logic. There was room for arbitrary acts of malevolence (especially on the part of the junior, less bureaucratic dead who had died more recently). But, afflicted with such malevolence, the Shang kings acted as if they could discover, by divination, the particular rule for any occasion, that is, the particular sacrificial contract that would propitiate the ancestor involved and remove the curse. The radical world optimism which Weber identified as a central Confucian value was already present in Shang religious belief.[20]

Generationalism

In Weberian terms, then, we can refer to the hierarchical, contractual, rational, routinized; mathematical, compartmentalized nature of Shang ancestor worship as bureaucratic.[21] But I am only led to use the anachronistic term "bureaucratic" because of the later development of bureaucracy in Chou and Han China. The Shang diviners did not regard themselves as proto-bureaucrats. To understand the true nature of the mentality revealed in the divinations about cult we must characterize it in terms that—had they made such distinctions explicit—would have been familiar to the Shang themselves. Since Shang religion, as we see it in the oracle inscriptions, was primarily a cult of the ancestors concerned with the relationships between dead and living kin, it is plausible to assume that the explanatory idioms we seek will involve such relationships.[22] I believe that the so-called bureaucratic logic of Shang religion can be discussed more accurately in terms of "generationalism," by which I mean the willingness, and probably the necessity, to conceive of the world in hierarchies of power based upon the relative age of generations.

The importance of generational ranking may be discerned in the Shang treatment of both the dead and the living. Until the reign of the last five kings, for example, Shang dynastic power generally remained within the same generation, passing from brother to brother before descending to the next generation.[23] In the system of ancestor worship, the "uncles" and "aunts" of the preceding generation were accorded important status.[24] And greater status was accorded those ancestors and ancestresses whose sons had become kings.[25] That is, those kings and queens who had advanced the dynasty by one generation were accorded "great tablet" status; those kings and queens whose sons had not become kings were accorded only "small tablet" status.[26] And the ancestors and ancestresses who did not qualify for major status were eventually dropped from the sacrificial schedule.[27]

There is further evidence of this generationalism in the divinations. The *pin* ceremony, for example (in which the king "received a spirit as a guest," or one ancestral spirit received another), was also regulated by generational status. Thus, junior ancestors offered *pin*-sacrifices only to more senior ancestors, and received the *pin*-sacrifice only from ancestors (or living kings) still more junior.[28] In the divinations, the ancestors were generally listed in order of decreasing seniority.[29] It was frequently the case that the older the ancestor the more he was honored, the more powerful he was thought to be, the larger his sphere of operations, and the larger his sacrifices.[30] From the viewpoint of such generationalism, in fact, death would have been a form of promotion in the generational hierarchy; the promotion conferred increased power. The longer an ancestor had been dead, the more seniority he had accumulated in the system.

It should also be stressed that the increased power of the senior generations was exercised in increasingly impersonal ways; that is, recently dead ancestors might plague living individuals (who would perhaps have known them when they were alive), but the dead of more distant generations affected the state as a whole by influencing harvests, droughts, and enemy invasions.[31] There is no evidence that the more powerful ancestors were still regarded as personalities with individual traits;[32] they had become abstractions, whose importance lay in their rank, not their person. Some were labeled "great" or "small" or were numbered, like "the fourth ancestor Ting" (*ssu tsu ting*).[33] And, as abstractions, we find that their names or titles varied both with their generational relationship to the sacrificer and with the nature of the sacrifice. Tsu Yi, "Ancestor Yi," for example, enjoyed at least six titles,[34] suggesting that more emphasis was placed upon terminological classification within the system than upon personal identity. Only certain ancestors received the cult titles,[35] so that the depersonalizing designation by title represented, itself, a promotion to the ranks of the elite.

This suggests that, to the extent that impersonality is characteristic of bureaucracy, these more powerful ancestors of the older generations were more bureaucratic, with Ti, the high god, being the most impersonal, most bureaucratic, of all. This is by no means fanciful, for it is a significant fact that (as recorded, at least, in the oracle inscriptions) the living kings appealed to Ti far less frequently than they did to the ancestors, and with far less sacrificial wealth.[36] Certain jurisdictions, like rain and warfare, were Ti's special concern,[37] but it was apparently not thought that he could be swayed by the *do ut des* contracts with which the ancestors were continually involved. The ancestors, despite their generational ranks, were still ancestors, still members of the royal family, and thus they responded to the bribes offered by their descendants below, partly because they were bribes, but mainly, perhaps, because they were offered by the descendants. Whether or not Ti was conceived of as the primordial ancestor of the Shang royal house we cannot tell.[38] But the lack of evidence of any kind of blood link, coupled with his relatively otiose role, suggests that while he stood at the apex of the generational hierarchy he did so, not for reasons of lineage, but for reasons of rank—generational rank, perhaps, since he was presumably conceived of as older than any of the Shang ancestors, but generational rank that was now divorced from any familial, particularistic significance—generational rank that verged, perhaps, on bureaucratic rank. It was precisely this impersonality which made it possible for Ti to harm the dynasty by sponsoring the attack of an enemy tribe[39] and which suggests that the Mandate-of-Heaven doctrine, usually regarded as a Chou invention—and which, because of its stress on promotion according to the stipulated criterion of merit, may be regarded as a bureaucratic doctrine—had its roots in Shang theology.[40]

The Religious Commitment

Religion itself, like political culture, is produced by society. That supernatural forces were conceived, for example, in terms of hierarchies of dead fathers whose wishes continued to be consulted through pyromantic divination implies much about the role of those fathers while alive; it was a role which, by its influence on the child, must have affected the adult's conceptions of authority in both the religious and secular sphere. The religious ranking of the Shang ancestors must have reflected the social system, with its own hierarchical obligations and attitudes, by which living relatives were classified; generationalism, like ancestor worship, derived from authority patterns among the living.[41] Such respect for gerontocratic power, with its implications of filial piety rather than generational strife, indicates that power and authority were accepted as the natural attribute of senior generations and were conceived of as flowing from senior to junior, down through the generational ranks. The natural acceptance of such a hierarchical yet nurturing relationship between generations legitimized superior and subordinate relationships among the living as well as the dead.

Similarly, the bureaucratic features of Shang religion must have been related to contemporary administrative practice. For Chinese administration may be regarded as already proto-bureaucratic in Shang times. Written documents certainly played a major role in the organization of the state.[42] The king issued orders to officers by their titles; administration was conducted through group assignments; such groups formed part of a hierarchical administration in which the king ordered individual officers, the officers ordered these groups, and the groups in turn directed the conscripts beneath them. And we can document, in some cases, a filiation between the titles of these Shang groups and the later bureaucratic titles of Chou times.[43]

Similarly, the religious concern with order and hierarchy is congruent with the intensely ordered style of much Shang hieratic art, devoted to the imposition of abstract, balanced, geometric patterns over entire surfaces. The style and the religious concerns reflect the emotional and intellectual dispositions of the Shang elite and the highly organized structure of their social conceptions.[44] The fact that Shang art is not naturalistic, that it displays great "psychical distance" between the style and the reality[45] so that it provides, for example, no visual information about political topics, the role of the king, or the appearance of the ancestors, is further evidence of the impersonal mode of both Shang religion and culture.[46]

The love of order may also be seen in the systematic nature of Shang divination, which frequently presented the divination topics in complementary, positive and negative forms carved on the turtle plastron with rigorous symmetry; and it may be seen in the ordered metaphysical conceptions those forms imply.[47] There was, in short, a congruence of function and expression between religious practice, political organization, kinship descent, artistic expression, and divination forms. Early Chinese culture as a whole was characterized by a remarkable love of, and perhaps a will to, order.

I am not arguing, therefore, that the origins of China's later secular political culture may be found in the logic and grammar of Shang religion, that Shang categories of understanding were necessarily "born in and of religion."[48] Nor am I arguing that the real origins of Shang religious classification are to be found in Shang kinship organization.[49] I believe rather that religious belief and practice had a social reality of their own, and that religion and society interacted synergetically (to borrow a term from biology), producing results which neither could have achieved without the other. The generational, hierarchical, and jurisdictional taxonomy by which the Shang kings classified their ancestors and the bureaucratic, contractual way in which the Shang kings negotiated with their ancestors undoubtedly were both analogous to, and served as analogies for, secular institutions and relationships. Sustained and enhanced by their religious role, bureaucratically ordered relationships came to be conceived of as the *sine qua non* of civilized life, satisfying not for utilitarian reasons alone (though those were certainly present), but for reasons of ultimate, religious significance, satisfying because, as Lévi-Strauss has said, they were "good to think."[50]

I am thus suggesting that there is a positive relationship between Shang religious belief and later bureaucratic conceptions. "Bureaucratic" ancestor worship does not explain the genesis of bureaucracy; but the religious logic by which the Shang confronted the *mysterium tremendum et fascinosum* of the ancestors may explain the paramount importance of bureaucratic values in traditional Chinese culture. The form that political authority, and the civil theology supporting it, eventually took as the political culture became increasingly secularized in Chou times continued to manifest a commitment to the hierarchical, authoritarian, quasimagical, bureaucratic features whose presence may be discovered in the characteristic generationalism and contractual logic of Shang ancestor worship.[51] Just as, to Weber, "Puritan wealth was an unintended consequence of the anxieties aroused by the doctrine of predestination,"[52] so, I would suggest, the high value that later Chinese placed on bureaucratic organization was partly an unintended consequence, not of the anxieties caused by fear of the ancestral dead, but of the way in which those anxieties were assuaged. This bureaucratic reaction was China's "stay against confusion." A religious faith in the validating efficacy of classification, hierarchy, number, and contract persisted, remaining behind in secular areas of life after the inundating flood of Shang religious belief had receded. This is one reason, perhaps, why in later times bureaucratic office, in Levenson's words, "could be taken to symbolize high culture, knowledge for its own sake, the terminal values of civilization," why "office-holding was clearly superior to any other social role," why "the bureaucratic end" was indeed "the end of life."[53] Faith in bureaucratic and social organization had become the functional equivalent of earlier, religious faith. Other civilizations have certainly developed centralized administrations that were more or less bureaucratic; it is only in China, however, that the bureaucratic role, with all its kin and ritual elements, has been so passionately cherished.

It could be said that what I have done is to give one more example of the truism that the Chinese bureaucratized their Heaven.[54] And there is no doubt that they did; religion is produced by society. But it is equally true, I submit, that the influence also worked the other way; that the habits of an optimistic, manipulating, and prognosticating religious logic endowed the order and structure of ranks and hierarchies, jurisdictions, contracts, and stipulated criteria which were emerging in Shang secular administration with special worth. We misunderstand the new, more differentiated values, attitudes, and institutions of Chou and Han if we view them in purely secular terms. The strength and endurance of the Confucian tradition, ostensibly secular though its manifestations frequently were, cannot be fully explained, or its true nature understood, unless we take into account the religious commitment which assisted at that tradition's birth and which continued to sustain it.[55]

Glossary of Chinese Characters

(The characters for Chinese and Japanese bibliographic references may be found in Keightley, Sources.)

fu 父

ling 令

ming 命

mu 母

pin 賓

Shang Chia 上甲

ssu tsu ting 四祖丁

Ta I 大乙

T'ang 唐．湯

Ti 帝

to-fu 多父

to-hou 多后

to-kung 多工

to-ma 多馬

to-pi 多妣

Tsu Chia 祖甲

Tsu I 祖乙

Tsu Keng 祖庚

tsung-fa 宗法

Tzu 子

Wu Ting 武丁

yü i-jen 余一人

Notes

A preliminary version of this paper, called "The Origins of Chinese Political Culture: The Religious Catalyst," was presented at the Annual Meeting of the Association for Asian Studios (New York, March 1972); it is now much changed. I am particularly grateful to my colleagues Irv Scheiner and Tu Wei-ming for their constructive suggestions.

1. Joseph Needham, with the collaboration of Wang Ling and Lu Gwoi-djen, *Science and Civilisation in China* (Cambridge, 1971) 4, pt. 3:90, n.a.
2. On the intermittent attention that even primitive societies pay to the spirit world, and on the theoretical character of traditional religious thinking, see Robin Horton, "African Traditional Thought and Western Science," *Africa* 37, no. 1 (January 1967): 59–60.

3. For an introduction to these documents, see David N. Keightley, *Sources of Shang History: The Oracle-Bone Inscriptions of Bronze-Age China* (Berkeley, 1978).

4. For a discussion of the historiographical issues, see ibid., chap. 5.

5. The description of Shang ancestor worship and government which follows is idealized. In particular, it ignores the presence of separate, and possibly competing, political-religious groups of dynastic claimants, diviners, and their followers and thus ignores the presence of ancestral theologies that may have varied in content if not in form. For an introduction to the problems involved, see Itō Miehiharu, "Indai ni okeru sosen saishi to teijin shūdan," *Kenkyū shigaku hen* 28 (March 1962): 23, 24, 28.

6. The phrase *yü-yi-jen*, "I the one man" (or, perhaps, "I the first man"), appears in the oracle-bone inscriptions (see Hu Hou-hsüan, "Shih 'yü yi-jen,'" *Li-shih yen-chiu*. no. 1 [1957], p. 75).

7. On the magical role of Shang divination, see David N. Keightley, "Legitimation in Shang China" (paper delivered at the Conference on Legitimation of Chinese Imperial Regimes, Asilomar, Calif., June 15–24, 1975), pp. 20–22, and "Shang Divination: The Magico-Religious Legacy" see below, pp. xxx

8. Tsung-tung Chang, *Der Kult der Shang-Dynastic im Spiegel der Orakelin-schriften: Eine paläographische Stralie zur Religion im archaischen China* (Wiesbaden, 1970), pp. 130, 146, 161. Chang's work is valuable as the first attempt in a Western language to present a detailed, comprehensive view of Shang religion based on contemporary Shang sources. I eite it frequently below on the assumption that it will be more accessible to many readers than scholarship written in Chinese and Japanese. For a critical review of Chang's translations, see Paul L-M. Serruys, "Studies in the Language of the Shang Oracle Inscriptions," *Toung Pao* 60, nos. 1–3 (1974): 12–120.

9. E.g., the inscriptions transcribed by Shima Kunio, *Inkyo bokuji sōrui*, 2d rev. ed. (Tokyo, 1971), pp. 467.4–468.1.

10. For a fuller treatment of the seminal role of religion in the Shang state, see Paul Whoatley, *The Pirot of the Four Quarters: A Preliminary Enquiry into the Origins and Character of the Ancient Chinese City* (Chicago, 1971), pp. 225–482.

11. Ibid., esp. pp. 305–16.

12. By bureaueratic I mean this actions or values characteristic of bureaucrats. And by bureaucrats I mean men or women, usually specialists, whose actions are validated by their titles and jurisdictions, systematically related to one another in relatively impersonal and routinized ways by a hierarchic system of defined regulations and duties, appointed and promoted on the basis of stipulated, written criteria, such as merit and seniority. This definition is derived from Reinhard Baulix, "Bureaucracy," *International Encyclopedia of the Social Sciences* (New York, 1968), 2:206 (hereafter *IESS*); and Peter M. Blau, "Theories of Organizations," *IESS*, 11:299.

13. On *do ut des*, see Émile Durkheim, *The Elementary Forms of the Religious Life*, trans. Joseph Ward Swain (New York, 1965), p. 33; see also E. R. Dodds, *The Greeks and the Irrational* (Berkeley, 1963), pp. 222, 241.

14. Chang, p. 70.

15. Ibid., p. 126.

16. Ibid., p. 130.

17. Ibid., p. 66; the attention paid to such distinctions is illustrated by the fact that no female animals were sacrificed to the ancestresses (p. 102).

18. The phrase is Mircea Eliade's; he uses it in his review of Samuel Noah Kramer, ed. *Mythologies of the Ancient World*, in *Journal of the American. Oriental Society* 82, no. 2 (April–June 1962): 218.

19. For some divisions of Function, see n. 37 below. That the jurisdictional power of the ancestors was a fundamental concern is confirmed by the Shang king's unconscious preoccupations. His dreams were caused by ancestors, and it was necessary to identify, by divination, the ancestor responsible, presumably so that a propitiatory sacrifice or purification ceremony could be offered (Chang, pp. 49–84, csp. 60; see the divinations listed by Shima, pp. 450.4–451.1).

20. Max Weber, *The Religion of China: Confucianism and Taoism*, trans. and ed. Hans. H. Gerth with an introduction by C. K. Yang (New York, 1964), pp. xxx, 235; see also 212, 227–28.

21. The argument as presented so far relies primarily on the language of Weberian analysis to link Shang religion to institutional developments. Further research will, I believe, show that the vocabularies of ancestor worship and administration overlapped significantly. For instance, the division of the ancestral tablets into right and left also appeared in official titles and in the organization of military units. Ti commanded (*ling*) wind and rain just as the Shang and Chou kings gave orders (*ming*) to their officers. Ancestors were sometimes classified in groups (the *to-hou*, "many consorts"; *to-pi*, "many grandmothers"; *to-fu*, "many fathers") just as officials were (the *to-kung*, "many artisans," *to-ma*, "many horse"). The prevalence of paternal and familial metaphors in later Confucian discourse, both moral and political, may also derive in part from the sacred value attached to such relationships in Shang theology. The secular calendar of Chou appears to have evolved from the sacrificial calendar of Shang, in which the names of sacrifices were also used to record secular dates or units of time (ef. Itō, pp. 6–8). Many other examples of continuity and concordance remain to be explored.

22. Sacrifices were offered to various nature powers such as the (Yellow) River, certain mountains, and earth spirits (Chang, pp. 167–210), but tho great bulk of Shang sacrificial wealth and divinatory attention was devoted to the ancestors.

23. Cheng Te-k'un, *Archaeology in China*, vol. 2, *Shang China* (Cambridge, 1960), pp. xxvi, 216–17; Chao Lin, *Marriage, Inheritance and Lineage Organization in Shang-Chou China* (Taipei, 1970), p. 22.

24. The terms *fu* and *mu* might designate either a king's biological father and mother or his father's brothers and sisters, i.e., his classificatory fathers and mothers (Chang, p. 34; Chao, p. 53; Cheng, p. 215).

25. Itō (pp. 10, 11) has stressed that the dead royal consorts, at least in Tung Tso-pin's periods II and V (on Tung's periods see Keightley, *Sources*, see. 4.2), possessed no independent divinity; only those consorts who had produced actual kings were worshiped. Conceivably, this was due to the influence of what, in imperial times, we would call the maternal clan of the Empress Dowager (ef. Itō, pp. 24–25), directing the sacrifices to the mother who had promoted the clan and thus validating its own political importance; see also n. 41 below.

26. Chao, pp. 22, 23, 25; this discussion of tablets refers to the system of sacrifices in use during the reign of Ti Yi, the penultimate ruler of the dynasty.

27. Cheng, p. 219; see also n. 41 below.

28. See the divinations listed by Shima, pp. 275.4–276.1; cf. Shima Kunio, *Inkyo bokuji kenkyū* (Hirosaki, 1958), p. 201.

29. E.g., the divinations cited by Chang, p. 100. For other cases of, as well as exceptions to, this rule, see Keightley, *Sources*, chap. 4, n. 22.

30. Chang, pp. 79, 139, 147, 258. King Wu Ting is an exception to this rule; he was apparently so powerful when alive that he was promoted immediately to a position

of power when dead (ibid., pp. 97, 147, 160). It may be that the power of a royal ancestor was related not simply to his generational status but also to the length of his reign (see ibid., pp. 24. 258) and to the value of his contribution to the lineage and dynasty; consider, for example, the great attention paid to Shang Chia, the predynastic progenitor of the lineage, and to T'ang (Ta Yi), the dynasty founder (see the inscriptions transcribed by Shima, *Sōrui*, pp. 511.1–514.3, 515.4–518.2).

31. Chang, pp. 79, 159–60, 258; cf. Chong, p. 219.

32. I find no evidence to support Chang's suggestion (pp. 133–35) that certain ancestors. in accepting the sacrificial meats, continued to display gourmet tastes they had shown while alive.

33. Cheng, p. 220; Shima, *Sōrui*, p. 531.3; Keightley, *Sources*, table 15, n. 1.

34. Cheng, p. 221; Tung Tso-pin, *Chia-ku-hsüeh liu-shih-nien* (Taipei, 1965), pp. 76–78; Keightley, *Sources*, table 15.

35. Chang, p. 132.

36. Ibid., p. 260.

37. Ibid., pp. 211, 214, 215, 218, 220. The oracle-bone inscriptions give evidence of some division of labor, of specialization of function, among the Shang ancestors and spiritual powers. Thus, Ti had dominion over rain, thunder, wind, drought, harvests, the fate of the capital, warfare, epidemics, and the king's person (pp. 211–20). Male ancestors had jurisdiction over harvests, rain, and livestock (p. 101). Ancestresses were responsible for royal childbirth and inflieting curses on the royal infants (p. 101); they were not prayed to for rain or harvest, which were apparently male concerns (Itō, p. 12). Nature powers also participated in the spiritual hierarchy with their own characteristic jurisdictions (Chang, pp. 167–210).

38. Cf. Kwang-ehih Chang, "Changing Relationships of Man and Animal in Shang and Chou Myths and Art," *Min-tsu-hsüeh yen-chiu-so chi-k'an* 16 (Autumn 1963): 142: Shang Ti "was not given a specific location, he was not to be sacrificed to, and his relations with the early, legendary ancestors of the Tzu clan were not very clearly defined.... I would ... suggest that, *the concept of Shang Ti was an abstraction*, whereas the ancestor doities represented substance" (italics added).

39. Chang, p. 239.

40. Ibid., p. 259; see also Keightley, "Legitimation," pp. 43–45, and my remarks in the *Journal of Asian Studies* 30, no. 3 (May 1971): 657–58.

41. Cf. Cheng, p. 223. Such considerations may explain the phenomenon noted earlier that only those royal ancestors whose sons became kings were accorded "great tablet" status. The genealogy of the Shang lineage, us it appears in the system of sacrifice, presumably served as "a calculus for the relationship of group members" of the living family. And the dropping of lesser ancestors from the sacrificial cycle may be regarded as a process of "telescoping" by which "those ancestors whose presence in the genealogy is inessential for the reckoning of contemporary relationships gradually disappear from memory" (Jack Goody, "Kinship: Descent Groups," *IESS*, 8:403). Itō (p. 22) provides an excellent example of such "telescoping" when he notes that in period I joint sacrifices to the ancestors were not addressed to the collateral kings who had inherited the throne as brothers rather than as sons; in period IIb, by contrast, joint sacrifices in the five-sacrifice system were offered to all kings, direct and collateral. He suggests the distinction was due in part to the fact that kings Wu Ting of period I and Tsu Keng of period IIa both succeeded their fathers to the throne, whereas Tsu Chia of IIb succeeded his elder brother. Collateral succession in this world may thus have encouraged sacrifices to collateral kings in the next, a practice

which presumably validated collateral succession on earth. Similar logic applied to the choice of royal consorts who were to receive sacrifice (ibid., p. 11; see also n. 25 above). It may well be, in fact, that the *tsung-fa* lineage system was consciously evolved in Late Shang times to legitimize the power of the direct, rather than collateral, descendants of the royal house (ef. Itō, pp. 18, 30, 31).

42. For an initial study, see David N. Keightley, "Public Work in Ancient China: A Study of Forced Labor in the Shang and Western Chou" (Ph.D. diss., Columbia University, 1969), pp. 349–51.

43. For an introduction to Shang proto-bureaucracy, see Ch'en Meng-chia, *Yin-hsü pu-tz'u tsung-shu* (Peking, 1956), pp. 503–22; Shima Kunio, *Kenkyū*, pp. 461–75; Herrlee G. Creel, *The Origins of Statecraft in China*, vol. I. *The Western Chou Empire* (Chicago, 1970). pp. 32–40; Chou Hung-hsiang, "Some Aspects of Shang Administration" (Ph.D. diss., Australian National University, Canberra, 1968); Keightley, "Public Work," pp. 10–20. and "The Temple Artisans of Ancient China: Part One: The *Kung* and *To-kung* of Shang" (paper delivered at the Modern Chinese History Project Colloquium, University of Washington, Seattle. December 17, 1970).

44. On Shang hieratic art. see William Watson. *Style in the Arts of China* (New York. 1974), pp. 25–52. On the relationship between art styles and social values, see J. L. Fisher, "Art Styles as Cultural Cognitive Maps," *American Anthropologist* 63, no. 1 (February 1961): 79–93. It may also be speculated, by analogy with Eskimo masks, that degree of formal abstraction, extreme in the Shang case, ref lects degree of sacredness (Joan M. Vastokas, "The Relation of Form to Iconography in Eskimo Masks," *The Bearer* [Autumn 1967], p. 30).

45. On this term see George Mills, "Art: An Introduction to Qualitative Anthropology," *Journal of Aesthetics and Art Criticism* 16. no. 1 (September 1957): 4–5; the article is reprinted in Charlotte M. Often, ed. *Anthropology and Art: Readings in Cross-cultural Aesthetics* (Garden City, N.Y., 1971) (see p. 72).

46. In other cultures, by contrast, naturalistic art may have developed to meet the needs of the ancestral cult (see Frank Willet, "Ifo in Nigerian Art," *African Arts/Arts d'Afrique* 1, no. 1 [Autumn 1967]: 34).

47. For an initial study, see David N. Keightley, "Shang Divination and Shang Metaphysics" (Included in this volume; see below).

48. Durkheim, pp. 21–22.

49. We cannot, say with certainty that the kinship classifications themselves were not equally derived from religious beliefs, rather than vice versa. Kinship is an objective fact, but its conceptualization may take various forms (see A. L. Kroeber, *The Nature of Culture* [Chicago, 1952], p. 219). Thus, Rodney Needham, taking issue with Durkheim, argues that there is no "evidence that hierarchical classification was based on ideas furnished by the family, clan, moiety…. In no single case is there any compulsion to believe that the society is the cause or even the model of the classification" (Émile Durkheim and Marcel Mauss, *Primitive Classification*, trans. Rodney Needham [Chicago, 1963], pp. xx, xxv; see also xli).

50. The phrase is cited by Clifford Geertz, "Religion: Anthropological Study," *1ESS*, 13:405. For a discussion which has aided my thinking about these issues, see Geertz, "Religion as a Cultural System," in *Anthropological Approaches to the Study of Religion*, ed. Michael Banton (London, 1966), pp. 1–46.

51. Secularization, as Wheatley (p. 315) has pointed out, does not necessarily imply a lessening of religious conviction. Kings and corporate warrior groups are distinguished from priesthoods by "their political goals rather than the methods employed

to attain them…. As such the importance of these groups lies not in a professed lesser intensity of religious conviction but in their willingness to extend the secular sphere of government operations, and to use their power in the prosecution of wholly secular aims." Modes of religious thought presumably expand into the secular sphere as part of the process of secularization.

52. Reinhard Bendix, "Max Weber," *IESS*, 16:496.

53. Joseph R. Levenson, "The Amateur Ideal in Ming and Early Ch'ing Society: Evidences from Painting," in *Chinese Thought and Institutions*, ed. John K, Fairbank (Chicago, 1957), p. 321.

54. E.g., C. K. Yang, *Religion in Chinese Society* (Berkeley, 1970), p. 150: "The organization of these super-natural authorities was patterned after the traditional temporal Chinese government" (cf. pp. 144, 181); Francis Hsü, *Americans and Chinese: Two Ways of Life* (New York, 1953), p. 220: "The Chinese world of the spirits is essentially like their world of men. In each the mass of common men are governed by a hierarchy of officials."

55. The probability exists that Shang ancestor worship, with its comparatively rational logic, may itself have served as a powerful secularizing agent, weakening other more disordered cults and superstitions. For the analogous role of Protestant Christianity, see Alasdair Macintyre, "Is Understanding Religion Compatible with Believing?" in *Faith and the Philosophers*, ed. John Hick (New York, 1964), pp. 131–32; the article is reprinted in *Rationality*, ed. Bryan R. Wilson (Oxford, 1974) (see p. 76).

5

LATE SHANG DIVINATION: THE MAGICO-RELIGIOUS LEGACY

David N. Keightley

Introduction

The figure of the high god Ti, ancestral rituals and sacrifices, the central value of filial piety, burial practices, the luni-solar calendar, the language and writing system—most aspects of Chou culture have their Late Shang antecedents. And by acknowledging in such catalogs the debts the Chou owed the Shang we may push the antiquity of Chinese culture back by at least two or three centuries.

But culture is not just content, it is also form. It is not just thoughts, it is ways of thinking. As Geertz has noted, "Culture patterns—religious, philosophical, aesthetic, scientific, ideological—are 'programs'; they provide a template or blueprint for the organization of social and psychological processes."[1] These culture patterns will be my concern in this essay. By studying the oracle-bone inscriptions of the Late Shang elite—the inscriptions, that is, from the reigns of the last eight or nine Shang kings (ca. 1200–1050 B.C. in my view)[2]—I hope to suggest ways in which the mental habits, psychological dispositions, and logical expectations which the Chou inherited from the Shang as part of an authoritative tradition influenced the nature of Chou thought and culture itself. By understanding the magico-religious origins (or, more exactly, the earliest documented instances) of some of the mental constraints within which the Chou operated, and which gave their thought much of its great power, we may gain fresh insights into the nature of Chou culture. The oracle-bones of Shang provide a fresh perspective from which to view the ancient Chinese, a fresh perspective from which to view the metaphysical-moral gulf, frequently unappreciated, that separates them from ourselves.[3]

It is not easy to make a distinction between the methods and goals of magic and religion, and there is no reason to think the Shang did so. For analytical purposes, however, I will assume that religion involves intercession, propitiation, and conciliation of supernatural beings, and that magic involves constraint, manipulation, and control of supernatural forces. Religious practices are far more expressive, making explanatory statements about the true nature of the world; magical practices are more instrumental.[4] But both kinds of activity are symbolic, a term which refers both to their nonrational (*not* irrational) character and to their supra-rational power. As Huizinga has put it: "From the causal point of view, symbolism appears as a sort of short-circuit of thought. Instead of looking for the relation between two things by following the hidden detours of their causal connections, thought makes a leap and discovers their relation, not in a connection of cause or effects, but in a connection of signification or finality."[5] And, as Gertz has pointed out, the peculiar power of symbols "comes from their presumed ability to identify fact with value at the most fundamental level, to give to what is otherwise merely actual, a comprehensive normative import."[6]

The oracle-bone inscriptions are not optimum documents for assessing the full range of Late Shang mentality, yet they have much to recommend them. Where divination flourishes, its logic and assumptions are not likely to be at variance with those of the rest of life.[7] Further, the Late Shang divined most aspects of life; the belief that the future could be divined was undoubtedly as real to the Shang as any other symbolic aspect of their culture. And it is clear, too, that the Shang elite devoted great amounts of time and energy to pyromancy.[8] For all these reasons, therefore—the "normal," comprehensive nature of their logic and assumptions, the scope of their concerns, and the attention paid to them—we are justified in studying the oracle-bone inscriptions for significant signals about the Late Shang worldview. In what follows, I shall first attempt to characterize significant aspects of Shang divination and its underlying conceptions; I will then consider their possible Chou legacies.

Late Shang Divination

The Rationality and Clarity of the Divination Charges

Shang divination was presumably a symbolic activity. It was entwined with magico-religious rituals that were both expressive and instrumental, and which shaped Shang views of reality and religious forces at the same time that they embodied the attempt to control them.[9] Rituals presumably rendered the divination efficacious (their magical, instrumental function); at the same time, they encouraged the view that all life could be and should be divinable (their religious, expressive function).[10]

There is nothing manifestly symbolic about the inscribed divination charges, however, which were recorded in straightforward, administrative prose—"it will rain"; "it will not rain"; "the king should ally with this tribe"; "the king should attack that one"; "the king's dream was caused by such-and-such an ancestor"; "there will be good harvest," etc. The function of the charges might vary (see pp. 105 below), but they were all recorded "in clear." An-yang was not Delphi, where the words of the Pythia had to be translated, frequently ambiguously, by priests.[11] Shang divination was "cool" and ordinary, uninspired and rational.

The fact that, in the reign of Wu Ting (Tung Tso-pin's period I),[12] the charges were frequently recorded as complementary charge pairs in the positive and negative mode ("Fu Hao's childbearing will be good/Fu Hao's childbearing will not perhaps be good")[13] reinforces our sense that the Shang diviners made contact with the supernatural not by relying on trance or the suspension of normal patterns of thought, but by proposing mundane, yes-no, positive-negative, alternatives. The supernatural powers were given little opportunity to inspire new solutions. Man proposed his simple, pedestrian (i.e., human) alternatives; the supernatural could only choose between them.[14] The "coolness" of the divination forms was congruent with the "coolness" of the language of the charges. It is true that the use of positive-negative modes may also have had symbolic significance, reflecting a metaphysical sense of *yin-yang* style complementarity, in which alternatives were inextricably entwined with one another,[15] but the fact remains that few if any charges were couched in this bifurcated mode after the reign of Wu Ting, and that all charges were precise and limited in the options they offered for consideration. The powers could only dispose in ways that man had already proposed.

The Order of the Divination Charges

There is an *ordnungswill* strikingly evident in the motifs and styles of Shang art, whose geometric patterns and highly formalized animal shapes are eloquent witness to the dominance of abstract order in the Shang worldview; such art was the pictorial and plastic expression of the structures of Shang thought and action, an expression of one of the *daimons* that gave the Shang their power and confidence.

The form of Shang divination, as well as its content, was also marked by a profound sense of order that must be taken as expressive of some fundamental view of reality and man's relation with the supernatural. Hollows were chiseled or bored into the backs of scapulas and plastrons with great care and effort so that the *pu*-cracks, which appeared on the front when the diviner burned the hollows, formed in their turn a series of preordained patterns. Unlike the free-form pyromancy of other cultures, where the bone might be thrown into the fire, or the heat applied to any point of the unprepared bone surface, there was nothing random about the pyromantic cracks of the Late Shang. Just as the clear, positive-negative charges imposed order on the powers, the hollows imposed order on the cracks. No crack could appear where the Shang diviner did not want it to. The powers could not reveal themselves in unexpected ways. The supernatural responses were rigorously channeled.

A similar sense of order may also be discerned in the content of divinations about ritual and sacrifice. Ancestors whose jurisdictions might overlap were ranked in a junior-senior hierarchy and sacrifices were offered to them according to an elaborate, fixed schedule. Divinations were concerned with offering the right number of the right kind of victims to the right ancestor on the right day. Even in the reign of Wu Ting, when the system of sacrifice was still developing, there was little opportunity for invention or spontaneity. By the reigns of Ti Yi and Ti Hsin (Tung Tso-pin's last period, period V), the Shang kings no longer sought approval for scheduled sacrifices. They simply informed the powers that the sacrifice was being offered and expressed the wish that there would be no fault or misfortune. Uncertainty had been replaced by pattern and order. System now gave as much reassurance as the auspicious approval of the powers had formerly done. And the powers themselves, presumably, were thought content with this solution. The existence and efficacy of order, particularly where time was concerned (see pp. 107–108 below), was a paramount article of Late Shang faith.

The Prophetic and Transcendental Worldview

All divination, to the extent that it predicts the future, or seeks to reveal the true, supernatural meaning of past events, is transcendental. It is the special quality of Shang prophecy—so different, say, from the ecstatic, personal, and frequently critical and unsettling prophecy of the Old Testament—that concerns me here. The Hebrew prophet announced a message or vision he had received from God; the Shang diviners announced their message to the spirits.[16] The difference is striking and critical.

During the reign of Wu Ting, Shang divination served several related functions. The charges and cracks were used to identify spiritual forces, to document the approval of the spirits, to pray for blessings and assistance.[17] The accompanying rituals energized the divinatory act. Faith in the efficacy of the procedure was also maintained by what I have called "display inscriptions" which recorded in large, bold calligraphy the accuracy of the king's forecasts. In a typical example, the king divined about whether there would be disaster or misfortune of some sort in the coming ten-day week; examining the cracks, he prognosticated that there would be a disaster; and, *mirabile dictu*, the verification records that disaster, such as an enemy incursion or a lunar eclipse, did occur as predicted.[18] Ostensibly at least, unknown events were assigned ominous significance *before* they had taken place.[19] Future events, explained before they occurred, demonstrated the efficacy of the king's mantic powers.

In addition to what we may call these "mantic, pre-facto portents," the Shang diviners under Wu Ting wore also concerned with more traditional, "inductive, post-factum portents"—as in divinations to discover which ancestor was responsible for a sickness or dream. In these cases, the past was explained so that some remedial, sacrificial action might be taken.

Divination as Magic

The bulk of Shang pyromancy, however, was not directed toward this kind of prophecy. "Divination" did not simply have the sense of forecasting or retrospective discovery that it has for us. After the reign of Wu Ting at least, Shang divinatory concerns were not generally focused on forecasts of unknown misfortunes that might befall the king (i.e., pre-facto portents), or on explications of specific misfortunes that had already befallen him (post-factum portents). Most of the divination charges stated to the spirits what it was that the king proposed to do—offer a sacrifice to an ancestor, attack an enemy statelet, hunt at a certain place on a certain day—and attempted to discover whether there would be "assistance," or "no misfortune," or "no regret," or "no disaster," if he indeed did so.

It is likely, however, that the Shang, in divining these statements, sought more than the pyromantic imprimatur of the powers. The evidence is not as strong as one would wish, but it seems reasonable to suppose that much Shang divination was incantatory in nature. When good and bad alternatives were proposed, the charge recording the bad or undesirable alternative usually contained the particle *ch'i* 其 which, it seems, weakened the force of the charge (and whose presence I indicate by a "perhaps"); such undesirable charges might also be weakened by being abbreviated.[20] Thus, a period I divination of the form "We will receive millet harvest" (right side) and "We will not perhaps receive millet harvest" (left side) should be regarded not simply as an attempt to *discover* whether or not there would be a good crop, but as an attempt to *ensure* that there would be.[21] The possibility that there would not be was weakened by the *ch'i* of the negative charge. The very fact that the charges were incised with great labor into the bone—that incising not being related, apparently, only to the desire to preserve the record for posterity (see p. 110 below)—may well have been due to the desire to "fix" the divinatory spell, "carve" it into the future, and render it efficacious.[22]

By period V, undesirable alternatives had virtually been excluded from the divination charges, which had become resolutely optimistic and desirable: "If the king hunts at Sang, going and coming there will be no disaster"; "In the (next) ten days there will be no disaster"; "This evening It will not rain"; "The king entertains and performs the *sui*-ritual; there will be no fault."[23] These charges may be regarded not just as religious applications for spiritual approval, but as magical charms to ensure that there would indeed be no disaster, no rain, no fault. The charges were not interrogative; they were assertive and impelling, informing the powers what the Shang were doing, what the Shang wanted, and attempting to ensure that the results would turn out as desired and forecast.[24] If, as has been said, "magic demands, religion implores,"[25] the late Shang charges may be seen as primarily magical and instrumental in intent, though, as we have seen, the rituals associated with them undoubtedly had their religious, expressive function. If one function of Shang divination was to encourage the occurrence of what had been forecast, then when what was forecast did happen, the event served in effect as a pre-facto portent, validating once again—though less explicitly than the display inscriptions of Wu Ting's reign had done—the king's role as seer and archimage. It should also be stressed that the king, as he appears in the inscription record, was generally an infallible prophet (and thus magus). Few if any verifications record that his forecasts or charms were proven wrong.[26]

The logic of the divination charges may also be characterized, like the view of reality which they divined, as magico-religious. That is to say, the correlation between two (or more) events linked together in a charge was spiritual, not human; the cause-and-effect depended on spiritual approval, not on empirically verifiable actions. It depended, in Huizinga's terms, on "a connection of significance or finality." Thus, to return to an example already cited, the charge, "If the king hunts at Sang, going and coming there will be no disaster," presents two ideas, juxtaposed by the act of divination itself. By calling the attention of the spirits to the hunt, and by performing the divinatory ritual, the king tried to ensure that there would be no disaster. But the result was contingent upon the approval of the spirits. In the most general terms, therefore, Shang divination, in which the charges proposed what were, in effect, pre-facto portents, was of the form "We do A and B will happen." The post-factum charges merely reversed the sequence: "B has happened and A did it." The "and" which correlated the events existed at the pleasure, and expressed the will, of the spirits. That pleasure, that will, could be divined by man and could be influenced or impelled by the divination charges and prayers, and by the attendant sacrifices. Man could propose his actions and the result that he wished; but it was the spirits who could make, or not make, the connection between the two.

By period V that connection was generally taken for granted; the perfunctory nature of the routine incantation suggests there was little doubt, or little concern, that the spirits would oblige. Though still primarily magical in its intent, divination was becoming more religious.[27] But for all its routineness, the cause-and-effect by which the world worked was conceived in symbolic terms.

The Categorical Unambiguousness of the Divination Charges

As I have already suggested, the divination charges were couched in terms that left little freedom for spiritual inspiration or invention. Under Wu Ting the complementary charge pairs generally offered only two options: "It will rain/it will not perhaps ruin," "We will receive assistance/we will not perhaps receive assistance," etc. By the late periods, a single option was the norm: "It will rain," "We will receive assistance." And to such restricted divinations, the cracks could give only three responses—auspicious, inauspicious, or neutral.[28] Some gradations were provided for—crack-notations might, for example, read "highly auspicious," "greatly auspicious," or "less auspicious"—but generally the world was conceived in sharply delineated alternatives, which either prevailed or did not. There was no room for subtle interpretations, paradoxical responses, or deceptive meanings concealed in obscure prognostications.[29] In this regard, Chaucer's lines,

> For goddes speken in amphibologies,
> And for o soth, they tellen twenty Lyes,

could hardly be applied to Shang divination. The ambiguities so characteristic of many other systems of divination, such as the Delphic one,[30] did not plague the mind of the Shang diviner, who saw—or at least recorded—a world in black-and-white, positive-negative, auspicious-inauspicious terms. Such a cast of mind is congruent with the strong sense of patterning and classification to which I have already referred.

The Flexibility of Timeliness

Such a system of divination—with charges and responses rigidly conceived and narrowly construed—would seem, to us at least, to have been a clumsy and unsatisfactory way for dealing with the supernatural. The interstices, the "greys" of human experience, unaccounted for by such a system, may well have been handled by other kinds of divination of which we have no Shang record; the *Yi-ching*, for example, with its enigmatic aphorisms, may well have arisen to fill this need (though even the *Yi-ching*, it should be remarked, presents a limited number of situations and responses).

The Shang diviners of Wu Ting's time, however, obtained some flexibility by the strong emphasis they placed upon timeliness. *Kuei*-day diviniations about the fortune of the coming ten-day week; divinations about performing sacrifice on the next *chia*, *yi*, or *ping* day and so on; divinations about rain from this day to that, or in this month; prognostications about childbearing or disaster that were verified on a later day—the endemic interest in time questions of this sort reveals what must have been a vivid and intense concern with time future, time forecast, time sanctioned by the approbation of the spirits. Time, as it appears in the inscriptions, was religious. The *kan-chih* calendar recorded in regular order the days on which rituals and sacrifices were offered to the ancestors (who were themselves named by the *kan* stems). The fundamental importance of religious, or cultic, time can be seen from the way in which late Shang inscriptions, on both bone and bronze, routinely date events in terms of the ritual cycle. But it is not so much the theology of time that concerns us here; it is the temporal dimension of Shang divination itself.

The fact that nearly every divination preface records the *kan-chih* date indicates that the time when the bone was cracked had significance. Presumably, the crack indicated the disposition of spiritual forces at that time; the prognostications, attached to the dated charge, applied only at that time. This interpretation is supported by the fact that the Shang would, on occasion, divine the same topic over a series of days; the repetition suggests that new results may have been expected as the day of divination changed.[31] Further, those cases in which the prognostication is more detailed than the original charge carved on the bone or shell—e.g., charge: "Fu Hao's childbearing will be good"; prognostication: "If it be a *ting*-day childbearing, it will be good. If it be a *keng*-day childbearing, it will be extremely auspicious"[32]—indicate that the Shang diviner assigned a specific day to each crack as he cracked it, even though such putative subcharges ("A *ting*-day childbearing will be good" ... crack! ... "A *keng*-day childbearing will be good"... crack! ..., etc.) were not recorded on the oracle-bone (see n. 28).

This concern with timeliness was characteristic of the divinations of Wu Ting, who reigned when the sacrificial schedule was still being formulated, when the date of each sacrifice might still be submitted for spiritual approval. By period V temporal flexibility had been lost. The ritual schedule was now rigidly formulated; the day on which a particular ancestor would receive sacrifice was already established; the divination was no longer concerned with determining the auspicious time, but only with announcing that the sacrifice would take place as scheduled.

This loss of temporal flexibility was also related to a reduction in the temporal scope of the charges. Under Wu Ting, the diviners might on occasion propose sacrifices twenty days in advance; but by the late period, the range of the divination never exceeds the ten-day week, and no sacrifices were divined in advance.[33] Timeliness was still essential, but it was no longer problematical. Time had been ordered, but a significant option for assessing degrees of, and changes in, spiritual approval had been lost—not lost, perhaps, to Shang culture (for other systems of divination may have emphasized the option of timeliness), but lost to the pyromantic record.

The Late Shang-Chou Transition: A Hypothesis

The scope of Shang divination had dwindled remarkably by period V. Divinations about the sacrificial schedule, the ten-day period and the night, and the hunt were still performed in great number, but dreams, sickness, enemy attacks, requests for harvest, the issuing of orders, etc., were divined far less frequently than they had been in period I, if at all.[34] This reduction, associated with the disappearance of positive and negative charge pairs, with the disappearance of inauspicious prognostications, and with the reduced temporal range of the forecasts, suggests that a major shift had taken place in magico-religious theology. We must assume, not that the Shang were no longer troubled by such questions as successful childbirth, victorious alliances, or the significance of dreams, but that other systems, like that represented by the *Yi-ching*, grew up to handle them. In period I, the king's toothache, for example, was regarded as the result of a spiritual curse; it was treated by determining, through divination, the ancestor responsible for the sick tooth, and by discovering which sacrifice, on which day, would lead to a cure.[35] The kings of period V presumably still suffered from toothache. The fact that they no longer divined about it suggests that a new explanation for curing toothache had been developed. Where a toothache (or drought, or accident, etc.) had formerly been considered a post-factum portent, symbolic of ancestral displeasure and requiring pyromantic spell and placatory ritual, it may now have been symbolic of something else.

I would suggest that, by the Late Shang, misfortunes were increasingly interpreted, not as the result of arbitrary or malicious actions taken by dead ancestors, but as the result of actions taken by their living descendants, explainable by a consistent set of religious values. A sickness would still have been a post-factum portent, but it might have been viewed as the result of human failing, a deficiency, at first, perhaps, in the attention given to the ancestors, and thus, by extrapolation, a deficiency in "virtue." What the content of that "virtue" may have been cannot be deduced with certainty from the oracle-bone inscriptions, though I would suppose, given the great attention the Shang paid to ancestral sacrifices, that virtue was related to ancestral sacrifices and, by extension, to filiality. Ethical action—the way one man treats another—would not yet have assumed major importance in the belief system, but the initiative in the relationship between man and the spirits, the responsibility for making the world work, would have been passing to man.

If these speculations are correct, the dwindling scope of the oracular record, together with the increasingly perfunctory nature of its routine incantations, may be seen as part of a shift from magic towards religion, from charm to prayer. In this view, the Late Shang came to rely increasingly on religion (human interces-sion) rather than magic (divinatory coercion) to deal with the shocks of life. To the extent that such religious action, which was undoubtedly highly ritualized, replaced pyromancy, the scope of Shang divination was reduced accordingly. But to the extent that such action was the functional analogue of divination, it con-tinued to have a mantic, magico-religious quality. Virtuous conduct, whatever its exact nature, would have been efficacious and desirable, not in its own right, but because of its symbolic, transcendental character. It was still a symbolic response not to misfortune or sickness per se, but to what was still seen primarily as a por-tent. Virtuous action had replaced actual pyromancy. But virtuous action itself was still an attempt to impel events by the old magical logic we have discerned in pyromantic divination.[36] And in both cases, divinatory or ethical, rituals were essential to proper action.

The Legacies, Metaphysical and Ethical

I have argued elsewhere the ways in which Shang ancestor worship may help explain the high value placed on bureaucratic modes of thought and action, the way in which the pervading sense of religious obligation was congruent with, and encouraged the development of, a work ethic based on obligations and duties rather than rights.[37] In what follows, I shall suggest some of the ways in which the magico-religious styles of Late Shang divination continued to affect the mental habits of later Chinese thinkers, especially in the area of metaphysics and ethics.

The fact that Shang divination appears to have involved no shamanistic flight to other realms, and that it employed normal language, normal conscious-ness, and normal systems of choice, may be related to the immanent metaphysics of later Chinese thought.[38] Just as heaven and man were later viewed as part of one existential continuum, so were man and the ancestors in Shang times; com-munication between them required no disruption of ordinary modes of existence. There is little evidence that the powers (and I am speaking here primarily of the ancestors, to whom the bulk of Shang religious attention was turned) were con-ceived as "wholly other."

The Shang did not reject transcendence—their world was quintessentially transcendent; it derived its significance from an endless succession of portentous events whose meaning could be discerned, and whose outcome could be influ-enced, by divination. Shang divination implied a unitary but transcendental metaphysics in which reality was pregnant with, inseparable from, immanent "sig-nification or finality." Reality had to be sought within phenomena, an approach strikingly different from that of the Western philosophers who have sought reality outside of phenomena.[39] But phenomena, if they were real, thus belonged to a larger system of sense and order. The later Confucian belief that a simple historical record (like *Ch'un-ch'iu*), or a man's ordinary actions, should be judged in transcen-dental, moral terms, the conviction that reality could be explained by *yin-yang* or *wu-hsing* theories, derives from this same Shang tradition which did not view the world in value-neutral terms, but as a series of phenomena whose true significance had to be divined. History and human conduct replaced divination as a means of foretelling the future;[40] past events and actions could be read as the Shang diviners had read the cracks. Didactic history was a record of pre-facto portents.

The whole tradition—which we may crudely characterize as the *chin-wen* view of reality—that has attempted to discern hidden meanings in mundane texts and events derives from, and takes strength from, the divinatory theology of the Shang elite. A view of reality, so long held and sanctioned by religious belief, would not easily have been discarded. Even in recent times, the desire to explain seemingly insignificant acts in terms of consistent, moral-political theories, to divine what a man's acts really mean, what his motives are, and, in so doing, to bring about changes in his behavior, is a characteristic feature of Chinese political culture. The explanatory power of the Marxist-Maoist portents ("Use the past to serve the present"), the political power of the *dazibao*, is not unrelated to the magico-religious power of the portents and the display inscriptions carved on the oracle-bones of Shang.

For it is likely that the Shang divination records served a rather different function from those kept, for example, in the ancient Near East. There, "the purpose was clearly to record experiences for future reference and for the benefit of coming generations."[41] Shang inscriptions, particularly the display inscriptions (see n. 18), may have served such a purpose for a while, but this was not, I suspect, the primary motive for incising them rather than merely writing them with a brush. The fact that many oracle-bones were stored underground with a variety of other Shang "junk" suggests they were not recorded for posterity.[42] And if the incised divination record itself was thought to have some magical power to help bring about what had been divined (see p. 15 above), then it may well be that this attitude affected later Chinese attitudes toward certain bodies of writing, which were not regarded simply as records or repositories of knowledge, but as accounts of what ought to happen, or what ought to have happened, i.e., accounts of not just facts, but "moral facts."

Similarly, the Shang concern with portents—with explaining reality in terms of the will of the powers—helps account for the fact that metaphysics did not develop as a major category of Chou thought. This was not because later thinkers were uninterested in metaphysical problems. But it is because, I would suggest, metaphysical questions were viewed as religious (and, by extension, moral) questions. The nature of reality was not an existential question but an essential question. Since reality was pregnant with meaning, the nature of reality was always conceived in terms of what it meant. Ethical speculation was a form of metaphysics. The study of reality without a study of its ethical significance would have had no meaning; it would have been like cracking an oracle-bone without caring about the result.

The categorical, yes-no, positive-negative, nature of the divination charges, another "cool" feature of Shang divination that allowed no surprise answers or inspired responses, also encouraged a view of reality in which there was only one right way; difficult or tragic alternatives were not the subject of philosophy. Fingarette has remarked on the absence of any well-developed, Western sense of choice in *Lun-yü*.[43] Some of the Confucian aphorisms, in fact, suggest the complementary forms of Shang divination pairs.[44] And one might remark too on the tendency to define ethical terms by their complementary opposites,[45] as though the complementary restraints of period I were still at work, so that one could only define bravery by contrast with fear, *jen* 仁 by contrast with *yu* 憂, etc.

I would suggest, too, that the Shang diviner's worldview, which dealt with the supernatural by compartmentalizing alternatives into discrete "bits"—day, ancestor, sacrifice, no assistance, etc.—encouraged a "coolness" of outlook which, like the "normalness" of the divinatory logic, may relate to the "failure" of abstract thinking to develop as markedly in classical China as it did, say, in classical Greece. The Shang diviner's concern was with specific forecasts, specific events, not with overriding insights or theories. Such modes of thinking were apparently so satisfying that the Chou philosophers, rational and secular though the content of thought may have been, did not discard the "oracular" forms of earlier thinking, with their emphasis on particular case histories viewed in symbolic terms. No sense of universal law could develop from such a religious view, only one of hierarchy and case-by-case bargaining.

The impelling, assertive mode of the Shang divination charges may also bear on this point.[46] Even when positive-negative alternatives were offered to the spirits, the Shang diviners did not ask a question of the powers. Their contact with the supernatural was indicative, not interrogative. They did not ask, "Today, will it rain?" They stated, "Today, it will perhaps rain/Today it will not rain." Divination was not just a matter of determining what the spirits wanted; it was a way of telling the spirits what man wanted, and of seeking reassurance from the fact the spirits had been informed. The moral certainty characteristic of Chou ethical thought, and related no doubt to the absence of any sense of original sin, is again a legacy of this confidence implicit in the Shang divination charges. Class interest may partly explain the high moral tone of some early Chou philosophy. But the impulse to tell others what to do, to let the *chün-tzu's* conscience guide everyone else's, surely stems in part from the belief that the enlightened man had the ability and charisma to issue oracular injunctions in this way.

Similarly, the faith in rectification of terms, the belief that good government involves the correct choice of words, and that reality will somehow come to accord with the words (*Lun-yü*, 13.7) may also be related to the magical, impelling character of the words of the divination charges. That the rectification was primarily ethical rather than metaphysical or logical,[47] is fully consonant with the transcendental Shang worldview. In this way, too, the philosophers of Chou were intellectual descendants of the diviners of Shang.[48]

The habit of not asking questions but of proposing answers, further evidence of a sense of self-confidence and optimism, served, as noted, to limit the kinds of answers that could be obtained. The answer, i.e., the charge that would be found auspicious, was known in advance. Symptomatic of the metaphysical incuriosity already referred to, this aspect of Shang mentality may explain the rather "close-lipped" nature of Confucianism, its disinterest in brainstorming, in imaginative speculation. One frequently has the sense in Chou philosophy that questions are only asked when the answer is known in advance. The *Kung-yang* or *Kuliang* commentaries represent, perhaps, an extreme version of what we may call "nonexploratory interrogation" whose origins may be found carved on the oracle-bones of Shang. I would not want to say that, as a result of this legacy, later Chinese culture has been characterized by an indifference to asking questions. But I would suggest that questioning did not have the same value or quality that it had, say, in ancient Greece. It did not raise the expectation of new revelations. New questions—new in the sense that they trespassed into unexplored ground—were not asked, because new answers were not foreseen. If we accept the remark that "trespassing is one of the most successful techniques in science,"[49] it may even be suggested that the "failure" of science to develop in China may have been related to the compartmentalized and limited nature of divination forms which gave no rhetorical or metaphysical support to the possibility of trespass. Shang divination charges, in the barriers they established, are metaphysical analogues of the ethical *li*.

Further, I would suggest that preference for chain-reasoning and analogical argument, again characteristic of much Chou thinking, may be related to the transcendental correlations of the oracle-bone charges. The content of Chou and Han thought was more ostensibly secular, but the way the world worked, the logical links between its elements, was still partly mystical and symbolic. There is, as Fingarette has noted, a significant, magical dimension to the thought of Confucius. "Is *jen* far away? As soon as I want it, it is here."[50] Similarly, the famous series of sorites in *Ta-hsüch* ending "When things are investigated, knowledge is extended; when knowledge is extended, the will becomes sincere ... when the family is regulated, the state will be in order; and when the state is in order, there will be peace throughout the world,"[51] belongs to the same logical tradition as the "We do A and B will happen" of the oracle-bone inscriptions. That B will happen is an article of magico-religious faith. The organic, synchronous worldview of the Chou and Han, with its emphasis on pattern and relation, on significant and moral juxtaposition, owed its inspiration to, and was congruent with, the divinatory logic of the Shang.[52] The Chou and Han knew the world worked this way because the Shang had known it before them.

Reasoning has been defined as "thinking enlightened by logic." In India and Greece, logic developed out of techniques for refuting arguments. To Plato, reason was the messenger of the gods.[53] To the ancient Chinese, quite clearly, it was something less exalted, less super-natural, less subject to inspiration; it was a problem-solving device, not an inspirational one. Reason was developed not in the refutation of arguments but in the stating of wishes.

The instrumental character of Shang divination may also have left its mark on the action-orientation of Confucian ethics. "Meng Yi Tzu asked what filial piety was. The master said, 'It is not being disobedient.'"[54] We see Confucius's mind acting like that of a Shang diviner, especially when we consider the Chinese text: *Meng Yi Tzu wen hsiao* 孟子問孝, "Meng Yi Tzu asked about 'Hsiao,'" i.e., he just proposed the word, the concept. Confucius, and one can almost sense the Shang mind at work, defined *hsiao* positively and negatively, "It is being obedient" and "It is not being disobedient," and then selected one of the two alternatives. Waley, in fact, translates the master's response, *wu wei* 無違, an imperative, "Never disobey!" And this I find extremely suggestive. For I have referred to the two alternative inscriptions of Shang complementary divinations as "charges."[55] The term seems accurate: since one or the other charge was to be the answer, it was, in many cases, an order or instruction as to what should be done.[56]

This feature of Shang divination may help account for the fact that, in Confucian rhetoric, answers to questions are not only circumscribed by the form of the question itself, but are frequently given as moral imperatives, or at least as answers which have the force of a forecast (as in *Tso chuan*) that should be implemented. Is involves ought. Here then may be a further legacy of Shang divinination forms which implied not only an answer, but action in accord with that answer. To divine, in fact, was to envisage and to commit oneself to eventual action, to involve oneself in the world. The characteristic action-orientation of Confucian ethics is congruent with the action-oriented form of the Shang diviner's charges and may have derived in port from mental patterns reinforced by the customs of divination. It may be objected that divination the world over is necessarily action-oriented. That is true. But there is an attitudinal difference between asking "Should the king hunt?" and stating "The king will hunt." The Shang king, by the very way he stated his charges, disposed himself to action in the way that a mere questioner would not have done.

The love of order and hierarchy, so characteristic of Shang art, Shang divination forms, and Shang ancestral theology, continued to flourish in later times. With the exception of the Taoists, the Chou thinkers were horrified by disorder.[57] The major goal of Chinese religion of imperial times was to realize the way of heaven by preserving a universal order.[58] The order, where social theory was concerned, could certainly be justified in secular terms. But the passionate attachment to orderly, hierarchical solutions may be partly explained in terms of a fundamental faith in order as a good, quite apart from its efficacy.[59] What the Shang loved, the Chou did not reject.

That Shang ancestor worship was essentially a family affair not only had metaphysical consequences, lessening any division between the human and the spiritual; it also meant that the hierarchies of the family tended to be imposed upon the larger world, whether of man or the spirits. And this "human" dimension to Shang religion had further consequences, I would suggest, for the character of later Chinese humanism. In the West, as Mote has noted, humanism developed in response to (or against) religious authoritarianism.[60] In China, on the other hand, it appears to have evolved smoothly from ancestor worship; magical care of the ancestors (ex-humans) leads to quasi-religious care of the parents (living humans), and may lead to ethical concern for other humans. And the humanistic values never lost the primacy attached to religious ones. But, on the other hand, evolving smoothly from, rather than against, religious belief, Chinese humanism was not anti-authoritarian, not anti-hierarchical. And this is one reason, perhaps, why Chinese social and political theory, even to this day, has encouraged the development of an "authoritarian humanism," benevolent, concerned with the social well-being of all, but dependent on, and administered by, a central, magico-religious father-figure, both priest and official—emperor, *hsien*-magistrate, sage, chairman—who confers assistance as the Shang ancestors did, whose role was religious as well as secular, and whose wisdom was mantic as well as conventional.

This linking of traditional political values and expectations to the "programs" of Shang divination is not fanciful. The "programs" and their legacies were not restricted to diviners and philosophers, but, as we have seen (cf. n. 6), may be taken to represent the mental attitudes of the elite as a whole, dominating their modes of thought and imagination. The oracular impulse lies deep in Chinese culture. One of the marks of the Confucian *chün-tzu*, the political-philosophical paragon from whom even a ruler could learn, was his ability to foresee and prognosticate. "The *chün-tzu* takes thought of misfortune and arms himself against it in advance," says *Yi-ching*.[61] "It is characteristic of the most entire sincerity to be able to foreknow," says *Chung-yung*.[62] And parts of *Tso-chuan* may be regarded as a Confucian divination text in which various prescient ministers, reading, if you will, the "cracks" in a man's character, are able to forecast, usually with astonishing success, the man's eventual and, in Confucian terms, thoroughly deserved fate.[63] Many of the stories in *Tso-chuan* are analogous to the display inscriptions of Shang, complete with charge, prognostication, and verification;[64] they record pre-facto portents which are always validated, and thus validate the status and ethics of the prognosticating *chün-tzu*. What makes a man's speech persuasive is his ability to speak with moral authority about the future. We find a similar emphasis in the myths of dynasty founders. It was one of the special powers of a new king to recognize a man's worth despite his insignificant birth or position, and before his worth was manifest to others.[65] In all these cases, the message was Confucian, but the medium, the forecasting trope with its magical over-tones, was a legacy of Shang. And it may even be suggested that aspects of Marxist-Maoist historiography (and of the orthodox tradition of the dynastic histories from which much modern historiography has not divorced itself) which found nothing new in the historical record, but only demonstrations of preconceived theory, belonged to the same tradition of metaphysical, ethical, and historical prescience.

Conclusions

There is plenty of evidence that Shang traditions and Shang culture were still vital a millennium after the fall of the dynasty. The states of Lu and Sung were regarded as repositories of Shang culture.[66] Confucius advocated riding in the state carriage of Yin.[67] Both Wang Mang and the Kuang-wu emperor enfoeffed a Yin heir.[68] Sacrifices to T'ang, the dynasty founder, only ceased with the start of the Later Han.[69] There are countless references to Shang customs in *Li-chi*. If the particulars flourished in this way, so did the ethos and worldview. Every idea, every pattern of thought, has its genealogy, and many of the mental habits central to Chou and Han culture can be traced back, as I have attempted to show, to the ideas and thought patterns of the Shang. There were evolutions and refinements, but the "set" of Chinese thinking had generally been established a millennium or so before the golden age of Chinese philosophy.

Chou secular culture may be conceived as a rationalized descendant of the magico-religious culture of Shang. The religious achievements of the one age shaped the secular concerns and solutions of the next. We see a shift from a magical, religious culture to a moral one, but the morality that evolved, and the ways of valuing human actions, were not without strong magico-religious overtones. If "religion is a man using a divining rod, and philosophy a man using a pick and shovel," the tools of the Chou philosophers, the vigor with which they were wielded, and the trenches they followed, owed much to the implements of their predecessors who had staked out the ground before them.

The fact that the magico-religious assumptions of Shang culture still played such a large role in the "inherited conglomerate" of Chou and Han suggests the degree to which these assumptions must have satisfied social and psychological needs. Whether or not the Shang diviners forecast or shaped the future with notable accuracy—and we might reflect on the record of modern economic forecasters before reaching too harsh a judgment—Shang divination clearly "worked" to satisfy the cultural demands of its, believers, worked so well that its underlying assumptions continued to play a role for a millennium and more. The continuities are remarkably strong.

The rationality and clarity, order and hierarchy of Shang divination; its prophetic treatment of a transcendental, portentous reality; its optimistic confidence that human action could impel religious favor; its belief that the human predicament could be diagnosed and managed on a case-by-case basis; its great attention to the timeliness of human action; its human confidence that man could propose solutions to the spirits, rather than vice versa—all these features thrive, in secular guises, in the thought and culture of the Chou. For the end could never be, as Norman Brown reminds us, "the elimination of magical thinking." The goal could only be "conscious magic, ... conscious mastery of those fires."[70] As we consider the philosophers of the Eastern Chou, or even of twentieth-century China, who dreamed and wrote of an ordered society, it is salutary to reflect that order itself, for all its pragmatic benefits, needs to be fueled by the fires of belief. The fires of Shang burned long; they may be smoldering still.

Notes

1. Clifford Geertz, "Ideology as a Cultural System," in *Ideology and Discontent*, ed. David E. Apter (New York, 1964), p. 62.
2. For the definition of this historical period and its absolute dates, see David N. Keightley, *Sources of Shang History: The Oracle-Bone Inscriptions of Bronze Age China* (Berkeley, 1978), pp. xiii, 171–76. Other chronologies have been proposed. Tung Tso-pin, for

example, would include twelve kings in this period for which we have inscriptions, and would date it to 1398–1112 B.C. (ibid., p. 226).

3. Frederick W. Mote, "The Cosmological Gulf Between China and the West," in *Transition and Permanence: Chinese History and Culture*, eds. David C. Buxbaum and Frederick W. Mote (Hong Kong, 1972), p. 6, has referred to "the Western failure to understand the basic nature of the Chinese world view." Different cosmologies, as he suggests, imply different views of reality, and they in turn are related to different ethical conceptions. It is the ethical-metaphysical conceptions that concern me in this essay.

4. Based on the discussions of: J. Goody, "Religion and Ritual: The Definitional Problem," *British Journal of Sociology* 12 (1961), 158–59; M. Fortes and G. Dieterlen, eds., *African Systems of Thought* (London, New York, Toronto, 1965), pp. 21, 24–25; John Middleton, ed., *Magic, Witchcraft and Curing* (Garden City, NY, 1967), p. ix.

5. J. Huizinga, *The Waning of the Middle Ages* (Garden City, NY 1954), p. 203.

6. Clifford Geertz, "Ethos, World-View and the Analysis of Sacred Symbols," in *Man Makes Sense: A Reader in Modern Cultural Anthropology*, eds. Eugene A. Hammel and William S. Simmons (Boston, 1970), p. 326.

7. "Dans les sociétés ou la divination ne revêt pas, comme dans la nôtre, le caractère d'un phénomène marginal, voire aberrant, où elle constitue une procédure normale, régulière, souvent même obligatoire, la logique des systèmes oraculaires n'est pas plus étrangère à l'esprit du public que n'est contestable la function du devin. La rationalité divinatoire ne forme pas, dans ces civilisations. un secteur à part, une mentalité isolée, s'opposant aux modes de raisonnement qui règlent la pratique du droit, de l'administration, de la politique, de la médecine ou de la vie quotidienne; elle s'insère de façon cohérente dans l'ensemble de la pensée sociale, elle obéit dans ses démarches intellectuelles à des normes analogue, tout de même que le statu du devin apparaît très rigoureusement articulé, dans la hiérarchie des fonctions, sur ceux des autres agents sociaux responsable de la vie du groupe. Sans cette double intégration de l'intelligence divinatoire dans la mentalité commune et des fonctions du devin dans l'organisation sociale, la divination serait incapable de remplir le rôle que lui ont reconnu les anthropologues de l'école fonctionaliste." J. P. Vernant, "Parole et signes muets," in *Divination et Rationalité*, ed. J. P. Vernant (Paris, 1974), p. 10.

8. I have estimated (*Sources of Shang History*, p. 89) that some fifty man-hours a day were devoted to scapulimancy and pyromancy during the reigns of the last eight or nine Shang kings.

9. There is not a great deal of contemporary evidence for Shang rituals directly concerned with the divinatory act. It is hardly likely, however, that the Shang contacted the supernatural without ritual. It is believed that the scapulas and turtle shells were ritually prepared before use, and that certain ritual rules governed the burning of the cracks (*Sources of Shang History*, pp. 12–17, 26, n. 120). That divination occurred in the ancestral temple (*Nan-pei*, "Ming" 729; *Chin-chang* 120; *Ch'ien-pien* 8.15.1 [all S270.2]; *Yi-ts'un* 131; *Hou-pien* 2.42.15; *T'ieh-yi* 1.10; *Ts'uo-pien* 12; *Chih-hsu* 64 [all S270.3]. Here and below, S refers to Shima Kunio 島邦男, *Inkyo bokuji sōrui* 殷墟卜辭類 [2d rev. ed., Tokyo, 1971]; the full bibliographic references for the abbreviations by which I cite oracle-bone inscriptions may be found in *Sources of Shang History* pp. 229–31), and that the verb for "divining" was written 𝍟 or 𝍞 , a simplified picture of a cauldron (modern *ting* 鼎), are further reasons for thinking that rituals were involved. Such a hypothesis is confirmed by the elaborate descriptions of plastromantic ritual in later texts such as *Chou-li* and *Li-chi*.

10. On the way in which ritual confers an aura of factuality on religious conceptions, see Clifford Geertz, "Religion as a Cultural System," in *Anthropological Approaches to the Study of Religion*, ed. Michael Banton (London, 1966), pp. 24–26.

11. Ambiguous prognostications, the diviner's defense against error, are common to many forms of divination around the world. "It was a notorious fact in antiquity that Apollo's oracular responses [at Delphi] were crooked and ambiguous" (H. W. Parke and D. E. W. Wormell, *The Delphic Oracle: Vol. 1: The History* [Oxford, 1956], p. 40). It was a recurrent theme in stories about prophecy in classical Greece "that the recipient should misunderstand the message and end in trouble, but that when the full facts are known the prophet's foreknowledge should be vindicated" (Antony Andrewes, *The Greeks* [London, 1967], pp. 242–43). There was no such tradition in China.

12. For an introduction to Tung Tso-pin's five periods, see *Sources of Shang History*, pp. 92–93, 203.

13. *Ping-pien* 247.1–2 (S140.1).

14. In this regard, the Shang diviners were by no means unique. Consider Alfred Guillaume, *Prophecy and Divination Among the Hebrews and Other Semites* (London, 1938), p. 47, on Sumero-Babylonian divination: "In all these oracles it is the schemes of men that are the concern of the gods, not the will of God that is the concern of man."

15. See the next essay in this volume.

16. For the Hebrew case, see Guillaume, *Prophecy and Divination*, pp. 107 ff.

17. See my paper, "Legitimation in Shang China," Conference on Legitimation of Chinese Imperial Regimes, 15–24 June 1975, Asilomar, California, mimeographed, pp. 9–24.

18. The essential characteristics of "display inscriptions" are: (i) bold, large calligraphy; (ii) the prognostication and verification are written as a single, continuous unit, and are usually placed immediately next to the charge; (iii) the verification, freqently detailed, confirms the accuracy of the prognostication. *Ping-Pien* 57.1; 247; *Ching-hua* 2, are typical examples; the last two are translated in *Sources of Shang History*, fig. 12, and p. 44.

19. This, at least, is the picture presented by the record. Whether the whole record was fabricated after the event, so that the forecast of misfortune was not recorded till after the misfortune occurred, need not concern us here. For an introduction to the issues involved, see *Sources of Shang History*, p. 46, n. 90.

20. On this function of the particle *ch'i*, see Paul L-M Serruys, "Studies in the language of the Shang Oracle Inscriptions," *T'oung Pao* 60.1–3 (1974) 25. I offer "perhaps" only as a functional indicator; Serruys himself (p. 58) rejects it as a translation. There is also some evidence that desired alternatives were placed on the right side of the turtle shell, undesired and abbreviated alternatives on the left (see *Sources of Shang History*, p. 51, n. 124, p. 52, n. 130).

21. Again, the Shang were not unique in this view of the diviner's function. "The whole of the Semitic world was permeated with the belief that the solemn pronouncements of accredited persons—whether priests, prophets, diviners, or magicians—possessed an authority not only over the mind, but also over the course of events, so that what such men said must surely come to pass because they spoke in the name, and with the authority, of a supernatural power. Theirs was ... the authority of the divine over the human; or, in reference to a more primitive stage, of what anthropologists call Mana" (Guillaume, *Prophecy and Divination*, p. 25).

22. The fact that, like the inscriptions, the *pu*-shaped stress cracks were, on occasion, themselves incised more deeply into the surface of the shell or bone (*Sources of Shang*

History, p. 53, n. 135), is suggestive. The motive may have been related to Arthur Waley's observation that "an omen is regarded as in itself a momentary, evanescent thing. Like silver-prints, it requires 'fixing'. Otherwise it will refer only to the moment at which it was secured" ("The Book of Changes," *Bulletin of the Museum of Far Eastern Antiquities* 5 [1933] 136).

23. *Ch'ien-pien* 2.31.4 (S293.4); S165.1–168.2; *Hsü-pien* 4.17.8 (S170.1); *Ching-chin* 5132 and others at S343.1. For an account of the way divination forms had evolved by period V, see *Sources of Shang History*, p. 122. It may be noted that some of the changes in Shang divination practice were linked to the difference between the Old School of diviners (periods I, IIa, IV) and the New (periods IIIb, V), though the exact division between them, especially in III and IV is not firmly established (*Sources of Shang History*, pp. 32, n. 18, 203).

24. For an initial study of the noninterrogative nature of the divination charges, see my paper, *"Shih Cheng* 貞卜 : A New Hypothesis About the Nature of Shang Divination," Asian Studies on the Pacific Coast Conference, Monterey, California, 17 June 1972, mimeographed; see too, *Sources of Shang History*, p. 29, n. 7.

25. The phrase, presumably deriving from Frazer, is quoted by Geoffrey Parrinder, *Religion in Africa* (Baltimore, 1969), p. 64.

26. This may help explain the terseness of the verifications in the later periods (*Sources of Shang History*, p. 118), for If the recorded result always validated the forecast the content of the verification could virtually be taken for granted.

27. The same trend may be discerned in ancient Near Eastern divination. "Everywhere there is a tendency for the priest to succeed the prophet, and for the formal rites of religion to replace and supersede *mana*" (Guillaume, *Prophecy and Divination*, pp. 37–38).

28. The evidence for the three responses was presented in Keightley, "How the Cracks Were Read: The Existence of the Subcharge," a paper prepared for the Annual Meeting of the American Oriental Society, Toronto, 12 April 1978.

29. Robin Horton, "A Definition of Religion, and Its Uses," *Journal of the Royal Anthropological Institute* 90.2 (July–December 1960), 208–9, has remarked on the way that "explicit definition of a limited number of permissible responses" reduces uncertainties and dangers of communication, especially when a large status difference distinguishes the participants. He finds such stereotyping typical of religious contexts and opposed to the flexibility of nonreligious ones. The forms of Shang divination, reflecting perhaps the keenly felt status differences between man and the spirits, appear to have carried such stereotyping to extreme limits.

30. See n. 11 above.

31. For a typical case, see *Sources of Shang History*, pp. 78–79, n. 86.

32. *Ping-pien* 247.1 (S140.1).

33. *Sources of Shang History*, p. 36.

34. For a general account of the reduced scope of Shang divination by period V, see *Sources of Shang History*, pp. 122, 177–182.

35. E.g., *Ping-pien* 12–21 as discussed in *Sources of Shang History*, pp. 76–90.

36. The pyromantic theology implied in *Shang-shu*, "Chin-t'eng," may represent this transitional stage—the reluctance to trouble the spirits, the initialive taken by the Duke of Chou, the *do ut des* bargaining with the spirits, the argument couched in terms of how human abilities might please the spirits; the emphasis is still magical, rather than religious, but human virtues are given prominence. For a study of nascent

Shang moral conceptions, see David S. Nivison, "Royal 'Virtue' in Shang Oracle Inscriptions," *Early China* 4 (1978–79) 52–55.

37. See the previous essay in this volume. See also Keightley, A Study of Forced Labor in the Shang and Western Chou," Ph.D. dissertation, Columbia University, 1969, pp. 340–46.

38. For possible links between shamanism, conceptions of the soul, metaphysics, and ethics, see E. R. Dodds, *The Greeks and the Irrational* (Berkeley, 1963), esp. pp. 139–40.

39. On this point, see T'ang Chün-yi 唐君毅, "Lun Chung-hsi che-hsüeh chung pen-t'i kuan-nien chih yi-chung pien-ch'ien pien-ch'ien 中西哲學中本體觀念之一種變遷," in T'angChün-yi, *Chung-hsi che-hsüeh ssu-hsiang pi-chiao yen-chiu* 中西哲學思想比較研究 (Shanghai, 1947), pp. 123–146. See too, n. 38 above.

40. Particularly apposite is the Mo-tzu comment quoted in *Shih-chi*: "I have heard it said that he who looks into the water will see the form of his face, but he who looks at men will know fortune and misfortune." As Burton Watson notes, the terms *chi* and *hsiung* are "part of the terminology of the ancient art of divination" (*Ssu-ma Ch'ien: Grand Historian of China* [New York, 1958], p. 136).

41. A. Leo Oppenheim, *Ancient Mesopotamia: Portrait of a Dead Civilization* (Chicago, 1964), p. 210.

42. The evidence, which I hope to present in a forthcoming study, suggests that in most cases used oracle-bones were stored above ground until they occupied too much room; they were then dumped into a storage pit, either by themselves, or along with raw bone materials and other debris of Shang life. Ssuma Ch'ien had heard that the Hsia and Yin threw away their divining stalks and shells after use because they felt that stored plastrons were not spiritually efficacious (*pu-ling* 不靈) (Takigawa Kametarō 瀧川龜太郎, *Shiki kaichū kōshō* 史記會注考證. [Tokyo, 1934], *ch.* 128, p. 3); I believe he was correctly informed.

43. Herbert Fingarette, *Confucius: The Secular As Sacred* (New York, 1972), pp. 18–36.

44. E.g., *Lun-yü*, 4.13; 10.1–2; *Chung-yung*, 20.2. (In these and the following citations to the Classics, I use the chapter and paragraph numbers of Legge's translations.)

45. E.g., *Lun-yü*, 9.28; 14.30. Cf. Fingarette, pp. 39, 43, 47.

46. The assertive self-confidence of early Chou religion is well demonstrated by the "Chou-sung" section of *Shih-ching*. There is no abasement before the powers. The major thrust is to proclaim the virtuous acts of the Chou, past and present, that have been, and should be, acceptable to the spirits.

47. Wing-tsit Chan, *A Source Book in Chinese Philosophy* (Princeton, 1963), pp. 40–41.

48. For the critical significance of this faith in *cheng-ming*, cf. Oppenheim, *Ancient Mesopotamia*, p. 231: "The fateful concept that reality should adjust to the requirements of a written corpus remains unknown to Mesopotamia—and probably to the entire ancient Near East. Only in a late and definitely peripheral development that sprang from the desire to create, for ideological reasons, a specific social context did Judaism succeed in creating such a pattern of behaviour."

49. W. Kohler, *The Place of Value in a World of Fact* (New York, 1938), p. 24.

50. *Lun-yü*, 7.29. Fingarette, pp. 3–4, argues that occasional comments in *Lun-yü* "seem to reveal a belief in magical powers of profound importance." The *chün-tzu* "simply wills the end in the proper ritual setting and with the proper ritual gesture and word; without further effort on his part, the deed is accomplished."

51. Chan, pp. 86–87.

52. Waley, p. 128, notes: "It is easy to see how the formula of folk-poetry (so often exemplified in the *Odes*) in which a series of statements concerning natural phenomena, trees, birds, etc., are correlated to a series of statements concerning a human situation grew up out of the omen formula." He is referring here to *Yi-ching* formulas, but the model for such correlations goes back to at least the divination charges of Shang.

53. These ideas about logic are taken from Donald M. Johnson, "Reasoning and Logic," in *International Encyclopedia of the Social Sciences*, ed. David L. Sills (New York, 1968), 13: 344.

54. *Lun-yü*, 2.5; Legge tr.

55. Modern scholars use the term "charge" (*ming-tz'u* 命辭) to refer to the topic of the divination inscription. That the term *ming* was used in Chou plastromancy suggests that it may have been a Shang term, or that it at least reflects the spirit of Shang divination. For further details, see *Sources of Shang History*, p. 33, nn. 20, 21.

56. On the obligatory mood of many Shang charges, see *Sources of Shang History*, p. 66, n. 44.

57. Love of order is particularly strong in thinkers such as Hsün-tzu, Han Fei-Tzu, and Shang Yang. It may also be found in *Lun-yü*. "Confucius' philosophy is that of a feudal kingdom, and of a cosmic order in which everything has its properly ordained place; insubordination is perhaps the chief crime, according lo the sage" (Herrlee Glessner Creel, "Was Confucius Agnostic?" *T'oung Pao* 29 [1932], 85).

58. See Jacques Gernet, *Daily Life in China on the Eve of the Mongol Invasion* (New York, 1962), p. 203; Mou Tsung-san 牟宗三, *Chung-kuo che-hsüch ti t'e-chih* 中國哲學的特質 (Hong Kong, 1963).

59. These considerations have some bearing on the picture of Hsün-tzu presented by Henry Rosemont, Jr., "State and Society in the *Hsün-Tzu*: A Philosophical Commentary," *Monumenta Serica* 29 (1970–71): 38–78. I suspect that Hsün-tzu was predisposed to seek solutions to social problems in the *li* and in hierarchy because such solutions were inherently attractive. His conclusions about the economy and society of Warring States China were culturally determined.

60. Frederick W. Mole, *Intellectual Foundations of China* (New York, 1971), p. 71.

61. Hexagram 63, the image; *The I Ching or Book of Changes*, The Richard Wilhelm Translation rendered into English by Gary F. Baynes (Princeton, 1969), p. 245.

62. *Chung-yung*, 24, Legge translation. On the foreknowledge of the *chün-tzu*, cf. Moss Roberts, "*Li, Yi*, and *Jen* in the *Lun Yü*: Three Philosophical Definitions," *Journal of the American Oriental Society* 88 (1968), 765–66.

63. For example, I count eight forecasts of this type for the year, Chao 1, seven for the year, Chao 3. See, too, n. 40 above.

64. A particularly apposite example is provided in *Shih-chi*, when Chi Tzu forecasts the degenerating behavior of his relative, the last Shang ruler (Takigawa, *ch*. 38, p. 6; Edouard Chavannes, trans., *Les Mémoires historiques de Sema Ts'ien* [Paris, 1967], 4: pp. 216–17).

65. For a detailed study of this theme, see Sarah Allan, *The Heir and the Sage: A Structural Analysis of Ancient Chinese Dynastic Legend* (San Francisco, 1980).

66. Tu Erh-wei 杜而未, "Lu-chün chien-chiao pien-cheng 魯君僭郊辨證," *Kuo-li T'ai-wan ta-hsüeh k'ao-ku jen-lei-hsüeh k'an* 國立臺灣大學考古人類學刊 25–26 (November 1965), 25–26; Barry Burden Blakeley, "Regional Aspects of Chinese Socio-Political Development in the Spring and Autumn Period (722–464 B.C.: Clan Power in a Segmentary State," Ph.D. dissertation, University of Michigan, 1970, pp. 330, 331.

67. *Lun-yü*, 15.10.

68. Hans Bielenstein, "The Restoration of the Han Dynasty: Vol. 3: The People," *Bulletin of the Museum of Far Eastern Antiquities* 39 (1967): 36, 37.

69. John K. Shryock, *The Origin and Development of the State Cult of Confucius* (New York, 1966), p. 100.

70. Norman O. Brown, *Love's Body* (New York, 1966), p. 254. Brown is writing of psychoanalysis, which "began as a further advance of civilized (scientific) objectivity; to expose remnants of primitive participation, to eliminate them.... But the outcome of psychoanalysis is the discovery that magic and madness are everywhere, and dreams is what we are made of." The same insight, I suspect, applies to the secularization of societies.

6

SHANG DIVINATION AND METAPHYSICS

David N. Keightley

The Shang have left us no explicit metaphysics. They transmitted no texts that systematically investigated the nature of first principles and the problems of ultimate reality. The Shang, however, did have an implicit ethos and world view, surmised perhaps rather than fully articulated, which derived from and reinforced certain principles and certain conceptions of reality that were accepted as inevitable and true. If we think of metaphysics as "the practice of rationality in its most theoretical form," then it is possible for the modern historian to infer from the archaeological, artistic, and written records of the Shang some of the theoretical strategies and presuppositions by which the Bronze Age elite of the closing centuries of the second millennium B.C. ordered their existence. In this article, I shall limit myself to deriving metaphysical concepts from only one of the institutions of Shang life—divination. And I shall limit myself, as far as possible, to the forms of Shang divination, leaving its language and the wider social, political, and religious implications of its contents, fruitful though these are for metaphysical insights, for treatment elsewhere.[1]

I choose divination, partly because it involved writing, and thus conscious and articulate intellectual activity; partly because it was one of the core institutions of the Shang elite, being one of the methods used to obtain consensus at the royal court;[2] and, above all, because it was the method for contacting the ultrahuman powers of the universe. If we can understand the mental assumptions underlying Shang divination, we can understand much about the Shang world view, and about the characteristic differences in mentality that separate the Shang from other cultures and from ourselves. The simple question "What did the Shang diviner think he was doing?" is well worth asking.

Shang Divination in the Reign of Wu Ting

Shang plastromancy and scapulimancy, as it was practiced during the reign of Wu Ting[d] (circa 1200–1181 B.C.), and probably in the succeeding reign of Tsu Keng[e], (circa 1180–1171 B.C.), proceeded as follows.[3] A topic was addressed to the turtle shell or bone in the form of a *charge,* which was frequently couched in either alternative (A or B) or in positive and negative (A not A) modes.

Thus, an initial inquiry about millet harvest might be divided into the two contrasting charges, "We will receive millet harvest" (*wo shou shu nien*[g]) and "We may not receive millet harvest" (*wo fu ch'i shou shu nien*[h]) (Figure 1). The charges were thus tentative predictions or statements of intent, proclaimed to the spirits for their approval or disapproval.[4] Single, unpaired charges, which, as we shall see, became more common with the passage of time, were predictions, even wishes—"In the next ten days there will be no disaster (*hsün wang huo*[m])" (Figure 2), for example—divined in order to test the reaction of the spirits.

As the charge was addressed to the shell or bone, a hot bronze poker or some other heat source was applied to a series of hollows or pits that had already been bored and chiseled into its back (Figures 1 and 3); the heat caused T-shaped stress cracks to form, with up to ten cracks being made in ten separate hollows for each question. Having been numbered (as in Figure 1, where they run from "1" to "5" on both sides of the plastron) and examined, the cracks, and thus the charges with

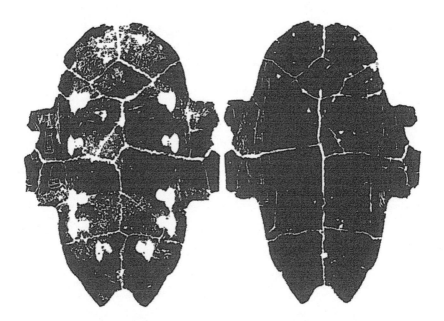

Figure 1 *Right.* Complementary positive and negative charges from the reign of Wu Ting. The inscription on the right side of the plastron reads: "Crack-making on ping-ch'en[i] (day 53), Ch'üeh[j] divined: 'We will receive millet harvest.'" The charge on the left side reads: "Crack-making on ping-ch'en, Ch'üeh divined: 'We may not receive millet harvest.'" *Left.* The inscription on the back of the plastron reads: "The king, reading the cracks, said: 'Auspicious. We will, in this case, receive harvest.'" Original plastron approximately 21 centimeters long. (*Ping-pien* 8–9)

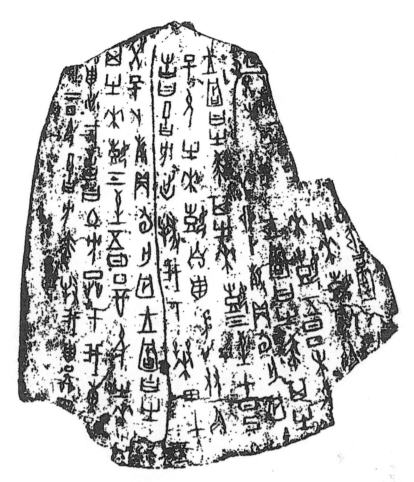

Figure 2 A display inscription, with detailed verification, from the reign of Wu Ting. The inscription on the left side of the scapula reads: "Crack-making on kuei-ssu (day 30), Ch'üeh divined: 'In the (next) ten days there will be no disaster.' The king, reading the cracks, said: 'There will be harm; there may be the coming of alarming news.' When it came to the fifth day, ting-yu (day 34), there really was the coming of alarming news from the west. Chih Kuo, reporting, said: 'The T'u-fang are besieging in our eastern borders and have harmed two settlements.' The Kung-fang also raided the fields of our western borders." Original scapula fragment approximately 22 centimeters long. (*Ching-hua* 2)

which they were associated, were interpreted, if possible, as lucky or unlucky to a greater or lesser degree. Thus, in Figure 1, *crack number* "4" on the left, negative, side has the auspicious *crack notation, erh kao*, literally, "two reports," inscribed in its lower angle.[5] *Prognostications,* when they were recorded, were frequently mere echoes of the divination charge, as in Figure 1: "The king, reading the cracks,

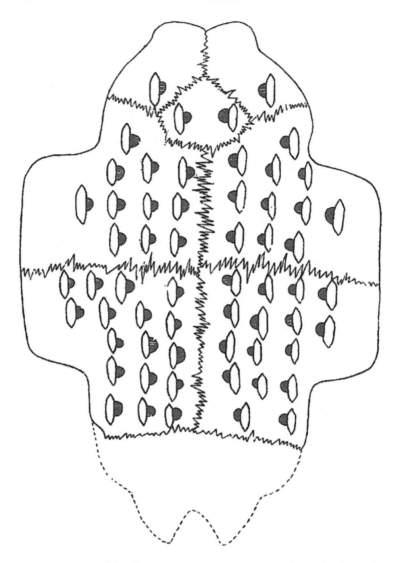

Figure 3 Drawing of the divination hollows carved into the back of a turtle plastron *(Chia-pien* 2124). Original plastron fragment approximately 23 centimeters long. (Tung Tso-pin, "Ta-kuei ssu pan k'ao-shih," *An-yang fa-chüeh pao-kao*[s] 3 (1931), facing p. 432, no. 1)

said: 'Auspicious. We will, in this case, receive harvest.'" And *verifications,* when they were recorded, confirmed the accuracy of the prognostication, so that a full divination would be of the form given in Figure 4, with (1) a charge in both the positive and negative modes, "It will rain" and "It may not rain"; (2) a prognostication, "It will rain, it will be a jen[v]-day"; and (3) a verification, "On the day jen-wu[w], it really did rain."

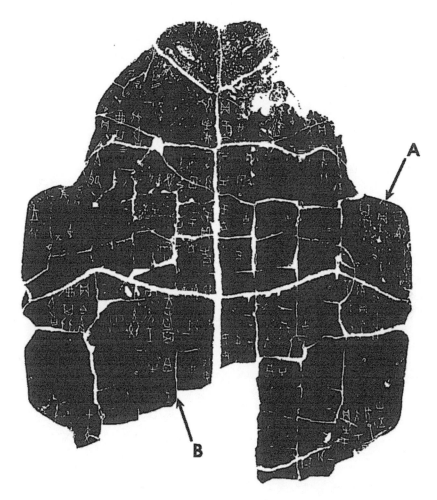

Figure 4 A display inscription from the reign of Wu Ting. The inscription (A) on the right side of the plastron reads: "Crack-making on chi-mao[u] (day 16), Ch'üeh divined: 'It may not rain.'" The inscription (B) on the left side reads: "Crack-making on chi-mao, Ch'üeh divined: 'It will rain.' The king, reading the cracks, said: 'It will rain; it will be a jen[v]-day.' On jen-wu[w] (day 19), it really did rain." Original plastron approximately 21 centimeters long. (*Ping-pien* 235)

The Magic of the Charges

The divination charges may be understood as spells applied to the future. In this view, cutting the potent words "We will receive millet harvest" into the bone or shell marked not only the divining medium, but the future itself, and induced, by analogical magic, the ripening of the millet. The magical nature of the charges is well demonstrated by divinations of the form *chin hsi wang huo*[x], "this night there will be no disaster,"[6] which were never paired and were always in the negative mode. Similarly, "whole day" divinations of the form *mei jih pu kou ta feng*[ab], "the whole day we will not encounter great wind," or "the whole day it will not rain," or "the whole day there will be no disaster," or "the whole day there will be no harm,"[7] which were common in the period from K'ang Ting to Wen Wu Ting[ac] (circa 1110–1096 B.C.), were always unpaired and always expressed the results desired. I regard all these routine divinations about no misfortune for the coming week, evening, or whole day as ritual incantations with a strong magical element, designed to ward off possible trouble. These charges were not primarily inquiries into the unknown. They were not genuine attempts to discover if there would be disasters; they were attempts to make sure that there would be no disasters.

The view that single charges, standing alone, served as spells fails to explain the existence of positive-negative charges that were paired. In such charges, as on the left side of the plastron reproduced in Figure 1, the negative, unwished-for outcome—in this case, "We may not receive millet harvest"—was also carved into the shell. If carved words had magical potency, the bad magic of the negative charge would seem, in these cases, to have cancelled the good magic of the positive charge. I believe that this did not happen because the undesirable charge, usually in the negative mode, was weakened in two ways: first, by the insertion of the modal particle *ch'i*[ad] (which I translate in this essay by using the subjunctive, so that *wo fu ch'i shou shu nien*[h] is rendered as "we *may* not receive millet harvest"); second, by a tendency to record the undesirable charge in a form more abbreviated than that of the desirable one.[8] The existence of these strategies suggests that the Shang diviners were indeed attempting to accentuate the positive.[9]

Legitimating Function

A significant number of inscriptions, mostly from the reign of Wu Ting, possess both prognostications and verifications. In virtually every case, the verification records how the prognostication was confirmed by later events. I refer to such records as *display inscriptions*, which, for the reign of Wu Ting, are characterized by: (1) bold, large calligraphy; (2) a prognostication that was written on the same bone or shell surface as a continuation of the charge and that usually was unfavorable or negated the charge; (3) a verification that was similarly written as a continuation of the prognostication and that, frequently in detail, confirmed the prognostication's accuracy. A typical example may be found in Figure 2, in which three similar divinations, which took place on days 30, 40, and 60 of the sixty-day cycle[10] and were carved on the same scapula, confirm the king's forecasts of misfortune with detailed verifications, such as "the T'u-fang went on campaign in our eastern border and destroyed two settlements." The inscribed verification validated, in bold calligraphy, the king's auguristic powers.[11] That the characters were frequently, as in this case, filled with vermilion pigment further indicates the importance the king attached to such inscriptions.[12]

I would stress in particular the spatial continuity of the record shown in Figure 2 and how it differs from the discontinuity of charge and prognostication shown in Figure 1; the latter divination does not qualify as a display inscription, not only because it lacks a verification, but because the prognostication was written separately, being on the back of the shell even though the charge was on the front. The fact that in all display divinations the prognostication was "run-in" to the charge and that the verification was also "run-in" to the prognostication suggests at least two conclusions: first, conceptually, that no sharp distinction was made between prognostication and verification, that what happened was indeed felt to be part of what was forecast, and, second, procedurally, that the entire inscription—charge, prognostication, and verification—had been written at one time, after the event.

These display inscriptions were not, in short, random divination records, a certain percentage of which would record wrong forecasts. They were, rather, a filtered record, a primitive form of legitimating historiography, selectively inscribed only after events had proven certain of the king's inauspicious forecasts correct. For we find no case, for example, in which the king forecast misfortunes and in which the verification then records that no misfortunes came. Wrong forecasts were passed over in decent silence; they were never explicitly identified as such.[13] All the display inscriptions, and probably all Shang inscriptions that contain both a prognostication and verification, represent a carefully edited ex post facto record that either served to confirm or did nothing to disconfirm what we may refer to as the "passive infallibility" of the royal diviner.

Complementary Charges and Their Metaphysical Implications

So far as metaphysics is concerned, one of the most significant features of many divinations of the Wu Ting period was the complementary, antipodal, balanced nature of the paired charges. I refer to charges as complementary when they complete the whole or mutually complete each other. Thus, the charges in Figure 1 form a complementary pair because the two inscriptions, "We will receive millet harvest" and "We may not receive millet harvest," complete the whole by embracing two contrary and incompatible possibilities. The positive and negative charges on the right and left sides of the shell are, furthermore, antipodal, not only because they are directly opposed in content, but because they are antipodal in placement, that is, at opposite sides of the shell. Further, they are balanced calligraphically, the characters being virtual mirror images of one another in their placement and, in the case of Ch'üeh, the diviner's name, even in the orientation of the graph. The concern with balance also extends to the pyromantic cracks associated with the charges, which were again formed as virtual mirror images. This symmetry of the cracks was fully intentional, for it depended on the symmetry with which the hollows had earlier been bored and chiseled into the back of the shell (Figures 1 and 3).

A large majority of all divination topics in the reign of Wu Ting was likely to be subjected to this symmetrical, positive-negative, complementary bifurcation. Divinations about disaster, distress, sickness, childbearing, rain and shine, floods, curses by ancestors or nature powers, harvest, divine protection and assistance, administrative orders, rituals and sacrifices, success in hunting, military strategy, capture of prisoners, urban construction, tours of inspection, sorties, trips, tribute payments, and so on were all, on occasion, paired in this way.[14] One naturally asks why. Why, when the Shang diviner proclaimed in his charge to the bone, and then inscribed, "We will receive millet harvest," did he also feel compelled to say and inscribe, "We may not receive millet harvest"?

The answer, I would suggest, is that the Shang diviners, and presumably the elites who employed them,[15] saw the world as a series of balanced dualisms, in which the auspicious and inauspicious, good and bad, harvest and dearth, victory and defeat, flood and drought, were seen as inextricably intertwined possibilities; the solutions that they proposed in their charge pairs were contrary, but, because they were both potentially true, they were not contradictory. The balanced cracks and charges dramatized, not the battle of good and evil, as they might have done in other cultures, but the essential symbiosis of good and bad fortune. They symbolized a metaphysical ambiguity that was presumably felt to be both desirable and true. Modern scholars have found in the *Yi-ching*[ai] (*The Book of Changes*) the suggestion of the theory that Gerald Swanson's discussion of the technical term *pien*[aj]-*hua*[ak], in the "Great Treatise" of the *Yi ching*, a term that he translates as "alternation and transformation," and in which he interprets *pien*, "alternation," as "ordered change of bipolar opposites," while *hua* is transformation . . . which is not reducible to bipolar opposition,"[17] suggests the degree to which Shang conceptions of change endured or were reborn in the *pien* of the Chou and Han diviners and philosophers.

> everything involves its own negation. . . . The universe is composed of pairs of opposites, such as good and evil, right and wrong, . . . positive and negative. . . . The phenomenon and its negation are necessary parts making up the whole. We cannot have, for instance, a positive without a negative, or vice versa. They are correlatives which involve each other. . . . [16]

To the Shang diviners, complementary opposition did not imply necessary contradiction. Alternative charges were presented because that was the way the world was viewed. There was a fundamental, organic tension between the possible choices facing man. Only by facing both possibilities, by giving each possibility, as it were, a fair chance, could Wu Ting's divinations themselves be fair, in accord with reality, and thus valid. The inscribed charges documented the fact that such fair chance had been given, that the divination had been metaphysically equitable, and hence realistic.[18]

This sense of realism may have had its practical uses. Despite the uniformly accurate predictions inscribed in the display inscriptions (see under "Legitimating Function"), the king's prognostications, especially in their prerecorded stage, cannot always have proved right. The balance and caution evident in the complementary charges appears to have served, therefore, the useful religious and political function of providing, in advance, a rationale for wrong forecasts. That the king might have forecast a millet harvest when the harvest subsequently failed was not a fatal challenge to his role as diviner and theocrat. Not only was the potentially embarrassing verification not recorded,[19] but the very possibility of an undesirable result (as opposed to an inaccurate forecast) had been acknowledged, and thus fore-knowledged. It had never been excluded; it had been incised on the shell in the form of the negative charge: "We may not receive millet harvest" (Figure l).[20] The display inscriptions may have been recorded to impress the king's supporters,[21] the complementary charges to impress the spirits.

It is instructive to compare the complementary charges of Shang divination with petal-plucking in our own culture, which also asks a question—"Does she love me?"—by breaking it up into repeated, complementary, positive and negative charges: "She loves me/She loves me not/She loves me/She loves me not," and so on. But notice the distinctions. First, we throw the petal away; the Shang did not. They treasured every alternative charge, every antipodal crack.[22] Second, we end with a right answer. Either she loves me or she does not; such finality is inherent in the form of the flower, which must eventually be reduced to its last petal. (Such finality is also inherent, one might add, in the mainstream of Western metaphysics.)[23]

To the Shang of Wu Ting's time there was less emphasis on polar opposites, one of which would triumph over the other. There was more concern, I would suggest, with momentary balance. Divination might reveal that the balance inclined to the positive or negative, but the balance was transitory and precarious, and the possibility, recorded antipodally on the other half of the shell, that the balance would swing back the other way was a reminder, carved into the record, of the changeable and inscrutable nature of reality and of man's rather humble role in attempting to understand or control it.

The contrast with the attitudes of the ancient Greeks is striking. The Delphic oracle was notorious for the ambiguity of its prognostications.[24] The response, "Croesus, having crossed the Halys, will destroy a great empire,"[25] was vindicated not by the destruction of the Persian empire, but of Croesus' own kingdom. To the Greeks, the future, reality itself, was held to contain a right answer, phrased though it might have been in temporarily deceptive terms. This was a divination, in short, that matched Plato's epistemological parable, in Book 7 of the *Republic,* of the shadows cast in the cave. There was a right answer, an ideal reality, but it was not easy to perceive.

The early Chinese had no such confidence in final solutions. Wu Ting's diviners would have expressed Croesus' question in terms that permitted no such ambiguity—"You will destroy the Persian empire/You may not (using the particle, *ch'i*[ad]) destroy the Persian empire"—but the prognostication, even if greatly auspicious, would have been colored, tinged, contaminated by the complementary possibility of great failure recorded by the negative charge. The king would have been warned by an ambiguity that depended not on the limitations of his own fallible reading of the oracle, but by an ambiguity inherent in even the most favorable cracks. The difference between the Delphic and Anyang mentality was undoubtedly one of degree. While the Greeks saw hubris, excessive human ambition, as leading to a man's downfall, the Shang of Wu Ting's time saw reversal, rather than downfall, as inherent in all the situations, both natural and human, for which they performed divination.

Such considerations may also apply to the muting of any tragic sense in early Chinese culture. Put crudely, we find in classical Greece a Platonic metaphysics of certainties, ideal forms, and right answers, accompanied by complex, tragic, and insoluble tensions in the realm of ethics. The metaphysical foundations being firm, the moral problems were intensely real, and as inexplicable as reality itself. To the early Chinese, however, if reality was forever changeable, man could not assume a position of tragic grandeur and maintain his footing for long. The moral heroism of the Confucians of Eastern Chou was not articulated in terms of any tragic flaw in the nature of the world or man. This lack of articulation, I believe, may be related to a significant indifference to the metaphysical foundation of Confucian ethics.

Oracle-bone divination, as practiced by Wu Ting, was no part of a theology of optimism. It offered no escape from the pains and uncertainties of life. But neither did it assume a theology of tragedy that affirms the painfulness of life. It subscribed instead to a theology and metaphysics that conceived of a world of alternating modes, pessimistic at times, optimistic at others, but with the germs of one mode always inherent in the other. Shang metaphysics, at least as revealed in the complementary forms of the Wu Ting inscriptions, was a metaphysics of yin and yang.

Binary Opposition and Complementarity

Binary modes of thinking and social organization are widespread in human culture. David H. P. Maybury-Lewis has proposed that

> societies which make systematic use of binary cosmologies, binary social classifications and binary social arrangements . . . are all concerned with the maintenance of cosmic and social equilibrium. They may feel that there is an immutable order in the grand scheme of things, but this is a cosmic equilibrium which offers small consolation to human beings, for humans are vulnerable to conflicting forces that could unbalance their individual and social lives in the short run. They therefore use their binary systems as a means of controlling the forces of chaos and conflict and maintaining a dynamic tension both in the cosmos and in their social lives.[26]

Such judgments could well be applied, I suspect, to the world of Wu Ting. Not only was the concern with good order, hierarchy, and harmony characteristic of Shang and later Chinese social and religious ideals,[27] but it also goes without saying that the principle of pairing, of bilaterality, of binary and symmetrical opposition, was characteristic of much Shang art,[28] of the placement of ancestral tablets from the Chou if not earlier,[29] and of Chou, if not Shang, military and bureaucratic organization.[30] Such pairing of opposites, accordingly, would not have been conceived merely to render pyromantic divination credible. It was evidently integral to the Shang world view, not for utilitarian reasons, but because, in Levi-Strauss's words, it was "good to think."[31]

Levi-Strauss, in fact, has stressed in his analysis of myth the ways in which many primitive peoples have used the conception of the union of opposites to further rather than hinder the integration of culture and society. He notes that "association by contrariety . . . is a universal feature of human thinking," and he has found in primitive religious rituals "the emergence of a logic operating by means of binary oppositions and coinciding with the first manifestations of symbolism."[32]

The most general model of this, and the most systematic application, is to be found perhaps in China, in the opposition of the two principles of Yang and Yin, as male and female, day and night, summer and winter, the union of which results in an organized totality (*tao*) such as the conjugal pair, the day, or the year.[33]

It is not my intention here to deal with binary oppositions in early Chinese cosmology and myth. I do not, however, detect any sense of the *union* of opposites in the processes of Shang divination. Complementarity, balance, alternation—these were the processes by which the Shang logic of binary opposition operated. Further, the kinds of opposition that Levi-Strauss cites—sky/earth, war/peace, upstream/downstream, red/white—are not as starkly antinomical as those of the Shang diviner—rain/not rain, curse/not curse, receive harvest/not receive harvest, go/not go, good/not good (birth)—which, by their original nature permit no possibility of union.

In the Wu Ting divination inscriptions we are dealing with nothing as unconscious as myth. The complementarity of the charge pairs was fully explicit and intentional. It meant something to the Shang, and it meant something *in its own terms.* The Shang had pondered such matters, and the responses they formulated—whatever the mythical or psychohistorical substratum—were theological and metaphysical in nature. They represent not myth but dialectics; they remind one less of Levi-Strauss's conclusions and more of Newton's third law of motion: "To every action there is always an equal and opposite, or contrary, reaction." The mechanistic, Newtonian analogy, inappropriate though it may seem when used to speak of an early Chinese world view that is usually regarded as "organismic,"[34] is apt in this regard: it reminds us that Shang divination was not concerned with the statics of social and metaphysical integration; it was concerned with the dynamics of decision-making and of how the world was constantly changing.

The Evolution of Shang Divinatory Practice and Belief

It is evident that, with the passage of time, the Shang diviners found some subjects, and thus, presumably, some aspects of reality, to be less complementary than others. Certain subjects tended not to be divined by means of complementary charges. They were offered either singly or as part of two or more inscriptions involving a choice, but not phrased in the complementary, positive-negative mode.

Among the significant topics which—particularly in the reigns of Lin Hsin and K'ang Ting, and after—were consistently not paired in this way was the ritual schedule.[35] Once a firm sacrificial schedule had been established by Tsu Chia[an] (circa,1170–1151 B.C.), divinations about the five major rituals were always unpaired and in the affirmative mood. They were affirmative, not in the sense that the charge did not contain a negative word, but in the sense that the charge affirmed that something desirable, like "there will be no disasters," would happen. Similarly, divinations about the offering of *lao*[ao] (penned cattle or sheep),[36] about the royal hunts and the weather to be encountered while hunting,[37] and about misfortunes for the ten-day week or for the night were rarely paired. A study of these and other noncomplementary inscriptions suggests the following rule: divination charges were not likely to be paired when (1) the king was required to do something, such as offer sacrifice or go hunting according to a predetermined schedule,[38] or (2) the king routinely wanted something not to happen, like misfortunes or bad weather.[39]

These unpaired charges, like the paired charges of Wu Ting, were, as we have already seen, not questions, but predictions, wishes, statements of intent in search of spiritual approval. They did not provide answers about what to do; that had already been decided. They provided reassurance about what was being done—the offering of a scheduled sacrifice, the conduct of a hunt, the wishing for no misfortune in the coming week, and so on.

I do not have the space to detail all the ways in which the divinations of the reigns of Ti Yi and Ti Hsin differed from those of Wu Ting, but the oracle-bone fragment reproduced in Figure 5 dramatizes some of the more fundamental changes.[40] This scapula strip from towards the end of the dynasty contains six complete inscriptions, made at ten-day intervals, of the general form: "On the kuei[bc] day (that is, the last day of the Shang ten-day week), the king made cracks and divined: 'In the next ten days there will be no disaster.' The king, reading the cracks, said: 'Auspicious.'"

One of the more obvious points to notice is the way in which the auspicious prognostications were now clustered together. All six divinations were, as we can tell from the remaining crack numbers, number "3" in the set.[41] It can hardly have been accidental that every time this routine divination was made, the third charge out of five happened to be the one that, for six weeks running, was always capable of prognostication and was always prognosticated favorably.[42]

It is equally striking that when the prognostication was *ta chi*[bd], "greatly auspicious," for one charge on a bone, it was usually also *ta chi* for all the other divinations on the same bone.[43] And by contrast, when one divination had no prognostication, it was generally the case that none of the other divinations on the same fragment had been provided with a prognostication either.[44] The divination procedures or records were evidently being manipulated. The prognostications for the ten-day divinations of the Ti Yi-Ti Hsin period were intentionally clustered; somebody had decided that all inscriptions on one bone should have "greatly

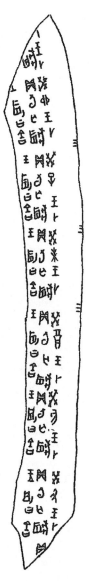

Figure 5 A series of divinations about the fortune of the coming week, from the reign of Ti Yi or Ti Hsin. The first inscription, at the bottom of the scapula fragment, reads: "On the day kuei-ch'ou[az] (day 50), the king, making cracks, divined: 'In the next ten days there will be no disaster.' The king, reading the cracks, said: 'Auspicious.'" The subsequent inscriptions, reading upwards, repeat these words exactly; only the date changes: "On the day kuei-hai[af] (day 60). . . ," "On the day kuei-yu[ba] (day 10). . . ," and so on, until the last full inscription, "On the day kuei-mao[bb] (day 40). . . ." Original fragment approximately 16.5 centimeters long. (*Hsü-ts'un* 2.972)

auspicious" prognostications, all inscriptions on another should have "auspicious" prognostications, and all inscriptions on yet another bone should have no prognostications whatever.[45]

Many other pieces of evidence indicate that the procedures of divination under the last two Shang kings, and thus the assumptions underlying them, had changed radically; the whole process had become more artificial, more routine, less spontaneous, less dramatic, less important. Calligraphy was small (Figure 5) rather than large (Figure 1);[46] prognostications were in every case auspicious, nonspecific, and frequently routine;[47] except in the case of the sacrifice schedule and hunt divinations, verifications were no longer recorded.[48]

Prognostications (unlike the one recorded in Figure 1) were invariably recorded on the same side of the bone or shell as the charge and, by contrast with the prognostications of Wu Ting's diviners, which could be remarkably detailed (as in Figure 2), they were invariably as brief and nonspecific as crack notations (as in Figure 5), whose function they may in part have assumed.[49] The period appears to have been characterized by a routine optimism that no longer required nongeneralized, documentary confirmation. It is particularly interesting that while the Ti Yi-Ti Hsin prognostications were uniformly auspicious, the number of auspicious crack notations declined to almost zero.[50] This is further evidence that Shang divination was losing its "working" nature by the closing reigns of the dynasty. If no bad forecasts were to be recorded, there would have been no need to record crack notations either. These trends all represent a routinization and simplification of the divination process, a paring away of time-consuming procedures, and, inevitably, a change in man's religious and metaphysical assumptions. One does not economize one's contacts with the supernatural unless the supernatural is assumed to approve the change.

With regard to metaphysics, the most notable feature of the Ti Yi-Ti Hsin inscriptions was the virtual abandonment of the use of complementary charges.[51] As we have seen (page 378), this trend had been developing since at least the reign of Tsu Chia. In the realm of divination, the use of complementary charges ceased not just because the world was no longer seen as paired; it also ceased because many of the more profound, more "metaphysical" areas of concern that had required complementary charges under Wu Ting were no longer subjects of divination.[52] In the reign of Wu Ting, for example, divinations about Ti[bg], the inscrutable and largely otiose supreme power of Shang, had been characterized by a high percentage of complementary charges. "Ti will/will not order rain," "Ti will/will not send down drought on us," "Ti will/will not harm the T'ang[bh] settlement," "Ti approves/does not approve the king," "Ti will/will not confer assistance on us," "It is/is not Ti who curses our crops," and so on.[53] The will of Ti was rarely divined after the reign of Wu Ting, and, when it was, it was not divined by means of complementary charge pairs. The entire scope of Shang divination, in fact, had become constricted remarkably by the closing reigns, so that many of the other problematical matters of Wu Ting's universe, such as rain, sickness, dreams, ancestral curses, requests for harvest, requests for progeny, and the luck of birth days were rarely, if ever, divined.

The bulk of the divinations under Ti Yi and Ti Hsin was concerned with three topics: the routine execution of the rigid sacrificial schedule, routine queries about the ten-day period (Figure 5), and routine queries about the king's hunts, which were also rigidly scheduled (see note 38). The charges no longer involved forecasts about what the ultrahuman powers might do to man, for example, by giving or not giving a millet harvest (Figure 1) or by permitting an enemy attack (Figure 2). The charges of Ti Yi and Ti Hsin were either routine charms, "In the next ten days there will be no disaster," or they were forecasts only in the sense that man forecast what he was going to do and then proclaimed in his almost automatically auspicious prognostications, legitimated by the hallowed cracking of shell and bone, that he expected good fortune in his enterprise.

Although, as I have argued, there was a magical, incantatory quality to these unpaired charges and prognostications, the magical element, as the miniscule calligraphy of Figure 5 indicates, was no longer as strong or assertive as it had once been. These later inscriptions record, I would suggest, the whisperings of charms and wishes, a constant bureaucratic murmur, forming a routine background of invocation to the daily life of the last two Shang kings, who were now talking, perhaps, more to themselves than to the ultrahuman powers.[54] In a sense, the oracle bone depicted in Figure 5 may still be regarded as a display inscription, but, unlike the display inscriptions of Wu Ting (Figure 2), its calligraphy was small rather than large, its prognostication was auspicious rather than inauspicious, and it lacked any recorded verification. Like the "fine print" in a modern contract, these late inscriptions documented the details of the Shang king's link with the supernatural. But they were now only details, whose ability to validate the theocrat's role was, like the size of the calligraphy, greatly reduced—reduced by the absence of crack notations, the absence of inauspicious prognostications, the absence of confirming verifications—the absence, in short, of all the elements that had made the earlier divination alive and dramatic. Wu Ting could forecast bad fortune and be vindicated by the record when it came (Figure 2). Ti Yi and Ti Hsin, by contrast, could record only forecasts of good fortune, and could do so only in vague and general formulas in which, with the exception of the hunt divinations, verifications were no longer worth recording. Optimistic ritual formula had replaced genuine metaphysical anxiety. Convention had tamed belief.[55]

These late divinations, in particular, may be likened to what modern philosophers have called "performatives," statements of intent or fact that satisfy the general rule that "saying so makes it so." When a Chinese householder inverts the auspicious character *fu*[bi] at his doorway, so that guests will be prompted to remark, "Ni ti fu tao (tao) le,"[bj] with the punning meaning of both "your 'good fortune' is upside down" and "your good fortune has come," he is relying on the efficacy of performatives. Herbert Fingarette's thesis, that "in the performative use of language the central burden of one's remark expressly *concerns the fact that one is making the remark* . . . it is the performance of the act *per se,* the making of the remark, which is *central to the message* of the remark,"[56] would certainly apply to the increasingly ritual nature of Shang divination, helping to explain the preference for the affirming, or desired mode, in the unpaired inscriptions. And his account of certain passages in the *Analects* "which seem to reveal a belief in magical powers" not only echoes my understanding of the magical qualities of the Shang charges (see earlier, "The Magic of the Charges") but suggests the degree to which Confucius may have been heir to the Shang tradition. By "magic," Fingarette writes,

> I mean the power of a specific person to accomplish his will directly and effortlessly through ritual, gesture and incantation. The user of magic . . . simply wills the end in the proper ritual setting and with the proper ritual gesture and word; without further effort on his part, the deed is accomplished.[57]

The Shang diviners may well have hoped that their cracks (the gesture) and charges (the word), performed with due ritual process, would have had similar, magical effect.

Metaphysics and Bureaucratic Procedure

It is important in closing this part of my discussion to address an objection that may already have occurred to the reader: On what grounds can we conclude that the use of positive-negative charge pairs was not purely a bureaucratic device, like "yes-no" or "true-false" boxes in a modern quiz, designed to render divination more efficient or foolproof, in which the negative charge on one side of the shell merely served to corroborate or contradict the results obtained from the positive charge on the other?[58] The binary opposition and complementarity of Shang divination in this view need have had no metaphysical dimension; the changes in divination procedure would have been simply bureaucratic; Wu Ting's diviners would have double-checked themselves in this way, the post-Tsu Chia diviners would not have done so.

Undoubtedly, such considerations did play a role, but for a number of reasons it would be reductionist to explain the forms of Shang divination purely in bureaucratic terms. First, even in the heyday of complementary divination under Wu Ting, one almost never finds a divination about disaster that included both the negative and positive, that is, the desired and unde-sired, version of the charge. The way in which this worked is worth dwelling on. In the case of "disaster" divinations, the positive charge *yu huo*[bk], "there will be disaster," was almost never balanced with the negative charge, *wang huo*[bi], "there will be no disaster."[59] It was this latter, unpaired formulation, that was almost universally used. Similarly, the routine, unpaired nature of the "this night there will be no disaster" charges (see "Magic of the Charges") also suggests that complementarity and noncomplementarity had more than a purely bureaucratic function.

In the case of the "harm" divinations, however, we find precisely the opposite situation: the charges, surprisingly, were couched only in the positive, undesirable mode, and with no weakening provided by the particle *ch'i*[ad]: *hsün yu ti*[bq], "In the next ten days there will be harm."[60] We almost never find a charge of the form **hsün wang ti*[br], "in the next ten days there will be no harm."[61] The reason is, I suspect, that the deleterious charge, "in the next ten days there will be harm," was designed precisely to serve as the first element in a display inscription (see "Legitimating Function") in which the king's pessimistic charge and prognostication about harm were confirmed by events: *wang chan yüeh yu ti*[bs], "the king, reading the cracks, said: 'There will be harm. . . ,'" with the nature of the harm being appended in validating detail (as in Figure 2).[62] The rigorous distribution of these unpaired divination formulas, in any event—some versions being expressed only in the desirable, others only in the undesirable mode—suggests once again that the charges were not formulated as pairs or nonpairs merely as the result of procedural routine.

Second, the fact that the particle *ch'i*[ad] almost invariably appeared only in the undesired charge and that the undesired charge tended to be abbreviated again indicates that the formulation of the charges had symbolic and not merely instrumental value. Third, it is striking that the general disappearance of complementarity was associated with a radical reduction in the scope of Shang divination; once again this correlation suggests more than a mechanical link between content and form. Fourth, it is significant that the early, interrogative charges of the Diviner Tui group (see note 4) did not reappear again in Late Shang charges, even after the complementary, positive-negative charges that had flourished under Wu Ting had lost their currency. Evidently, the Shang diviners found some value in the indicative, as opposed to the interrogative, mode. The Late Shang kings and their diviners were not asking questions, they were expressing wishes. All these considerations, in short, suggest that the form in which the charges were couched had meaning.

Finally, I would suggest that any attempt to separate Late Shang bureaucratic and metaphysical concerns is anachronistic. Even in our own culture, the use of multiple-choice tests implies much about the world view of the testers. Surely this was far truer of the Shang, where divination and knowledge were inseparable, and where the techniques for apprehending reality were inseparably linked to the forms of what was being apprehended (see note 15). Shang divination was not just a false science. It was, to take one scholar's definition of divination in another culture, "a procedure employed, within a framework of certain beliefs, to throw light on hidden or unknown facts."[63] The procedures created the forms of the world as much as the forms created the procedures; neither would have been thinkable without the other. They endowed the Late Shang world with meaning.

That the Shang diviners were able to change the ways in which they grappled with the present and future over the course of some one hundred and fifty-five years (circa 1200–1045 B.C.) suggests that they were not insensible to the fundamental assumptions of their culture and that they consciously practiced a certain intellectual introspection, the kind of self-conscious use of concepts, in fact, that may be associated with the development of literacy.[64] Whether they actually articulated the philosophical principles of understanding that we can discern in the evolving metaphysical paradigms described here, our present inscriptional data do not permit us to say.

A final analogy with our own culture may prove helpful. That Wu Ting's diviners frequently made anywhere from ten to twenty cracks, half for the positive charge, half for the negative, and that Ti Yi and Ti Hsin's diviners routinely made five cracks per unpaired charge,[65] calls to mind our own "statistical" approach to fortune-telling when we toss a coin, opting for two out of three, or best of five, and so on, rather than accepting the result of the first toss. It is true that few if any of us have any explicit metaphysical or theological explanation for our choice in such matters, but there are at least two reasons why the Shang case, I would suggest, must have been different. First, under the reign of Wu Ting, the Shang king divined about virtually everything he did; he was not merely engaging in an occasional coin toss, an activity that we usually reserve for trivial matters in which the choice "really won't make much difference." To the Shang of Wu Ting's time, the choice made all the difference in the world. Second, the Shang diviners consistently and rigorously followed the same divinatory procedures day after day, year after year. At the very least, we have to acknowledge the existence of a custom that, to endure in this way, must have had a strong rationale behind it. The oracle-bone inscriptions provide but a pale reflection of whatever metaphysical assumptions may have undergirded Shang culture. Nevertheless, the reflection is there. We may legitimately treat the inscriptions as clues to the half-thoughts and only partly articulated certainties that undoubtedly played a role in Shang thinking about the nature of the world.

Concluding Speculations

One can only guess at the reasons for the evolution in both divinatory practice and metaphysical assumptions proposed in the pages above. Perhaps, on the basis of the oracle-bone data—a point of historiographical caution that must always be borne in mind—the last two Shang kings were less dependent on, more skeptical about, religious explanations. This secularization and routine ritualization of the world may have been related to the confidence engendered by at least a century of successful dynastic rule. Man, rather than Ti and the ancestors, may have been thought to be increasingly capable of handling his own fate.[66]

One can see that accompanying this secularizing trend, there would probably have been a tendency for a divination record that had already been stringently edited, and thus artificial, under Wu Ting, to have become more pro forma, and metaphysically emptier and less urgent, with the passage of time. The possibility that an Yi ching-style of divination, based upon the manipulation of numbers and the generation of hexagrams, was beginning to replace pyromancy may also help explain the change in the content and form of the oracle-bone inscriptions.[67]

If we consider the evolving forms of divination, the following psychohistorical or psychotechnical hypothesis seems plausible.[68] Neolithic man would have felt himself to be at the mercy of numerous unknowable forces, many of them destructive, harmful, and difficult to understand. Neolithic divination, therefore, would have been single-mindedly concerned with warding off the undesirable, with magical attempts to forestall disaster. The primitive forms of Late Neolithic pyromancy in China—which presumably originated with the burning of sacrificial meat to the spirits[69]—offer some support for this view. It is clear that in pre-Shang pyromancy, heat was applied to the bone surface in a haphazard manner. Some bones were burned with no advance preparation whatever, the heat being applied directly to the unworked natural surface; others did have pits, which varied greatly in size and shape, bored into their surface (sometimes into both front and rear surfaces), but the arrangement of the pits was crowded and higgledy-piggledy.[70]

We may draw two kinds of "metaphysical" conclusion from this evidence. First, given the primitive techniques with which the bones were prepared for cracking, when they were prepared at all, it would seem likely that the Neolithic diviners were not always able to produce a crack by the application of heat, and that they were certainly not able to control its shape or direction. Hence the diviners, influenced by the technical inadequacy of their divination procedures, may have believed that the spiritual forces of the world were not always communicative, were not always willing to respond to man's search for reassurance, were not predictable or open to regular control.

Second, given the absence of any regular arrangement of pits and cracks—the absence, that is, of a sense of symmetry or pairing—we may tentatively suppose that, when responses were indicated by cracks, they were definite and unequivocal. No yin-yang sense of complementarity, of balance, of paired alternation, such as I have discerned in the inscriptions and hollows of Wu Ting's diviners, was present in the forms of Late Neolithic divination. Such a sense may, therefore, also have been absent in the Late Neolithic world view.[71]

The introduction of turtle plastrons into Shang divination, which may per-haps be associated with the Upper Erh-li-kang phase at Cheng-chou (carbon-14 dated to circa 1600 B.C), introduced a new divinatory medium, symmetrical about its bifurcating central axis, with conveniently marked matching zones to right and left.[72] This new medium may eventually have encouraged the develop-ment of symmetrical divination forms.[73] It was only with the development of the double hollows, however, which were formed by combining the bored round pit with a chiseled oval pit (as in Figures 1 and 3), that diviners would have found that they were consistently able to produce T-shaped cracks and to determine the direction in which they would run. This was probably a development that took place around the time of the Jen-min park phase at Cheng-chou, a phase that is thought to be slightly prior or chronologically equivalent to the Late Shang occu-pation at An-yang. That the double hollows, with their circular and oval pits (as in Figure 3), could be used to determine the direction of the crack does not appear to have been appreciated at first, for on the Jen-min park shells and bones the bored circular pit was placed to either the right or the left of the chiseled oval so that there was no consistent direction to the cracks formed on any one oracle bone. At An-yang, by contrast, as we have seen, the double hollows of Wu Ting's reign were prepared in such a way that the cracks formed on one side of the shell would all run according to a predetermined, symmetrical pattern (Figure 1).[74]

By the reign of Wu Ting, at the start of the twelfth century B.C., agricul-ture, metalworking, writing, and stable government had all progressed to the point that the world could be viewed, in the complementary divinations, in terms of a yin-yang-style balance between positive and negative forces, in which the good had almost as much chance as the bad to predominate. Pyromantic divination was being used—as it may long have been—not simply to forecast the future, but also to justify the diviner. Divination had become more sophisticated, more service-able politically, just as Shang society as a whole had been growing more sophisti-cated and more political, with its entry into an age of writing, bronze-making, and dynastic kings. The Shang diviners now explicated the puzzles and paradoxes of existence by the use of contrastive, alternative, and hence alternating, relationships. They sought for certainty, but for a certainty that, by the way in which the diviner defined it, was acknowledged to be uncertain and changeable. That uncertainty, however, was neither total nor disordered. The diviner patterned the changeability by confining it within the contrasting limits defined by the complementary words of the divination charges. The desired was presented against the undesired, and the undesired, were it to occur, was not unexpected. Such a view of the world may be described as cautious, pragmatic, undemanding, even perhaps a trifle cynical, in the sense that later Taoist *wu-wei*[bx] doctrine was sardonic, amused, and relaxed. But such a view, firmly held, permitted the Shang of the early twelfth century B.C., when faced with problems of meaning, suffering, and choice, to endure.

A century later, in the reigns of Ti Yi and Ti Hsin, with the continued advance of culture, and, perhaps, the increasing strength of the dynastic institution, the world—to the extent that it was still conceived in a divinatory context at all—could be seen primarily in terms of positive, desirable alternatives, with negative and undesirable ones suppressed and unrecorded. There was a shift, to employ the terms of Swanson's analysis (mentioned earlier), from an emphasis on *pien*[aj], "alternation," to one on *hua*[ak], "transformation ... not reducible to bipolar opposition."

I would suggest that the *pien*-like proto-yin-yang metaphysics, discernible in the complementary divinations of Wu Ting, may already have been a tradi-tional, conservative expression of earlier conceptions of thought that had been developing as the Shang emerged from the Neolithic stage.[75] Such a thorough-going "Taoist" complementarity, was, as I have indicated, not only a doctrine for executives or powerful dynasts; it was also a doctrine for metaphysicians. The optimistic-pessimistic patterns of thought associated with the paired charges, therefore, may have been in retreat in the reign of Wu Ting, beginning to be replaced by the *hua*-like unpaired, unbalanced charges that were also present in his reign, and that, in their positive or affirmative forms, were to become predomi-nant by the closing reigns of the dynasty.

The reign of Wu Ting, in this view, would have represented a unique, transitional stage—that in which sophisticated yet ancient, religious, and meta-physical conceptions were apparently integrated for a time into the business of government. It was undoubtedly an age of perplexity as the Shang kings strove to establish methods of spiritual communication, firm ritual schedules, and bureau-cratic procedures of control that would take account both of their older religious conceptions of the world and their new political position in it.[76] The balance of caution against confidence, of negative doubt against the need for positive action, of religious reflection against secular activity, of Neolithic pessimism against Bronze Age optimism, appears, with the passage of time, to have shifted in favor of optimism, confidence, and human control.[77]

This shift may be further discerned in the increasing use of *Yi-ching*-style forms of divination which eventually, if not originally, allowed more scope for human reflection and interpretation. And it may also be discerned in the eventual moralization of political theory involved in the Chou doctrine of the Mandate of Heaven. It is for this reason, perhaps, that Confucian morality seems, to the Western reader, narrow, one-dimensional, and assertive— closer, perhaps, to the incantatory, nonmetaphysical mentality of Ti Yi and Ti Hsin's diviners than to the complementary "Taoist" mentality of Wu Ting's. The very humanism of the Confucian thinkers helped to remove man from his metaphysical environment. That removal may be traced in part to the "humanism" of the Ti Yi-Ti Hsin period, in which man asserted his ability to control the world by narrowing his concerns and ignoring the non-human and inexplicable. The dreamy and quizzical "man-as-butterfly or butterfly-as-man" metaphysics at the end of *Chuang Tzu's* chapter 2, by contrast, seems far closer to the assumptions of Wu Ting's diviners.

The glimpse that the oracle-bone inscriptions afford us of metaphysical conceptions in the eleventh and tenth centuries B.C. suggests that the philosophical tensions that we associate primarily with the Taoism and Confucianism of Eastern Chou had already appeared, in different form, in the intellectual history of China, half a millennium earlier. When the philosophers of Eastern Chou turned to metaphysical and cosmological concerns, the resources of the world views of the Shang—complementary and changeable under Wu Ting, more assertive and confident under Ti Yi and Ti Hsin—could once again be employed or rediscovered in texts such as the *Yi ching,* the *Lao Tzu,* and the *Chuang Tzu,* and in Confucian texts like the *Lun-yü* (see note 18).

Whatever the validity of the hypotheses offered here, there is, I believe, much knowledge and insight to be gained from a study of the forms of Late Shang divination. Shang China lies well within the realm of Chinese intellectual history. The origins of much that is thought to be characteristically Chinese may be identified in the ethos and world view of its Bronze Age diviners.

Notes

1. For metaphysics as "rationality in its most theoretical form" see Jack Goody, *The Domestication of the Savage Mind* (Cambridge: Cambridge University Press, 1977), p. 48. The present article is a considerably revised version of a much longer paper, "Shang Divination and Shang Metaphysics (With An Excursion into the Neolithic)" (March 1973); a short version of that paper, entitled "Shang Metaphysics," was delivered at the annual meeting of the Association for Asian Studies in Chicago on 30 March 1973. I am grateful to Roger T. Ames and Henry Rosemont, Jr. for their critical comments offered on that earlier draft and to David S. Nivison for his comments on a later one; I have done my best to take advantage of their good advice. For

my initial studies of the religious and philosophical implications of Shang divination, see Keightley, "The Religious Commitment: Shang Theology and the Genesis
of Chinese Political Culture," *History of Religions* 17 (1978): 211–224; "Late Shang
Divination: The Magico-Religious Legacy," in Henry Rosemont, Jr., ed., *Explorations
in Early Chinese Cosmology,* Journal of the American Academy of Religion Studies
50, no. 2 (1984): 11–34; pp. 20–26 deal, in part, with the metaphysical legacies.
Without necessarily invoking the Sapir-Whorf hypothesis of linguistic relativity, one
can still imagine that the grammar of the Shang inscriptions has much to tell us about
Shang conceptions of reality, particularly about the forces of nature. For introductions
to Shang grammar, see, among their other writings, Paul L-M. Serruys, "Towards a
Grammar of the Language of the Shang Bone Inscriptions," in *Chung-yang yen-chiu-
yüan kuo-chi Han-hsüeh hui-yi lun-wen-chi* [a] (Taipei: Academia Sinica, 1981), pp.
313–364; K. Takashima, "Two Copulas or One Copula in Proto-Sino-Tibetan?: *Wei* [b]
and *Hui* [c] in Oracle-Bone Inscriptions," to appear in *Monumenta Serica* 38.

2. On the consensus-building role of Shang divinations, see Keightley, "Legitimation in
Shang China" (Paper prepared for the Conference on Legitimation of Chinese Imperial Regimes, Asilomar, 15–24 June, 1975), pp. 11–12.

3. For a fuller account of Shang pyromancy, see Keightley, *Sources of Shang History:
The Oracle-Bone Inscriptions of Bronze Age China* (Berkeley, California: University of
California Press, 1978). For estimated dates of the Shang kings, see ibid., "Appendix
4: Absolute Chronology: A Brief Note," pp. 171–176. New advances in our understanding of relative chronology now indicate that the so-called Diviner Pin [f] group
inscriptions, which in my book I placed only in the reign of Wu Ting, may well
have extended into the reign of Tsu Keng. See, Edward L. Shaughnessy, "Recent
Approaches to Oracle-Bone Periodization: A Review," *Early China* 8 (1982–83):
1–13, esp. pp. 6, 8. My references to divination in the reign of Wu Ting in what follows, accordingly, should be read with this probable extension in mind.

4. For the argument that the charges were statements, not questions, see Keightley,
Sources, p. 29, n. 7. See, too, David S. Nivison, "The 'Question' Question" (Paper
prepared for the International Conference on Shang Civilization, Honolulu,
7–11 September 1982). As Li Hsüeh-ch'in has noted ("Kuan-yü Tui tsu pu-tz'u ti
yi-hsieh wen-t'i," *Ku-wen-tzu yen-chiu* [k] 3 (1980): 39–42), the Tui diviner group
inscriptions (which now appear to be the earliest found at An-yang) rather commonly used interrogatory final particles. This raises the possibility that the earliest divination charges may indeed have been true questions and that it was only
by the reign of Wu Ting that the indicative charges had replaced the interrogative ones. On this point, see Shaughnessy, "Recent Approaches," p. 11, n. 17. A
fuller discussion of these issues will be found in Ch'iu Hsi-kuei, "Kuan-yü Yin-hsü
pu-tz'u ti ming-tz'u shih-fou wen-chü ti yen-chiu!" (in press; originally delivered
at the International Conference on China's Yin-Shang Culture, Anyang, 7–16
September 1987).

5. The precise meaning or function of the *erh kao* notation has not yet been established;
see Keightley, "Reports from the Shang: A Correction and Some Speculations," *Early
China* 9–10 (1983–1985): 20–54.

6. For a list of such divinations, spanning all reigns from Wu Ting to the end of the
dynasty, see Shima Kunio, *Inkyo bokuji sō rui* [y], 2d rev. ed. (Tokyo: Kyūko Shoin,
1971), pp. 161.4–162.1. This invaluable reference is hereafter cited as S. *Chia-pien*
3917 is from the period (ca. 1150–1125 B.C.) of Lin Hsin [z] and K'ang Ting [aa], and
is an excellent example of such a routine divination; it records twenty-six identical

charges, divined on twenty-six consecutive days: "This night there will be no disaster." (In citing inscriptions, I use the abbreviations given in Keightley, *Sources,* pp. 229–231, and p. vi of the 1984 reprint.)

7. S104.4–105.2.

8. For the view that the undesirable charge tended to be abbreviated, see Keightley, *Sources,* p. 52, n. 130; for some examples of such abbreviation, see note 52 following. That the undesirable charge was not always abbreviated, however, is well illustrated by the left-hand inscription reproduced in Figure 1.

9. On the magic of the divination charges and the weakening of the undesirable charge, see Keightley, "Late Shang Divination," pp. 15–16. On the general topic of word magic in the Han and earlier, see Donald Harper, "Wang Yen-shou's Nightmare Poem," *Harvard Journal of Asiatic Studies* 47 (1987): 239–283.

10. The inscription in the middle of the plastron does not record the preface or charge. It is clear from the reference in the verification to the "seventh day, *chi-ssu*[ac] (day 6 in the cycle)" that the charge must have been divined on *kuei-hai*[af] (day 60).

11. For further discussion of these display descriptions and their audience, see Keightley, "Legitimation," pp. 13–17.

12. On the pigmentation of the inscriptions, see Keightley, *Sources,* pp. 54–56.

13. Chi Te-wei (David Keightley), "Chung-kuo chih cheng-shih chih yüan-yüan: Shang wang chan-pu shih-fou yi-kuan cheng-ch'üeh?[ag]" *Ku-wen-tzu yen-chiu* 13 (1986): 117–128. A revised English manuscript of this paper, "The Origins of Legitimating Historiography in China: Were the Shang Kings Always Right?" (November 1984), is available.

14. For a description and examples of such divination topics, see Keightley, *Sources,* pp. 33–35. Specific examples of positive-negative charge pairs would include: *Disaster. Ping-pien* 5.1–2, 7–10; 111.3–4; 203.22–23; 264.5–6. *Distress: Chia-pien* 2996.1–4; *Chui-ho* 274; *Ping-pien* 340.3–4. *Sickness: Ping-pien* 106.18–29; 190.1–4; 334.2–3, 4–5. *Childbearing: Ping-pien* 190.5–6; 249.2–3; 506.2–3. *Rain and shine: Ping-pien* 3.15–16; 87.6–7; 93.1–2; 155.5–6; 368.1–2. *Floods: Hsü-pien* 4.28.4; *Shih-to* 2.476. *Curses by ancestors: Ping-pien* 217.6–9; 394.1–2. *Curses by nature powers: Ping-pien* 203.20–21; *Yi-pien* 920; 4265; 5313. *Harvest:* Figure 1; *Hsü-ts'un* 1.179 (= *Wai-pien* 457). *Divine protection and assistance: Ping-pien* 171.5–6. *Administrative orders: Chia-pien* 2124.20–21, 25–26; *Chui-ho* 244; 320; *Ping-pien* 264.7–8. *Rituals and sacrifices: Ping-pien* 37.3–6; 43.14–15; 52.5–6, 8–13; 90.1–2. *Success in hunting: Chia-pien* 3919.12–13. *Military strategy: Ping-pien* 1.1–2, 13–14; 26.1–2; 76.3–6. *Capture of prisoners: Yi-pien* 865. *Urban construction: Ping-pien* 93.4–7. *Tours of inspection: Ping-pien* 148.1–2. *Sorties and trips: Ping-pien* 26.3–4; 165.3–4, 10–11, 14–15; *Yi-pien* 7768. *Tribute payments: Ping-pien* 47.7–8; 227.3–4; 342.2–3; 379.3–4. The most comprehensive record of this "pairing syndrome" is Chou Hung-hsiang, *Pu-tz'u tui-chen shu-li*[ah] (Hong Kong: Wan-yu, 1969), from whose pages some of the preceding examples were derived.

15. For the view that the logic and assumptions of Shang divination were likely to resemble those current in other aspects of life, see Keightley, "Late Shang Divination," p. 12, n. 7. Consider, too, the judgment of J. J. Finkelstein, in "Mesopotamian Historiography," *Proceedings of the American Philosophical Society* 107, no. 6 (December 1963): 463, that "the Mesopotamian form of learning known as 'divination' was rooted in, and is most characteristic of, the fundamental cognitive mode of the Mesopotamian intellect." A similar judgment, broad though it is, could, I believe, be reached about Shang divination.

16. Ch'u Chai, with Winberg Chai, ed., "Introduction" to *I Ching: Book of Changes,* translated by James Legge (New York: Bantam, 1969), pp. lxxvi–lxxvii.

17. Gerald Swanson, "The Concept of Change in the *Great Treatise,"* in Henry Rosemont, Jr., ed., *Explorations in Early Chinese Cosmology,* Journal of the American Academy of Religion Studies 50, no. 2 (1984): 73.

18. Such a view of the metaphysics of Shang divination is strikingly reinforced by Roger T. Ames's conclusion that what he calls "polarism"—"a symbiosis: the unity of two organismic processes which require each other as a necessary condition for being what they are"—is a "major principle of explanation in the initial formulation and evolution of classical Chinese metaphysics" ("The Meaning of Body in Classical Chinese Thought," *International Philosophical Quarterly* 24 (1984): 41). Benjamin Schwartz had earlier employed the metaphor of polarity in presenting what he regarded as a series of inseparable complementarities in classical Confucianism ("Some Polarities in Confucian Thought," in David S. Nivison and Arthur F. Wright, eds., *Confucianism in Action* (Stanford, California: Stanford University Press, 1959), pp. 51–52). Richard J. Smith, *China's Cultural Heritage: The Ch'ing Dynasty, 1644–1912* (Boulder, Colorado: Westview, 1983), pp. 85–86, 102–105, also summarizes the traditional polarities.

19. For a discussion of this matter, see the scholarship cited in note 13.

20. Similar considerations would also apply to the series of charges that propose sacrificing a certain number of victims—ten, fifteen, or twenty, say—to a particular ancestor (e.g., *Ping-pien* 455.2, 6, 7; *Yi-ts'un* 208). Presumably, only one of these numbers was finally chosen, yet the unused numbers were also incised into the surface of the oracle bone. I suggest that the impulse in this case was also protective. In the event that the sacrifice failed in some way, the record showed that the king and his diviners had considered other numbers or kinds of victims.

21. Keightley, "Legitimation," pp. 16–17.

22. Not only were the positive and negative charges inscribed; the cracks, too, might be cut more deeply into the surface of the bone or shell. Cracks and inscriptions, as we have seen (n. 12), were also frequently filled with colored pigment, presumably to make them stand out.

23. Although the evidence, strictly speaking, falls outside the confines of this article, the content of the Shang oracle-bone inscriptions indicates that Shang divination was not shamanic, that there was no transcendent world of ideal forms to which the diviner might voyage or where he might find final solutions (Keightley, "Royal Shamanism in the Shang: Archaic Vestige or Central Reality?" (Paper prepared for the Chinese Divination and Portent Workshop, Berkeley, 20 June–1 July 1983). See also, Keightley, "Late Shang Divination," pp. 20–21.

24. Keightley, "Late Shang Divination," pp. 12–13 and n. 11.

25. On the exact wording of this Delphic response, see H. W. Parke and D. E. W. Wormell, *The Delphic Oracle: "Vol. 1: The History* (Oxford: Oxford University Press, 1956), p. 133. These authors argue, in fact (pp. 135, 136), that the original prognostication was not ambiguous in this way and that the story we now have was a later, ex post facto, invention. This does not affect the general point being made here.

26. "On Theories of Order and Justice in the Development of Civilization," *Symbols* (December 1985): 18.

27. See, e.g., Keightley, "Religious Commitment," pp. 220–223; and "Late Shang Divination," pp. 13–14.

28. If, on the basis of Shang divination, we associate right and left complementarity with alternating or balanced positive-negative modes, it is possible to suggest that the so-called *t'aot'ieh*[al], "monster mask," designs on Shang bronzes, whatever they may have represented, were neither hostile nor beneficent, but half of each. Such a view would accord with the findings of art historians that many of the masks and figures of Pacific Basin art suggest "a duality of good and evil, and the aversion of harm by means of the power to harm" (*Early Chinese Art and the Pacific Basin: A Photographic Exhibition* [New York: Intercultural Arts Press, 1968], p. 19; see too, pp. 31–32).

29. Kwang-chih Chang has done much to identify binary features in Shang culture; see, e.g., his "Some Dualistic Phenomena in Shang Society," *Journal of Asian Studies* 24, no. 1 (November 1964): 45–61; and *Shang Civilization* (New Haven, Connecticut: Yale, 1980), pp. 165–189. See, too, Marcel Granet, "Right and Left in China," in Rodney Needham, ed., *Right and Left: Essays on Dual Symbolic Classification* (Chicago, Illinois: University of Chicago Press, 1977), pp. 43–58.

30. I am thinking here primarily of the common use of "right" and "left" in official titles. Sung Chen-hao has discerned the existence of a three-crack system of divination that included inscriptions about the right crack and the left crack ("Lun ku-tai chia-ku chan-pu shang ti 'san pu' chih"[am] (in press; originally delivered at the International Conference on China's Yin-Shang Culture, An-yang, 7–16 September 1987).

31. Claude Levi-Strauss, *Totemism* (Boston, Massachusetts: Beacon, 1963), p. 89.

32. Ibid., pp. 88–90.

33. Ibid., p. 89.

34. On "organism" as a "key-word in Chinese thought," see, e.g., Joseph Needham, with the research assistance of Wang Ling, *Science and Civilisation in China. Volume 2. History of Scientific Thought* (Cambridge: Cambridge University Press, 1956), pp. 280–281.

35. Wu Ting's divinations about sacrifices or rituals, which were not yet subject to divination in a routine way, could be presented as pairs of positive and negative charges; see, e.g., *Ping-pien* 50.1–2; 57.1–2, 9–14; 338.1–10.

36. Charges might propose "two *lao*" or "three *lao*" as alternatives (e.g. *Jimbun* 1785, 1786; *Yi-ts'un* 208, etc.; see the abbreviated list of inscriptions at S213.1–2), but the complementary pair "Offer *lao*/Not offer *lao*" was never proposed.

37. Divinations of the form *wang wang t'ien*[ap], "the king goes to hunt," or *wang ch'i t'ien X wang tsai*[aq], "If the king hunts at X; there will be no disaster" (rare under Wu Ting); or *wang ch'i t'ien wang lai wang tsai*[ay], "If the king hunts, coming and going there will be no disaster" (S77.2–4; 79.1; 289.3–297.1) were almost never paired and were usually in the affirming mode. The only exceptions I have found to this statement are the hunting pairs, *Yi-pien* 4538 (S77.2) and *Yeh-yi* 2.40.1 (= *Ching-chin* 3454; see Chou Hung-hsiang, *Pu-tz'u tui-chen shu-li*, p. 60), from the reigns of Wu Ting and Tsu Keng-Tsu Chia, respectively.

38. For an introduction to the five-ritual schedule, see, e.g., Ch'en Meng-chia, *Yin-hsü pu-tz'u tsung-shu*[as] (Peking: K'e-hsüeh Ch'u-pan-she, 1956), pp. 385–392; Tung Tso-pin, *Chia-ku-hsüeh liu-shih-nien*[at] (Taipei: Yi-wen, 1965), pp. 109–113. Matsumaru Michio, "Inkyo bokujichū no denryōchi ni tsuite—Indai kokka kōzō kenkyū no tame ni," *Tōyō bunka kenkyōjo kiyō*[au] 31 (1963): 1–163, demonstrates that the last two Shang kings generally hunted according to a fixed schedule, for only five days out of every ten. Our understanding of Shang ritual practice is complicated by Li Hsüeh-ch'in's recent discovery of a relatively small number of records (as opposed

to divination charges), carved only on scapulas. These appear to indicate that certain rituals, including three of the five regular rituals of Tsu Chia, were already being performed under Wu Ting (or, more precisely, under the ruler who presided over these diviner-Pin inscriptions), even though the rituals were not yet being subjected to divination ("Lun Pin-tsu chia-ku ti chi-chung chi-shih k'e-tzu"[av] (in press; originally delivered at the International Conference on China's Yin-Shang Culture, Anyang, 7–16 September 1987). Among the inscriptions Li cites are *Ho-chi* 1262, 1263, 1770, 10410, and 12333. Li's discovery reminds us once again of the historiographical limits of the divination inscriptions; their silence can only tell us that something was not being divined, not that it was not being performed.

39. Charges of the form, *wang ch'i t'ien pu kou ta yü* (or *feng*)[aw], "If the king hunts he will not encounter great rain (or wind)" (S, 290.4–291.) are common from the reigns of Tsu Chia to Wen Wu Ting; in these reigns they were generally unpaired and affirming. The standard formula, *hsün wang huo*[m], "In the next ten days there will be no disaster" (S, 165.1–166.3 has an abbreviated listing), runs as a constant refrain through the divinations from Wu Ting to Wen Wu Ting; by the reigns of Ti Yi[ax] (ca. 1095–1076 B.C.) and Ti Hsin[ay] (ca. 1075–1045 B.C.), it had become fully incorporated into the records of the ritual schedule (S, 166.4–168.2). These divinations were never paired, and the charge was virtually always in this negative, but affirming, mode.

40. Evidence that documents these changes may be found in Keightley, *Sources,* p. 122; "Appendix 5: Relative Chronology: The Periodicity of Divination Topics and Idioms," pp. 177–182.

41. For the nature of inscription sets, see Keightley, *Sources,* pp. 37–40.

42. Such examples, in which cracks of the same number uniformly have the same prognostications, are not easy to find, due to the failure of crack numbers to appear on many of the fragments we have. In addition to *Hsü-ts'un* 2.972 (Figure 5), I would cite *Hsü-ts'un* 1.2580, 1.2684, 2.929 (?); and *Yi-chu* 246.

43. E.g., *Hsü-ts'un* 1.2689 contains three charges and three "run-in" *ta chi* prognostications; *Chin-chang* 334, *Hou-pien* 1.19.4, and *Ch'ien-pien* 5.16.2 + 4.6.5 (S, 167.4) all contain four charges and four "run-in" *ta chi* prognostications; *Yi-chu* 243 contains six charges and six "run-in" *ta chi* prognostications; and *Yi-chu* 244 contains seven charges and seven "run-in" *ta chi* prognostications.

44. The contrast between *Yi-chu* 277 (seven charges, seven auspicious prognostications) and *Hsü-ts'un* 2.964 (seven charges, zero prognostications) is particularly notable. Other examples: *Hsü-pien* 3.29.3, *Hsü-ts'un* 2.966, and *Yi-chu* 217 all have four charges; *Hsü-ts'un* 2.971 and *Yi-chu* 245 both have five charges; Ch'en Meng-chia, *Yin-hsü pu-tz'u tsung-shu,* pl. 21.3 and *Chui-ho* 65 both have six charges; *Hsü-ts'un* 2.964 has seven charges. Yet in every case there are no prognostications (or crack notations) whatsoever.

45. Only one out of twenty-one Wu Ting bone fragments in *Jimbun* with ten-day or evening divinations on them actually contains a prognostication; this is in contrast to the sixteen out of thirty-one fragments for the Ti Yi-Ti Hsin bones in the same collection. Furthermore, that one fragment (*Jimbun* 848) is not "homogenous," i.e., it contains seven ten-day divinations, all number "2" in their sets, only two of which have prognostications; in addition, the scapula contains three auspicious crack notations, a feature that is present on none of the ten-day fragments from the reigns of Ti Yi and Ti Hsin. See, too, *K'u-fang* 1595, a Wu Ting fragment that contains four ten-day divinations, all numbered "2" in their respective sets, but only one of which has a prognostication, and that

one unfavorable. A count of all Ti Yi-Ti Hsin divinations from S166.4–168.2 indicates that of the fifty-nine ten-day divination fragments that contain two or more charges, 41 percent had no prognostication at all, 41 percent had charges which were all linked to auspicious prognostications; and only 18 percent were nonhomogenous, i.e., contained charges, some of which had prognostications, some of which did not.

46. On the evolution of oracle-bone calligraphy, see Keightley, *Sources,* pp. 104–109.

47. Keightley, *Sources,* pp. 117–118. It is striking that no *hsün wang huo*[m] inscriptions appear with an auspicious prognostication until the reigns of Ti Yi and Ti Hsin.

48. Keightley, *Sources,* pp. 118–119. The practice of appending records of sacrifices performed to "ten-day" divinations about the coming week started under Tsu Chia (S166.3–166.4); it became common under Ti Yi and Ti Hsin (S166.4–168.2). Presumably these records of sacrifices performed served as a form of verification to show that there had been "no disaster."

49. The abbreviated listing of fourteen *wang chan yüeh*[bc] ("the king, reading the cracks, said") inscriptions from the Ti Yi and Ti Hsin period, recorded at S311.2–311.3, were all inscribed on the same side of the bone as the charge.

50. Keightley, *Sources,* p. 121, n. 137.

51. One of the rare, complementary charge pairs from the Ti Yi-Ti Hsin period is *Ch'ien-pien* 3.17.5 (S41.2): "On the next wu[bf] day, it will not rain"/"It will rain."

52. In the Ti Yi - Ti Hsin divinations we do find, curiously, a significant number of charges of the form, "The king will hunt at X and will not encounter rain (or great wind)," paired with, "He will encounter rain (or great wind)"; e.g., *Hou-pien* 1.20.1; *Ch'ien-pien* 2.44.1; 2.43.5, etc. (S457.1); *Ch'ien-pien* 2.30.6; *Hou-pien* 1.30.8 (S455.4). It is worth noting that in every case it was the undesirable charge ("He will encounter rain [or great wind])" that was abbreviated; this suggests that, although the king was genuinely seeking a weather forecast, he was at the same time attempting to make the desirable forecast ("He will not encounter. . . .") the stronger of the two by presenting it in fuller form. Although these late divinations were not, in terms of the discussion earlier, complementary, they were still, as the complementary pairs of Wu Ting's reign had been, metaphysically and magically unbalanced.

53. For these inscriptions see, in order: *Chui-ho* 115 (S157.1); *Ping-pien* 67.7–8 (S157.2), cf. *Hsü-pien* 5.2.1; *Yi-ts'un* 36 (S157.3); *Ping-pien* 108.5–6 (S157.3); *Chui-ho* 323 (S48.2); *Yi-pien* 3787 (S157.4); *Yi-pien* 7456 (S158.1).

54. Keightley, "Legitimation," p. 50.

55. I see no evidence in the inscriptional or archaeological evidence from the reigns of Ti Yi and Ti Hsin of the disorderly, dissolute behavior that the theory of the dynastic cycle subsequently imputed to "bad last" rulers. Wu Ting's diviners, had they still been alive, might have been shocked by the "shallow" optimism I discern in the divinatory theology of this period, but, so far as we can tell from the inscriptions, the state and its system of ancestral rituals were functioning in a regular manner.

56. Herbert Fingarette, "Performatives," *American Philosophical Quarterly* 4 (1967): 39, 40–41; italics in original.

57. Herbert Fingarette, *Confucius: The Secular as Sacred* (New York: Harper and Row, 1972), p. 3. On pp. 11 to 15 Fingarette further develops the performative quality in Confucius' teachings. On the endurance of this Shang tradition, see, too, Keightley, "Late Shang Divination," p. 23.

58. Certain features of Ifa divination in Nigeria, for example, appear to have adopted this procedure, in which "questions are posed in terms of two statements, the first

affirmative and the second negative" (William Bascom, *Ifa Divination: Communication Between Gods and Men in West Africa* (Bloomington, Indiana: Indiana University Press, 1969), p. 51; see, too, p. 53). It will be noted that the Ifa "translation" of the question into two statements, positive and negative, is analogous to the way in which the complementary charges of Shang worked. The analogy is hard to pursue after that point, however. In the first place, the Ifa diviner made no attempt to record the statements, which were not a primary feature of the divination process, but served only to clarify and supplement the message contained in the divination verses; second, the statements were not divined in multiple fashion as the Shang charges, with their sets of cracks, were; third, there was no attempt to weaken one statement at the expense of the other (see earlier, "The Magic of the Charges").

59. Only two fragments *(Hsü-ts'un* 1.2201 and *Ts'ui-pien* 1417)—not from the reign of Wu Ting, where one might expect to find them, but dated to the period after Tsu Chia but before Ti Yi—contain the charge in the positive mode, *hsün yu huo*[bm], "In the next ten days there will be disaster." These two exceptional cases may have been the result of scribal error (Kuo Mo-jo, interestingly, erroneously transcribes the *yu*[bn] as *wang*[bo] in his *Ts'ui-pien* commentary). Error, I would suggest, was encouraged because such divinations were becoming so routine that it hardly mattered how they were written. The routine nature of these "ten-day" inscriptions is further suggested by the fact that a few from the earlier period *(Yi-pien* 70, 80, 1121, 8496, 397, 403; S168.2–3) had already been abbreviated to the single-character charge, *hsün*[bp], "In the next ten days," indicating that the content of these divinations was already so stereotyped that a full record did not always need to be inscribed.

60. S209.4–210.1.

61. The only exceptions to this generalization are *Ch'ien-pien* 6.17.7 (S209.4) and *Yi-pien* 6408 (where the *ti* of the *hsün wang ti* was presumably on a missing fragment of shell).

62. Figure 2 is not, in fact, precisely of the type proposed here, since the charge read *hsün wang huo*[m], not *hsün yu ti*[bq]. Most of the *hsün yu ti* charges at S209.4–210.1 are found on relatively small shell fragments, so that they cannot be directly connected to the prognostications (such as those at S210.2) that employ the *wang chan yüeh yu ti*[bs] formula. It appears that this particular charge formula was primarily (though not invariably) divined on turtle plastrons and not on bovid scapulas.

63. Erika Bourguignon, "Divination, transe et possession en Afrique transsaharienne," in André Caquot and Marcel Leibovici, eds., *La Divination* (Paris: Presses Universitaires de France, 1968), vol. 2, p. 331.

64. Goody, *Domestication,* p. 48.

65. See Keightley, *Sources,* pp. 38–40, on the number of cracks per set of charges.

66. For additional reflections on what I there characterized as "part of a shift from magic towards religion, from charm to prayer," see Keightley, "Late Shang Divination," pp. 19–20.

67. For a discussion of hexagram-like numbers found on Late Shang and early Chou oracle bones, see Zhang Ya-chu and Liu Yu, "Some Observations About Milfoil Divination Based on Shang and Zhou *bagua* Numerical Symbols," trans, by Edward Shaughnessy, *Early China* 7 (1981–82): 46–55; Keightley, "Was the *Chou Yi* a Legacy of Shang?" (Paper presented at the annual meeting of the Association for Asian Studies, Chicago, 3 April 1982).

68. For a different, though by no means contradictory, view of the increasing rationalization of early Chinese osteomancy, see Léon Vandermeersch, "De la tortue à

l'achillée," in Jean-Pierre Vernant and others, *Divination et Rationalité* (Paris: Editions du Seuil, 1974), pp. 38–39.

69. This is the plausible hypothesis of Shirakawa Shizuka, "Bokuji no sekai," in Kaizuka Shigeki, ed., *Kodai In teikoku*[bt], 2d ed. (Tokyo, 1967), p. 197.

70. See, e.g., Li Chi, ed., *Ch'eng-tzu-yai: The Black Pottery Culture Site at Lung-shan-chen in Li Ch'eng hsien, Shantung Province,* Yale University Publications in Anthropology, no. 52 (New Haven, Connecticut, 1956), p. 149.

71. For Late Neolithic evidence of pyromancy, as reported to the end of 1977, see Keightley, *Sources,* p. 3, n. 3. Many more finds have been reported since then. See, e.g., the table of finds provided by Hsiao Liang-ch'iung, "Chou-yüan pu-tz'u ho Yin-hsü pu-tz'u chih yi-t'ung ch'u-t'an," in Hu Hou-hsüan, ed., *Chia-ku-wen yü Yin-Shang shih*[bu] (Shanghai: Ku-chi, 1983), pp. 276–280.

72. For the introduction of plastromancy, as opposed to scapulimancy, see the evidence cited at Keightley, *Sources,* p. 8, nn. 23–26.

73. Lin Yun has suggested that there was a connection between the hollow shapes of the late Erh-li-kang oracle-bones found at Cheng-chou, and those of the Diviner Tui group, which are thought to be the earliest of the inscriptional corpus excavated at Anyang ("Hsiao-t'un nan-ti fa-chüeh yü Yin-hsü chia-ku tuan-tai,"[bv] *Ku-wen-tzu yen-chiu* 9 (1984): 122); Laura Anne Skosey, trans., "Lin Yun's 'The Xiaotun *nandi* Excavation and the Periodization of Yinxu Oracle Bones'" (Master's thesis, Far Eastern Languages and Civilizations, University of Chicago, 1987), pp. 24–25.

74. Itö Michiharu, "In izen no ketsuen shoshiki to shükyö," *Tō hō gakuhō*[bw] 32 (1962): 259.

75. It will be obvious that some of the changes in divination form that I have described here can be related to Tung Tso-pin's theories of alternating Old and New Schools of divination, in which Wu Ting's diviners followed Old School practice, and Ti Yi and Ti Hsin's diviners followed those of the New School. Although Tung's vision of alternating ritual schools has been superseded by more recent analyses, there is little doubt that reforms did take place in the reign of Tsu Chia that were concerned with rationalizing the system of cult by making it more orderly and systematic. Wu Ting's sacrificial practice, at least as it appears in the divinatory charges, seems to have been less organized, and less predictable, than that of his successors. For an introduction to the Old and New School controversies, and to Tsu Chia's reforms, see Keightley, *Sources,* p. 32, n. 18; p. 108, n. 68; and pp. 115, 178. For some of the more recent studies that further challenge Tung's model, see Shaughnessy, "Recent Approaches," and Skosey, "Lin Yun's 'The Xiaotun *nandi* Excavation'," esp. pp. 3–15.

76. The possibility that Wu Ting was already performing certain rituals without subjecting them to divination (see n. 38) suggests the degree to which the religious system was still in flux.

77. Maybury-Lewis, in a suggestive passage, argues that "In relatively small societies, that are not subject to the central authority of the state, the effect of dual organization is to guarantee justice, since it constrains the social system within the parameters of cosmic equilibrium. This delicate balance is threatened by state formation, unless the rulers themselves subscribe to the theory and put some form of it into practice. . . . In a small scale society the theory and practice of dual organization acts as a restraint. It prevents the society temporarily . . . from transforming itself. In an empire, the ideology is no longer sufficient restraint. It has to be supported by force. We are therefore dealing with the passage from a controlling ideology to an ideology backed up by control" ("On Theories of Order and Justice," p. 19). A similar shift may have been occurring in China between the more traditional reign of Wu Ting and the more statist reigns of Ti Yi and Ti Hsin.

a 中央研究院國際漢學會義論文集

b 隹

c 叀

d 武丁

e 祖庚

f 賓

g 我受漆年

h 我弗其受漆年

i 丙辰

j 殷

k 李學勤, "關於𠂤組卜辭的一些問題, "古文字研究

l 裘錫圭, "關於殷墟卜辭的命辭是否問句的研究"

m 旬亡禍

n 癸巳

o 丁酉

p 沚𢦔

q 土方

r 吾方

r 董作賓, "大龜四版考釋," 安陽發掘報告

s 二告

t 己卯

u 壬

v 壬午

w 今夕亡禍

x 島邦男, 殷墟卜辭綜類

y 𡥓辛

z 康丁

aa 湄日不遘大風

ab 文武丁

ac 其

ad 己巳

ae 癸亥

af 吉德燧, "中國之正史之淵源:商王占卜是否一貫正確?"

ag 周鴻翔, 卜辭對貞述例

ah 易經

ai 燮

aj 化

ak 燹燹

al 宋鎮豪, "論古代甲骨占卜上的'三卜'制"

am 祖甲

an 牢

ap 王往田

aq 王其田 x 亡災

ar 王其田往來亡災

as 陳夢家, <u>殷虛卜辭綜述</u>

at <u>甲骨學六十年</u>

au 松丸道雄, "殷墟卜辞中の田獵地について──殷代国家構造研究のために," <u>東洋文化研究所紀要</u>

av "論賓組胛骨的幾種記事刻辭"

aw 王其田不遘大雨(風)

ax 帝乙

ay 帝辛

az 癸丑

ba 癸酉

bb 癸卯

bc 癸

bd 大吉

be 王固曰

bf 戊

bg 帝

bh 唐

bi 福

bj 你的福倒(到)了

bk 又禍

bl 亡禍

bm 旬又禍

bn 又

bo 亡

bp 旬

bq 旬又 / 虫祟

br 旬亡祟

bs 王固曰虫祟

bt 白川静, "卜辞の世界," 貝塚茂樹, 古代殷帝国

bu 蕭良瓊, "周原卜辭和殷墟卜辭之異同初探," 胡厚宣, <u>甲骨文與殷商史</u>

bv 林澐, "小屯南地發掘與殷墟甲骨斷代"

bw 伊藤道治, "殷以前の血緣組織と宗教," <u>東方學報</u>

bx 無爲

7

THE MAKING OF THE ANCESTORS: LATE SHANG RELIGION AND ITS LEGACY

DAVID N. KEIGHTLEY

I argue in this article that the dynastic elites of the Late Shang 商—who flourished ca. 1200–1045 B.C. in the area of northern Henan, southwest Shanxi, and western Shandong—*made* their ancestors, that they made them in a way that had significant impact on the making of early Chinese culture in general, and that one can put a date on that act of making, and even, perhaps, a name on the makers.[1] Those Shang elites are important because they left us the first body of written materials yet available in East Asia—the oracle-bone inscriptions. And they are important because many of the cultural choices they made and the institutions they devised were to prove ancestral to subsequent Chinese practice. One of their most significant legacies was the creation of the ancestors (and ancestresses). "The dead," it has been noted, "have no existence other than that which the living imagine for them."[2] The way in which the Shang imagined the dead and the consequences of that imagining are the subject of this article.

Ancestor Worship Defined

The word "religiosity" might be substituted for "religion" in the subtitle of this article because the Late Shang records available to us provide access primarily to the extrinsic ritual routines of Shang religious activity; they tell us little about inner, "spiritual" experience (see, e.g., the discussion on p. 189 below). The distinction between religion and religiosity, however, is by no means clear cut, and although the degree to which extrinsic religiosity may serve as an index of intrinsic religious orientation is hard to determine, I do assume, in my discussions below, that the attitudes and orientations generated in the external sphere of religious activity both shaped and were shaped by subjective experience.[3]

Even the category of "religion" itself may sacrifice the emic realities of Late Shang experience to the etic needs of modern analytical convenience. In Late Shang, the royal lineage served as the central axis of the dynastic state, a state in which religious, political, and social idioms and institutions were largely undifferentiated.

"All aspects of Shang life could be impregnated, as the occasion arose, with religious significance," and "the homogeneity of the Shang world view that this implies reinforces the assumption that Shang religious conceptions were the conceptions of Shang life as a whole."[4] As Patricia A. McAnany has written of the ancient Maya,

> Communing with deceased progenitors was not a religious experience divorced from political and economic realities ...; rather, it was a practice grounded in pragmatism that drew power from the past, legitimized the current state of affairs (including all the inequities in rights and privileges), and charted a course for the future. Ancestors resided at that critical nexus between past and future, and their presence both materially and symbolically lent weight to the claims of their mere mortal descendants.[5]

Her characterization of ancestral veneration as "living with the ancestors" has much relevance for the Shang.[6]

Ancestor veneration or worship involved, in ancient China and elsewhere, a "belief in the empowered dead with the attendant practices stemming from that belief."[7] The key word in this definition would be "empowered." For the commemoration of dead kin does not, of itself, qualify as ancestor worship. The anthropologist Meyer Fortes has argued that ancestor worship should be regarded as "a representation or extension of the authority component in the jural relations of successive generations.... It is not the whole man, but only his jural status as the parent ... vested with authority that is transmuted into ancestorhood."[8] As Fortes has also written, "Ancestorhood is fatherhood made immortal.... Death palpably removes fathers; but it is not assumed to extinguish fatherhood." In a culture where ancestor worship flourishes, accordingly, "a person never escapes from authority."[9]

Fortes' definitions, which derive from his work among the Tallensi in West Africa (Ghana), work well for ancient China, where ancestor worship did "not involve the perceptual commemoration of the total personality of the deceased," but "involve[d] an appeal to certain powers that the deceased [was] conceived as possessing."[10] In the "Tan gong 檀弓" chapter of the *Liji* 禮記, compiled in late Zhou and Han, Confucius' disciple Zi You 子游 is reported to have noted that, "When a man dies, there arises a feeling of disgust (at the corpse). Its impotency makes us turn away from it (人死斯惡之矣, 無能也, 斯倍之矣)."[11] It was the "impotency," *wu neng* 無能, of the corpse that the ancestors were able, through proper ritual treatment, to transcend. Shang ancestor worship—which involved the scheduled offering of meat, blood, grain, ale, and so on—preserved the potency of the ancestral persona.[12] The Shang regarded their ancestors as ritually abstracted anthropomorphic beings who had particular powers.

The Neolithic Background

The roots of Shang ancestor worship lay far back in the past, mainly discernible to us today in the remarkable care with which the inhabitants of Neolithic China treated their dead.[13] The ritual treatment of the corpse—with particular attention to its posture, orientation, and furnishings—is evident from as early as the fifth millennium B.C. And by the third millennium B.C., the graves of elites, with the elegance of their construction and the wealth of their grave goods (many of which, like the ritual jades found in Liangzhu 良渚 burials, would have required much labor to produce), evidently reflect the considerable differences in wealth and status that were developing in the cultures of the Late Neolithic. Where the cult of the ancestors was concerned, one can posit a shift from the egalitarian and communitarian cults of the early Neolithic, to the increasing individuation of particular lineage groups, followed by the dominance of some and the special treatment of their lineage dead.[14] It may also be noted that the presence of oracle-bones in or near certain Late Neolithic graves suggests that divination was involved in the mortuary rituals and, possibly, that the mourners were using the divination bones to communicate with the recently dead.[15]

The Shang Pantheon

Modern scholars may, for analytical purposes, divide the Shang Powers into six groups: (1) Di 帝, the High God; (2) Nature Powers, like He 河 (the River Power), Yang 羔 (the Mountain Power), and Ri 日 (the sun); (3) Former Lords, like Nao 夒 and Wang Hai 王亥, who were apparently ex-humans whom the cultists now associated with the dynasty;[16] (4) predynastic ancestors, like Shang Jia 上甲 (P1) and the three Bao 報 (P2–P4)[17] who received cult ahead of Da Yi 大乙, the dynasty founder, in the Period V ritual cycle;[18] (5) the dynastic ancestors, starting with Da Yi 大乙 (K1), who could be grouped in a number of ways (p. 166 below); and (6) the dynastic ancestresses, the consorts of those kings on the main line of descent. The worship of the non-dynastic Powers (groups 1 to 3 above), whether natural or human (a distinction that might not have been easy or even desirable to make), presumably strengthened the king's position by enlarging the scope of his influence in the spiritual world. It may be regarded as a form of "spiritual imperialism" in which the spirits worshiped by local populations were coopted into the official Shang theology, frequently being placed in the shadowy, and relatively "empty," pre-dynastic ritual space before Da Yi (K1), the founder.[19]

The distinctions between these groups, especially the Nature Powers, Former Lords, and predynastic ancestors—whom I shall call, collectively, the High Powers[20]—were by no means rigid; the Shang ritualists conceived of the High Powers as sharing many essential features. Furthermore, the cultists also regarded some of the High Powers as ancestors. Thus, the Former Lords, Nao (as in *Heji* 30398, 30399, and 33227) and Wang Hai, were called *gao zu*, "High Ancestor," in Periods II to IV, as in

[1] 其告于高祖王亥三牛

"(We) will offer a report to High Ancestor Wang Hai,[21] (with) three cows." (II–IV. Nameless Royal) (*Heji* 30447; Y1246.1)[22]

[2] 乙巳貞：大禦其陟于高祖王亥

On *yisi* (day 42) divined: "In performing the Great Exorcism, (we) will offer it in the presence of the High Ancestor Wang Hai."[23] (II. Li 2) (*Heji* 32916; Y1246.1)

He, the River Power, was also so honored, on one occasion, as *Gao Zu He* 高祖河, in Period II (e.g., *Heji* 32028; II, Li 2). Whether the kin relationship so implied was fictive or not, the Shang ritualists sought, by the use of *zu*, to associate the Nature Powers and Former Lords with the highest levels of their ancestral pantheon.[24]

The Shang distinguished the High Powers and the dynastic ancestors by the differing ritual treatments and functions they assigned them. Although the Shang kings might occasionally host (*bin* 賓) a Nature Power, the ritual practioners never established for the Nature Powers or Former Lords the regular schedule of hostings (as in [3], [4], [20], [21A–C], [23], [24]) that characterized the later ancestral cult.[25] Furthermore, the Shang ritualists never conferred upon Di, the Nature Powers, and the Former Lords the *gan* 干-stem temple names that were essential to the orderly functioning of the ancestral cult (see p. 162 below).[26] The dynastic ancestors were also distinguished from the High Powers by the way in which rituals to the ancestors were regularly offered not only to the main-line kings but also to their consorts;[27] the consorts of most of the High Powers, by contrast, were not divined about, and we do not know, in most cases, their consorts' names or if they even had consorts. That the ritualists occasionally included the consorts of Shi Ren 示壬 (P5) and Shi Gui 示癸 (P6) in the ritual cycle,[28] as in,

[3] 庚辰卜貞：王賓示壬奭妣庚翌日亡〔尤〕

Crack-making on *gengchen* (day 17), divined: "His Majesty, performing the hosting ceremony for the *yi* day-ritual to Shi Ren's (P5) consort Ancestress Geng, will have no [fault]."[29] (V. Huang) (*Heji* 36183; Y1373.1)

---

[4]〔甲〕辰卜貞：王賓示癸奭妣甲卷日亡尤

Crack-making on [*jia*] *chen* (day 41), divined: "His Majesty, performing the hosting ceremony for the *xie* day-ritual for Shi Gui's (P6) consort Ancestress Jia, will have no fault." (V. Huang) (*Heji* 36190; Y1374.1),

accords with the liminal nature of these most junior, and most recent, of the predynastic ancestors, who were accorded, but only irregularly, this defining feature of main-line dynastic status.

In terms of functions, Di, the Nature Powers, and a few of the Former Lords, like Huang Yin 黃尹 (Y977.1–78.2), tended to affect the dynasty or the country as a whole, influencing the weather, the crops, and warfare; by contrast, the ancestors were more directly concerned with the king's personal activities: his illnesses ([10AB]), his well-being ([11]), and the fault-free management of the rituals ([20], [21A–C]). And in all cases of pyromantic enquiry, even when no ancestral Power was explicitly implicated, my study of Shang divinatory theology has suggested that the ancestors were deeply involved in generating the oracular cracks in bone and shell, speaking to their descendants through the sounds made by the cracks as they formed.[30] The High Powers presumably occupied a middle ground, between Di, on the one hand, and the ancestors on the other, unable to emulate Di by commanding (*ling*) 令 natural phenomena, but still having large impact on the weather and the crops.[31]

One has a sense, in fact, that the diviners distinguished the High Powers, unsystematically to be sure, by the degree of "ancestralization" they accorded them. In this view, the Shang liturgists would have ancestralized a Power by incorporating it into the ritual system, providing the Power with the temple name and regular schedule of cult that characterized their treatment of the regular ancestors. By this standard, some High Powers were more ancestral than others. Di, for example, had minimal ancestral status. He issued commands in a way that none of the other High Powers or ancestors could;[32] he received little or no cult; and he was given no temple name and no ancestral designation. The Nature Powers were more ancestral; they received some sacrifices, often through the *di* 禘-ritual, which appears to have involved requests for rain, for pacifying the wind and locusts, and for good harvests,[33] and they were occasionally given ancestral titles (as in *Heji* 32028 with its reference to Gao Zu He 高祖河, "High Ancestor River"). The Former Lords were still more ancestral; they received cult, although irregularly, on certain *gan* days (see n. 26 above), which suggests an incipient system of *gan* temple names, and they were also given ancestral titles.[34] The predynastic ancestors were more ancestral yet again and were indeed accorded many of the ritual privileges attached to true kin. They were given temple names, such as Shang Jia (P1) and Bao Yi 報乙 (P2), and they received cult, on their *gan* days, as participants in the regular ritual cycle. The consorts of Shi Ren and Shi Gui, furthermore, were, as we have seen, also honored with cult on their appropriate *gan*-named days (as in [3] and [4]); since Shi Ren and Shi Gui were the most recent of the predynastic ancestors, one sees the increasing "ancestralization" of these figures as they grew closer to the ancestors themselves. The ancestors, finally, were all given temple names; they received rich sacrifices. And cult was offered to them—and to the consorts of the main line kings—on the appropriate *gan* days in a schedule that grew more systematic with time.

Arthur Wolf, in his study of religion in modern Taiwan, made at least two observations that may bear on the Shang situation.

> [Maurice] Freedman has argued that ancestors are not feared in China as in some West African societies because the living are not conscious of having displaced their ascendants from coveted positions of power.... A simpler explanation might be that Chinese ancestors are not feared because they are not conceived of as powerful beings. The African societies Freedman discusses are stateless societies in which the senior men of the lineage dominate the social landscape. In traditional China the authority of senior kinsmen was overshadowed by the far greater power of the imperial bureaucracy. People did not attribute great events to the spiritual remains of kinsmen because kinsmen were not capable of controlling the course of events. Great events were more appropriately attributed to gods, gods who were modeled on the imperial bureaucracy.[35]

While presumably true for the bulk of the Chinese peasantry in late Imperial times, it is worth noting that these judgments do not describe the far earlier situation of the Shang royal ancestors and their descendants. The ancestors were powerful, and they were powerful precisely because they had been powerful when alive, and because their descendants still were. The Shang ancestors, in Wolf's terms, would have been part of "the imperial bureaucracy" (i.e., the dynastic apparatus) and they were fully capable, as the divination inscriptions amply demonstrate, of "controlling the course of events." The living might have been, in Freedman's terms, less "conscious of having displaced their ascendants from coveted positions of power" precisely because the ancestors were indeed still powerful. They had not been displaced, they had been promoted.

Wolf also commented on the contractual nature of the bargaining that takes place between modern Taiwanese and their gods:

> When a man appeals to an ancestor he appeals to a kinship relationship involving a certain degree of mutual dependence, but when he appeals to a god he negotiates for his good will just as he would in attempting to secure a favor from a magistrate or policeman. He makes a small sacrifice and promises a larger one if the god will grant his petition. If divination reveals that the god is not inclined to grant the petition, he then promises a more substantial gift, repeating the process until the god finally agrees…. the larger gift is not produced until after the desired outcome

This kind of bargaining is, in my view, evident in the Shang divination inscriptions of Wu Ding's period, in which the *ce* 冊 ritual was used to "pledge" offerings to ancestors on account, as in:[37]

[5] 貞：禦于父乙斯三牛冊三十伐三十宰

Divined: "In making Exorcism in the presence of Father Yi (K20), (we) will cleave three cows and pledge thirty dismembered victims and thirty penned sheep." (I. Bin) (*Heji* 886; Y891.2)

The "on account" model assumes that if the Exorcism in this case worked (i.e., if the living human who was being "defended" in this way recovered), the king would actually offer the large numbers of humans (thirty dismembered victims) and animals (thirty penned sheep) he had pledged; in the meantime, he offered only three cows. As Shirakawa originally noted, the discrepancy between the small number of victims offered in other ways and the large number offered in the *ce* 冊 ritual is striking, as in:[38]

[6] ☒卜爭貞：燎冊百羊百牛百豕穀五十

Crack-making on …, Zheng divined: "In making burnt offering, (we) pledge one hundred sheep, one hundred cows, one hundred pigs, and piglets, fifty." (I. Bin) (*Yingcang* 1256; Y1135.1)

The Shang generally offered such pledges to their ancestors and ancestresses (see the inscriptions at Y1133.1–35-1), as in [5] and:

[7] 貞：冊妣庚十𠬝劉十牢

Divined: "Pledge to Ancestress Geng ten captives, split open ten penned cows."
(I. Bin) (*Heji* 698f; Y1133.1)

Although no divination charges indicate that certain ancestors, such as Shang Jia
(P1) and Da Yi (K1), the dynasty founder, were bargained with in this way, many
of the other kings, chiefly on the main line of descent, but also some collaterals,
were offered the pledge ritual.[39] One has the impression that king Wu Ding was
ready to bargain with most of his ancestors, but that he tended to do so more
frequently with those who were closer to him in time (see the inscriptions cited in
n. 39), particularly with his father, Xiao Yi 小乙 (the Fu Yi 父乙 of [5]; see too the
Xiao Yi inscriptions cited in n. 39), and also, in all likelihood, with the consorts
who had been married to those more recent kings.[40]

Wu Ding occasionally offered pledges to a small number of Nature Powers
and Former Lords, but he evidently regarded them as more distant, less open to
this kind or human negotiation.[41] The only notable exception to this generalization, in fact, is the striking inscription:

[8] 甲子卜爭貞：禱年于口⿱十⁹牛曲百⁹牛

Crack-making *on jiazi* (day 1), Zheng divined: "In praying for harvest to the Sun,[42]
(we) will cleave ten dappled cows and pledge one hundred dappled cows." (I. Bin)
(*Heji* 10116; Y530.2)

The inscription appears to record "a major harvest prayer, offered to the sun (or
suns) on the first day of the cycle (*jiazi*, day 1), in which ten cows were offered
(one for each sun of the ten-day week?) and one hundred more were pledged (ten
for each sun?)."[43] I know of no other cases in which the Shang king attempted to
bargain with the Sun Power in this way.

I conclude, in short, that the Shang conceived of the Nature and the Ancestral
Powers as occupying a hierarchy of negotiability, with the close ancestors and ancestresses of the pantheon being most open to this kind or pledging, and the higher
Powers, both ancestral and natural, being less approachable in this way. This conclusion, as we shall see, accords well with the general impersonalization of the ancestors
that appears to have taken place as they became increasingly senior (see pp. 174 ff.
below).

Shang Ancestor Worship: Theology and Structure

We would today, I think, find the actual experience of Shang ancestor worship
rather a shock. The cries of the animal and human victims, the blood streaming
down, the body parts, the decapitated heads, the horrible uncertainties and dangers
of the environment, the use of magic and spells, the awe and fear with which the
ancestors and other Powers were regarded, the intense concern about lucky and
unlucky days—all these "realities" should not be forgotten.[44] But neither should
they blind us to the significance of the attempts that the Shang ritualists were
making to bring order and sense to their world, some three thousand years ago.

And the search for significance invites us to focus primarily on the structures and implicit theological assumptions of Shang ancestor worship, rather than on the dramatic experience.

Late Shang cult, as it was recorded in the oracle-bone inscriptions, involved not mere veneration or commemoration, but actual worship.[45] By this I mean that the cult was thought to be operational and pragmatic. The regular offerings, sacrificial pledges (pp. 160–62 above), appeals, reports, and so on, by which the Shang kings sustained, appeased, and informed their ancestors, were not simply marks of respect. They were attempts to influence the religious power that the ancestors possessed, either by the offering of victims or by the expressions of hope that, if the Shang king performed certain rituals, there would, for example, be "no disasters" (*wang huo* 亡禍), there would be "no fault (or troubles)" (*wang you* 亡尤), we would "receive harvest" (*shou nian* 受年), and we would "receive assistance" (*shou you* 受又). Thus, ancestor worship was inextricably tied to the successful exercise of power, both spiritual and political. This undoubtedly was one of the reasons that participation in the worship was limited to members of the royal lineage.[46] The worship of the ancestors not only validated status; it gave access to power.

Temple Names

The living Shang elites conferred upon each of their ancestors and ancestresses a "temple name" (modern Chinese *miaohao* 廟號) as a posthumous ritual title. These temple names might combine either a kin term, like *fu* 父, "Father," or *zu* 祖, "Ancestor," or other descriptive prefixes like *da* 大, "Big, Greater," and *xiao* 小, "Small, Lesser," with a *gan* 干 or "stem" suffix (see the royal genealogy presented in Fig. 1). One can think of the *gan* stems—*jia* 甲, *yi* 乙, *bing* 丙, *ding* 丁, and so on—like the numbers from 1 to 10, or like the first ten letters of the alphabet, A to J, used to sequence and categorize items. Since the ten *gan* or "stems" were also the names of the ten days that composed the Shang week— also called *jia* 甲, *yi* 乙, *bing* 丙, *ding* 丁, and so on—it became possible for the Shang liturgists, particularly after the reign of Zu Jia 祖甲 ("Ancestor Jia" [K23]; Period IIb), to link the ancestors' temple names to the name of the day by offering cult to the ancestors almost invariably on the day of the ancestors' temple names (as in [3], [4], [20], [21A–C]; see too Fig. 2). Thus Da Yi 大乙 ("The Greater Yi"), for example, received cult on *yi*-days, Zu Ding 祖丁, "Ancestor Ding," on *ding*-days, Fu Jia 父甲, "Father Jia," on *jia*-days, Bi Geng 妣庚, "Ancestress Geng," on *geng*-days, and Mu Xin 母辛, "Mother Xin," on *xin*-days. These posthumous temple names, which were commonly used, for both the royal ancestors and also for certain non-royal elites,[47] served to pigeonhole and classify the ancestors. The ancestors were no longer referred to by their personal names, the names the living had presumably used. They were now known, and worshipped, by their ritual names that classified them and scheduled them in the system of ancestral cult.

Temple Name		Generation
P1 Shang Jia 上甲		1
P2 Bao Yi 報乙		2
P3 Bao Bing 報丙		3
P4 Bao Ding 郣丁		4
P5 Shi Ren 示壬 = Bi Geng 妣庚		5
P6 Shi Gui 示癸 = Bi Jia 妣甲		6
K1 Da Yi 大乙 = Bi Bing 妣丙		7
K2 Da Ding 大丁 = Bi Wu 妣戊		8
K3 Da Jia 大甲 = Bi Xin 妣辛	K4 Bu Bing 卜丙	9
K5 Da Geng 大庚 = Bi Ren 妣壬	K6 Xiao Jia 小甲	10
K7 Da Wu 大戊 = Bi Ren 妣壬	K8 Lü Ji 呂己	11
K9 Zhong Ding 中丁 = Bi Ji 妣己 = Bi Gui 妣癸	K10 Bu Ren 卜壬	12
K12 Zu Yi 祖乙 = Bi Ji 妣己 = Bi Geng 妣庚	K11 Jian Jia 戔甲	13
K13 Zu Xin 祖辛 = Bi Geng 妣庚 = Bi Jia 妣甲	K14 Qiang Jia 羌甲	14
K15 Zu Ding 祖丁 = Bi Ji 妣己 = Bi Geng 妣庚	K16 Nan Geng 南庚	15

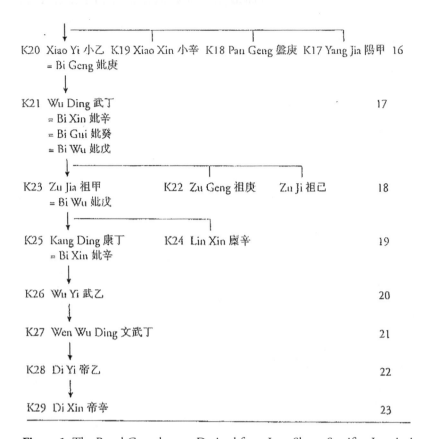

Figure 1 The Royal Genealogy as Derived from Late Shang Sacrifice Inscriptions

P = predynastic ancestor; K = king. The ↓ indicates the main line of father-to-son descent known traditionally as the *dazong* 大宗.

Sources: For the Shang kings, see Keightley (*Sources of Shang History*, 185–87, 204–09), whose notes should be consulted for particular problems involving the reconstruction of the list. For the consorts, see Chang Yuzhi, *Shangdai zhouji zhidu*, 103–04, who limits her consorts to those who received cult as part of the regular five-ritual cycle. Occasional references, in either oracle-bone or bronze inscriptions, to consorts who were not included in the cycle, do indicate, e.g., that the consort of Qiang Jia (K14) was Bi Geng (*Heiji* 23325; Chang Yuzhi, *Shangdai zhouji zhidu*, 94; see too, Keightley, *Sources of Shang History*, 187, n.f) and that the consort of Wu Yi (K26) was Bi Geng (Chen Menjia, *Yinxu buci zongshu*, 384; Chang Yuzhi, 100, n. 1). But no evidence indicates that these royal women received regular cult in association with their royal husbands. Chang Yuzhi (p. 118) provides a useful tabulation of the king and consort numbers proposed by various scholars: she herself identifies 31 kings (including Shang Jia) and 20 consorts; Dong Zuobin, by contrast had identified 33 kings and 24 consorts, Chen Mengjia had identified 34 kings and 22 consorts, etc.; Keightley ("At the Beginning," 58–60) identifies 29 kings and 19 consorts (plus 2 more, if one includes the consorts of the two pre-dynastic ancestors Shi Ren [P5] and Shi Gui [P6]; see p. 159 above).

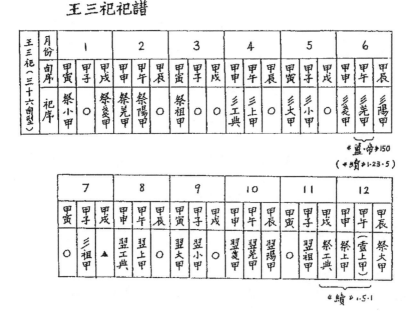

Figure 2 A reconstruction of the "third ritual cycle" calendar year. (Chang Yuzhi, *Shangdai zhouji zhidu*, 230.)

The reliance on generic temple names rather than individual personal names over a long period of time—we are looking, in the case of the Shang royal lineage, at a claimed time depth of some twenty-three generations (Fig. 1)—would necessarily have encouraged the impersonalization of the ancestors. Since six predynastic ancestors, from Shang Jia (P1) to Shi Gui (P6), and twenty-nine kings, from Da Yi (K1) to Di Xin (K29), had to be squeezed into only ten slots—that is, into the ten *gan* of their temple names and into the ten days of the week used for their cult—duplication of temple names (as in the case of the ancestresses; see n. 40) was inevitably involved, particularly since some temple names—notably Jia, Yi, and Ding—were more auspcious, and hence more popular, than others.[48]

It thus became necessary for the Shang to disambiguate their ancestors by a variety of distinguishing prefixes. The Shang created seven Jia ancestors (Fig. 1): Shang Jia 上甲, Da Jia 大甲, Xiao Jia 小甲, Jian Jia 戔甲, Qiang Jia 羌甲, Yang Jia 陽甲, and Zu Jia 祖甲, all of whom received cult on a *jia*-day as their turn in the ritual schedule came round. Note that the honorific prefixes—"Greater" (K3) and "Ancestor" (K23)—were reserved for the main-line kings; the collateral Jia kings were either prefixed with "Lesser" (K6) or with names that may have represented ethnic affiliation (K11, K14, K17). The Shang similarly created seven Yi ancestors: Bao Yi 報乙, Da Yi 大乙, Zu Yi 祖乙, Xiao Yi 小乙, Wu Yi 武乙, and Di Yi 帝乙, all of whom received cult on an *yi*-day; and they created six Ding ancestors: Bao Ding 報丁, Da Ding 大丁, Zhong Ding 中丁, Zu Ding 祖丁, Wu Ding 武丁, and Wenwu Ding 文武丁, all of whom received cult on a *ding*-day.[49] So impersonal was the naming system in fact, that Zhong Ding (K9) was also known as San Zu Ding 三祖丁, "Third Ancestor Ding"—as he was coming later than Bao Ding (P4) and Da Ding (K2). And Zu Ding (K15), "Ancestor Ding," the next Ding-named ancestor, was similarly known as Si Zu Ding 四祖丁, "Fourth Ancestor Ding" (as in [20]). (That none of the collateral kings were given the temple name of Yi or Ding suggests the importance attached to those two *gan*.)

It may also be noted that all of these ancestors, in the generation after their death, would presumably have been honored with the prefix of Fu 父, "Father," so that the seven Jia ancestors, for example, would all, at one point in their ancestral careers, have been accorded the same temple name of Fu Jia 父甲, "Father Jia," the six Yi ancestors would have all been Fu Yi 父乙, "Father Yi," and so on.[50] The ritual naming of the ancestors thus de-emphasized their individual personalities. To become an ancestor, in fact, you had to be renamed, and the name had to be limited to one of the ten *gan* allowed by the system; your name when dead was not, except in the case of one significant and temporary exception (see n. 96 below), a name that you had used while alive.

Ancestral Clusters

The Shang lineage, so far as we can discern it in the oracle-bone inscriptions, functioned as a corporate descent group that cooperated in ritual, political, and social activities.[51] Its importance is demonstrated by the Shang practice of addressing rituals and requests not just to individual royal ancestors but to groups of them. Fathers and more senior ancestors were among the royal kin who could be clustered in this way, with some offerings being made to "The Three Fathers" (San Fu 三父)—probably a reference to three of the four "fathers" in the generation preceding Wu Ding—and to "The Three Ancestors" (San Zu 三祖; see p. 181 below).[52] The ancestral groups sometimes consisted of some or all of the ancestors on the main line of descent, that is, those kings whose sons had, in their turn, become kings (e.g., K1, K2, K3, K5, K7, and the other kings below and above a ↓ in Fig. 1). Some rituals, in fact, were addressed to a lengthy list of ancestors, as in:

[9] □未卜：禱雨自上甲大乙大丁大甲大庚〔大戊〕中丁祖乙祖辛祖丁十示率牡

Crack-making on … *wei*: "In praying for rain to (the ancestors) from Shang Jia (P1) (to) Da Yi (K1), Da Ding (K2), Da Jia (K3), Da Geng (K5), [Da Wu (K7),] Zhong Ding (K9), Zu Yi (K12), Zu Xin (K13), and Zu Ding (K15), the Ten Ancestors,[53] (we will) lead-in-sacrifice (?) a ram."[54] (I. Shi) (*Heji* 32385; Y1376.1)

Few modern readers, I imagine, could claim to extend their own "ancestral tree" back that far in time, listing a group of "Ten ancestors" for a period of over fifteen generations (on the assumption that Da Yi represented the seventh generation after Shang Jia, and Zu Ding the ninth generation after Da Yi).

The Shang ritualists also clustered their ancestors in generic groups referred to by such terms as Da Shi 大示 (Y398.2–99.2), "The Greater Ancestors," and Xiao Shi 小示 (Y399.2), "The Lesser Ancestors." Other terms were also used in the inscriptions, such as Yuan Shi 元示, "The Primary Ancestors," Shang Shi 上示, "The Superior Ancestors," Zhong Shi 中示, "The Middle Ancestors," and so on.[55] The label Da Shi referred to the six direct-line ancestors: Shang Jia, the first predynastic ancestor, and the first five dynastic kings whose temple names were prefixed with Da 大, "Greater," i.e., Da Yi (K1), Da Ding (K2), Da Jia (K3), Da Geng (K5), and Da Wu (K7). They received more cult than other ancestors.[56] The Shang, mainly in the time of Wu Ding, appealed to The Greater Ancestors, for example, in connection with a variety of major topics:

[10A] ☑王疾隹大示

"… His Majesty's illness is not due to The Greater Ancestors." (*Heji* 13697Af; Y398.2)

[10B] 貞：王疾隹大示

Divined: "His Majesty's illness is due to The Greater Ancestors." (I. Bin) (*Heji* 13697Bf; Y398.2)

---

[11] 貞：不隹大示害王

Divined: "It is not The Greater Ancestors who are harming His Majesty." (1. Bin 1) (*Heji* 14833f; Y398.2)

---

[12] 丁酉卜古貞：大示五牛九月

Crack-making on *dingyou* (day 34), Gu divined: "(To) The Greater Ancestors (we offer) five cows." Ninth moon. (I. Bin 2) (*Heji* 10111; Y398.2)

---

[13] 甲申卜：于大示告方來

Crack-making on *jiashen* (day 21): "To The Greater Ancestors (we) make ritual report that the Fang (enemy) are coming." (II. Li 2) (*Tunnan* 2432; Y399.1)

[14A] 庚申貞：王其告于大示

On *gengshen* (day 57) divined: "His Majesty will make ritual report to The Greater Ancestors."

[14B] 庚申貞：王于父丁告

On *gengshen* divined: "His Majesty will, to Father Ding, (i.e., Wu Ding, K21) make ritual report." (IIa. Li 2 B) (*Heji* 32807; Y399.1 [partial])

---

[15] 庚午貞：于大示禱禾雨

On *gengwnu* (day 7) divined: "If to The Greater Ancestors (we) pray for harvest, it will rain." (II. Li 2) (*Heji* 33320; Y399.1)

The title of Xiao Shi 小示 ("The Lesser Ancestors"), by contrast, was probably a collective title for the kings who were not on the main line of dynastic descent; it appears to have included the five predynastic ancestors from Bao Yi (P2) to Shi Gui (P6).[57] They received less cultic attention than the Da Shi and were frequently assigned a coordinate and sometimes subordinate ritual status, always being listed after The Greater Ancestors, Ten Ancestors, or Six Ancestors, and often receiving smaller sacrifices, as in [16]–[19]:

[16] ☒〔又〕伐自上甲大示☒五羌小示羊

"… [in offering] dismembered victims, to The Greater Ancestors, starting from Shang Jia (P1), … five Qiang (captives), to The Lesser Ancestors a sheep. (I–II. Li 2?) (*Tunnan* 1113; Y399.2)

[17A] 己亥貞：劉于大(示)其十牢下示五牢小示三牢

On *jihai* (day 36) divined: "(In offering) the split-open victims ro The Greater (Ancestors), (we) will (use) ten penned cows, to The Lower Ancestors, five penned cows, to The Lesser Ancestors, three penned cows."[58]

[17B] 庚子貞：伐劉于大示五牢下示三牢

On *gengzi* (day 37) divined: "(We) dismember and split open to The Greater Ancestors five penned cows, to The Lower Ancestors three penned cows." (I–II. Li 2) (*Tunnan* 1115; no transcription in Y)

---

[18] 乙未貞：其禱自上甲十示又三牛小示羊

On *yiwei* divined: "In praying to The Thirteen Ancestors, starting from Shang Jia, (we offer) a cow, to The Lesser Ancestors (we offer) a sheep." (I. Li) (*Heji* 34117; Y399.2)

---

[19] 丁未貞：禱禾自上甲六示牛小示盤羊

On *dingwei* divined: "In praying for harvest to The Six Ancestors starting from Shang Jia (P1), (we offer) a cow; (to) The Lesser Ancestors (we) cut up (and offer the blood of) a sheep." (II. Li 2) (*Heji* 33296; Y399.2)

The Shang appealed to such ancestral groups mainly in Periods I and II. Presumably such appeals represented an attempt to invoke the joint favor of their most powerful ascendants, acting in concert. But such appeals were never as common as those addressed to particular ancestors. Such "package deals," in fact, may have involved a theological problem, because they meant, as in the case of [9]–[19] and other inscriptions,[59] that most of the ancestors clustered together in this way would not have been receiving cult on their name-day. By Period V, in fact, such joint hostings, prayers, and offerings were becoming less common;[60] it had become, by then, standard practice for the Shang king to host just one ancestor at a time, as in

[20] 丁巳卜貞：王賓四祖丁骘日亡尤

> Crack-making on *dingsi* (day 54), divined: "His Majesty, performing the hosting ceremony for the *xie* day-ritual to Fourth Ancestor Ding (= Zu Ding, K15), will have no fault." (V. Huang) (*Heji* 35713; Y265.2)

One has the impression, in fact, of a liturgical system whose centrally-important "hosting" ritual was becoming increasingly regularized and routine, with the routineness indicated in part by the minuscule calligraphy that was characteristic of the Period V inscriptions. The ancestral groupings of Period I and II were replaced by a more strictly scheduled and narrowly focused series of individual observances. To benefit from the full potency of an ancestor (or ancestress),[61] the Shang reformers were now offering cult to that single ancestor on his (or her) particular name day. Every ancestor and ancestress had his or her own ritual slot.

The Five-Ritual Cycle

Starting with the reign of Zu Jia (K23) (Period IIb) if not earlier,[62] and also extensively practiced in the reigns of Di Yi (K28) and Di Xin (K29) (Period V), a schedule of five regular rituals, performed in conjunction with the hostings that were offered to the individual patrilineal royal ascendants, formed the core of the Shang system of ancestor worship.[63] The cycle, as reconstructed by a number of scholars, started with the *yi* 翌 (or *yi ri* 翌日, "*yi* day-") rituals offered to the royal ancestors (and ancestresses) in sequence, followed by the *ji* 祭 *zai* 劇 (or 貴), and *xie* 骘 (or *xie ri* 骘日, "*xie* day-") rituals performed as a unit, and concluding with the cycle of the *rong* 彡 (or *rong ri* 彡日, "*rong* day-") rituals performed separately.[64] Once the cycle to a particular ancestor was completed, ending with the *rong*, the cycle to that ancestor started again with the *yi*. And by the end of the dynasty it was the case that the entire cycle of the five rituals took some 360 days to perform, with the *yi* 翌 ritual cycle (beginning with Shang Jia [P1]) starting at the beginning of Week 2, the *ji* 祭 ritual cycle starting at the beginning of Week 13, the *zai* 劇 (or 貴) ritual cycle starting at the beginning of Week 14, the *xie* 骘 ritual cycle starting at the beginning of Week 15, and the *rong* 彡 ritual cycle starting at the beginning of Week 26.[65] In each case, the first ancestor to receive the new ritual was Shang Jia, on *jia*-day of that week, and the subsequent ancestors received their cult according to the schedule, so that Da Yi (K1) and Da Ding (K2) received the *yi*-ritual on the second and fourth days of Week 3, Da Jia (K3) and Bu Bing (K4) received the *yi*-ritual on the first and third days of Week 4, Xiao Jia (K6) received the *yi*-ritual on the first day of Week 5, and so on.[66] Although, given the overlapping of three of the rituals, many of the five rituals might be performed to different ancestors or ancestresses in the course of any one ten-day week, it was apparently the rule that a particular recipient was to receive only one of the five rituals in any one week.[67]

The complexity of the five-ritual cycle can be demonstrated by a considera-tion of how the three linked rituals—reconstructed here, to simplify matters, just for the Jia-named ancestors—were scheduled during the course of one thirteen-week period (Fig. 3), starting with the *ji* 祭 ritual to Shang Jia (P1) at the start of the second week, with the *zai* 飢 (or 壹) ritual to Shang Jia at the start of the third week, and the *xie* 魯 ritual to Shang Jia at the start of the fourth week.[68] Each of the three cycles, in this example, then proceeded down the kinglist, lagging the previous ritual by a week: the *ji* to Shang Jia started Week 2, the *zai* to Shang Jia started Week 3, and the *xie* to Shang Jia started Week 4. It may be noted that, in Week 9, three separate Jia ancestors would have been offered cult on the same *jia*-day: Yang Jia (K17) would have been offered the *ji*-ritual, Qjang Jia (K14) would have been offered the *zai*-ritual, and Jian Jia (K11) would have been offered the *xie*-ritual. It can also be shown that the cycle of rituals offered to the ancestresses lagged behind that of their consorts by one week, so that the kings received cult one week ahead of their consorts.[69] Maintaining such a complex schedule of wor-ship must have required assiduous attention on the part of the ritual specialists at the Shang court, who no doubt derived much of their own status from their ability to guarantee the beneficial and orderly progress of the rituals and sacrifices.

The Shang offered the five regular rituals to both main-line kings and collat-eral kings, but, where the royal consorts or queens were concerned, the Shang intro-duced another important criterion: they only offered the five rituals to the consorts whose husbands had been kings on the main line of descent, as in [3], [4], and

[21A] 辛巳卜貞 ：王賓武丁奭妣辛飢亡尤

Crack-making on *xinsi* (day 18), divined: "His Majesy, performing the hosting cere-mony for the *zai*-ritual to Wu Ding's consort, Ancestress Xin (i.e., the deceased Fu Hao 婦好; see n. 102), will have no fault."

[21B] 癸未卜貞 ：王賓武丁奭妣癸抓飢亡尤

Crack-making on *guiwei* (day 20), divined: "His Majesty, performing the hosting ceremony for the *zai*-ritual to Wu Ding's consort, Ancestress Gui, will have no fault."

[21C] 戊子卜貞 ：王賓武丁奭妣戊飢亡尤

Crack-making on *wuzi* (day 25), divined: "His Majesty, performing the hosting cere-mony for the *zai*-ritual to Wu Ding's consort, Ancestress Wu, will have no fault." (V. Huang) (*Heji* 36268; Y1426.1)

祀典＼祀序＼旬	祭	壹	劦	祀組祀序
第一旬	祭工典			祭工典
第二旬	祭上甲	壹工典		祭上甲壹工典
第三旬	空旬	壹上甲	劦工典	壹上甲劦工典
第四旬	祭大甲	空旬	劦上甲	祭大甲劦上甲
第五旬	祭小甲	壹大甲	空旬	祭小甲壹大甲
第六旬	空旬	壹小甲	劦大甲	壹小甲劦大甲
第七旬	祭戔甲	空旬	劦小甲	祭戔甲劦小甲
第八旬	祭羌甲	壹戔甲	空旬	祭羌甲壹戔甲
第九旬	祭陽甲	壹羌甲	劦戔甲	祭陽甲壹羌甲劦戔甲
第十旬	空旬	壹陽甲	劦羌甲	壹陽甲劦羌甲
第十一旬	祭祖甲	空旬	劦陽甲	祭祖甲劦陽甲
第十二旬		壹祖甲	空旬	壹祖甲
第十三旬			劦祖甲	劦祖甲

Figure 3 The schedule of three linked rituals offered to the Jia-named ancestors during the course of one thirteen-week period, starting with the *ji* 祭 ritual to Shang Jia (P1) at the start of the second week. (Chang Yuzhi, *Shangdai zhouji zhidu*, 168.)

The consorts of the collateral kings were not honored in this way (and hence we generally do not know their consorts' names), so that, by Period V, the living Shang king was worshipping 31 dead kings (including Shang Jia), but only 20 dead consorts.[70] Once again, one sees the application of an impersonal criterion; the personality of the individual consort did not matter. The liturgists only included her—or, more properly, her ancestral persona—in the five-ritual cycle if she had married a king who was the son of a king and if she had become the mother of a king.

Furthermore, it should be noted that, as in the case of the kings, the rituals were offered to the consorts on the *gan*-days of their temple names (thus [21A], about the offering of cult to Ancestress Xin, had been divined on *xinsi*, [21B], about the offering of cult to Ancestress Gui, had been divined on *guiwei*, and so on; see too [3] and [4]). But there was an important difference where the kings were concerned. The Shang kings were generally awarded the auspicious name-days at the start of the week (i.e., *jia, ding, yi, geng*; see the number of Jia, Yi, and Ding kings pp. 162 and 165–66); the temple names awarded to the royal women tended to link them to the inauspicious name-days at the end of the week, such as *xin, ren,* and *gui*. Conceivably, the women had their own (*yin* 陰?) system of lucky and unlucky days, but the fact remains that it differed from, and appears to have been the inverse of, the (*yang* 陽?) system used for the male ascendants.[71] Once again, the liturgists were classifying the dead according to general and impersonal criteria—in this case, gender—not according to individual personality. The men got their own set of lucky days; the women got another set, whose quality, at least as we can judge it from the divination record, was, in the view of the kings and their diviners, far less auspicious.

The cycle of five-rituals that comprised the scheduled ancestral cult emerged in the divinations of the Chu 出-diviner group of King Zu Jia (K23) (Period IIb), and had become standard by Period V. By Period V, and even earlier, in fact, the five-ritual divinations linked to the hosting of the consorts had become so well-ordered that, where consorts were involved, each oracle-bone was usually reserved for charges about only one of the five rituals (as in the case of the plastron fragment [21A-C]), devoted to the *zai*-ritual), even though various ancestral consorts, were specified; divinations about any of the other rituals addressed to consorts were divined on other bones.[72]

The divination bones, in other words, were now ritual specific. And the cult had become so regular that the Shang diviners recorded particular rituals in the postfaces to the divination charges as a way of identifying the particular week. The Period V ritual cycle had become so predictable that it was used to fix the date for other inscriptions, such as the routine divinations, always performed on the *gui*-day, the last day of the week, about "no disasters" in the week to come:

[22A] 癸巳王卜貞 ：旬亡禍。王固曰 ：吉。在十月又二甲午魯日上甲
祭大甲

On *guisi* (day 30), His Majesty made cracks and divined: "In the (next) ten days, there will be no disasters." His Majesty read the cracks and said: "Auspicious." (*Postface:*) In the twelfth moon (divined for the coming week in which on) *jiawu* (day 31) (we were to offer) the *xie* day-ritual to Shang Jia (P1) and the *ji*-ritual to Da Jia (K3).

Similarly,

[22B] 癸卯王卜貞 ：旬亡禍。王固曰 ：吉。在十月又二甲辰飙大
甲祭小甲

On *guimao* (day 40), His Majesty made cracks and divined: "In the (next) ten days, there will be no disasters." His Majesty read the cracks and said: "Auspicious." (*Postface:*) In the twelfth moon (divined for the coming week in which on) *jiachen* (day 41) (we were to offer) the *zai*-ritual to Da Jia (K3) and the *ji*-ritual to Xiao Jia (K6).[73] (V) (*Heji* 35530; Y1386.2)

The offering of the cult, on schedule, had become so routine that it could be used in this way to locate and disambiguate each week in ritual time. And one may note too that, particularly by the end of the dynasty, the days were getting crowded. Each ancestor received cult on the day of his temple name, but in this case, there were two Jia ancestors scheduled to receive cult on the same *jia*-day: Shang Jia and Da Jia on *jiawu* ([22A]) in Week 4, Da Jia and Xiao Jia on *jiachen* ([22B]) in Week 5.

The attention that the Late Shang paid to the temple-name requirements of the ritual schedule is also revealed by their performance of anticipatory cult on the evening prior to an ancestor's cult day. Thus:

[23] 丙辰卜貞：王賓中丁彡夕亡尤

Crack-making on *bingchen* (day 53), divined: "His Majesty, performing the hosting ceremony for the *rong*-eve-ritual to Zhong Ding (K9), will have no fault." (V. Huang) (*Heji* 35630; Y1289.1)

———————

[24] 己巳卜貞：王賓祖庚彡夕亡尤

Crack-making on *jisi* (day 6), divined: "His Majesty, performing the hosting ceremony for the *rong*-eve-ritual to Ancestor Geng (K22), will have no fault." (V. Huang) (*Heji* 35878; Y1289.2)

The inscriptions that employed the *xi* 夕, "eve" or "evening," in this way were all preparatory, divined on the eve of the day in which the "day" ritual was to be performed. Thus the *rong*-eve-ritual of [23] was divined on *bingchen* (day 53), the night before the *rong*-day-ritual to Zong Ding was to be performed on *dingsi* (day 54); the *rong*-eve-ritual of [24] was divined on *jisi* (day 6), the night before the *rong*-day-ritual to Ancestor Geng was to be performed on *gengwu* (day 7).[74] The scheduled rituals cast a temporal shadow before them, requiring divinatory and ritual attention even before the day of the ritual itself had dawned.

This understanding of the day-related character of the temple names is further supported by a series of Di Yi-Di Xin oracle-bone inscriptions that specifically refer to cult being offered on the day of the ancestor concerned, as in:

[25] 丙戌卜貞：文武丁宗□其牢

Crack-making on *bingxu* (day 23), divined: "On the day of the Wen Wu (Ding) ancestor (presumably *dinghai*, day 24), (we) will offer a penned cow."[75] (V. Huang) (*Heji* 36154; Y1432.1)

The graph for *ri* 日, "day," however, was generally omitted, not only in the bronze inscriptions (see below), but also in the bone inscriptions, as in

[26] 丙戌卜貞：文武宗其牢

Crack-making on *bingxu* (day 23), divined: "(On the day of the) Wen Wu (Ding) ancestor (presumably *dinghai*, day 24), we will offer a penned cow." (V) (*Heji* 36156; Y1432.1)

A number of bronze inscriptions that employed the formula, "ancestral term + day + *gan*," also associate an ancestor or ancestress with a particular day of cult. The formula was in fairly common use in Late Shang and early Western Zhou.[76]

One can cite as an example the Neng Tao zun 能匋尊, a Late Shang or early Western Zhou vessel:

[27] 能匋用作文父日乙寶尊 𢀛

Neng Tao thus made this honored *zun* vessel for his 'deceased' father whose (cult) day is *yi*. Insignia.[77]

Such formulas were also used for women in the Late Shang-early Zhou period. On the various Fu Bin (?) 婦闌, "Lady Bin," vessels—*ding* 鼎, *xian* 甗, *jia* 斝, *guang* 觥, *jue* 爵, and *yu* 盂—for example, which are thought to be of Late Shang date, one finds, as on the *Fu Bin* (?) *You* 婦闌盂:

[28] 婦闌作文姑日癸障彝 𢀛

Fu Bin (?) made this honored vessel for her 'deceased' aunt whose day is *gui*. Insignia.[78]

It may be noted, incidentally, in light of the previous discussion (p. 172), that the aunt's day was *gui*, the last day of the Shang week; only one of the Shang predynastic ancestors, Shi Gui (P6) had been given the temple name of *gui*, and none of the dynastic kings had. *Gui*-days were generally reserved for the temple names of royal consorts.[79]

Such inscriptions, in short, if we assume continuity of practice between Late Shang and early Western Zhou (but Shang-style) ancestor dedications, further demonstrate how the *gan* designations served to link ancestors and ancestresses to particular days of cult, with particular ritual bronzes being cast specifically for a *gan*-named ancestor and for use on a particular *gan*-day.

It would be anachronistic to refer to the Shang liturgists as clock watchers, but the evidence shows they were certainly calendar, day, and sun watchers, whose temporal and jurisdictional concerns were sanctified by profound religious assumptions.[80] The ritual cycle, as they located the cult to fifty-plus impersonalized royal ancestors and ancestresses in their appropriate time slots, demanded informed attention. The cycle, with its claims to ritual efficacy, presumably represented esoteric knowledge that served to validate the role of the king, as chief sacrificer, and his ritual experts.

Impersonalization of the Dead

I have suggested at several points the important role that impersonalization of the dead played in Shang ancestor worship. This is indicated by the generic temple names, like Jia, Yi, and Ding, that were assigned to the royal dead, and by the "ranking" names like "Third Ancestor Ding" and "Fourth Ancestor Ding." It is indicated by the greater sacrificial wealth offered to the Da Shi, "Greater Ancestors." It is indicated by the occasional Shang willingness to treat ancestors as a group and by the highly formalized nature of the five-ritual cycle in which all the ancestors (and ancestresses too, if they qualified as the consorts of main-line kings) were offered an identical sequence of rituals according to a rigid schedule. It is indicated by the assigning of the temple-names to lucky days, for the ancestors, and to unluckier days—at least by the ancestors' standards—for the ancestresses. By Period V, there was nothing ad hoc or unpredictable about the cult. It was highly structured. And there was no individuation. There is no indication in the divination inscriptions that the liturgists credited the ancestors with any personal preference for one kind of ritual, one kind of sacrifice, one kind of victim, over another.[81] When the ancestors' day-name arrived, he (or she) received the scheduled *yi*-ritual; and he or she was then put aside until the next of his or her rituals—the *ji, zai, xie,* or *rong*—was due on the appropriate name day. The Shang were, one might say, "equal opportunity" worshippers. Once a dead king or consort met the criteria, they became an ancestor or ancestress, were given their temple name, and were treated like all the other ancestors or ancestresses in the five-ritual cult cycle. It was the good order represented by the ancestors that was paramount, not their individual personalities.

The Shang tendency to impersonalize their ancestors can also be seen in the ritual distinction that I discern in the cultic treatment that distinguished fathers from grandfathers and mothers from grandmothers. Generally speaking, dead fathers and mothers, the parents of the reigning king, were not offered cult in the system of the five rituals. It was only when two generations separated the king and his ascendants that, now known as "grandfather/Ancestor" (Zu 祖) and "grandmother/Ancestress" (Bi 妣), they were given their place in the cycle.[82] Those whom the Shang admitted to the roster of the ancestors and ancestresses, in short, were generally those whom the king would have known, if at all, only as his parents' parents. To become an ancestor required a degree of generational and personal distance. Impersonalization involved the passage of time. The ancestors of Shang did not become ancestors the moment they died; they had to grow into, be promoted to, the status.

The tendency to categorize the Shang royal dead generically is also seen in the way certain dead were assigned jurisdictions on the basis of their generational, gender, and dynastic status. The role and the influence of the royal ancestors were, in fact, circumscribed. Unlike Di and the Nature Powers at the top of the Pantheon, for example, whose impact affected the entire dynastic community, the ancestors' attention was focused more squarely on the king himself (p. 158 above). And there were evidently generational hierarchies that existed among the ancestors themselves; it was mostly, for example, the ancestors from Zu Yi (K12) on down who, during the reign of Wu Ding, were thought to be capable of harming the king. The role and the influence of the ancestresses, too, were circumscribed. They were offered, with rare exceptions, no prayers for rain and harvest; prayers for rain and harvest were generally only directed to the Predynastic Ancestors or Nature Powers or to large groups of ancestors (as in [9] or *Tunnan* 2359 [Y531.2]).[83] The ancestresses' jurisdiction was not agricultural fruitfulness but human reproduction. It was to them, and not to the ancestors, that the king offered his prayers for the progeny (*sheng* 生) whose good fortune was vital to the success of the dynasty.[84] The royal women, like the royal men, in short, had their jurisdictions; both groups were treated generically, stereotypically.

A similar kind of sorting can be seen in the nature of the ritual reports (*gao* 告) (that the Shang king made to the dead. He frequently made reports to his ancestors about a large number of topics—such as the rituals he offered, locusts, floods, enemy attacks, and illness—but he rarely offered such reports to an ancestress; evidently the authority of the ancestresses did not extend to such matters.[85] No doubt, such distinctions reflected, as they reinforced, the social and cultural arrangments among the living, but, once again, one's sex and status while alive, rather than one's personality, determined one's treatment after death. The Shang made ancestors of their dead by "compartmentalizing" them. And such treatment presumably had its emotional benefits: both serving to distance the living from the dead but also providing a structure for the working out of filial and ancestral obligations in culturally accepted and regularly ordered ways.

It may not be uninstructive to compare the Shang treatment of the dead with the treatment of the dead in medieval Europe:

> Christian attitudes toward the dead, as the medieval church intended to define and impose these altitudes, were entirely contained within the notion of the *memoria*, the "remembrance of the dead." This was a liturgical remembrance, reinforced by inscribing the names of those dead who were worthy of being commemorated into *libri memoriales*, necrologies, and the obituaries of monasteries and convents. The liturgical Memento was recited specifically on the occasion of the masses said for the salvation of the dead person, especially on the anniversary of the death. But this word "remembrance" is in fact misleading, for the goal of the *memoria* was to help the living separate from the dead, to shorten the latter's stay in purgatorial punishment (or in purgatory), and finally, to enable the living to forget the deceased. The rhythm of masses and prayers was therefore increasingly relaxed, and they lasted a limited amount of time: three days, seven days, a month, or a year, rarely longer than that. The inscription of a name in the *liber memorialis* did not promise that the deceased would be glorified forever—this was reserved for saints and kings—but that the deceased would be rapidly included in the anonymity of past generations.[86]

The Shang had no fear of purgatory, and their royal ancestors were evidently in the position of the Christian saints and kings. Nevertheless, some of the Shang impulses may been similar. It is instructive to consider, in particular, that

> the *memoria*, as a form of collective memory, was a social technique of forgetting. Its function was to "cool off" the memory under the guise of maintaining it, to sooth the painful memory of the deceased until the memory became indistinct. A classifying technique, the *memoria* put the dead in their rightful place so that the living, if they should happen to recall the names of the dead, could do so without fear or emotion.[87]

The Shang royal dead, like Christian saints, had power that could be invoked. And they were not remembered just "for three days, seven days, a month, or a year," but for the duration of the dynasty. Within both cultures there was evidently a strong impulse to classify, impersonalize, and order the dead, but the ways in which that was done differed characteristically and significantly.

The Impact of Ritual

Mary Douglas has noted that the "framing and boxing" involved in ritual "limit experience, shut in desired themes or shut out intruding ones." Ritual, it has also been said, reorganizes experience, providing

> a kind of learning, through which the world is simplified for the individual: the complex world of experience is transformed [through ritual] into an orderly world of symbols. At the same time, there is also a transformation of the individual, who acquires new understandings, or ... "new cognitive structures," and a new transformed identity.[88]

The liturgy of Shang ancestor worship would have had such an impact, encouraging the internalization of the theological assumptions described above and validating new cognitive structures and a particular sense of Shang identity.

With regard to the cultural impact of such a religious system, the complexity of the five ritual cycle (see Fig. 3), to say nothing of the practices of Shang divination, would presumably have required a considerable degree of training.[89] The overlapping schedules of the ancestors, ancestresses, and their sequential sacrifices would have had to be mastered by the liturgists and at least understood by the elites who attended the king's court. The engravers, if not the diviners, would have had to learn how to write so that they were at least functionally literate where the ancestral cult was concerned. Certain elites, in other words, were being trained in the assumptions and skills that underlay the structure of Shang ancestor worship, and were being rewarded, with occupation and status, for what they had learned and what they performed.

The latent consequences of the discipline and impersonalization that the cycle required would have been considerable. Roy A. Rappaport, who used "the term 'liturgical order' to refer not only to individual rituals, but to the more or less invariant sequences of rituals that make up cycles and other series as well," argued that "The primary function or metafunction of liturgical performances is not to control behavior directly, but father to establish conventional understandings, rules and norms in accordance with which everyday behaviour is *supposed* to proceed." And he observed "that those whose activities are organized by common liturgical orders thereby constitute social entities of some sort. Indeed, coordination of ritual performances may actually define discrete social groups."[90] I believe that the impact of the Late Shang liturgy should be understood in these terms. It was one of the elements of Shang culture that defined, as it created, what it meant to be Shang.

The Roles of Zu Jia 祖甲 and Wu Ding 武丁

It may be possible to situate the cultural reforms I have been describing in time, and even to attribute them to one or more historical actors, particularly the 23rd king, Zu Jia, and his subordinates. Under the 21st king, Wu Ding (d. ca. 1189 B.C.),[91] the Shang had engaged in a series of major wars against the Tufang

土方 and Gongfang 舌方 to their northwest. They had been involved in frequent struggles with the Qiangfang 羌方, and had obtained a series of military victories in Shanxi, west of the Taihang 太行 mountain range.[92] Under his son, the next king, Zu Geng 祖庚 (K22), the Shang armies proved less successful in their battles with the Shaofang 召方 (Y958.1–2) and Gongfang (Y269.2–72.2), and the Shang's western alliances began to crumble. And by the end of the dynasty, the divination record represents the king as the major military leader, still powerful but more isolated than his predecessors had been.[93] The Shang had been able to stabilize the situation closer to home, but the Shang sphere of influence had grown considerably smaller.

One has the sense—and, given the present state of our knowledge, both archaeological and epigraphical, it can only be a sense—that the 23rd king, Zu Jia, in particular, would have found it necessary to, as we would put it today, improve efficiency and modernize his administration, or, as I suspect he would have put it, he would have found it necessary to bring better order to his attempts to invoke the power of his ancestors and encourage the consistent assent and support of the members of the royal lineage.[94] For it is under Zu Jia (ca. 1177–1158 B.C.) that the ritual system becomes regularized.[95] The king and his liturgists, as we have seen, now tied the ancestors rigidly to their day-names; the liturgists regularized the five-ritual cycle of sacrifices, so that each ancestor and ancestress, as it were, and each celebrant, knew his and her place. There was, accordingly, no more wasting time in determining the right day on which sacrifices were to be offered; there was less room for personal idiosyncracy, either on the part of the living or the dead.[96] Martin Kern, in writing of the role of the impersonator (*shi* 尸) in Zhou rituals, has proposed that

> This mediated communication structure between the clan and the spirits is itself a ritual device of control: the living and the dead remain carefully separated from each other. For the living, ritual form thus creates distance and probably also a certain security in dealing with the spirits.[97]

The disciplines of Zu Jia's ritual reform would have given the Shang increasing control over their negotiations with their ancestors. And for the elites, these religious constructions involved the definition or redefinition of "humanity" in the ways I have been suggesting. The structures and values of Shang ancestor worship no doubt imitated, as they helped to shape and render meaningful, the social experiences of contemporary Shang life.[98] And the fact that, in the Zhou, as in the Shang,

> There was no provision in Chinese ritual language for naming a living king; until he received a posthumous title, the word for him was the word for all kings, and he was indistinguishable, at least on the level of language and ideals, from that generalized role,[99]

is a further indication of the synergy that existed between the naming of the high-status living and the high-status dead.

Not all the credit, however, should go to Zu Jia. It can be shown, convincingly I believe, that the first Shang king to be laid to rest in the royal cemetery at Xibeigang 西北岡 was Wu Ding (K21), Zu Jia's father, who had been buried in M1001.[100] This conclusion by itself might permit us to assume that it was in the generation of his sons, Zu Geng and Zu Jia, that the ritual shift occurred, for it was they who would have buried their royal father there. However, it can also be argued that two of the large tombs at Xibeigang, the so-called "great tomb at Wuguan" (武官大墓) and the as yet unexcavated tomb to its southwest from which the *Simu Wu ding* 司母戊鼎 was taken, were slightly earlier than M1001 in date. They, it is thought, would have been the tombs of Wu Ding's consorts, Bi Gui 妣癸 and Bi Wu 妣戊, both buried at Xibeigang either late in the reign of Wu Ding or slightly after his death.[101] And it can also be shown, from the sequence and number of the divinations about ritual offerings recorded in the oracle-bone inscriptions of Period II, that, of Wu Ding's three consorts, it was Mu Xin 母辛, "Mother Xin"—thought to be the temple name of Fu Hao 婦好—who had died first.[102] So we have a situation in which Wu Ding buried Fu Hao, the first of his consorts to die, in a tomb, M5, close to the temple-palace residential complex at Xiaotun 小屯 where he dwelt; but also a situation in which Wu Ding, or his sons, buried his other two consorts, and also selected the site of his own burial, in the new royal cemetery across the Huan 洹 River. This segregation of the dead may, I think, be seen as one more example of the way in which the dead were being impersonalized. Wu Ding wanted to have Fu Hao buried close at hand; he himself and his other consorts were buried at a distance. To the distance in time that it required to become an ancestor was now added distance in space.[103] And it is worth remarking that crossing the Huan River, both to bury the royal dead and to offer cult at the grave site, would have represented something of a challenge, especially during the summer rains.

I would conclude, in short, that the initial impulses towards formalization of Shang ancestor worship were present under Wu Ding (K21), who was, in fact, occasionally recording some of the five rituals of the five-ritual cycle (n. 62 above), as in,

[29] [乙]亥彡大乙

On [*yi*]*hai* (day 12) (we) performed the *rong* ritual to Da Yi (K1). (I. Bin) (*Heji* 1262; Y1286.1)

and was even more occasionally divining them as in:

[30] 辛卯卜亘貞：彡酚于上甲亡害九月

Crack-making on *xinmao* (day 28), Xuan divined: "In performing the *you*-cutting sacrifice for the *rong* ritual to Shang Jia (P1), there will be no harm." (*Postface*:) Ninth moon.[104] (I. Bin) (*Heji* 1184; Y1286.1)

It is worth noting that while the Period I offering of the *rong* ritual to Da Yi was recorded as having taken place on an *yi*-day ([29]), the divination about offering the *rong* ritual to Shang Jia had not been divined on or about a *jia*-day ([30]). The routine, scheduled divination of these initiatives would only have come to fruition under Wu Ding's son, Zu Jia. Such a model makes good historical sense, for it sees the Zu Jia reforms as an intensification of trends already under way, and stimulated by the powerful figure of Wu Ding himself, rather than as an invention *de novo* by his son.

Given the historical importance I wish to assign to the ruler whose temple name was Zu Jia, "Ancestor Jia," it will not be inappropriate to look at him in person, if we can. Of course, the very idea of "in person" runs counter to the thrust of my analysis. Zu Jia's very success at impersonalizing the ancestors now makes it hard to de-impersonalize the image of him that appears in the bone inscriptions. I would note, first of all, that his own temple name was generic. That is, he would of course have first been called Fu Jia 父甲, "Father Jia," in the generation of his sons—a title that would have earlier been applied, as we have seen, to Shang Jia, Da Jia, Xiao Jia, Jian Jia, and Yang Jia, by their sons. And, to pursue the theme of generic labeling, it should be noted that when, in Period IV, he was given the title of Zu Jia, Ancestor Jia, he was taking over a title that earlier, in Period II, he himself had used to refer to Yang Jia (K17).[105] Zu Jia was also to be classified as one of the "San Zu" (三祖), "The Three Ancestors," namely the three brothers, sons of Wu Ding: Zu Ji 祖己 (who died before he could assume the kingship; see n. 114), Zu Geng (K22), and himself.[106]

Zhou texts give a disappointingly stereotyped view of Zu Jia.[107] According to the "Wuyi 無逸" chapter of the *Shangshu* 尚書, for example,

> At the start, when he came to the high position, then he knew the sufferings of the small people. He could give protection and kindness to the common people, and he dared not insult widowers and widows. Thus Zu Jia's enjoyment of the realm lasted for 33 years.[108]

The passage, however, is problematic, both in terms of its meaning,[109] and in terms of the identity of the Zu Jia referred to.[110] Various traditions about Zu Jia's campaigns and administration were recorded in the *Jinben Zhushu jinian* 今本竹書紀年, which also records, as does the *Guben* 古本 *Zhushu jinian*, that his name was Dai 戴,[111] but the historicity of these accounts is problematic. The personalizing detail that he might have been named Dai appears, as we would expect, nowhere in the oracle-bone inscriptions.

The traditional texts, in fact, do not agree in their assessment of Zu Jia's reign. The "Wuyi," as we have seen, presents him as a charitable sovereign who ruled for thirty-three years. Sima Qian's *Shiji* 史記, "Yin benji 殷本紀," however, following a tradition found in the *Guoyu*, a text compiled about the 4th century B.C., gives him short shrift: "Emperor Jia was licentious and disorderly and Yin again declined" (帝甲淫亂殷復衰); and that is all Sima Qian has to say.[112] No traditional text, in fact, refers to any ritual reforms conducted under Zu Jia. Since the oracle-bone inscriptions clearly indicate that such reforms were instituted, the silence of the later texts reminds us of how little their compilers knew of Shang history. The accusation of being "licentious and disorderly" (*yinluan* 淫亂) seems particularly inappropriate. Zu Jia's rituals were anything but disordered; and, unlike his father, who had three,

Zu Jia is recorded in the bone inscriptions as having had only one consort, Bi Wu 妣戊, "Ancestress Wu." The accusation of disorder may, of course, have represented a propaganda charge, either by the predynastic Zhou who might have seen Zu Jia's reforms as a threat, or by discontented elements within the Late Shang sphere of influence, who resented Zu Jia's "new fangled" ways that would in part have validated and strengthened the main-line of descent at the expense of the collaterals. Or one might even speculate that the rigor of Zu Jia's ritual activities represented a form of compensation for the license of his other activities. But the discrepancy between the oracle-bone evidence and the traditional accounts is striking.

The situation is no better in the case of Wu Ding. Late texts, such as the *Jinben Zhushu jinian* and the *Da Dai Liji* 大戴禮記, indicate that he may have engaged in ritual reforms, but texts, like tlie *Shangshu* or *Shiji*, mostly provide a series of standard, moralizing anecdotes.[113] Only the "Gao Zong rong ri 高宗肜日" chapter of the *Shangshu* implies that Zu Ji 祖己 (a figure who does appear in the oracle-bone inscriptions)[114] exhorted Wu Ding "典祀無豐于暱." Legge, in a loose translation that accords well with the theme of this article, offers "attend to the sacrifices (to all your ancestors), and be not so excessive in those to your father."[115] Karlgren, however, gives, "In the standard sacrifices (sc. to the royal spirits), do not perform rites in familiarity,"[116] a reading that better accords with the usual meanings of *ni* 暱. A translation of "In the rituals that are registered (i.e., the five-ritual cycle?), do not over-indulge in being close (to your ancestors)" might be possible. But the evidence is too uncertain in both its meaning and its historicity for any useful conclusions to be drawn from it.

The Ancestors and Their Legacy

Conceiving the Ancestors

It would appear that

> an inverse relationship exists between the degree to which an ancestor cult is articulated and the degree of attention paid to the actual, personal circumstances of the soul in the afterlife. In this view, cultures, like that of early Greece, that provide imaginative depictions of the afterworld, and also of this one, may not need a well-structured ancestral cult. Indeed, they may well depict post-mortem existence in detail precisely because the "ancestors" are missing. The presence of an impersonalized ancestral cult in early China, by contrast, would help explain the classical texts' general lack of interest in the particulars of death and the afterlife.... In this view, early Chinese elites would have felt less need for the precision of event and personality and for the existential details that are such notable features of the art and mythology of early Greece precisely because they did not primarily conceive of their ancestors, and thus of the human personality, in these ways.[117]

In the ideology of the early Chinese elites, the depersonalized dead were the ordered dead. There was no need to tell their individual stories, for the "quirkyness" of the individual personalities would, precisely, have threatened the good, impersonal order that was desired. It is certainly possible that all levels of Shang society may also have subscribed to far more lively, disordered, and dramatic visions of gods, spirits, and the afterlife, as we know to have been true of later Chinese culture. The point is, however, that the elites of Shang and Zhou did not sanctify such subversive alternatives in the texts that they honored and transmitted.

In considering the degree to which the Shang impersonalized their ancestors, and considering too the legacy of Shang custom, it may also be helpful to consider the treatment of the ancestors in later texts. The "Pan Geng 盤庚" chapter (probably written during the Western Zhou) of the *Shangshu* provides, for example, a clear instance of a Shang ruler who was conceived as using his ancestors as authority figures to legitimate his decision, which was evidently unpopular with his people, to remove the capital to Yin. Not only was Pan Geng represented as appealing to the wise and benevolent government of the former kings when they had been alive, but he spoke of the continuing relationship—entirely jural and impersonal—among the dead ascendants. Speaking to his recalcitrant people, he said:

> Now when I offer the great sacrifices to the former kings (*xian wang* 先王), your ancestors (*er zu* 爾祖) are present to share in them. (pt. 1, para. 14)

> … If you, the myriads of the people, do not attend to [my commands] … the former rulers (*xian hou* 先后) will send down on you great punishment for your crime, and say, 'Why do you not agree with out young descendant, …?' When they punish you from above, you will have no way of escape…. Our former rulers will restrain your ancestors and fathers (*zufu* 祖父), (so that) your ancestors and fathers will reject you, and not save you from death…. Your ancestors and fathers urgently report (*gao* 告) to my High Rulers (*gao hou* 高后), saying, 'Execute great punishments on our descendants.' (pt. 2, paras. 11–14)[118]

Thus was the Shang king thought to have assigned functions to the dead, both royal and non-royal, so that they would both approve his demands and impose sanctions on those who would oppose him. Here the dead have virtually become coercive police officers in the service of the living king. Pan Geng does not name or otherwise identify, except by their status, a single one of the former rulers or ascendants. Although these dead have jural power, they have no individual personality. Nor, it may be noted, does Pan Geng; we know nothing of his physical appearance or personal idiosyncracies. He too is presented entirely as a jural figure, issuing commands.

The *Huainanzi* 淮南子, compiled in the 2nd century B.C., to cite another example, notes that

逌股子不思其父，無貌於心也。不夢見像，無形於目也

> A son born after his father's death will not long for his father, because there is no image (of the father) in his mind. He will not see his image in his dreams, because the external shape is not in his (mind's) eye.[119]

The point seems obvious enough; it would be hard to long for, or to resurrect the image of, a father that you had not known. But no such experiential hindrance prevented the Shang from dreaming of the influence of ancestors who might have lived as many as eight generations back, ancestors whom they could never have known face to face,[120] as in the case of:

[31A] 貞 ：王夢隹大甲

"His Majesty's dream was due to Da Jia (K3)."

[31B] 貞 ：工夢不隹大甲

"His Majesty's dream was not due to Da Jia." (I. Bin) (*Heji* 14199 = *Bingbian* 212. 5–6; Y1186.1)

The Shang found no difficulty in worshipping ancestors as many as twenty-one generations back (in the case of Shang Jia, when offered cult in Period V). Clearly, there was no need to revivify ancestral features when worshipping them, just as there was no evident need to create images of the Shang kings, living or dead. Indeed, as we have seen (p. 175 above), the dead fathers (and mothers), such as those to whom the *Huainanzi* passage referred, were not generally offered cult in the Shang five-ritual system, which was directed to the grandparents and beyond; Shang ancestor worship did not emphasize the close parent-child bond.

Just as Shang ancestor worship emphasized order and structure, rather than naturalistic, idiosyncratic, personalizing detail, so too were Shang bronzes decorated with geometric, abstract, non-naturalistic, highly patterned animal mask motifs, motifs that may have had their origins in the designs found on the jade *cong* 琮 tubes and jade axes of the Neolithic cultures to the southeast.[121] We have no way of knowing what Zu Jia looked like, but it is probable that the generations of his grandchildren and later had no naturalistic images of him to consult either.[122] In other cultures, naturalistic art may have developed to meet the needs of the ancestral cult,[123] but that was evidently not true for the ancestors of the Late Shang. The Shang did not individualize their ancestors, either theologically or artistically. And their preference for the non-figurative would have had significant cultural consequences. The choice that the Chinese of Zhou and later times made, for example, to not erect life-size, naturalistic—if not individualistic—representations of the dead at the grave site or in sanctuaries, analogous to the tens of thousands of *kouroi* erected in the Greek world of the seventh century B.C.,[124] "with their inscrutable 'Archaic smile'" and with the pubic hair added in paint,[125] or to not decorate their coins with human heads or other representations of their rulers, was presumably prompted and reinforced by the non-individual, non-representational cultural dispositions of earlier times. Early Chinese representations of the dead, with their emphasis on impersonal, non-naturalistic order and hierarchy, were strikingly different.

The conceptualization of the ancestors was also addressed in the classical ritual texts. According to the *Liji*, the purpose of the ancestral shrine was, in the words of K.E. Brashier, twofold: "to give order to one's ascendants near and far;"

and, secondly, "to foster remembrance, to 'return to the origin and never forget the progenitor.'"[126] For I am not denying that the Shang remembered their dead, but I am urging that they constructed their rituals so as to shape the memory and the persona of the dead in particular ways. The *Liji*, "Tan Gong-檀弓" chapter, notes, in fact, that

銘明旌也。以死者為不可別已。故以其旗識之。愛之斯錄之矣。
敬之斯盡其道焉耳

> The name and prename of the deceased are written on the funerary banner. Because the deceased can no longer be distinguished, his son uses this banner to commemorate him. Because he loves him, he inscribes his name and prename; because he respects him he renders him all possible honor.[127]

We are dealing here with written names, not with representational images characterized by individualizing features.

The use of non-descriptive, non-representational ancestral tablets, in fact, as opposed to effigies or images of the dead, was probably as old as the Shang dynasty. A small number of stone and jade "plumb-bob" shapes, 7 cm long, excavated in 1991 from M3, a looted burial at Hougang 後岡 (1.5 km to the southeast of the cult center at Xiaotun), with temple-names, such as Zu Jia 祖甲 and Fu Xin 父辛, written on them in red, are thought to have been Shang ancestral tablets.[128] It was the non-representational tablet, standard in form and inscribed with the temple name, that was taken to stand for the ancestor (as in "The Ten Ancestors" of [9]; see n. 53). The cultural dispositions for these kinds of religious choices have been strong. An ethnographer who worked early in the twentieth century, for example, recorded that, "In Sichuan there are ceremonies by which the soul is enticed into the ancestral tablet, which becomes its dwelling place. Afterward the ancestral tablet is regarded as the ancestor himself, and is treated as such."[129]

According, once again, to the *Liji*,

稱情而立文。因以飾群。別親疏貴賤之節。

> The different rules for the mourning rites were established in harmony with [men's] feelings. By means of them the differences in social relations are set forth, and the distinctions shown of kindred as nearer or more distant, and of ranks as more noble or less.[130]

The three years' mourning of Late Zhou, in other words, was designed to exemplify and validate the distinctions of political and social status; it was not primarily designed to revivify the memory of the deceased.[131] I cite these various later passages to indicate that the Zhou and Han Chinese elites would have found the kind of impersonalization I have described for Shang ancestor worship congenial to their understanding of how the dead should be treated. Confucius's advice, 務民之義，敬鬼神而遠之，可謂知矣，"Devote yourself to what is proper for people, respect the ghosts and spirits, but keep them at a distance; this can be called wisdom" (*Lunyu* 論語 6.20), may have derived in part from the same source.

My discussion in no sense implies that early Chinese elites did not find the death of loved ones a matter of anguish and disorder. But the point is that the ideological response, the enduring ritual constructions, that these elites developed to deal with such such crises generally sought to downplay the personal and emotional in favor of the impersonal and well-ordered. As Zi You 子游 made explicit in the "Tan gong 檀弓" chapter of the *Liji*,

禮有微惜者,有以故興物者。有真情而徑行者戎狄之道也。禮道則不然。

> In the rituals there are some intended to lessen the (display) of feeling, and there are others which purposely introduce things (to excite it). To give direct vent to the feeling and act it out as by a short cut is the way of the Rong and Di. The way of the rituals is not like this.[132]

And the *Liji* does address the emotional and more personal side of ancestor worship. The "Ji yi 祭義" chapter, for example, argues that:

是故先王之孝也。色不忘乎目。心志嗜欲不忘乎心。致愛則存。致愨則著

> The filial piety taught by the ancient kings required that the eyes of the son should not forget the looks (of his parents), nor his ears their voices; and that he should retain the memory of their aims, likings, and wishes. In the fullness of his love, they lived again; in the fullness of his reverence, they stood out before him.[133]

There is certainly a strong personal note in this that seems to run counter to the view of ancestors as juridical abstractions. It is possible to regard such passages as an attempt to repersonalize and revitalize a ritual that, by Eastern Zhou and Han times, had perhaps become too impersonal, too pro forma. Consider for example a passage in the "Wen sang 問喪" chapter of the *Liji* about how the mourning son should act right after the death of his father—

惻怛之心痛疾之意,傷腎乾肝焦肺,水漿不入口,三日不舉火

> In the bitterness of his [the mourner's] grief, and the distress of his thoughts, his kidneys were injured, his liver dried up, and his lungs scorched, while water or other liquid did not enter his mouth, and for three days fire was not kindled (to cook anything for him).[134]

The intensity of the practice being prescribed raises the possibility of a contemporary situation in which mourners had not been thought to be showing suitable emotional reactions. More to the point, however, I would note that these passages refer only to the worship and commemoration of one's parents.[135] The practical inability, as the *Huainanzi* had noted (p. 183 above), of calling to mind someone whom the mourner had never known would evidently have prevented any further personalization of the more senior dead.

Already in the Shang, the more senior ancestors had been likely to take a less personal interest in the king than the more recently dead, the generation of the "fathers," would do:

> The increased power of the senior generations was exercised in increasingly impersonal ways; that is, recently dead ancestors might plague living individuals

(who would perhaps have known them when they were alive), but the dead of more distant generations affected the state as a whole by influencing harvests, droughts, and enemy invasions.[136]

If, for example, one looks at the charges that sought to identify the Power responsible for various "harms" (*hai* 害; oracle-bone 𡆥) inflicted on the Shang king himself, no ancestor more senior than Zu Yi (K12), four generations prior to Wu Ding, was ever identified as a possible source of harm (based on the inscription sample at Y683.1–2); the more senior ancestors evidently had more important, less personal matters with which to concern themselves. It was the recently dead Fathers (Fu 父), Mothers (Mu 母), Ancestresses (Bi 妣), and Brothers (Xiong 兄), who were primarily thought responsible for harming the king (Y684.1–2.) and, as we have seen (p. 160). were thought to be suitable recipients of the "pledge" ritual with its implied interest in negotiation.[137] And it was not until the generation of the grandfathers and grandmothers that the Shang incorporated their dead into the regular ancestral cult, treating them as personas rather than as persons.

When we consider the difficulty involved in conceiving distant ancestors, one of the most striking features of Shang ancestral cult is, in fact, its generational depth. By the time of Di Yi and Di Xin, the Shang were still performing cult on a regular basis to ancestors from Shang Jia on down, up to twenty-one claimed generations distant. If we estimate that a generation, in recent historical time in the West, lasts some forty years, that means that modern readers, were we in the position of the late Shang kings, would, five times a year, have been worshiping a first ancestor who had died in the 12th century A.D., shortly after the Norman Conquest in the West or at the time of the Southern Song in China. Shang generations, even the generations of the Shang kings, may well have been shorter,[138] but the remarkable generational depth claimed for the Shang ancestors on the main-line of descent was presumably a prerogative of royalty. Whatever the time interval, real or claimed, involved, the more ancient ancestors must surely have been regarded as juridical, impersonalized stereotypes, not as personalities. They were conceived, one might say, as "impersonalities."

Later elites, in fact, continued to think in terms of impersonalization, and also in terms—startling to those who accept the Western notion of an eternal soul— of eventual extinction. By Han times, for example, the *Chunqiu fanlu* 春秋繁露, attributed to Dong Zhongshu 董仲舒 of the second century B.C., though its authenticity is in some dispute, "depicts the fading of the ruler's soul as an elaborate series of promotions" in which "the soul not only diminishes by degrees, it also loses its individuality," becoming impersonalized, "as it joins larger and larger groups."[139] Once again, the dead were being ordered and arranged in generational terms and, finally, depersonalized to the point of exclusion from any ancestral role.

It may be noted, finally, that even in modern China the same understanding of the dead obtains. As Rubie Watson, basing herself upon the work of Maurice

Freedman, has noted of the distinction between funeral rites and grave rites, "in the funeral rites"—the rites, presumably, for parents —

> the dead continue to be individuals; they retain their kinship, gender, and marital status. The longer the ancestor remains in the grave, however, the more depersonalized he becomes. His flesh rots; eventually his bones may be cleaned and reburied; in the end he becomes a symbol not a person. Eventually the ancestor in his grave becomes passive, incapable of volition or of real harm, but he does not pass out of human concern altogether. His grave may become a rallying point for powerful agnatic groups ... The ancestor in his grave is perhaps best seen as a pawn to be manipulated by descendants for their own political benefit.[140]

Arthur Wolf has also remarked of the dead in Taiwan that "once a soul is installed as an ancestor, it loses many of its human appetites."[141] The legacy of the early Chinese customs that the Shang had articulated and formalized has indeed been enduring.

Legacies and Cultural Consequences

The later ramifications of Shang theology as we can discern it in the divinatory treatment of the ancestors, and thus in the Shang dynasts' conceptions of themselves as ancestors-to-be, are manifold, I can only, in the space remaining, indicate a few areas that reveal the depth of the Shang legacy.

I have suggested elsewhere that there was a homology between "the hierarchical, contractual, rational, routinized, mathematical, compartmentalized nature of Shang ancestor worship" and the value attached to bureaucratic forms of organization.[142] As Mark Lewis has subsequently written,

> The world of the spirits became the first imaginary double of the emerging state.... In short, the structure of the ancestral cult established the precedent of a graded hierarchy in which position took priority over personal character and each named individual moved through a series of roles. Thus the Shang-Zhou ancestral cults, which determined the structure of both state and kin groupings, anticipated several of the basic principles attributed to bureaucracy in the later state.[143]

The present essay attempts to document the genesis of these impulses, particularly the emphasis on the impersonality of roles, in more detail.

I am also struck by the homology between the ancestral organization described above and the modular forms of production, depending upon the standardization of units, that Lothar Ledderose has referred to as representing "a distinctly Chinese pattern of thought." "The Chinese started working with module systems early in their history and developed them to a remarkably advanced level. They used modules in their language, literature, philosophy, and social organizations, as well as in their arts." He concludes that modular production has contributed "its share toward forging and maintaining structures of an organized society, and [promoting] a powerful bureaucracy." And he further notes that "To Chinese artists, mimesis was not of paramount importance.... Rather than making things that *looked* like creations of nature, they tried to create along the *principles* of nature."[144] The ritual compartmentalization, standardization and impersonalization of the Shang ancestors, and the lack of concern with their naturalistic representation, are entirely congruent with, and were presumably deeply implicated in, the genesis of the modular imagination that Ledderose describes.

Within the tradition that came to be known as Confucian, the emphasis in all the texts was on humans as social beings, with responsibilities and obligations to the larger group, rather than on humans as unique individuals. And within that tradition, the idioms of kinship continued to exercise a powerful attraction. In the *Shijing* (Mao nos. 172, 251), the *junzi* 君子, the "Noble man," is referred to as *min zhi fu mu* 民之父母, "the father and mother of the people." And in the *Liji*, "Ji tong 祭統" chapter, the perfect homology between filiality and loyalty to the ruler is presented as the highest cultural ideal:

忠臣以事其君，孝子以事其親，其本一也。上則順於鬼神，外則順於君長，內則以孝。如此之謂備

> There is a fundamental agreement between a loyal subject in his service of his ruler and a filial son in his service of his parents. Above, to be in harmony with the spirits; externally, to be in harmony with the ruler and elders; domestically to serve with filiality—this is what is called perfection.[145]

Such teachings derive to a significant degree from the religious values elaborated if not created by the Late Shang. Fatherhood, to recall Meyer Fortes' phrasing (p. 156 above), was indeed not dead.

The continuing strength of the classifying impulse is evident in the *Zuozhuan*, which can be seen as a text in which "narrative drive was subordinated to generic classification";[146] it is evident in the way that the historian Ban Gu 班固, compiling his *Hanshu* 漢書 (1st century A.D.), ranked 1,998 major protagonists in Chinese history on a moral scale of 1 to 9 in his "Gujin renbiao 古今人表" ("Table of Ancient and Recent People").[147] The rather stereotypical way in which heroes and protagonists were often presented in Zhou texts also accords with the impersonalization of the dead; such modes of representation singled out the continuing social importance and relevance of categories of great men, by stressing their powers and accomplishments over their personalities, by stressing what they had done, not who they had been.[148]

I would also suggest, finally, that because the ancestors do not die, but only slowly fade away as they are replaced by their more numerous descendants, they cannot be regarded as tragic figures. Ancestor worship, in short, provided no reinforcement for a tragic impulse in early Chinese literature, an impulse that was already weakened by the relatively impersonal way in which living protagonists were represented.

It will, of course, be up to historians working in each subsequent period, particularly in the Zhou and Han, to consider how the Shang models played themselves out, how they were accepted, modified, and rejected in the religion and society at each significant moment in historical time and in particular regional contexts. The Western Zhou kings, after all, claimed to have overthrown the Shang dynasty, thus challenging the efficacy of the ancestral cult described above. And the Western Zhou rulers, with the Shang model before them, tended to privilege Heaven over the ancestors, as they appealed to the Powers above. And yet, while the Zhou propaganda directed at the conquered Shang stressed the iniquity of the last Shang ruler, Di Xin, it is also of interest that a significant part of that iniquity was couched in terms of his failure to continue the cult to his ancestors, and that there were later traditions to the effect that the Zhou continued the Shang ancestral sacrifices.[149] The Zhou clearly thought that ancestors still mattered.

And it must be admitted that not all the post-Zu Jia kings practiced the five-ritual cult with equal intensity (see n. 63 above). Late Shang society would have been far more complex, less tidy, than I have presented it in this essay.[150] It must be recognized, moreover, that both the grave goods in Shang burials and the Shang oracle-bone inscriptions represent someone's idealized view of the way the world should have worked. When we see the kinds of changes in Shang theology that I have been describing, we are seeing, first of all, only changes in what the diviners and ritualists did. The extent to which the king and his elites, say, promoted, accepted, or resisted the assumptions and practices of his ritualists and diviners is uncertain. One can, if extremely cynical, conceive of a situation in which a Period V king says to his diviners, "Yes, I know it's a *jia*-day tomorrow, but I want to sleep in. You handle the divination to Zu Jia. I can't be bothered. Just put my name on the form." The minuscule handwriting of the Period V texts could lend support to such a scenario.[151] And one can well imagine that, as suggested by the *Liji* passages cited earlier (pp. 185–186), a tension existed, even in the Late Shang, between a more personal, emotional form of kinship commemoration, which may have been more prevalent in, say, the reign of Wu Ding, and the more systematic, impersonal structures developed under Zu Jia.

Zu Jia's reforms, to be sure, may represent only one part of an emotional and theological spectrum, and may have been needed and insisted upon with such rigor precisely because actual Shang practice, at least until that point, had been rather less ordered, rather less "efficient." Such cautions, however, do not persuade me that the patterns established under Zu Jia did not have a major cultural impact. There may have been occasional faltering, but I believe that the diffused impact of elite Shang religiosity and ritual discipline on social, political, and cultural life would have been considerable.[152] The material wealth lavished on the royal tombs; the extravagant use of bronze in the vessels cast for the ancestral cult, which undoubtedly stimulated the technical achievements of the Shang metallurgical industry; the large numbers of sacrificial victims offered to the ancestors and buried near the royal dead; the great expense of time and manpower involved in divining, performing, and recording the ancestral rituals; the subsequent character of Chinese culture in which some form of ancestor worship usually played a strategic role—these considerations all suggest that Shang ancestor worship as I have described it, for all its idealizing nature, would have been a powerful shaper of early Chinese values, or kinship conceptions, of conceptions about the nature of the individual personality.

Just as there was a "disciplinary revolution" associated with the Calvinist wing of the Reformation in the West, so, I would suggest, was there a disciplinary revolution in the reforms of Zu Jia, a revolution that would have "operated at a number of levels," including a more rigorous "code of systematic ethical action" involving reverence for seniors and ancestors, "new institutions" such as the ritual cycle "capable of enforcing the code" and demonstrating its efficacy, and strengthened "solidary organizations" such as the corporate descent group that were "strong enough to influence political and economic developments."[153] Peter Brown, in tracing how the cult of the saints developed in late antiquity, has written of "a group of *impresarios*, taking initiatives, making choices, and, in so doing, coining a public language that would last through Western Europe deep into the middle ages."[154] The same analysis could, I believe, be applied to Wu Ding, Zu Jia, and their liturgists, who similarly developed a language of religious and political discourse that would last, and be refined, through the Zhou and Han and beyond.

Religious belief can change the way men think. "Religion," in the words of Robert Bellah, "provides the indispensable element of cultural codes, not only for the institutionalization of new social forms but, when internalized in personality systems, for new forms of individual motivation as well."[155] And I do believe that for many in the Late Shang, the ancestors, as the kings and their supporters conceived them, were a real, if almost routine, presence, heard in the cracking of the bones, present at the offering of the "hosting" and other rituals, acknowledging the sacrifices, presiding, on schedule, over the days of their temple names, ensuring that there would be "no troubles," "no fault." Their claim to cultural "fatherhood," to an authority that could not easily be escaped, is well justified. The Shang did indeed make their ancestors and they had made them useful. The living had put the dead to work. And the dead had responded in kind.

Notes

An initial version of this article was presented as the The Walker-Ames Lecture at the University of Washington, Seattle, on 23 February 1999. I am particularly grateful for the thoughtful comments subsequently offered by John Kieschnick, John Lagerwey, Edward Shaughnessy, and Melvin Thatcher, some of which I have incorporated in this revised version. The article's faults remain my own.

1. It is of some interest that the *International Encyclopedia of the Social Sciences* (David L. Sills ed., New York: Macmillan and Free Press, 1968) has no index entry for "Ancestors" or "Ancestor Worship." And Franz Schurmann's article on "Chinese Society" makes scant reference to it, as in "the Zhou religion was essentially a politically oriented ancestor worship which tended to develop locally rather than nationally, thus impeding the formation of a unified high culture" (2: 410; here as elsewhere I convert Wade-Giles and other romanization systems to pinyin).
2. Jean-Claude Schmitt, *Ghosts in the Middle Ages: The Living and the Dead in Medieval Society*, 1, Chicago: University of Chicago Press, 1998.

3. For an introduction to these issues, see, e.g., the discussion of "religion-religiosity" at James E. Dittes, "Religion: Psychological Study," in David L. Sills ed., *International Encyclopedia of the Social Sciences*, 13: 418, New York: Macmillan and Free Press, 1968.

4. David N. Keightley, "The Religious Commitment: Shang Theology and the Genesis of Chinese Political Culture," *History of Religions* 17 (1978): 212. Essay 4 in this volume.

5. Patricia A. McAnany, *Living With the Ancestors: Kinship and Kingship in Ancient Maya Society*, 1 (Austin: University of Texas Press, 1995).

6. But consider the qualification proposed at n. 103 below.

7. Elizabeth Bloch-Smith, *Judahite Burial Practices*, 150, Sheffield, England: JSOT Press, 1992.

8. Meyer Fortes, "Some Reflections on Ancestor Worship in Africa," 133, in M. Fortes and G. Dieterlen eds., *African Systems of Thought*, London: Oxford University Press, 1965. He refers to the remark of Hilda Kuper, "The Ancestors are the ideal not the actual personality" (*An African Aristocracy*, 188, London: Oxford University Press, 1947).

9. Meyer Fortes, "Pietas in Ancestor Worship," *Journal of the Royal Anthropological Institute* 91.2 (1961): 182, 184, 185.

10. David N. Keightley, "Clean Hands and Shining Helmets: Heroic Action in Early Chinese and Greek Culture," in Tobin Siebers ed., *Religion and Authority*, 2XX, Ann Arbor: University of Michigan Press, 1993. Essay 10 in this volume.

11. Translation based on James Legge tr., *The Sacred Books of China: The Texts of Confucianism. Part III. The Li Ki*, 1: 177, Delhi: Motilal Banarsidass, [1885] 1966. See too Séraphin Couvreur tr., 禮記 *Li ki, Mémoires sur les bienséances et les cérémonies*, 1: 217, Ho-kien-fou: Mission Catholique, 1899; reprint, Paris: Cathasia, 1950.

12. One dictionary defines "persona" as "The personality assumed by an individual for purposes of concealment, defense, deception, or adaptation to his environment" (*Funk & Wagnalls Standard College Dictionary* [New York: Funk & Wagnalls, 1977]), another as "The role that one assumes or displays in public or society; one's public image or personality, as distinguished from the inner self" (*The American Heritage Dictionary of the English Language* [Boston: Houghton Mifflin, 1992]). That the word derives from Latin *persôna*, "mask," makes the word particularly appropriate to the discussion of Shang ancestor worship that follows. For the view that "spirit ghosts of ancestors ... were envisioned as anthropomorphized animal masks" see Elizabeth Childs-Johnson, "The Ghost Head Mask and Metamorphic Shang Imagery," *Early China* 20 (1995): 79.

13. On the origins of ancestor worship in China, see, e.g., David N. Keightley, "Shamanism, Death, and the Ancestors: Religious Mediation in Neolithic and Shang China (ca. 5000–1000 B.C.)," *Asiatische Studien* 52.3 (1998): 774–93; Li Liu, "Who Were the Ancestors?: The Origins of Chinese Ancestral Cult and Racial Myths," *Antiquity* 73 (1999): 602–04.

14. For a recent account of religious, economic, and sociopolitical development in the Neolithic, see Li Liu, "Settlement Patterns, Chiefdom Variability, and the Development of Early States in North China," *Journal of Anthropological Archaeology* 15 (1996): 237–88.

15. See Li Liu ("Development of Chiefdom Societies in the Middle and Lower Yellow River Valley in Neolithic China—A Study of the Longshan Culture from the Perspective of Settlement Patterns," 65, 66, Ph.D. diss., Harvard, May 1994) on the divination bones found in association with Kangjia 康家 burials (in Lintong 臨潼, Shaanxi), an indication that "divination may have taken place during the burial process."

On the divination bones associated with burials at Qinweijia 秦魏家 and Dahe zhuang 大何莊 in east central Gansu, see Keightley, "Shamanism, Death, and the Ancestors," 790–91. Zhang Zhongpei 張忠培 ("Kuitan Lingjiatan mudi 窺探淩家灘墓地;" *Wenwu* 文物 2000.9: 55–58) has even identified the spread of "osteomantic religion" (骨卜宗敎) as a major cultural development during the Neolithic, with much of the evidence based on the scapulas and turtle shells found in burials.

16. The modern term for "Former Lords" is *xian gong* 先公; they are to be distinguished from the *xian wang* 先王 ("Former Kings"), a category that includes both the predynastic and dynastic ancestors. See, e.g., Itô Michiharu, "Part One: Religion and Society," in Itô Michiharu and Ken-ichi Takashima eds., *Studies in Early Chinese Civilization: Religion, Society, Language, and Palaeography*, 1:1, Hirakata: Kansai Gaidai University Press, 1996.

17. The P and K numbers indicate the regnal sequence of the Predynastic ancestors (P1 indicates the first predynastic ancestor) and the dynastic Kings (Kl indicates the first dynastic ancestor); see Fig. 1 on p. 163.

18. On the ritual cycle, see p. 169. For an introduction to the periodization of the oracle-bone inscriptions, see David N. Keightley, *Sources of Shang History: The Oracle-Bone Inscriptions of Bronze Age China*, 91–133, Berkeley: University of California Press, 1978; Edward L. Shaughnessy, "Recent Approaches to Oracle-Bone Periodization," *Early China* 8 (1982–83): 1–13.

19. Itô Michiharu 伊藤道治, "Shûkyômen kara mira Indai no ni-san no mondai: In ôchô no kôzô, sono ni 宗敎面から見た殷代の二三の問題：殷王朝の構造，その二" *Tôyôshi kenkyû* 東洋史研究 20 (1961): 268–90; see too Itô Michiharu, "Part One: Religion and Society," 85–86.

20. For the use of the modern term, "Power," see David N. Keightley, *The Ancestral Landscape: Time, Space, and Community in Late Shang China* (*ca. 1200–1050 B.C.*), 5, n. 16, Berkeley: Institute of East Asian Studies, 2000; see, too, Mu-chou Poo, *In Search of Personal Welfare: A View of Ancient Chinese Religion*, 6, 28, Albany, N.Y.: State University of New York Press, 1998. "High" is justified by the Shang use of the title *gao zu* 高祖, "high ancestor," for certain members of this group, as in inscriptions [1] and [2].

21. In this inscription, the graph for Hai was written by combining the *hai* phonetic and a bird element; on this, see Keightley, *The Ancestral State*, 110, n. 44.

22. *Heji* is an abbreviated reference to Guo Moruo 郭沫若 ed.; Hu Houxuan 胡厚宣 ed. in chief, *Jiagmven heji* 甲骨文合集, 13 vols., N.p.: Zhonghua shuju, 1978–82. Y is an abbreviation for Yao Xiaosui 姚孝遂 and Xiao Ding 肖丁, *Yinxu jiagu keci leizuan* 殷墟甲骨刻辭類纂, Beijing: Zhonghua, 1989; "Y1246.1" means that a hand copy of the inscription in question (transcribed in both oracle-bone and modern script) may be found in the top register of p. 1246.

23. Xu Jinxiong, in his commentary to an earlier publication of this bone, as *Menzies* 2312, suggests that the diviners used *zhi* 陟, "to ascend, raise," because Wang Hai was more distant than the close ancestors in whose presence the Exorcism ritual was usually performed. For the abbreviations by which I cite collections of oracle-bone inscriptions, see Keightley, *Sources of Shang Hisory*, 229–31 (there romanized in Wade-Giles); *The Ancestral Landscape*, 159–62.

24. Itô Michiharu 伊藤道道 ("Bokuji ni mieru sorei kannen ni tsuite 卜辭た見える祖靈觀念たついて," *Tôhô gakuhô* 東洋學報 26 [1956]: 27) makes a similar point. Later legends about He Bo 河伯, the Lord of the Yellow River (see, e.g., Chen Mengjia 陳夢家, *Yinxu buci zongshu* 殷虛卜辭綜述, 72, Beijing: Kexue, 1956; Bernhard

Karlgren, "Legends and Cults in Ancient China," *Bulletin of the Museum of Far Eastern Antiquities* 18 (1946): 320; Arthur Waley, *The Nine Songs: A Study of Shamanism in Ancient China*, 48–52, London: Allen and Unwin, 1955), confirm this tendency to anthropomorphize the nature Powers by sometimes incorporating them into the system of kin and political status.

25. The Shang hosted the River Power in *Tunnan* 1116 (Y493.1), but it is uncertain that they hosted the Mountain Power (see the inscriptions at Y469.1–2, where the syntax differs from that of the usual formula), and there is no evidence that they ever divined about hosting the Former Lords, Nao and Wang Hai.

26. Although the Former Lords were not formally given temple names, there appears, in some cases, to have been an affinity between a particular lord and a particular *gan* day for cult. As K. C. Chang (*"T'ien kan: A Key to the History of the Shang,"* in David T. Roy and Tsuen-hsuin Tsien eds., *Ancient China: Studies in Early Civilization*, 36, Hong Kong: Chinese University Press, 1978) has noted, for example, the Shang generally offered cult to Wang Hai on a *xin*-day (as in *Heji* 14732, 32028, and *Tunnan* 1116); this suggests to Chang that Wang Hai, had he been awarded a temple name, "would have been called Gao Zu Xin" (高祖辛, "High Ancestor Xin"). The implied use of the ancestral *gan* suggests the liminal role of the Former Lords—part ancestor, part other. It is also possible, however, that the Shang ritualists preferred a *xin*-day for their rituals to Wang Hai (and also, to a degree, for their burnt offerings to the River Power; see the inscriptions at Y488.2–83.2) because, during the reign of Wu Ding, the period when most of these rituals were divined, the *xin*-day was not overburdened with cult to Xin-named ancestors and was thus "open" for Powers who had not been given temple names.

27. See David N. Keightley, "At the Beginning: The Status of Women in Neolithic and Shang China," *Nan Nü: Men, Women and Gender in Early and Imperial China* I.1 (1999): 35–46.

28. Chang Yuzhi 常玉芝, *Shangdai zhouji zhidu* 商代周祭制度, 87, [Beijing:] Zhongguo shehui kexueyuan, 1987.

29. For the *bin* 賓, "hosting" ceremony, as a stage in the offering of the rituals of the five-ritual cycle, see Zhang Yujin 張玉金, "Lun bin ziju de jufa jiegou 論賓字句的句法結構," *Gu Hanyu yanjiu* 古漢語研究, 19 (1993.2): 1–8.

30. David N. Keightley, "Divination and Kingship in Late Shang China" (book ms., 1991, chapter 2; "In the Bone: Divination, Theology, and Political Culture in Late Shang China," talk, Pre-Modern China Seminar, Fairbank Center, Harvard University, 17 October 1994; "Making a Mark (2): Why *Did* the Shang Inscribe Their Oracle-Bone Inscriptions?," 21–23, paper prepared for the conference on "Ritual and Text in Early China," Princeton University, 20–22 October 2000.

31. See, e.g., *Heji* 378f, 10076, 10085f, 10105, 10109, 10111, 10116.

32. See, e.g., *Heji* 672f, 776f, 900fb, 6746, 10976f, 14138, and *Yingcang* 1133.

33. Shima Kunio 島邦男, *Inkyo bokuji kenkyū* 殷墟卜辭研究, 203, Hirosaki: Hirosaki daigaku Chūgoku kenkyūkai, 1958; Itô Michiharu, "Part One: Religion and Society," 64. For examples of divinations about the *di*-ritual, see *Heji* 14295 and 32012, translated at Keightley, *The Ancestral Landscape*, 70, 73; see too 74, n. 51.

34. See, e.g., *Heji* 30398, 30399, 30447, 32916, 33227.

35. Arthur P. Wolf, "Gods, Ghosts, and Ancestors," in Arthur P. Wolf ed., *Religion and Ritual in Chinese Society*, 168, Stanford: Stanford University Press, 1974.

36. Wolf, "Gods, Ghosts, and Ancestors," 162.

37. The Shang graph 冊 (Y1133.1) may have depicted wooden writing slips over a mouth or placed in a box (Shirakawa Shizuka 白川靜, "Sakusatsu kô 作冊考," in his *Kôkotsu kimbungaku ronsô* 甲骨金文學論叢 2: 14, Kyoto: Self-published, 1955). On the basis of Shang usage 1 regard *ce* as a verb of cult (it was used less frequently as a noun; see Liu Xinfang 劉信芳, "Ce, ce, ce, ce huishi 冊, 冊, 禰, 圓彙釋," *Kaogu yu wenwu* 考古與文物 1990.2: 41.) in which large or important offerings were made ritualist's prayer had been answered, or (ii) consisting only of the "paper" pledge. For a fuller discussion, see Keightley "Divination and Kingship," 432–34, the "Glossary" entry for *ce* 冊; Matsumaru Michio 松凡道雄 and Takashima Ken-ichi 尚腦謙—, *Kôkotsumoji jishaku sôran* 甲骨文字字釋綜覽, no. 0585, Tokyo: Tokyo University Press (1993, not for sale), 1994; this work is hereafter abbreviated as *Sôran*.

38. Shirakawa, "Sakusatsu kô," 8–9. For more on the *ce* ritual, see Keightley, *The Ancestral Landscape*, 29, n. 44.

39. The main-line king recipients of the pledge ritual included (see the inscriptions at Y1133.1–35.1) Da Jia (K3; *Heji* 908, 1440), Da Geng (K5; *Heji* 895B), Da Wu (K7; *Heji* 19834), Zu Yi (K12; *Heji* 140b, 898, 9l4f, 6947f), Zu Xin (K13; *Heji* 959, 1732, 7026, *White* 139), Zu Ding (K15; *Heji* 914f, 915b), Xiao Yi (K20; *Heji* 271f, 702f, 709f, 713, 886, 924f, 2212, 2213f, 4116, 6664f, *Yingcang* 83, l49f). The collateral recipients included Qiang jia (K14; *Heji* 1793f, *White* 43), Han Geng(K16; *Yingcang* 38), Yang Jia (K17; *Heji* 19914). One predynastic ancestor, Shi Ren (P5) may also have been the recipient of the pledge ritual (*Yingcang* 1236; Y1135.1). For the genealogical status of all these ancestors, see Fig. 1.

40. Because the same temple name was often conferred on more than one of the royal consorts (e.g., four of the main-line kings had consorts who had been awarded the name of Ancestress Geng [Bi Geng 妣庚]: Zu Yi 祖乙 [K12], Zu Xin 祖辛 [K13], Zu Ding 祖丁 [K15], and Xiao Yi 小乙 [K20]; see Keightley, "At the Beginning," 58–60), it is not possible, in the *ce* inscriptions, to identify them with certainty. But it is plausible to assume that the Ancestress Geng (*Heji* 438f, 720f, 723f, 724fb, 772f, 773A, 779f, 893f, 2468f, 2469, 2470f, 2472, 22229, 22231) and the Ancestress Ji (Bi Ji 妣己; *Heji* 707f, 716f, 718f, 719f, 784, 2424, 22231, *Tunnan* 3058; see the inscriptions at Y1133.1–35.1) who were commonly the recipients of pledge rituals in the Wu Ding divinations were the consorts of Xiao Yi (K20) and Zu Ding (K15) respectively (see Fig. 1).This Bi Geng and Bi ji would have been Wu Ding's mother and grandmother, logical recipients of the Exorcism rituals often associated with Wu Ding's pledge offerings.

41. On two rare occasions Wu Ding may have made a pledge to the River Power; see *Heji* 5522f (Y1134.1) and 14521 (Y1132.2). But that may have been because the River Power was, in fact, thought of as a "High Ancestor" (p. 159). He did make a pledge to the Former Lord, Huang Yin 黃尹 (*Heji* 6945 [Y1134.1]) and on two occasions, he offered a pledge to 𓏁 (*Heji* 6947f [Y1134.1], *Tunnan* 1458 [Y1135.1]); for 𓏁 as the name of an ancestor or Nature Power, see Keightley, *The Ancestral Landscape*, 61, n. 14). He twice made pledges to E 娥 (*Heji* 14780, 14807f [Y1134.1]), who may have been a Power of some sort (sec the entries at *Sôran*, no. 1428). He made no pledges, however, to the Mountain Power or to the Former Lords Nao 夔 and Wang Hai 王亥. Nor, with the one possible exception of Shi Ren (see n. 39 above), did he even make pledges to the Predynastic Ancestors, who were presumably thought to be too distant to be swayed in this way.

42. For the argument that the □ of this and similar inscriptions should be read not as *ding* 丁 but as *ri* 日, "sun," see David N. Keightley, "Graphs, Words, and Meanings: Three Reference Works for Shang Oracle-Bone Studies, With an Excursus into the Religious Role of the Day or Sun," *Journal of the American Oriental Society* 117.3 (1997): 517–24.

43. Keightley, "Graphs, Words, and Meanings," 518.

44. David N. Keightley, "The Science of the Ancestors: Divination, Curing, and Bronze-Casting in Late Shang China," *Asia Major* 14.2 (2001): 186.

45. On this distinction in modern Chinese religion, see Maurice Freedman, *Chinese Lineage and Society: Fukien and Kwangtung*, 153–54, London: London School of Economics: Monographs on Social Anthropology 33, 1966.

46. David N. Keightley, "The Shang: China's First Historical Dynasty," in Michael Loewe and Edward L. Shaughnessy eds., *The Cambridge History of Ancient China: From the Origins of Civilization to 221 B.C.*, 271–72, New York: Cambridge University Press, 1999.

47. For non-royal temple names in divination inscriptions, see, e.g., *Heji* 31993 (= Zhongguo shchui kexueyuan kaogu yanjiusuo 中國社會科學院考古研究所, *Xiaotun nandi jiagu. Shangce, diyi fence* 小屯南地甲骨, 上冊, 第一分冊, Fu 附 3, Shanghai: Zhonghua, 1980). The temple names of the ancestors and ancestresses incribed on this scapula, such as Zu Wu 祖戊, Bi Yi 妣乙, and Bi Ding 妣丁, do not appear to be those of the usual kings and consorts who received regular ancestral sacrifices. These and other features suggest that the divinations using this bone were performed, not by the court diviners, but by another group of diviners; see Keightley, "Shang Oracle Bone Inscriptions from Anyang, Henan Province," in Xiaoneng Yang ed., *The Golden Age of Archaeology: Celebrated Discoveries from the People's Republic of China*, 184–85, Washington: National Gallery of Art, 1999. For such non-royal names in the bronze inscriptions, one should consult the at least 1300 Shang bronze inscriptions that record temple names. Roswell S. Britton (*Fifty Shang Inscriptions*, 73, Princeton: Princeton University Library, 1940) tabulated 1301 Shang cases from the two collections, *Yinwen cun* 殷文存 and *Xu Yinwen cun* 續殷文存; Zhang Guangzhi 張光直 ("Tan Wang Hai yu Yi Yin de jiri bing zailun Yin-Shang wangzhi 談王亥與伊尹的祭日並再論殷商王制," *Zhongyang yanjiuyuan minzu yanjiu suo jikan* 中央研究民族學研究所集刊 35 [1973]: 116; reprinted in Zhang Guangzhi, *Zhongguo qingtongqi shidai* 中國青銅器時代, 111, Hong Kong: Zhongwen daxue, 1982), tabulated 1285 cases, 1102 of which may be dated to the Shang, 191 to the Western Zhou (only 19 of which may be dated to the period after Cheng Wang 成王 and Kang Wang 康王), with 2 of uncertain date. More recent discoveries of Shang bronzes would raise the number of cases. Virginia C. Kane has suggested that the Shang royal practice of casting posthumous *gan* designations into bronzes was "in the course of the Anyang occupation, adopted by the lesser aristocratic clans (including those of the pre-Conquest Zhou principality)" ("The Chronological Significance of the Inscribed Ancestor Dedication in the Periodization of Shang Dynasty Bronze Vessels," *Artibus Asiae* 35 [1973]: 337). Edward L. Shaughnessy (*Sources of Western Zhou History: Inscribed Bronze Vessels*, 167, Berkeley: University of California Press, 1991) has noted that "It is now clear … that the Shang convention of ancestor titles continued to he used, in at least some families, well into the Western Zhou."

48. For the preference for particular *gan* temple names, see n. 71 below.

49. Li Xueqin 李學勤 and Peng Yushang 彭裕商 (*Yinxu jiagu fenqi yanji* 殷墟甲骨分期研究, 179, Shanghai: Guji chubanshe, 1996) note that the addition of honorifics like

Wu 武 and Wen 文 was first practiced in the late Yinxu period, so the disambiguating title of Wu Ding 武丁 is mainly seen in the Huang 黃 Diviner-group inscriptions of Period V (as in [21A-C]).

50. I am assuming, in making this argument, that these ancestral titles had indeed been in use since the time of the first Shang kings. It is possible, in the absence of contemporary records from, say, the 16th century B.C., that Da Yi and the other early kings were—in their very essence or at least in their ritual incarnations—a construction of the Late Shang liturgists of the 12th century B.C., who were simply creating a ritual past that was modeled on their current practice.

51. Keightley, "The Shang: China's First Historical Dynasty," 269–72. For the situation in the Chunqiu period, see Melvin P. Thatcher, "Lineage in Spring and Autumn China," ms (October 1998).

52. Chen Mengjia, *Yinxu buci zongshu*, 494–95; he also cites examples of rituals to the "The Two Fathers" (Er Fu 二父), "The Four Brothers" (Si xiong 四兄), "The Three Brothers" (San Xiong 三兄), etc.

53. In oracle-bone usage, *shi* 示, as a noun, meant "Ancestor." The word may have been a synecdoche, a tablet or altar stand used for "Ancestor"; see the scholarship cited at Keightley, *Sources of Shang History*, 17, n. 71. For the view that oracle-bone *shi* should be understood as *zhu* 主, the ancestral tablet, see Yang Shengnan 楊升南, "Cong Yinxu buci zhong tic 'shi', 'zong' shuodao Shangdai de zongfa zhidu 從殷墟姬卜辭中的'示','宗'說到商代的宗法制度," *Zhongguo shi yanjiu* 中國史研究 1985.3: 3 and the scholarship cited there. The 1995 article by Liu Zhao (cited in n. 128 below), also summarizes the scholarship on this point. I capitalize "Ancestor" to indicate that *shi* referred to the Ancestors in their ritual embodiment.

54. For the possible meanings of the word that I have transcribed as *shuai* 率, "lead," see *Sônm*, no. 1567.

55. For these terms, see Chao Fulin 晁福林, "Guanyu Yinxu buci zong de 'shi' he 'zong' de tanrao—Jianlun zongfazhi de ruogan wenti 關于殷墟卜辭中的「示」和「宗」的探討 —— 兼論宗法制的若干問題," *Shehui kexue zhanxian* 社會科學戰線 1989.3: 158–66. For the inscriptions see Y399.2–400.1, 396.2, 397.1.

56. Chao Fulin, "Guanyu Yinxu buci zong de 'shi' he 'zong' de tantao," 158–59; Zhu Fenghan 朱鳳翰, "Lun Yinxu buci zhong de 'dashi' ji qi xiangguan wenti 論殷墟卜辭中的「大示」及其相關問題," *Guwenzi yanjiu* 古文字研究 16 (1989): 40, 42, 45; "Yinxu buci suo jian Shang wangshi zongmiao zhidu 殷墟卜辭所見商王室宗廟制度," *Lishi yanjiu* 歷史研究 1990.6: 5–6. I would also note that, if one excludes Shang Jia and the predynastic ancestors from Bao Yi to Shi Gui, the five "Greater" ancestors were the first Shang kings to be accorded their particular *gun* temple names; Da Yi, accordingly; would have been "The Greater Yi," because he was the first ruler of the Yi designation, and so on.

57. Zhu Fenghan, "Lun Yinxu buci zhong de 'dashi' ji qi xiangguan wenti," 44. Chao Fulin ("Guanyu Yinxu buci zong de 'shi' he 'zong' de tantao," 162), by contrast, suggests that the distinction between the Da Shi and the Xiao Shi was temporal rather than genealogical; he proposes that the title of Xiao Shi referred to the younger or junior ancestors.

58. As the *Shiwen* to *Tunnan* 1115 notes, this charge indicates that, contrary to earlier opinion, the Xiao Shi and Xia Shi were not identical, nor were the Da Shi and Shang Shi.

59. See, e.g., the hosting (*bin* 賓) ritual offered to "the ancestors from Zu Yi (K12) down to Father Ding (i.e., Wu Ding, K21)" (自祖乙至于父丁) (*Heji* 22899 [Y917.2]); see too *Heji* 35436 (Y186.1).

60. Of the 26 "from such-and-such an ancestor (down to)" charges transcribed at Y238.2–39.1, only 3 are from Period V. This sample is incomplete, but a search for the "from Shang Jia" charges in Shima Kunio's 島邦男 concordance (*Inkyo bokui sôrui* 殷墟卜辭綜類, 513.2–14.3, Tokyo: Kyûko, 1971, 2d rev. ed.) reveals a similar pattern: 6 Period V charges out of the total of the ca. 205 "miscellaneous" Shang Jia charges from all periods collected there. I find no Period V charges about The Greater or Lessee Ancestors.

61. For the ritual treatment of the ancestresses, see Keightley, "At the Beginning," 31–46.

62. For evidence that the five-ritual cycle was being practiced during the time of the Bin-group diviners, but was apparently not being regularly divined, as it was to be in Period IIb, see Li Xueqin 李學勤, "Lun Binzu jiagu de jizhong jishi keci 論賓組甲骨的幾種記事刻辭; On Some Bin Diviner Group Record Inscriptions Engraved on Ox Scapulae," in Li Xueqin, Qi Wenxin 齊文心, and Ai Lan 艾蘭 (Sarah Allan) eds., *Yingguo suocangjiaguji. Xia bian* 英國所藏甲骨集.下編. *Oracle Bone Collections in Great Britain. Vol. II*, 161–66 (Chinese), 167–76 (English), London and Beijing: School of Oriental and African Studies and Institute of History, Chinese Academy of Social Sciences; Beijing: Zhonghua Shuju, 1991. See too Itô Michiharu, "Part One: Religion and Society," 1: 95.

63. The fate of the five-ritual cycle in Periods III and IV is not clear; possibly it fell into disuse, or it was practiced but was not divined, or the cache of relevant bone inscriptions has not yet been unearthed. See, e.g., Itô Michiharu, "Part One: Religion and Society," 1:142. For the situation in Periods IVb and V, see Chang Yuzhi, *Shangdai zhouji zhidu*, 227–305; Wang Hui 王暉, "Zhouyuan jiagu shuxing yu Shang Zhou zhi ji jili de bianhua 周原甲骨屬性與商周之際祭禮的變化," *Lishi yanjiu* 歷史研究 1998.3: 14–20; David N. Keightley, "Five in Five, Or What Happened to the Five-Ritual Cycle in Oracle-Bone Period V?," ms., 12 February 1999. As Li Xueqin and Peng Yushang (*Yinxu jiagu fenqi yanjiu*, 179) note, records of the five-ritual cycle ate only numerous in the inscriptions of the Chu 出 and Huang 黃 diviner groups.

64. For an introduction to the cycle, see, e.g., Itô Michiharu, "Part One: Religion and Society," 1: 92–95. The relevant inscriptions are listed at Y706.1–2, 1288.2–90.2, 265.1–66.2. See too the discussion of the *yi ri* ritual at Chang Yuzhi, *Shangdai zhouji zhidu*, 20–21. I adopt the order of the rituals given by her and by Xu Jinxiong 許進雄, *Yin buci zhong wuzhong jisi de yanjiu* 殷卜辭中五種祭祀的研究, 55–73, Taibei: Guoli Taiwan daxue wenxueyuan, Wenshi congkan zhi ershi liu, 1968.

65. For how the ritual cycle lasted approximately one year (though it was not synchronized to the luni-solar calendar) see Chang Yuzhi, *Shangdai zhouji zhidu*, 256–57, who provides a reconstruction of the "first" through the "fifth" ritual cycles of what she calls "the first ritual system." Thus, the first ritual cycle would have started with the *yi* 翌 ritual to Shang Jia on day *jiashen* at the start or the first ten-day week of the eighth moon of one year, with the next *yi* ritual to Shang Jia recurring again on the day *jiawu* of the middle ten-day week of the eighth moon of the following year.

66. Chang Yuzhi, *Shangdai zhouji zhidu*, 191–93. She provides a useful chart, reconstructing the year-long "third ritual cycle" on p. 230 (reproduced as Fig. 2).

67. Chang Yuzhi, *Shangdai zhouji zhidu*, 42; see, e.g., the ritual schedule provided in Fig. 3.

68. See Chang Yuzhi, *Shangdai zhouji zhidu*, 168.

69. Keightley, "At The Beginning," 39–40.

70. See the note to Fig. 1 on xxx.

71. Ji Dewei 吉德煒, "Zhongguo gudai de jiri yu miaohao 中國古代的告日與廟號," *Yinxu bowuyuan yuankan (chuangkan hao)* 殷墟博物苑苑刊 (創刊號) 1989: 20–32; see, in particular, tables 2–4 on p. 27.

72. Chang Yuzhi, *Shangdai zhouji zhidu*, 31. See, e.g., *Heji* 36184, 36226, 36269, 36281 (Y96.2–97.2).

73. See Chang Yuzhi, *Shangdai zhouji zhidu*, 41. Notice that the week referred to in [22A] would have been Week 4 in the *ji*-ritual cycle; the week referred to in [22B] would have been Week 5. See Fig. 3.

74. For divinations about *rong*-day-rituals offered to those two ancestors on the days of their temple names, see (for Zhong Ding) *Heji* 35629 and 35630 (Y1392.2), and (for Ancestor Geng) *Heji* 35877 (Y1427.1).

75. *Zong* 宗 should be understood as "ancestor"; see Bernhard Karlgren, *Grammata Serica Recensa*, no. 1003, Stockholm: Museum of Far Eastern Antiquities, 1957; Léon Vandermeersch, *Wangdao ou la voie royale: Recherches sur l'esprit des institutions de la Chine archaïque. Tome I. Structures cultuelles et structures familiales*, 43, n.3, Paris: École fraçaise d'Extrême-Orient, 1977. The graph depicted an ancestral altar strand enshrined under a roof, hence the related meaning, "temple." The usage, "On the day of such-and-such an ancestor," was, I believe, far more common in Di Yi-Di Xin inscriptions than has been realized because the oracle-bone graph □ has generally been read as *ding* 丁; for the view that it should, in many cases, and particularly in cases like [25], be read a graphic simplification of *ri* 日, "day, sun," see n. 42 above.

76. Shirakawa Shizuka 白川靜 (*Kumbun tsûshaku* 金文通釋 56: 285, Kobe: Hakutsuru bijutsukan, 1984) lists sixteen inscriptions of the *gan ri* 干日 variety. For further discussion of the practice of naming ancestors after the days of the ten *gan* see Shaughnessy's account (*Sources of Western Zhou History*, 7) of Guo Moruo's 1934 study of a passage in the *Liji*, "Daxue 大學," which, when properly understood, appears to have referred to a bronze inscription that recorded ancestor dedications to "Elder Brother Day Xin, Grandfather Day Xin, and Father Day Xin (兄日辛, 祖日辛, 父日辛)." There are also the three ritual halberd blades, of uncertain authenticity, reputedly found in the 1920s at Baoding 保定 or some other area of the Henan-Hebei border, which were apparently used for services to a series of ancestors, and which follow the same formula. The blade dedicated to the "grandfathers," for instance, included the names of "the Great Grandfather whose days is *ji*, the grandfather whose day is *ding*, the grandfather whose day is *geng*, the grandfather whose day is *yi* (大祖旧己，祖日丁，祖日庚，祖日己), etc."; see Wang Guowei 王國維, *Dingben Guantang jilin* 定本觀堂集林, 18. 1a–b, Wucheng, Zhejiang: 1923; Chen Mengjia, *Yinxu buci zongshu*, 500–501. As K. C. Chang ("*T'ien kan*," 24, n. 19) notes, many scholars regard these inscriptions as fake. Other attested finds, however, support the view that such formulas would have been in use. On the basis of three bronze inscriptions excavated from burials M93 and M907 in Area no. 7 of the Yinxu West cemetery, for example, Noel Barnard has concluded that the *gan* symbols *jia*, *yi*, and *xin* are, in these inscriptions, to be read as abbreviations of the formulas *ri jia* 日甲, *ri yi* 日乙, and *ri xin* 日辛, respectively ("A New Approach to the Study of Clan-sign Inscriptions of Shang," in K.C. Chang ed., *Studies of Shang Archaeology: Selected Papers from the International Conference on Shang Civilization*, 145, Fig. 23; 150–51, New Haven; Yale University Press, 1986). See too the further examples and discussion at David N. Keightley, "Whose Names, Whose Graves?: Temple Names and Late Shang Yuppies," 12–23, paper prepared for the Association for Asian Studies meetings, San Francisco, 26 March 1988.

77. Akatsuka Kiyoshi, *Chûgoku kodai no shûkyô to bunka: In ôchô no saishi* 中國古代
˙ɩ宗教˙〇文化 ： 殷王朝 ˙ɩ宗祀, 826–27, Tokyo: Kadokawa, 1977. I follow
Lothar von Falkenhausen ("The Concept of *Wen* in the Ancient Chinese Ancestral
Cult," *Clear* 18 [1996]: 1–22) in treating *wen* 文 in such contexts as a word associated with ritual experience whose precise meaning is yet to be determined. It is
not out of the question—and would well suit the argument of this essay—that *wen*
meant "ritualized," i.e., somebody "deceased" who had been ritually converted to
ancestral status and who thus merited the appropriate ritual treatment. Such figures
would have been *wen* because they were more ordered, more cultured, more accomplished, than they had been in real life. For an introduction to the 𐀴 insignia, sec
William Watson, *Ancient Chinese Bronzes*, 72–73, London; Faber and Faber, 1962,
2d ed. 1977; Yu Xingwu, "Shi ju 釋𐀴," *Kaogu* 考古 1979.4:353–55; Qin Jianming
秦建明 and Zhang Maorong 張橄鎔, "Shuo zi 說𐀴," *Kaogu yu wenwu* 考古與
文物 1984.6: 80–82.

78. Akatsuka, *Chûgoku kodai no shûkyô to bunka*, 804–08; Wang Shimin 王世民,
"Ji Riben Chuguang meishuguan shoucang de woguo Yin-Zhou tongqi, 記日本出
光美術館收藏的我國殷周銅器," *Guwenzi yanjiu* 古文字研究 12 (1985): 196–97.

79. Ji Dewei, "Zhongguo gudai de jiri yu miaohao," 27, table 4, 28, table 7.

80. Chang Yuzhi (*Shangdai zhouji zhidu*, 307) reaches a similar conclusion.

81. Similar considerations were to govern the nature of Eastern Zhou sacrifice as presented
in the *Zuozhuan* 左傳 and *Guoyu* 國語, where as characterized by David Schaberg (*A
Patterned Past: Form and Thought in Early Chinese Historiography*, 129, Cambridge:
Harvard University Asia Center, 2001), "Personal taste cannot determine the details
of sacrifice." He cites (374, n. 19) an anecdote from the *Guoyu*, "Chuyu 楚語," 1.3,
in which "Qu Dao 屈到, a Chu minister and a lover of caltrop (*ji* 〔芰〕), asks that that
vegetable be included among the items offered to him after his death. His son later for-
bids the family elders to implement the change, insisting that no variation is permitted
in the canon of sacrifice, particularly for one who in life was a model to his subjects."

82. Note, for example, how the list of ancestors in the Period-I inscription [9] stopped
with Zu Ding (K15), Wu Ding's grandfather. Chang Yuzhi (*Shangdai zhouji zhidu*,
104) also notes that the consort cycle of the Chu diviner group (Period II) stopped
with the grandmother's generation and that the mother's generation was not given
sacrifice. With regard to "Fathers," there are certainly a few exceptions to this dis-
tancing, particularly in the case of "Father Ding," i.e., Wu Ding (K21), who was
offered the five ritual sacrifices during the generation of his son, Zn Jia (K23). See,
e.g., *Heji* 23243 (Y706.1) for the *yi*-ritual; *Heji* 23256 (Y350.2) for the *ji*-ritual; *Heji*
223120 (Y264.2), 36129 (Y266.1) for the *xie*-ritual; *Heji* 23239, 23240, 23241f,
25076 (Y1287.1) for the *rong*-ritual. I find, however, no offering of the five rituals
to any other Fathers. It is of interest, in this regard, that the Period II diviners also
divined about offering some of the five rituals to Elder Brother Ji (Xiong Ji 兄己)
(*Heji* 23241f) and to Elder Brother Geng (Xiong Geng 兄庚) (*Heji* 23483, 23486).
Evidently, as the ritual cycle was being established in Period II, the recently dead—
especially when they appear to have been powerful rulers, like Wu Ding—were also
included in the ancestral cult cycle.

83. The only exceptions I have found involved: a prayer for rain, addressed to
Da Yi (K1), the dynasty founder (*Yingcang* 1757 [Y565.1]); and prayers for harvest
addressed to Zu Ding (K15) (*Heji* 28275 [Y531.1], *Tunnan* 2359 [Y531.2]).

84. Keightley, "At the Beginning," 41–42.

85. Keightley, "At the Beginning," 44.

86. Schmitt, *Ghosts in the Middle Ages*, 5.

87. Schmitt, *Ghosts in the Middle Ages*, 5–6.

88. Erika Bourguignon, *Psychological Anthropology: An Introduction to Human Nature and Cultural Differences*, 243, New York: Holt, Rinehart, and Winston, 1979, citing A. F C. Wallace, *Religion: An Anthropological View*, 239, New York: Random House, 1966.

89. Chang Yuzhi, *Shangdai zhouji zhidu*, 170.

90. Roy A. Rappaport, *Ritual and Religion in the Making of Humanity*, 169, 123, 190, New York: Cambridge University Press, 1999 (italics in the original).

91. I take the dates of the Lace Shang kings from Edward L. Shaughnessy, "Calendar and Chronology," in Loewe and Shaughnessy eds., *The Cambridge History of Ancient China*, 19–29. The Xia-Shang-Zhou chronology project has dated Wu Ding's death to 1192 B.C. (Xia Shang Zhou duandai gongcheng congshu bianji weihuanhui ed., *Xia Shang Zhou duandai gongcheng: 1996–2000 nian jieduan chengguo baogao; Jianben* 夏商周斷代工程：1996–2000 年階段成果報告; 簡本, 60, Beijing: Shijie tushu chuban gongsi, 2000).

92. On the location of these enemy groups, see, e.g., Zheng Jiexiung 鄭杰祥, *Shangdai dili gailun* 商代地理概論, 284–86, 314, 319, 325, Zhengzhou: Zhongzhou guji chubanshe, 1994.

93. Taken, with minor alterations, from Keightley, "The Shang: China's First Historical Dynasty," 288–89. For the research on which these judgments are based, see Edward L. Shaughnessy, "Extra-Lineage Cult in the Shang Dynasty: A Surrejoinder," *Early China*, 11–12 (1985–87): 187–90; Xia Hanyi 夏含氣, "Zaoqi Shang Zhou guanxi ji qi dui Wu Ding yihou Yin Shang wangshi shili fanwei de yiyi 早期商周關係及其對武丁以後殷商王室勢力範圍的意義," *Jiuzhou xuekan* 九州學刊 2.1 (1987): 20–32. See also Wang Yuxin 王宇信, "Wuding qi zhanzheng buci fenqi de changshi 武丁期戰爭卜辭分期的智試," in Wang Yuxin ed., *Jiaguwen yu Yin Shang shi. Di san ji* 甲貴文與殷商史 · 第三輯, especially 174, table 1, Shanghai: Shanghai guji, 1991; Fan Yuzhou 范碴周, "Yindai Wuding shiqi de zhanzheng 殷代武丁時朋的戰爭," in Wang Yuxin ed., *Jiaguwen yu Yin Shang shi. Di san ji*, 175–239. For one reconstruction of Zu Jia's campaigns against the Renfang 人方, see Yan Yiping 跟一萍, *Yin Shang shiji* 殷商史記, 3: 1380–1409, Taibei: Yiwen, 1989.

94. I cannot resist here quoting Garrison Keillor, who reported that Bill Gates had said in an interview, that "Just in terms of allocation of time resources, religion is not very efficient. There's a lot more I could be doing on a Sunday morning," To which Keillor responded, tongue-in-cheek, "And that's why LOL—Lutherans on Line—tries to bring you a Sunday morning worship matrix that maximizes religious benefits per unit of time expended" ("A Prairie Home Companion," originally broadcast on National Public Radio on 28 June 1997).

95. Much scholarship, from Dong Zuobin onwards, supports this view. For one recent account, see Itô Michiharu. "Part One: Religion and Society," 1: 27, 44, 49, 53, 99, 99–100. Itô, in fact, concludes that under Zu Jia, "the ancestral spirits became better defined entities than they had been in Period I" (p. 185). At least they so appear to us in the divination record.

96. Significant in this regard is the change in the way the dynasty founder, the first king, was referred to. In Periods I and II, the Shang bad referred to him as Cheng 成, "The Achiever" (?) (Y1378.2–79.2) and as Tang 唐 (Y1379.2–82.1), but already in Period I, and increasingly with the IIb ritual reforms of Zu Jia, they regularized the name of the dynasty founder as Da Yi 大乙, "The Greater Yi" (Y1374.1–78.2) (as in [9]). See, e.g., Keightley, *Sources of Shang History*, 204, 207, n. a.

97. Martin Kern, "*Shi Jing* 詩經 Songs As Performance Texts: A Case Study of 'Chu ci' 楚茨 ('Thorny Caltrop')," ms. p. 18, to appear in *Early China* 25. For the view, speculative in my opinion, that the *shi*, "personator," is recorded in a number of Shang bone inscriptions, see Fang Shuxin 方述鑫, "Yinxu buci zhong suojian de 'shi' 殷墟 卜辭中所見的'尸'" *Kaogu yu wenwu* 考古與文物 2000.5: 21–24, 27. Fang cites, in particular, *Heji* 32285 (= *Cuibian* 519).

98. In this connection, the observation of Fortes ("Pietas in Ancestor Worship," 184) that "It is often impossible to tell, when Tallensi speak of a farther or a grandfather, whether they are referring to a living person or to an ancestor" is suggestive. The personality types, evidently, were not distinct in modern Africa; they may not have been distinct in Late Shang China.

99. David Schaberg, "Command and the Content of Tradition," in Christopher Lupke ed., *The Magnitude of Ming: Command, Lot and Fate in Chinese Culture* (Honolulu: University of Hawaii Press, in press). As Schaberg notes, "Kings did have personal names; but it appears that only they and their family elders used them."

100. Cao Dingyun 曹定云, *Yin Shang kaogu luncong* 殷商考古論鑑, 49–67, Taibei: Yiwen, 1996. See too Alexander C. Soper, "Early, Middle, and Late Shang: A Note," *Artibus Asiae* 28 (1966): 5–38; K.C. Chang, *Shang Civilization*, 118, New Haven: Yale University Press, 1980.

101. Cao Dingyun, *Yin Shang kaogu luncong*, 60. The Mu Wu, "Mother Wu," whose temple name was cast into the *Si Mu Wu ding*, would have been Bi Wu 姚戊, "Ancestress Wu" (identified as Wu Ding's consort in [21C] above).

102. That Fu Hao received cult on a *xin* day (*Heji* 32757) makes it likely that her temple name, whether Mu Xin or Bi Xin, was Xin; see Li Xueqin 李學勤, "Lun 'Fu Hao' mu de niandai ji youguan Wenwu 論'婦好'墓的年代及有關問題," *Wemon* 文物 1977.11: 35. For the order in which the consorts died, see Chang Yuzhi, *Shangdai zhouji zhidu*, 105, n. 2; she also cites Li Xueqin 李學勤, "'Zhong Ri Ou Mei Ao Niu suo jian suo tuo suo mo jinwen huibian' xuanshi '中日歐美 懊紐所見所拓所摹金文彙編' 選擇," *Guwenzi yanjiu lunwenji* 古文字研究論文集, 10 (1982): 41. See too Keightley, "At the Beginning," 41–42.

103. This conclusion bears on Patricia McAnany's phrase, "living with the ancestors" (quoted on p. 156 above). Mortuary practice in early China differed from that of the Maya. The Maya had "interred their ancestors under the floors of their houses, in residential shrines, and within large funerary pyramids right in the center of their cities and villages" (McAnany, *Living With the Ancestors*, 1). "In North China and the Northwest," by contrast, "the Neolithic adult dead were removed from the living, with adult graves clustered outside the residence area and sometimes separated from it by a ditch, perhaps for symbolic reasons…. The practice of extramural burial continued into the early Bronze Age" (David N. Keightley, "Dead But Not Gone: The Role of Mortuary Practices in the Formation of Neolithic and Early Bronze Age Chinese Culture, ca. 8000 to 1000 B.C.," 5–6, paper prepared for the conference on "Ritual and the Social Significance of Death in Chinese Society," Oracle, Az., 2–7 January 1985).

104. See the discussion of this and related inscriptions at Wen Mingrong 溫明榮, Guo Zhenlu 郭振祿, and Liu Yiman 劉一曼, "Shilun buci fenqi zhong de jige wenti 試論卜辭分期中的幾個問題," in Zhongguo kaoguxue yanjiu bianwei hui 中國考古學研究編委會 ed., *Zhongguo kaoguxue yanjiu—Xia Nai xiansheng kaogu wushi nian jinian wenji* 中園考古學研究——夏鼐先生考古五十年紀念文集, 164, Beijing: Wenwu, 1986.

105. Keightley, *Sources*, 209, n. ai.

106. Chen Mengjia, *Yinxu buci zongshu*, 494; Qu Wanli, *Yinxu wenzi: Jiabian kaoshi*, no. 627. The relevant inscriptions are *Heji* 4933, 32617, 32690.

107. For a compilation of early textual references to Zu Jia, see Zhou Hongxiang 周鴻翔, *Shang Yin diwang benji* 商殷帝王本紀, 147–50, Hong Kong: 1958; Yan Yiping, *Yin Shang shiji*, 1:175–83.

108. Bernhard Karlgren tr., *The Book of Documents*, 58, Stockholm: Museum of Far Eastern Antiquities, 1950.

109. There is some disagreement about the words 其在祖甲不義惟王 that precede this passage. Karlgren offers: "When (it rested with Zu Jia =) the turn came to Zu Jia, it was not (right, reasonable =) to be expected that he should become king (sc. two brothers preceding him to the throne), and for long he was (one of) the small people" ("Glosses on the Book of Documents II," *Bulletin of the Museum of Far Eastern Antiquities* 21 [1959], 108–09, no. 1840). That interpretation is attractive for it suggests that the unexpectedness or irregularity of his succession might have given Zu Jia particular interest in how he was to be remembered as an ancestor, claiming the status of main-line descent for himself and relegating his two brothers—Karlgren refers to Zu Ji (seen. 114 below) and Zu Geng (K22)—to collateral status. James Legge (tr., *The Chinese Classics, Volume III: The Shoo King or the Book of Historical Documents*, 467, London: Frowde, 1865), however, follows the more traditional view and offers: "he would not unrighteously be emperor, and he was at first one of the inferior people."

110. Karlgren rejected as "amusing" and "absurd" the view, which he traces back to 6 B.C., that the Zu Jia of the passage did not refer to K23 at all but to Tai Jia 太甲 (i.e., Da Jia 大甲, K3), Da Yi's grandson ("Glosses on the Book of Documents II," 108, no. 1840). Cai Zhemao 蔡哲茂, however ("Lun 'Shangshu, Wuyi' 'Qi zai Xu Jia, bi yi wei wang' 論 '尚書, 無逸' '其在祖甲, 不遄悱王,'" in Lishi yuyan yanjiusuo; Taiwan Shida guowenxi eds., *Jiaguwen faxian yibai zhounian xueshu yantaohui* 甲骨文發現一百周年學術研討會, 85–100, Taibei: 10–12 May 1998), concludes that the Zu Jia in the "Wu yi" was, without question, Da Jia.

111. Legge tr., *The Shoo King*, 136; Wang Guowei 王國維, "Jinben Zhushu jinian shuzheng 今本竹書紀年疏證," Shang 上:32b, in Yang Jialuo 楊家駱, ed., *Zhushu Jinian ba zhong* 竹盅紀年八重, Taibei: Shijie, 1963; Fan Xiangyong 范祥雍, ed., *Guben Zhushu jinian jijiao dingbu* 古本竹書紀年訂補, 22, Shanghai: Shanghai Renmin chubanshe, 1962.

112. Takigawa Kametarô 瀧川太郎, *Shiki kaichû kôshô* 史記會注考証, 3: 24, Tokyo: Tôhô bunka gakuin, 1934; Édouard Chavannes tr., *Les Mémoires historiques de Sema Ts'ien. Tome Premier*, 197, Paris: Ernest Leroux, 1895; reprint, Paris: Adrien-Maisonneuve, 1967; cf. William H. Nienhauser Jr. ed., with Tsai-fa Cheng, Zongli Lu, and Robert Reynolds trs., *The Grand Scribe's Records. Volume I. The Basic Annals of Pre-Han China by Ssu-ma Ch'ien*, 49, Bloomington: Indiana University Press, 1994.

113. For a compilation of the relevant texts, see, e.g., Zhou Hongxiang, *Shang Yin diwang benji*, 129–40; Yan Yiping, *Yin Shang shiji*, 1: 157–73. The *Guben Zhushu jinian* contains no information about Wu Ding whatever; see Fan Xiangyong, ed., *Guben Zhushu jinian*, 21.

114. He is thought to have been a son of Wu Ding; see Keightley, *Sources of Shang History*, 206, 208, n. ad.

115. Legge tr., *The Shoo King*, 266. Chavannes (tr., *Les Mémoires historiques de Sema Ts'ien*, I, 196, n. 5), commenting that the *Shangshu* account is clearer than the *Shiji* version, read the text much as Legge had done: 'Wu Ding had shown too much zeal in

sacrificing to his dead father, to the detriment of the earlier ancestors who had right to the same honors.'

116. Karlgren tr., *The Book of Documents*, 26. In his "Glosses on the Book of Documents," *Bulletin of the Museum of Far Eastern Antiquities* 20 (1948): 216–17, no. 1492, Karlgren cites several traditional interpretations in which the phrase in question means "in regard to the sacrifices, do not be over-rich in the (near one =) father's shrine" or some version thereof.

117. Keightley, "Clean Hands and Shining Helmets," See Essay 10, below.

118. Translation based on Karlgren tr., "Book of Documents," 21, 24; "Glosses On the Book of Documents," 202, no. 1463; Legge tr., *The Shoo King*, 230, 238–240.

119. Chen Yiping 陳一平, *Huainanzi: jiao zhu yi* 淮南子 ： 校注譯, *j.* 17, "Shuolınxun 說林訓," 846, Guangzhou: Guangdong renmin chubanshe, 1994; from Christoph Harbsmeier, "Elementary Exercises in Ancient Chinese Conceptual History No. 1: The Ancient Chinese Concept of the Heart," ms. (ca. March 1996): 25, tr. adj.

120. Keightley, *The Ancestral Landscape*, 101–102.

121. See the scholarship cited at David N. Keightley, "Art, Ancestors, and the Origins of Writing in China," *Representations* 56 (Fall 1996): 93, n. 26. On masks, see too n. 12 above. Wu Hung's comment ("All About the Eyes: Two Groups of Sculptures From the Sanxingdui Culture," *Orientations* 28.8 [September 1997]: 64) that "it seems that by distorting the natural human form, the [Bronze-Age] artist could bestow his creation with supernatural qualities" also suggests that the impersonalization I have been describing in Late Shang theology was a way of enhancing and sanctifying the powers of the dead.

122. For the possibility that the Zhou songs refer to images of the ancestors, see Edward L. Shaughnessy, "From Liturgy to Literature: The Ritual Contexts of the Earliest Poems in the *Book of Poetry*," in Shaughnessy, *Before Confucius: Studies in the Creation of the Chinese Classics*, 189, n. 16, Albany: State University of New York Press: 1997. He proposes that *xiang* 相 in "Qing miao 清廟" (Mao no. 266), which is usually understood as sacrificial "assistants," referred instead to "images" (*xiang* 象) of the ancestors in the temple. Even if this is true for the Zhou, any such images, if they existed, have not been preserved. And for the Shang at least, we appear to have some examples of their ancestral tablets, inscribed not with images but only with temple names (p. 37). And as John Kieschnick has observed (email communication of 22 June 1999), "In general religious icons were not the focus of worship before Buddhism entered China. It makes sense that since the ancestors were impersonal, they were not represented in anthropomorphic form."

123. Frank Willet, "Ife in Nigerian Art," *African Arts/Arts d'Afrique* 1.1 (Autumn 1967): 34. See, too, Keightley, "The Religious Commitment," 221–22.

124. *Kouroi* were "archaic Greek marble statues of naked, striding, beardless males … made to body forth a specific metaphysic of masculinity, of masculine presence as such" (Andrew F. Stewart, *Art, Desire, and the Body in Ancient Greece*, 63, 67, Cambridge: Cambridge University Press, 1997). The *kouros* was "the rendering not of a particular man but of the idea of a man—an archetype that can stand for all…. Though it does not realistically portray the aristocratic dead, it embodies and memorializes him at the height of his beauty and *aret*'" (Jeffrey M. Hurwit, *The Art and Culture of Early Greece, 1100–480 B.C.*, 197, 200, Ithaca: Cornell University Press, 1985). Stewart estimates that "*several thousand* kouroi stood in Attica by the end of the sixth century—and perhaps ten times as many in the Greek world as a whole" (pp. 63–64, italics in the original).

125. Hurwit, *The Art and Culture of Early Greece*, 26; Stewart, *Art, Desire, and the Body*, 65.

126. K.E. Brashier, "Death as Controlled Transformation in the Han," 2, paper presented at the Association for Asian Studies Meetings, Washington, D.C., April 1995. He cites the *Liji*, "Ji yi 祭龜," in which "(The sages) built halls and established ancestral temples so (the people) could distinguish between recent ascendants and remote ascendants, between those closely related and those distantly related. They taught the people to revert to antiquity and return to the origin, never forgetting their progenitor" (築為宮室設為宗桃以別親疏遠邇,教民反古復始不忘其所由生也). For variant translations, see Legge tr., *The Li Ki*, 2: 221; Couvreur tr., *Li ki*, 2: 290–91. See too K.E. Brashier, "Han Thanatology and the Division of 'Souls,'" *Early China* 21 (1996): 154.

127. Translation derived from Couvreur tr.,禮記 *Li ki*, 1: 200–01, and Legge tr., *The Li Ki*, 1: 168. Shaughnessy (personal communication, 4 March 1999) proposes "considering the deceased as not departed" for 以死者為不可別已.

128. Liu Zhao 劉剑, "Anyang Hougang Yin mu suochu 'bing xing shi' yongru kao 安陽後岡殷墓所出 '柄形飾' 用途考," *Kaogu* 考古 1995.7: 623–625, 605.

129. David Crockett Graham, "Religion in Szechuan Province, China." *Smithsonian Miscellaneous Collections* 80, no. 4 (1928): 12.

130. Legge tr., *The Li Ki*, 2; 391, "San nian wen 三年問."

131. Cf. the discussion of the Christian *Memoria* on p. 28.

132. Based on Legge tr., *The Li Ki*, 1: 177.

133. Legge tr., *The Li Ki* 2: 211, tr. adj.; see too Couvreur tr., *Li ki* 2: 274.

134. Based on Legge tr., *The Li Ki*, 2: 375; see too Couvreur tr., *Li ki*, 2: 552.

135. Similarly, Arthur Wolf had noted that, in modern Taiwan, "Many families make effort to respect the personal tastes of individual ancestors" ("Gods, Ghosts, and Ancestors," 177), but the examples he cites only involve a mother-in-law and father-in-law, and on the anniversary of the deathday, not more distant ancestors as they are being offered cult according to a Shang-style timetable.

136. Keightley, "Religious Commitment," 218.

137. For an expression of such "generationalism" in later ritual texts, which distinguished between recent and remote ascendants, see n. 126 above.

138. According to C.W. Bishop, the average reign length of the kings and state rulers of the Zhou was twenty years; see the discussion at Keightley, *Sources of Shang History*, 175.

139. Brashier, "Death as Controlled Transformation," 3–4. For Dong Zhongshu, he cites Su Yu 蘇輿, *Chunqiu fanlu yizheng* 春秋繁露義證, "Sandai gaizhi zhiwen 三代改制質文," 7.18a-b, Taibei: Helu tushu, 1974: 故聖王生則天于,崩遷則 存為三王 ,紬減則為五帝 ,下至附庸,紬為九皇 ,下極其為民, "Thus, a sage-king is the 'son of heaven' when he is alive, but when he dies and (his tablet) is moved (to the ancestral shrines), he is preserved as (one of) the 'three kings.' He gradually diminishes (to the level of) the 'five emperors', declining to the level of a dependency. He diminishes to (the level of) the 'nine august ones' and is then reduced all the way down to (the level of) the people.'" See too Legge's approving summary (tr., *The Chinese Classics, Volume V: The Ch'un Ts'ew with The Tso Chuen*, 233, London: Trübner, 1872) of the discussion of Zhou rulers' mourning rites by the Qing scholar, Mao Qiling 毛奇齡, in which "At the conclusion of the mourning, the new tablet was taken to its proper shrine in the temple, and one of the older ones was removed;—in the form and order prescribed."

140. Rubie S. Watson, "Remembering the Dead: Graves and Politics in Southeastern China," in James L. Watson and Evelyn S. Rawski eds., *Death Ritual in Late Imperial and Modern China*, 205, Berkeley: University of California Press, 1988, citing Maurice Freeman, *Chinese Lineage and Society*, 140–43, London: Athlone, 1966.

141. Wolf, "Gods Ghosts, and Ancestors," 151.

142. Keightley, "Religious Commitment," p. 93.

143. Mark Edward Lewis, *Writing and Authority in Early China*, 13, 16, Albany: State University of New York Press, 1999.

144. Lothar Ledderose, *Ten Thousand Things: Module and Mass Production in Chinese Art*, 2, 5, 7, Princeton: Princeton University Press, 2000.

145. Translation based on Legge tr., *The Li Ki*, 2: 236-37; Couvreur tr., *Li ki*, 2: 318.

146. David Johnson, "Epic and History in Early China: the Matter of Wu Tzu-Hsü," *Journal of Asian Studies* 40 (1981): 271.

147. *Hanshu, j.* 20. See Derk Bodde, "Types of Chinese Categorical Thinking," in Charles Le Blanc and Dorothy Borei eds., *Essays in Chinese Civilization*, 147–60, Princeton: Princeton University Press, 1981 (originally published in *Journal of the American Oriental Society* 59 [1939]: 200–19); Cho-yun Hsu, *Ancient China in Transition: An Analysis of Social Mobility, 722–222 B.C.*, 25, Stanford: Stanford University Press, 1965.

148. See, e.g., Keightley, "Clean Hands and Shining Helmets," 15–51.

149. Wang Hui, "Zhouyuan jiagu shuxing," 5–20. Wang cites, in part, such passages as the following from the *Mozi*, "Ming gui, xia 明鬼,下": "In ancient times, having captured Yin and punished Zhou, Wu Wang let the great lords share in the sacrifices (to the Shang ancestors). He said, 'Let those more closely related partake in the domestic rituals and those more distantly related in the external rituals'" (昔者武王之攻殷誅紂也，使諸候分其祭曰: 使親者受內祀，疏者受外祀). One notes the continuing emphasis on kin-based jurisdictions.

150. Chang Yuzhi (*Shangdai zhouji zhidu*, 304) has noted, for example, that because cult to Wu Yi (K26) and Wen Wu Ding (K27) was not divined on bones that also recorded cult to other kings or consorts, it is not possible to situate these two kings in the ritual cycle; they certainly were offered the five rituals of the cycle, but not, it seems, as part of the regular five-ritual calendar.

151. Keightley (*Sources of Shang History*, 108) refers to "the general trend toward a neat, standard page design and neat, small standardized graphs" that "reached its fruition in the routine divination inscriptions of Period V."

152. Consider, in this regard, Rappaport's comments (*Ritual and Religion in the Making of Humanity*, 123, 124 [italics in original]): "That a liturgical order is accepted in its performance does not ... guarantee that the performer will abide by whatever rules or norms that order encodes.... *it is not ritual's office to ensure compliance but to establish obligation.*"

153. My characterization of the "disciplinary revolution," together with the words enclosed in quotes, is taken from Robert N. Bellah, "Prologue," 11, in his "Religious Evolution" (unpublished ms., January 1999). He cites Philip Gorski, "The Protestant Ethic Revisited: Disciplinary Revolution and State Formation in Holland and Prussia," *American Journal of Sociology* 99.2 (1993): 253–316; S.N. Eisenstadt, "Origins of the West: The Origin of the West in Recent Macrosociological Theory: The Protestant Ethic Reconsidered," *Cultural Dynamics* 2.3(1990): 119–53.

154. Peter Brown, *The Cult of the Saints: Its Rise and Function in Latin Christianity*, 49, Chicago: University of Chicago Press, 1981.

155. "Prologue," 14. He cites S.N. Eisenstadt, "Axial Age Sectarianism and the Antinomies of Modernity," in S. A. McKnight and G.L. Pierce eds., *Politics, Order and History*, Sheffield: Sheffield Academic Press, 1999. Paul Wheatley (*The Pivot of the Four Quarters: A Preliminary Enquiry into the Origins and Character of the Ancient Chinese City*, 318–19, Chicago: Aldine, 1971) had provided a similar model for the genesis of the early Chinese city, arguing that though there is "no single autonomous cause ... one activity does seem in a sense to command a sort of priority. Whatever structural changes in social organization were induced by commerce, warfare, or technology, they needed to be validated by some instrument of authority if they were to achieve institutionalized permanence. This does not imply that religion ... was a primary causative factor, but rather that it permeated all activities, all institutional change, and afforded a consensual focus for social life." See, too, the discussion at Rappaport, *Ritual and Religion in the Making of Humanity*, 173–75.

8

THEOLOGY AND THE WRITING OF HISTORY: TRUTH AND THE ANCESTORS IN THE WU DING DIVINATION RECORDS

David N. Keightley

Abstract

Close reading of the oracle-bone inscriptions can provide insights into the work habits of the Shang diviners and their commitment to the keeping of accurate historical records. Most inscriptions from the reign of Wu Ding (ca. 1200 to ca. 1189 B.C.E.) either show that the king's forecasts were accurate, with the verification confirming the royal prognostication, or they provide insufficient information for the king's successes as a diviner to be judged. In a small but significant number of cases, however, Wu Ding did forecast that a certain event might occur on a certain day and yet the verification records that the event took place on another day. Analysis of these "discomfiting" divinatory scenarios reveals the modest and fallible nature of the king's abilities as seer. Although records in which the king "missed" the day might be considered potentially damaging to the king's legitimacy, they must be understood not simply in terms of secular historiography but also in terms of a Shang ancestral theology in which it was important to record the particular days and—by implication, the ancestors associated with those particular days—that the king's forecast had invoked. Despite their specialized nature, the Shang divination inscriptions throw valuable light on one important system, presumably influential, of early Chinese record-keeping.

The oracle-bone inscri ptions of the Late Shang dynasty (ca. 1200 to ca. 1045 B.C.E), can on occasion provide us with an immediate sense, remarkable at a remove of over three thousand years, of the work habits and motives of the Shang diviners and record-keepers.[1] In this essay, I will focus on a small number of inscriptions from the reign of Wu Ding 武丁 (ca. 1200–1189 B.C.E.) that bear on the diviners' commitment to the keeping of records that were not only historically accurate but that appear to have preserved more of the truth than, in the best interests of the king, they needed to. The evidence, when read closely, throws light on the diviners' historiographical and theological concerns.

Divination Records Under Wu Ding

Since Wu Ding's religious, political, and economic authority rested upon his routine ability to assert his status within the royal descent group, it is no surprise that a significant number of his divination records served an explicitly validating function. Successful divinations—defined as those in which Wu Ding's forecasts, whether of good or bad fortune, had been confirmed by the subsequent events—demonstrated his mantic powers. And auspicious forecasts, whether confirmed by the event or not, presumably demonstrated the temporary approval of the religious Powers, revealed in the pyromantic cracks, as the king prayed for rain and good harvests, commanded his subordinates, and mobilized conscripts for his economic and military ventures.[2]

Given divination's validating role, Wu Ding, one may suppose, would not have been likely to employ engravers who recorded on scapula or plastron that a royal forecast had been unsuccessful. This may explain why the vast majority of the verifications, the *post-facto* records of what actually transpired, confirm the king's forecasts (Ji Dewei 1986:118–119, 127, n. 4; Keightley 1988:372–373). It may also help explain why, in many other cases, forecasts and results—many of which had presumably failed to confirm the king's forecasts—were not recorded at all (see note 30 below).

Three representative divinations exemplify Wu Ding's legitimating successes:

[1A] 己卯卜殻貞 : 不其雨

Crack-making on *jimao* (day 16), Que divined: *(Charge:)* "It may not rain."[3]

[1B] 己卯卜 殻貞 : 雨 . 王固 : 其雨佳壬 . 壬午允雨

Crack-making on *jimao*, Que divined: *(Charge:)* "It will rain."
(Prognostication:) The king read the cracks and said: "If it rains, it will be on a *ren*-day." *(Verification:)* On *renwu* (day 19), it really did rain." (I. Bin)[4] (*Bingbian* 235.1-2 = *HJ* 902f)[5]

In this case, the king, having proposed two complementary charges, one positive ([1B]) and one negative ([1A]), had forecast rain for a *ren*-day, and, sure enough, the verification recorded that "on *renwu* it really did rain." A record of full success! Similarly:

[2] 癸巳卜殻貞 : 旬亡禍 . 王固曰 : 出咎其出來嬉 . 乞至五日丁酉
允出來嬉自西正戟告曰土方征于我東鄙𢀛二邑舌方亦侵我西鄙田

Crack-making on *guisi* (day 30), Que divined: *(Charge:)* "In the (next) ten days there will be no disasters." *(Prognostication:)* The king read the cracks and said: "There will be calamities: there may be (someone) bringing alarming news." *(Verification:)* When it came to the fifth day, *dingyou* (day 34), there really was (someone) bringing alarming news from the west. Zhi Guo reported and said: "The Tufang have attacked in our eastern borders and have seized two settlements. The Gongfang likewise invaded the fields of our western borders." (I. Bin) *(Jinghua* 2 = *HJ* 6057f)

In four other instances on this scapula the engravers recorded prognostications that were identical to that of [2]: 王固曰 ： 出咎其出來嬉, "The king read the cracks and said: 'There will be calamities: there may be (someone) bringing alarming news.' And in each case, the verification documented, with news of various enemy invasions, that the king's pessimistic forecast had been correct. Again, full success.

Finally, a charge-pair involving childbirth, in which Wu Ding's forecast had been vindicated by the event:

[3A] 辛未卜殷貞 ： 婦妓娩嘉 . 王固曰 ： 其佳庚娩嘉 . 三月庚戌娩嘉

Crack-making on *xinwei* (day 8), Que divined: *(Charge:)* "Lady Nuan's childbearing will be good." *(Prognostication:)* The king read the cracks and said: "If it be a *geng*-day childbearing, it will be good." *(Verification:)* (In) the third moon, on *gengxu* (day 47), she gave birth; it was good."

[3B] 辛[未]卜殷貞 ： [婦]妓挽[不]其嘉

Crack-making on *xin[wei]*, Que divined: "[Lady] Nuan's childbearing may [not] be good." (I. Bin) *(Bingbian* 257.1-2 = *HJ* 454f)

In this inscription the king's forecast of a "good" *geng*-day birth, proved accurate forty days later. One need not be overly cynical to suppose that the king had had three previous chances to be right—on *gengchen* (day 17), *gengyin* (day 27), and *gengzi* (day 37)—before the birth of a son on *gengxu* (day 47) vindicated his "any *geng*-day" approach. Nevertheless, given the terms of the prognostication, the divination had been a success.

Wu Ding's verifications, however, were not all simply self-congratulatory records of his successes as diviner. A small number of the verifications reveal a commitment to truthful record-keeping, in which the record itself appears to call into question the king's divinatory success. Most of the cases involve scenarios in which the king's recorded forecast about a particular day or days was not confirmed by the recorded results, as in the following case of royal childbirth (Figure 1):

[4A] 甲申卜殷貞 ： 婦好娩嘉 . 王固曰 ： 其佳丁娩嘉其佳庚娩引吉.
三旬又一日甲寅娩不嘉佳女

(Preface:) Crack-making on *jiashen* (day 21), Que divined: *(Charge:)* "Lady Hao's childbearing will be good."[6] *(Prognostication:)* The king read the cracks and said: "If it be a *ding*-day childbearing, it will be good; if it be a *geng*-(day) childbearing, there will be prolonged auspiciousness." *(Verification:)* (After) thirty-one days, on *jiayin* (day 51), she gave birth; it was not good; it was a girl.

Figure 1 Rubbing of *Bingbian* 247 = *HJ* 14002f, discussed in the text as [4AB]. Original length 13.4 cm.

[4B] 甲申卜殼貞 : 婦好娩不其嘉. 三旬又一日甲寅娩允不嘉隹女

(Preface:) Crack-making on *jiashen*, Que divined: *(Charge:)* "Lady Hao's child-bearing may not be good." *(Verification:)* (After) thirty-one days, on *jiayin* (day 51), she gave birth; it really was not good; it was a girl. (*Bingbian* 247.1-2 = *HJ* 14002f)

[4C] 王固曰 : 其隹丁娩嘉. 其庚引吉其隹壬戌不吉

(Prognostication:) The king read the cracks and said: "If it be a *ding*-(day) child-bearing, it will be good; if (it be) a *geng*-day (childbearing), there will be prolonged auspiciousness; if it be a *renxu* (day 59) (childbearing), it will not be auspicious."[7] (I.Bin) (*Bingbian* 248.7 = *HJ* 14002b)

In this case, the king made the contingent forecast that Lady Hao's childbearing would be auspicious if it occurred on a *ding*-day or a *geng*-day ([4A] and [4C]), not auspicious if it fell on *renxu* ([4C]). In fact, she gave birth on a *jia*-day and, because she gave birth to a girl, the birth was "not good"—a verification recorded in both [4A] and [4B]. Strictly speaking, the king's accuracy as a forecaster was not invalidated by the inauspiciousness of the result, for the actual birth, on *jiayin*, occurred on a day for which he had, in these prognostications, made no forecast at all. In effect, the king had said—or, more precisely, was recorded as having said— 'I can only tell you about births on *ding*-days, *geng*-days, and *renxu*; I have no information about other days.' One could accordingly argue that, given the terms of the prognostication, the divination had been a success. Nevertheless, it would seem that, to the extent that Wu Ding's forecasts about *ding*-days, *geng*-days, and *renxu* had entirely "missed" the event on *jiayin*, they had, as forecasts, been largely rendered "irrelevant."

Understanding of this particular divinatory scenario can be improved by situating it within a wider context. Que had, eighteen days later, divined a second charge-pair, involving what appears to have been the same birth (Figure 2):

[5A] 壬寅卜殼貞 : 婦[好]娩嘉．王🔲曰 : 其隹[庚?]申娩吉嘉其隹甲寅娩不吉．退隹女

(Preface:) Crack-making on *renyin* (day 39), Que divined: *(Charge:)* "Lady [Hao's] childbearing will be good." *(Prognostication:)* The king read the cracks and said: "If it be on [*geng?*]*shen* (day 57?)[8] that she give birth, it will be auspicious and good. If it be on *jiayin* (day 51) that she give birth, it will not be auspicious." *(Verification:)* It was delayed. It was a girl.

[5B] 壬寅卜殼貞 : 婦好娩不其嘉．王🔲曰 : 特不嘉其嘉不吉于𚿬 若茲 迺死

Crack-making on *renyin* (day 39), Que divined: "Lady Hao's childbearing may not be good." The king read the cracks and said: "If (we) seize (the baby) (?) (or, If [she] hold [the baby] [?]), it will not be good. If it is good, it will not be auspicious." *(Verification:)* At the ..(?) ..,[9] it was like this and then (the baby?) died. (I. Bin) (*Yibian* 4729 = *HJ* 14001f)

On the assumption that the inscriptions on the two plastrons both refer to the same event—and there can be little doubt that this is so[10]—it would appear, on the face of it, that in the second prognostication, [5A], made eighteen days after the missed prognostications of [4AB], the king got it right, forecasting with accuracy that a birth on *jiayin* (day 51) would not be "auspicious." And the verifications of [4AB], confirming that the *jiayin* birth had not been "good," documented that this second forecast had been uncannily accurate. (For the possibility that the

Figure 2 Rubbing of *Yibian* 4729 = *HJ* 14001, discussed in the text as [5AB]. Original length 9 cm.

precision of this forecast had been retroactive and thus spurious, see the discussion of [6AB] and [7AB] on page 214 below.) Wu Ding's "missing" the day in his forecasts of [4AC] had thus been "corrected" or compensated for by the accuracy of his [5A] forecast eighteen days later.[11]

Three conclusions may be drawn from [4ABC], [5A], and a few similar cases in which there was a temporal disjunction between the forecast and verification.[12] First, Wu Ding's forecasts seem to have been modest in their expectations; the king's forecasts were often contingent. The relatively weak legitimation that the record of [4ABC] appears to have provided—showing that the king hazarded a forecast for two *gan* days and one *ganzhi* day, but that the result fell on another day—suggests both the reliability of the record-keeping and the king's modest claims to foreknowledge.

Second, the way in which the engravers recorded that the king had missed the day (or that the day had missed the king?) indicates the degree to which these inscriptions were not created merely for propaganda purposes. That is, one can imagine a variety of treatments that would have bolstered the king's reputation as seer more effectively: the record-keepers of [4AC] could have incised, *post facto*, the prognostication that "If it be a *jia*-day childbearing, it will not be good" (as the record-keepers of [5A] in effect were to do), which would have been confirmed by the results; or the record-keepers could have omitted the verification entirely; or they could have omitted both the prognostication and the verification. But they adopted none of these expedients.[13] Similarly, the [5A] prognostication had also recorded a "superfluous" forecast, "If it be on *gengshen* (?) that she give birth, it will be auspicious and good." Since the king had, once again, missed the day in this case, that particular prognostication had also proved irrelevant. Yet the diviners, once again, had not omitted this part of the forecast from the record. That they did not do so appears to reveal their commitment, in this and a relatively small number of other cases, to keeping a record of what the king had actually said.

Third, the existence of [5AB] reminds us that what was to prove a "miss" in one divinatory scenario ([4ABC]) could be rectified by later divination. It seems unlikely, however, that in this case the king had deliberately designed the second divination to rectify the first, for the second try ([5AB]) had been attempted on day 39, twelve days before the missed outcome (on day 51) of the day 21 divination of [4AB] would have been known to the king. The king, in short, was not just following the principle of "If at first you don't succeed, try, try again"; he was evidently observing some other rationale (see pages 217–218 below).

Records of forecasts in which Wu Ding missed the day were not limited to divinations about birth, as the following example demonstrates:

[6A] 癸酉卜㱿貞：臣得．王固曰：其得隹甲乙．甲戌臣涉舟延㠯弗告旬又
五日丁亥執．十二月

Crack-making on *guiyou* (day 10), Xuan divined: *(Charge:)* "The Servitors will (get =) catch (the enemy?)." *(Prognostication:)* The king read the cracks and said: "If they catch them it will be on a *jia*-day or *yi*-day (probably day 11 or 12)." *(Verification:)* On *jiaxu* (day 11), the Servitors, by ford and by boat (?), continued to trap (them) (or, went on to Xian?), but did not report; on the fifteenth day, *dinghai* (day 24), (the Servitors) shackled (them)." Twelfth moon.

[6B] 癸酉卜㐸貞：[臣]不其得

Crack-making on *guiyou* (day 10), Xuan divined: *(Charge:)* "[The Servitors] may not catch (the enemy?)." (I. Bin) *(Bingbian 243.3-4 = HJ 641f)*[14]

In this case, the verification clearly did not record a royal success, and yet, the verification was, once again, not entirely a record of failure.

Although they had not caught the enemy on the *jia*- or *yi*-day forecast, the Servitors had, nevertheless, taken some action (continuing to trap the enemy, or continuing on to Xian) on *jiaxu*, one of the days for which a fortunate result had been foretold in [6A]. This relatively detailed verification, which recorded their activities, may thus have been intended to minimize the failure of the forecast: the enemy were not caught on the *jia*-day; nothing happened on the *yi*-day, the other day for which a forecast had been made; and the actual capture occurred on a *ding*-day, a day that—like the birth day of the baby girl in [4A] and [4B]—had not been mentioned in the original prognostication. Once again, the forecast had been contingent and cautious, making forecasts for only two out of a possible ten days ("If they catch [them], it will be on a *jia*-day or *yi*-day"). The verification was seemingly a true record of the way the king had missed the day, thus demonstrating that the cautious approach had been justified. And, once again, the diviners had not doctored the record. They could, for example, have included a *ding*-day forecast in the prognostication, but they did not do so. They could have omitted the *yi*-day from the prognostication, for nothing whatever happened on that day; but they did not do so. The record, though it need not have done so, demonstrated the king's limitations. It demonstrated, once again, a commitment to recording what the king had actually said.

This scenario too needs to be considered in fuller context, for the [6AB] charge-pair that Xuan had divined and the king had prognosticated on *guiyou* (day 10) and that, by *dinghai* (day 24), had led to an outcome whose timing the king had not forecast, appears to have been related to another charge-pair, recorded on another plastron excavated from the same storage pit, YH 127. These charges were divined by Bin, on *guisi* (day 30), and divined, it would seem, in ignorance of the outcome that had already transpired on day 24, six days earlier:[15]

[7A] 癸巳卜賓貞：臣執．王固曰：吉其執隹乙丁．七日丁亥既執

Crack-making on guisi (day 30), Bin divined: *(Charge:)* "The Servitors will shackle (the enemy?)." *(Prognostication:)* The king read the cracks and said: "Auspicious; if they shackle (them) it will be on an *yi*-day or a *ding*-day."[16] *(Verification:)* Seven days (earlier), on *dinghai* (day 24), they had (finished shackling =) already shackled (them).

[7B] 貞 ： 臣不其執

Divined: *(Charge:)* "The Servitors may not shackle (the enemy?)." (I. Bin) (*Yibian* 2093 = *HJ* 643Cf)

In this case, the contingent forecast of [7A], "if they shackle (them) it will be on an *yi*-day or a *ding*-day"—unlike the contingent forecast of [6A], "If they catch (them) it will be on a *jia*-day or *yi*-day"—was successful, for it was confirmed by the verification, which recorded that the enemy had been shackled on a *ding*-day, *dinghai*, as forecast. Yet the engraver of [7A] had recorded a royal forecast of a possible *yi*-day shackling that had, in the event, proved irrelevant. The [7A] prognostication thus provides, once again, a fuller and more faithful record of the king's forecasts than it needed to have done had the intent simply been to demonstrate the king's divinatory success. The engravers had still cut the king's *yi*-day forecast into the bone, even though the shackling had not taken place on an *yi*-day.

In this case, moreover, the forecast and verification of [7A] had been retroactive. The record shows the king making forecasts about events that had, in fact, already taken place. That is, he is shown in [7AB] to have divined on day 30 about events that had already transpired: on day 24—"Seven days (earlier),[17] on *dinghai* (day 24), they had already shackled (them)"; the verification, with its reference to that "seven day" interval, and its use of *ji* 既, the verb of completion, clearly documented the *post-facto* nature of the forecast, which thus demonstrated Wu Ding's ignorance of events at the time that he had divined. There had evidently been no reluctance to record the limited nature of the king's mantic insights.

It is also probable that, in this case, some editorial manipulation of the record may have occurred, for it seems that the verification of [6A]—"on the fifteenth day, *dinghai* (day 24), (the Servitors) shackled (them)"—may not have been inscribed until at least day 30 when, on the basis of the [7A] verification, "Seven days (earlier), on *dinghai* (day 24), they had already shackled (them)," we may suppose that the news of the day-24 success had reached the Shang capital. The change in wording provides the clue. The verb of the day-10 charge of [6A] was *de* 得 "get, catch," but the verb of the day-24 verification of [6A]—part of the same inscription unit—was *zhi* 執, "shackle," precisely the term used in the day-30 charges, forecast, and verification of [7AB]. Having heard, prior to day 30, that the victory of day 24 had involved "shackling" the enemy (as we know from the verification of [7A]), it seems probable that the king or his record-keepers had improved the wording of the day-30 charges ([7AB]), which, following the use of *de* in the [6AB] charges, might originally have employed the verb, *de*. More significantly, the diviners appear to have improved the wording of the verification attached to the day-10 charge ([6A]) so as to accord with results that the king now knew had already taken place on day 24. Such an explanation would account for the anomalous use of different verbs, *de* and *zhi*, in the charge and verification of [6A].[18] Even though the verification of [6A] seems to have been edited in this way to better accord with the reality represented by the verification of [7A], the very disjuncture between the *de* (in the charges of [6AB]) and the *zhi* (in the verification of [6A]) suggests, once again, a commitment to recording, at least in the case of the first charge, what the king had said, i.e., that he had used *de* rather than *zhi*. The record-keepers could quite easily have manipulated the record far more extensively in the king's favor—by, for example, using *zhi* in the charges of [6AB] or by omitting the missed *jia*- or *yi*-day in the prognostication of [6A] or the missed *yi*-day in the prognostication of [7A]—but they did not do so. The king's limitations as diviner were not entirely concealed. His formulations were permitted to change, as the shift from *de* to *zhi* indicates, with a change in circumstances.

It is possible that a similar editorial manipulation may have taken place in the case of the two childbearing divinations, [4ABC] and [5AB], considered above. That the bad and inauspicious [5A] forecast made on day 39, "If it be on *jiayin* (day 51) that she give birth, it will not be auspicious," was so precisely confirmed by the verification, "not good; it was a girl," recorded for that same day 51 by the verification of [4AB], at least raises the suspicion that the prognostication of [5A] had not been recorded, with its suspicious precision, until after the "bad" birth had taken place and the date was known. But there is no way to confirm such a suspicion.[19]

Cases in which the record, such as the verification of [6A] or the prognostication of [5A], may have been incised into the bone several days, or even weeks, after the date of the original divination and prognostication, are important because they suggest that the divination inscriptions are not, strictly speaking, primary sources.[20] The primary sources would have been interim records in which the original charges and prognostications were transcribed as spoken; written on perishable materials like bamboo or silk, it is these "diviners' notebooks" that would have formed the basis for the engravers' work.[21] In this view, the shift from *de* to *zhi* in [6A] implies the existence of an original notebook record in which both the charge and the prognostication would have used *de*. Similarly, the engravers of the superfluous *ding*-day, *geng*-day, and *renxu* forecasts of [4AC], or of the *yi*-day forecast in [7A], for example, would have copied these day-dates from the original notebook account of the king's prognostication.

Finally, one set of inscriptions, in which the days of the forecast and day of the verification did not match, implies, more clearly than any other case, a royal divinatory failure. Once again, the following verifications did not flatly contradict the royal forecast, but the detailed record suggests a sustained (and eventually unsuccessful) effort to avoid acknowledging the failure of that forecast.

[8A] 癸巳卜爭貞：今一月雨．王固曰：[隹]丙雨

Crack-making on *guisi* (day 30), Zheng divined: *(Charge:)* "In the present first moon, it will rain." *(Prognostication:)* The king read the cracks and said: [It will be] on the *bing-day* that it rains."[22]

[8B] 癸巳卜爭貞：今一月不其雨

Crack-making on *guisi*, Zheng divined: *(Charge:)* "In the present first moon, it may not rain."

[8C] 旬壬寅雨甲辰亦雨

(*Verification:*) In the (next) ten-day week, on *renyin* (day 39), it rained; on *jiachen* (day 41), it also rained. (*Bingbian* 368.1-3 = *HJ* 12487f)

[8D] 己酉雨辛亥亦雨

(*Verification:*) On *jiyou* (day 46), it rained; on *xinhai* (day 48), it also rained."
(I. Bin) (*Bingbian* 369.1 = *HJ* 12487b)

In divination [8A] the king, on day 30, forecast that it would rain on a *bing*-day (i.e., days 33, 43, 53, etc.); the two verifications—[8C] on the front of the plastron and [8D] on the back—record that it rained on four other days—days 39, 41, 46, and 48. There is no record, however, that rain fell on a *bing*-day.

For the record-keepers of [8A-D] to have recorded rainfall over an eighteen-day period was unusual, particularly during the first moon, a time when little if any rain falls today in North China.[23] (The existence of such inscriptions, incidentally, is one indication that the Late Shang climate was warmer and wetter, and the growing season longer, than it is today [see, e.g., K.C. Chang 1980: 136–41].) I suspect that in [8CD] the verification process was being "kept open"—even to the extent of continuing to record the third and fourth verifications on the back of the plastron ([8D])—in the hopes that rain would eventually fall on a *bing*-day, as forecast in [8A]. Having waited in vain through nearly two full ten-day weeks, the diviners finally closed the case. The king's forecast had not come true.

Such a record, once again, did not directly delegitimize Wu Ding. The verifications confirmed that the king, as the general tester of the spiritual "climate," had been sufficiently right—rain, after all, had fallen on four separate occasions, as recorded in [8CD]—even though he might have been wrong about the precise day. This might have sufficed to save some royal face. In no other Shang oracle-bone inscription, however, did the verification so nearly give the lie to the king's forecast as the [8CD] verifications do.[24] And even in this case, the failure of the king's forecast had been indicated by omission; the engraver had not recorded the direct rebuttal: 丙不雨, "On the *bing*-day, it did not rain." Such precise rebuttals, in fact, were never recorded as a response to a specific forecast about events not under Shang control. We never find verifications of the form, "On the *jia*-day she did not give birth," "On the *yi*-day the Servitors did not catch them," and so on, that would have directly refuted the royal forecast. It was evidently in the interest of neither the king nor his diviners to record such discomfiting results so explicitly. The engravers recorded what had happened; they never, in such cases, recorded what had not happened. It was up to the readers to draw their own conclusions about the success or failure of the forecast.[25]

That the diviner, Zheng, of the [8A-D] rainfall inscriptions had "closed the case" with a verification for the eighteenth day (day 48) after he had performed the original divination (on day 30) suggests that further light can be thrown on Shang divinatory practice by considering the timing of such extended prognostications or verifications. In the divinations of [4A-C] and [5AB] about Lady Hao's childbearing, the king had forecast "If it be a *ding*-day childbearing, it will be

good; If it be a *geng*-day childbearing, there will be prolonged auspiciousness …
if it be a *renxu* (childbearing), it will not be auspicious." With the charges being
divined on *jiashen* (day 21), the next two *ding*-days would have been *dinghai*
(day 24) and *dingyou* (day 34); the next two *geng*-days would have been *gengyin*
(day 27) and *gengzi* (day 37). Evidently, Que, the diviner, had waited eighteen
days until those four days had passed with no birth, and he had then redivined the
topic, in [5AB], on *renyin* (day 39). He evidently had not been prepared to wait
for a birth on *renxu* (day 59), the third day for which the king had made a forecast. The same temporal range may also be observed in the case of the Servitors
shackling the enemy ([6AB]), in which, on *guiyou* (day 10), Wu Ding prognosticated: "If they catch them it will be on a *jia*-day or *yi*-day." Evidently, the suitable
days, *jiaxu* (day 11) and *yihai* (day 12) of the first subsequent week, *and jiashen*
(day 21) and *yi-you* (day 22) of the second, had passed without result, so the king
had waited till the end of that second week and had then divined the topic again
([7AB]) on *guisi* (day 30), twenty days after the original divination.[26] And the
same pattern had obtained, as we have seen, in [8A-D], where the case had been
closed after eighteen days. It seems likely, accordingly, that, in cases where the king
was attempting to determine the date of some anticipated event, the efficacy of a
forecast was thought to extend for up to two ten-day weeks; if no outcome had yet
materialized, the king might then divine the topic again.[27]

     This scrutiny of prognostications, verifications, missed days, primary and
secondary sources, and timing suggests at least two conclusions. First, as we have
seen, Wu Ding himself made no exaggerated claims to infallibility; many of his
recorded forecasts specified a number of possible days rather than a single one; as
in [2], he frequently couched his charges and forecasts in general terms—such as
"There will be no disasters" and "There will be calamities; there may be (someone)
bringing alarming news"[28]—rather than specific ones; he did not forecast who
would be coming, the specific day within the ten-day week on which that person
would arrive, or what the news would be. Second, although the royal desire for a
legitimating history—as demonstrated by the large number of verifications that
did validate the Shang king's auguristic powers (Ji Dewei 1986: 118–119; 127,
n.4)—dominated the recording of the king's divinations, that desire was not given
unrestrained expression. Certain divinations in which the king's forecast had
been partially or entirely "off the mark" such as [4AC], [5A], [6A], [7A], and
[8A-D]—*were* recorded. That their number was small may be partly explained
by the accidents of archaeological recovery; when part of a plastron or scapula
is missing, it is often impossible to reconstruct a complete divinatory scenario
from preface to verification. It is still harder, given the great gaps in the corpus
of inscriptions that remains to us,[29] to establish scenarios that may have spanned
several bones. The small number of missed forecasts may also be explained by
the nature of Shang record-keeping itself, which often recorded neither a prognostication nor a verification so that we have no way to discover what the king
had forecast or what had then happened.[30] Such omissions are, of course, further
grounds for thinking both that Wu Ding made no claims to infallibility and that
his record-keepers did not wish to document his fallibilities explicitly. The very

rareness of the discomfiting cases discussed above demonstrates how the Shang engravers generally presented a record of the king's success or made it impossible to assess the degree of his success.[31]

Theology and History

The cases in which the Shang did keep a true record should not, of course, be considered in terms of a purely secular historiography. The oracle-bone inscriptions record a series of ritual acts, and the theology of those acts affected the nature of the records kept. Just as, on occasion, Wu Ding's engravers recorded more, discomfiting information about the king's prognostications than they needed to—as in the case of [4AC], [5A], [6A], [7A], and [8A]—so, it is important to remember, did they regularly record both the desired and the undesired charges, cutting into the bone statements of both what they wanted to have happen ([IB], [2], [3A], [4A], [5A], [6A], [7A], and [8A]) and what they did not want to have happen ([1A], [3B], [4B], [5B], [6B], [7B], and [8B]). I have explored elsewhere the possible significance of the "metaphysical balance" represented by these positive-negative charge-pairs:

> To the Shang diviners, complementary opposition did not imply necessary contradiction. Alternative charges were presented because that was the way the world was viewed. There was a fundamental, organic tension between the possible choices facing man. Only by facing both possibilities, by giving each possibility, as it were, a fair chance, could Wu Ting's divinations themselves be fair, in accord with reality, and thus valid. The inscribed charges documented the fact that such fair chance had been given, that the divination had been metaphysically equitable, and hence realistic (p. 130 in this volume).

It was evidently important to the validity of the divination process itself that such—to the modern eye, unnecessary or superfluous—records of undesirable charges be incised into the bone.

I would suggest, though there is no way to document this with certainty, that the commitment to recording "superfluous" or "unsuccessful" forecasts was related to similar assumptions about the nature of reality and the nature of the divinatory process. The Shang ritualists came to associate each day (or sun) of the Shang ten-day week with the day (or sun) of the ancestor or ancestors whose temple-name was the name of the day—so that Zu Jia 祖甲, for example, received cult on *jia*-days, Zu Yi 祖乙 on *yi*-days, and so on.[32] Forecasts, accordingly, for births on *ding*- or *geng*-days, as in [4AC], or for successful military operations on *jia*- or *yi*-days, as in [6A], or for rain on a *bing*-day, as in [8A], would have implicitly acknowledged the influence of the ancestors associated with those days. The king and his diviners, having thus invoked in their forecasts the day-names of particular ancestors, could not, and indeed probably would not have wished to, neglect the ancestors' days as they created the ritual record. The ancestors' names, once invoked in an oral prognostication, could no more be omitted from the recorded prognostication than the undesired charges could be omitted from the record of the positive-negative charge-pairs. It was important, in both cases, to document the contacts that had been made with the religious forces and meta-physical balances of the world.

In this connection, the very fact that Wu Ding's diviners made and recorded contingent forecasts, as in [3A], [4AC], [5A], [6A], and [7A], documents the power of the day, the power of the ancestor, to confer significance upon events and to affect their outcome. I cite just one more example of such a contingent, day-related prognostication:

[9] 王固曰：丁丑其有蠽不吉其隹甲有蠽吉其隹[辛]有蠽亦不吉

The king read the cracks and said: "On *dingchou* (day 14), if there is thunder,[33] it will be inauspicious. If it be on a *jia*-day that there is thunder, it will be auspicious. If it be on a (*xin*-day) that there is thunder, it will likewise be inauspicious." (I. Bin) (*Bingbian* 19.9 = *HJ* 6485b)

Whatever the charge to which this prognostication may have been a response,[34] it provides one further example of the way in which the good or bad fortune of an outcome was thought to be profoundly influenced by the *gan*-day on which it occurred. Thunder, in this case, would have been auspicious on *jia*-day, inauspicious on *dingchou* or *xin*-days. The prognostication served as a "spiritual scoreboard."

Whether, in the event, such contingent forecasts proved right or wrong, they did possess a sanctity that, if it was decided to record them at all, appears to have required the kind of "full disclosure" discussed above. Such an explana-tion is supported by the consideration that it was only in the case of verifications involving day-dates that Wu Ding's diviners recorded such divinatory misses. This raises the possibility that it was only prognostications and verifications involving religious time that required such scrupulous reporting. If one supposes that, to use a modern analogy, every time the White House forecast the growth-rate for the economy, each monthly projection were to involve the patronage of a saint, one may get some sense of how these Shang prognostications may have been regarded. They might be omitted entirely from the record (see note 30), but those that were recorded testified, whatever the eventual outcome, to the range and religious importance of the efforts that had been made.

It may also be noted that "missed-day" forecasts of the kind presented above were no longer recorded after Wu Ding. Under the so-called "New School" ritual reforms instituted during the reign of Zu Jia 祖甲 (ca. 1170–1151 B.C.E.), the schedule of the ancestral cult, which matched the ancestors to their *gan*-days, became more rigorous than it had been previously.[35] With each ancestor now routinely fixed in place, the ad hoc acknowledgments of ancestral influence that had occasionally been recorded in the prognostications of Wu Ding may no longer have been needed. At the same time, positive-negative charge-pairs were now rarely used; the post-Wu Ding kings and their diviners simply divined the desirable outcome and found no need to divine the undesirable alternative. It had evidently become less important to record the full range of divinatory options, and the range of options and topics itself appears to have shrunk (Keightley 1978: 122; 1988: 378–383).

It may be instructive to close with a reminder that the entirely rational pressures for forecasters and record-keepers to conform to cultural expectations are not unknown in the modern United States. The Senate or Defense Department pressures upon the State Department's "diviners" who "lost China" or who tried to forecast the outcome of the Vietnam war with accuracy are well-known.[36] I cannot resist ending, in fact, with the following newspaper account of a modern diviner in Los Angeles whose dilemma his Shang predecessors might well have understood:

> A radio weather forecaster who predicted rain for a Rush Limbaugh event ran into a storm of opposition from station management and was fired for not altering his forecast, according to the *Los Angeles Times*.
>
> Forecaster Sean Boyd was quoted in yesterday's editions of the *Times* as saying he had been fired by his boss at KMJ, one of the top three markets in the country for Limbaugh's syndicated morning show, after he refused to change his weather forecast of a chance of rain for an outdoor function honoring the conservative commentator....
>
> Boyd told the *Times* his boss asked him to "fudge" his forecast by predicting a greater possibility of sunshine rather than a chance of rain, as the latter might keep people away from the event....
>
> On the day, Boyd had the last word, the heavens opened and it poured....
> (Reuters 1995)

It is impossible for us to tell, of course, the degree to which Wu Ding or his diviners might have falsified their own prognostications in response to political or other pressures of this sort. The divinatory record carved into the bones was not constructed to convey that kind of information. Indeed, the record was, with the exception of the few rather unusual cases considered above, a partial record constructed precisely not to convey that kind of information. Divinatory misses, if they occurred, were rarely remarked. One can see that Shang practice in this regard may have anticipated the historiographical principle of "concealing yet revealing" (*yin er zhang* 隱而章) that the Song scholar Su Xun 蘇洵 (1009–1066 c.e.) and others have discerned in the work of Sima Qian 司馬遷.[37] Wu Ding's divination inscriptions represent the impulse to present the king, his ancestors, and the divinatory institution itself in the best possible light; the omissions in the record— of prognostications and verifications—generally afforded a simple and effective way to do this. Even the occasional records of royal failure can be understood as reflecting this larger impulse. Missed forecasts were thus not irrelevant; they documented the religious significance of the efforts that the king had made.

The oracle-bone records, shaped as they were by the theological concerns of the divinatory enterprise itself, represent only one form of early record keeping. One should not, accordingly, generalize too easily from the bone inscriptions of Shang to the historiographical traditions of Zhou and Han. The bone inscriptions may be analyzed, as I have attempted to do in this essay, as historical records, but the reality that they recorded, the divination process itself, was narrow and specialized. As they do for the genesis of the high culture in general, Wu Ding's pyromantic inscriptions can throw only a partial light on the genesis of orthodox historiography in the Chinese Bronze Age. At the same time, however, these divination records can, when read closely, bring modern readers into close contact with the traditions of one system of bureaucratic record-keeping that undoubtedly influenced, as it was influenced by, the writing of other, more secular, records.[38]

Notes

Although I did not appreciate it at the time, one of K.C. Chang's relatively early publications (Chang 1964) may have done much to attract me to the field of ancient Chinese studies. I was then a student of modern China, but K.C.'s ability, in that article, to discern significant new anthropological patterns in the Shang evidence impressed and attracted me in ways that must have influenced my decision to desert, as it were, Mao for Yao, and to eventually take up my own study of the Shang. I had the pleasure of first meeting K.C., eleven years later, when he welcomed me late in the evening of 18 May 1975 to the Beijing Hotel. I was a late-arriving member of the Paleoanthropology Delegation that was about to tour archaeological sites and institutions in the People's Republic. His acute observations and sensitivity to Chinese culture taught me much in the month that we traveled together. Since that time, I, like many others, have benefited from his guiding presence in various conferences on early China. These would include the 1978 conference on the Origins of Chinese Civilization (which led to the publication of Keightley [ed.] 1983), the 1982 International Conference on Shang Civilization (which led to the publication of K.C. Chang [ed.] 1986), and the 1986 conference on Ancient China and Social Science Generalizations. K.C.'s published research on Neolithic and Shang culture has, of course, taught me more than I can specify in this short space. The essay that follows represents a small contribution to our knowledge of China's first historical dynasty, a dynasty that K.C. has (particularly in Chang 1980) so notably introduced to the world of Western scholarship.

1. This essay, which refines and develops some, of the conclusions reached in Keightley 1975 and Ji Dewei 1986, derives from part of a talk, "In the Bone: Divination, Theology, and Political Culture in Late Shang China," that I gave to the Pre-Modern China Seminar, Fairbank Center, Harvard University, on 17 October 1994. I am grateful for the perceptive criticisms of Edward L. Shaughnessy who commented on an early draft of the essay; its mistakes remain my own.

2. On Shang legitimation, see Keightley 1975; 1988:372–373. Lin Yun (1979:330–331) provides a useful statement of the king's role; Zhu Fenghan (1990:10, 14–19) demonstrates the links between royal authority and the Shang temple system.

3. The way in which *qi* 其 functioned in the bone inscriptions is still under review. I continue to treat it in this article, where it only appears in the charge-pairs and prognostications of Wu Ding, as a preverbal modal particle of tentative expectancy. For a recent discussion and review of the scholarship, see Takashima 1996, who argues (p. 4) that "*qi* functions as a kind of adverbial particle, conveying a variety of modal as well as aspectual meanings"; see too Nivison 1996, who counters (p. 276) that "in most of the common cases it doesn't matter whether *qi* is used or not."

4. I periodize the inscriptions by reference to Dong Zuobin's five-period system and by the name of the diviner group. Thus, the charge-pair [1AB] may be dated to Dong's period I and to the Bin 賓 diviner group. For an introduction to Dong's oracle-bone periodization and to diviner groups, see Keightley 1978: 92–94 and Shaughnessy 1982–83.

5. *HJ* is an abbrevated reference to Guo Moruo, ed., and Hu Houxuan, ed.-in-chief 1978–82, the *corpus inscriptionum* of oracle-bone inscriptions (see Keightley 1990: 39–51); the number following *HJ* indicates the number of the rubbing in that collection; the letters f and b refer to the front and back of the bone. For other oracle-bone collections, such as *Bingbian*, cited by abbreviated title in this essay, see Keightley 1978:229–231 (where the abbreviarions and citations are romanized in the Wade-Giles system).

6. For an introduction to Lady Hao (or Lady Zi), Wu Ding's most prominent consort, whose unrifled tomb was excavated in 1976, see C.L. Chang 1986; K.C. Chang 1980: 87–90.

7. The transcription I give for [4C] follows that of Zhang Bingquan (1962:322) in his commentary to *Bingbian* 248.7, rather than that given by Yao Xiaosui and Xiao Ding eds. 1988: 324.2.

8. Since the plastron is broken at this point, there is no way to reconstruct with certainty the missing *gan* graph that preceded the *shen*. A reconstructed *gengshen* date as the "auspicious and good" birth day, however, would provide another link with the [4AG] prognostications: "if it be a *geng*-(day) childbearing, there will be prolonged auspiciousness." That the date was *gengshen* (day 57) rather than *wusken* (day 45) is also suggested by the [4C] prognostication, "if it be a *renxu* (day 59) (childbearing), it will not be auspicious." The combination of the *jiayin* birth (day 51) and the *renxu* forecast (day 59) suggests that the king was focusing his attention on that particular ten-day week; it is less likely, accordingly, that he would have invoked *wushen* (day 45), which fell in the previous week, rather than *gengshen* (day 57), which fell in the same week.

9. The Shang graph Ψ appears only in this inscription. For the limited scholarship, see Matsumaru and Takashima 1994, no. 5407.

10. The following considerations support this conclusion: (I) Both plastrons were found in the same pit, YH 127. (2) Both the charges, on days 21 and 38, were divined by Que. (3) The calligraphy and "layout" of the characters on the two plastrons are virtually identical (see Figures 1 and 2). (4) The forecasts about birth days on the two plastrons are not contradictory. (5) The bad and inauspicious forecast made on day 39 about day 51 of [5A] on the second plastron is confirmed by the events recorded for day 51 by [4AB] on the first plastron.

11. It is curious that this second plastron, *HJ* 14001fb, on which the [5AB] inscriptions were recorded, appears to contain no verification that would have documented Wu Ding's accuracy as a forecaster; to discover that a "not good" birth had indeed occurred on *jiayin* as forecast in [5A], it is necessary to turn back to the verifications of [4AB] on the first plastron (Figure 1). I suspect, however, that a verification to [5AB] had indeed been recorded on the back of the second plastron, *HJ* 14001b. The rubbing is virtually illegible (and the original rubbing, *Yibian* 4730, is little better), but I can make out a *jia* 甲 graph (ignored by Yao and Xiao 1988) in its center; this might have formed part of a verification that recorded what had happened on *jiayin*.

12. For another childbearing divination in which Wu Ding missed the day, see *HJ* 14009f; he forecast a "good" birth on a *geng*-day; the birth actually occurred on a *xin*-day, but was recorded as "good" anyway.

13. Similarly, the engravers of [3A] had not sought to improve the record by doctoring the prognostication, "If it be a *geng*-day childbearing, it will be good," to read: "If it be a *gengxu* childbearing, it will be good." The king's claims to precise accuracy had, in this case, also been relatively modest.

14. My translation of [6A], which is tentative at several points, generally follows that proposed by Takashima 1973: 218–219.

15. Hu Houxuan (1976: 12–13) links the two plastrons in this way; both he and Huang Tianshu (1991:325) note the retroactive nature of the [7AB] record.

16. Note the absence of any forecast for the intervening *bing*-day. *Bing*-days were generally regarded as unlucky; see Ji Dewei 1989:20, Table 1.

17. Wu Ding's diviners generally used an inclusive day count, so that the interval from day 24 to day 30 was counted as seven days.

18. It would thus follow that the language of the [7AB] charges, with their use of *zhi* rather than the *de* of [6AB], would not have been recorded on the bone until after the outcome (the verification of [7A], with its use of *zhi* rather than *de*) was known to the record-keepers.

19. That the verification of [4A] spoke of the birth as "not good," whereas the prognostication of [5A] forecast that such a birth would "not be auspicious," suggests, as in the case of *de* and *zhi*, that the truth of the record was more important than editorial consistency.

20. For an introduction to the question of how long after the divination was performed the inscription was incised, see Keightley 1978:45–46, nn. 89–91.

21. In this connection, see Li Xueqin 1991, who shows how the records inscribed on *HJ* 390 indicate that the scapula was in use for a span of over one hundred days. It is likely that the original notations of its early use, involving the initial sacrifice of the bovid and the sanctification of its scapula, must have first been recorded on some other medium before being transferred to the bone at the end of that period. (I am grateful to Bobby Shih for pointing this out to me in an undergraduate seminar in Spring 1996).

22. Zhang Bingquan's transcription makes no provision for the possibility, but the rubbing of *Bingbian* 368.1 (which is clearer than either the *HJ* 12487f version or the original *Yibian* 1922 and 2691) suggests, as the transcription in Yao and Xiao (eds. 1988: 290.2) indicates, that a graph has been obliterated between the *yue* 曰 and the *bing* 丙 of the prognostication. The remaining traces of the graph suggest that it would have been the copula *wei* 隹 (oracle-bone form 𢓓); cf. the prognostication, 其隹丙[雨], on *HJ* 12511f; see too the use of *wei* in the prognostication to [6A].

23. It is generally, though not universally, thought that—following Zhou and Han accounts, and in accordance with the practice of Chinese calendars that have traditionally started with or near the winter solstice—the first Shang moon started with the new moon after the winter solstice; for judicious summaries of the technical issues and scholarship, see Zhang Peiyu 1986. In this view, the Shang "first moon" would have fallen within the period of modern January and February. I know of only one other case, a verification on *HJ* 10976f, which also records rainfall over an eighteen-day period, although not by specific days. That verification, furthermore (no prognostication is found on the incomplete plastron), was recorded in the ninth Shang moon (i.e., September to October), a period when rain would normally have been more plentiful.

24. For the differential discoloration of the plastron fragments upon which the [8A-D] inscriptions were recorded and the conclusion that the plastron was broken apart

before it was placed in pit YH 127, see Zhang Bingquan's (1962:436) commentary to *Bingbian* 368. Such fragmentation raises the possibility that the king or his diviners may have wished to destroy this record of divinatory failure—but, if so, only after they had made the record in the first place!

25. There is no space here to discuss the audience who may have read the inscriptions. The need to inscribe crack-notations (which indicated whether or not a particular crack was auspicious), the large size of much of the Wu Ding calligraphy, and the practice of filling the graphs with colored pigment, all suggest that the inscriptions were intended to be read by, or at least shown to, an audience of the king's supporters (dead or alive) after the initial divination had ended. On these features, and on the character of what I have called "display inscriptions" (represented in this essay by [1AB], [2], [3AB], and [7AB]), see Keightley 1978:40, 46, n. 90, 53–55; 1988: 372–373.

26. That the *HJ* 14002 plastron was bigger than the *HJ* 14001 plastron (see Figures 1 and 2), and the *HJ* 641 plastron was bigger than the *HJ* 643 plastron, at least raises the possibility that "repeat" divinations were performed on smaller bones than the original ones.

27. The relative infreqency with which the Shang engravers recorded the moon or month number—as they did in the verification to [3A], the postface to [6A], and the charges [8AB]—also suggests that the diviners were accustomed to dealing with matters in the relatively short term. Modern usage is similar in this regard; one says "on the seventeenth" rather than "on March seventeenth," if it is assumed that everything is going to be resolved within the next few days, and certainly within the same month.

28. See, too *HJ* 914f, 4264b, 4735b, 7075b and other prognostications transcribed at Yao and Xiao [eds.] 1989:831.1, 839.2–840.1.

29. My latest crude calculations suggest that we now possess some 20 percent of the inscriptions originally made; see Keightley 1978: 165–169 and the supplementary figures presented at Keightley 1990:40, 47, n. 46, 49.

30. On the difficulties involved in quantifying the number of charges that were recorded without prognostications or verifications, see Keightley 1978: 41, n. 67. Tedious and crude calculations, based on the number of inscriptions recorded in *Heji* and adjusted to account for charge-pairs, sets, and other divinatory records, suggest that the Bin-group diviners recorded only one prognostication for every 83 divinations for a prognostication-per-episode rate of 1.2 percent.

31. The verification to *Jinghua* 1=*HJ* 10405f, which records that both the king and Prince Yang (Zi Yang 子央) fell out of a chariot while hunting, confirms that records of royal discomfiture were not entirely banned. (For two translations of the inscription, which presents some difficulties, see Shaughnessy 1988:214 and Kolb 1991:24.) Even in this case, however, the king—following the model of [2] above—had indeed forecast, in his prognostication, that there would be calamities; the recording of the chariot accident, accordingly, validated his powers as a diviner.

32. On the temple-names and days, see K.C. Chang 1980: 168–175; Ji Dewei 1989. On the role of the sun in Shang religion, see Allan 1991: 19–56.

33. I follow Xu Zhaoren 1989 and Zhan Yinxin 1983 in reading oracle-bone 乍 as *zuo* 鑿, literally, "chisel." For the translation of "thunder," based largely on contextual rather than philological grounds, see Keightley 1978: 80, n. 91; Serruys 1986: 207, no. 24; Takashima 1990: 79–80, n. 20; 1996a: 140–141. For additional scholarship on the word, see Matsumaru and Takashima 1994, no. 3661.

34. I have elsewhere suggested (Keightley 1978: 88) that Wu Ding, in the case of [9], was forecasting the weather he might expect when offering sacrifice to his Father Geng.

35. For an introduction to these reforms and the scholarly problems involved, see Keightley 1978:32, n. 18; Shaughnessy 1982–1983. It is not necessary to accept Dong Zuobin's theory of *alternating* "Old" and "New" Schools to agree that a marked regularization of ritual practice took place under Zu Jia and later kings.

36. See, e.g., Esherick (1975: xx) who notes that John S. Service, John Carter Vincent, John Patton Davies, and O. Edmund Clubb were forced from the State Department because "these were the men who had predicted the defeat of Chiang Kai-shek." For the difficulties of State Department officers who foretold trouble ahead in Vietnam, see, e.g., Sarris 1995.

37. Watson 1958: 96–98; but see too Liu (1967:110) for Ouyang Xiu's contribution.

38. On the links between Shang divination, theology, and bureaucratic forms of organization, see Keightley 1978a.

References Cited

Allan, Sarah (1991). *The Shape of the Turtle: Myth, Art, and Cosmos in Early China.* Albany: State University of New York Press.

Chang, Cheng-lang (1986). "A Brief Discussion of Fu Tzu." In K. C. Chang (editor), *Studies of Shang Archaeology: Selected Papers from the International Conference on Shang Civilization,* pp. 103–119. New Haven: Yale University Press.

Chang, K. C. (1964). "Some Dualistic Phenomena in Shang Society." *Journal of Asian Studies* 24:45–61.

Chang, K. C. (1980). *Shang Civilization.* New Haven: Yale University Press.

Chang, K. C. (editor) (1986). *Studies of Shang Archaeology: Selected Papers from the International Conference on Shang Civilization.* New Haven: Yale University Press.

Esherick, Joseph W. (1975). "Introduction." In Joseph W. Esherick (editor), *Lost Chance in China: The World War II Despatches of John S. Service,* pp. xiii–xxiii. New York: Vintage.

Huang Tianshu 黃天樹 (1991). *Yinxu wang buci de fenlei yu duandai* 殷墟王卜辭的分類與斷代. Taibei: Wenjing.

Hu Houxuan 胡厚宣 (1976). "Jiaguwen suo jian Yindai nuli de fan yapo douzheng 甲骨文所見殷代奴隸的反壓迫鬥爭." *Kaogu xuebao* 考古學報1976.1:1–18.

Ji Dewei 吉德煒 (David N. Keightley) (1986). "Zhongguo zhi zhengshi zhi yuanyuan: Shang wang zhanbu shifou yiguan zhengque? 中國之正史之淵源：商王占卜是否一貫正確?" *Guwenzi yanjiu* 古文字研究 13:117–128.

Ji Dewei (David N. Keightley) (1989). "Zhongguo gudai de jiri yu miaohao 中國古代的吉日與廟號." *Yinxu bowuyuan yuankan* 殷墟博物苑苑刊 · 創刊號 (Inaugural issue): 20–32.

Keightley, David N. (1975). "Legitimation in Shang China." Paper presented at the Conference on Legitimation of Chinese Imperial Regimes, Asilomar, CA., 15–24 June 1975.

Keightley, David N. (1978). *Sources of Shang History: The Oracle-Bone Inscriptions of Bronze Age China.* Berkeley: University of California Press.

Keightley, David N. (1978a). "The Religious Commitment: Shang Theology and the Genesis of Chinese Political Culture." *History of Religions* 17:211–224 (Chapter 4 in this volume).

Keightley, David N. (editor) (1983). *The Origins of Chinese Civilization.* Berkeley: University of California Press.

Keightley, David N. (1988). "Shang Divination and Metaphysics." *Philosophy East and West* 38:367–397 (Chapter 6 in this volume).

Keightley, David N. (1990). "Sources of Shang History: Two Major Oracle-Bone Collections Published in the People's Republic of China." *Journal of the American Oriental Society* 110.1 (1990):39–59.

Kolb, Raimund Theodor (1991). *Die Infanterie im Alten China: Ein Beitrag zur Militärgeschichte der vor-Zhan-Guo-Zeit.* Mainz: Philip von Zabern.

Li Xueqin 李學勤 (1991). "Lun Binzu jiagu de jizhong jishi keci 論賓組胛骨的幾種記事刻辭; On Some Bin Diviner Group Record Inscriptions Engraved on Ox Scapulae." In Li Xueqin, Qi Wenxin 齊文心, and Ai Lan 艾蘭 (Sarah Allan) (eds.), *Yingguo suocang jiaguji* 英國所藏甲骨集, *Oracle Bone Collections in Great Britain.* Vol. II, pp. 161–166 (Chinese), 167–176 (English). Beijing: Chinese Academy of Social Sciences, Institute of History; and Zhonghua Shuju; London: School of Oriental and African Studies.

Lin Yun 林澐 (1979). "Cong Wu Ding shidai de jizhong 'Zi buci' shilun Shang dai de jiazu xingtai 從武丁時代的幾種「子卜辭」試論商代的家族形態." *Guwenzi yanjiu* 古文字研究 1:314–336.

Liu, James T. C. (1967). *Ou-yang Hsiu: An Eleventh-Century Neo-Confucianist.* Stanford: Stanford University Press.

Matsumaru Michio 松丸道雄 and Takashima Ken-ichi 高島謙一(1994). *Kōkotsumoji jishaku sōran* 甲骨文字字釋綜覽. Tokyo: Tokyo University Press [1993, not for sale].

Nivison, David S. (1996). "Replies and Comments." In P. J. Ivanhoe (editor), *Chinese Language, Thought, and Culture: Nivison and His Critics*, pp. 267–277. Chicago: Open Court.

Reuters (1995). "Forecaster Fired—Predicted Rain." *San Francisco Chronicle*, 29 April 1995:8.

Sarris, Louis G. (1995). "McNamara's War, and Mine." *New York Times* 5 September 1995:Section A, p.13.

Serruys, Paul L-M. (1986). "Notes on the Grammar of the Oracular Inscriptions of Shang." In John McCoy and Timothy Light (eds.), *Contributions to Sino-Tibetan Studies*, pp. 203–257. Cornell Linguistic Contributions 5. Leiden: Brill.

Shaughnessy, Edward L. (1982–1983). "Recent Approaches to Oracle-Bone Periodization." *Early China* 8:1–13.

Shaughnessy, Edward L. (1988). "Historical Perspectives on the Introduction of the Chariot into China." *Harvard Journal of Asiatic Studies* 48.1:189–237.

Takashima, Ken-ichi (1973). "Negatives in the King Wu-ting Bone Inscriptions." Ph.D. dissertation, Department of Asian Languages and Literature, University of Washington, Seattle.

Takashima, Ken-ichi (1990). "A Study of the Copulas in Shang Chinese." *The Memoirs of the Institute of Oriental Culture* 112:1–92. Tokyo: University of Tokyo.

Takashima, Ken-ichi (1996). "Toward a New Pronominal Hypothesis of *Qi* in Shang Chinese." In P. J. Ivanhoe (editor), *Chinese Language, Thought, and Culture: Nivison and His Critics*, pp. 3–38. Chicago: Open Court.

Takashima, Ken-ichi (1996a). "Part Two: Language and Palaeography." In *Studies in Early Chinese Civilization: Religion, Society, Language, and Palaeography. Volume 1: Text. Volume 2: Tables and Notes*, by Itô Michiharu and Ken-ichi Takashima, pp. 179–505. Hirakata: Kansai Gaidai University Press.

Watson, Burton (1958). *Ssu-ma Ch'ien: Grand Historian of China*. New York: Columbia University Press.

Xu Zhaoren 徐兆仁 (1989). "Shi zuo 釋乍." *Guwenzi yanjiu* 17:223–229.

Yao Xiaosui 姚孝遂 and Xiao Ding 肖丁 (editors) (1988). *Yinxu jiagu keci moshi zongji* 殷墟甲骨刻辭摹釋總集. 2 vols. Beijing: Zhonghua.

Yao Xiaosui and Xiao Ding (editors) (1989). *Yinxu jiagu keci leizuan* 殷墟甲骨刻辭類纂. 3 vols. Beijing: Zhonghua.

Zhang Bingquan 張秉權 (1962). *Xiaotun dierben: Yinxu wenzi: bingbian* 小屯第二本：殷墟文字：丙編. Vol. 2, pt. 1 (1962). Taibei: Zhongyang yanjiuyuan lishi yuyan yanjiusuo 中央研究院歷史語言研究所.

Zhan Yinxin 詹鄞鑫 (1983). "Shi xin ji yu xin youguan de jige zi 釋辛及與辛有關的幾個字." *Zhongguo yuwen* 中國語文 1983.5:369–374.

Zhu Fenghan 朱鳳瀚 (1990). "Yinxu buci suo jian Shang wangshi zongmiao zhidu 殷墟卜辭所見商王室宗廟制度." *Lishi yanjiu* 歷史研究 1990.6:3–19.

Zhang Peiyu 張培瑜 (1986). "Yinxu buci lifa yanjiu zongshu 殷墟卜辭曆法研究綜述." *Xian Qin shi yanjiu* 先秦史研究 12:1–14.

9

MARKS AND LABELS: EARLY WRITING IN NEOLITHIC AND SHANG CHINA

David N. Keightley

The question must be not only What does the inscription say? but What function did it serve to say it? What did the record keeper think he was doing? (Keightley 1978:154)

The Neolithic Background

The inhabitants of early China, in all likelihood, did not import their logographic writing system from abroad; it would be hard to demonstrate any genetic connection between the signs scratched or painted on Neolithic pots, found usually in burials of higher status (Yang Xiaoneng 2000 provides a pictorial catalog of the evidence) or the oracle-bone graph forms of the Late Shang on the one hand, and Sumerian, Egyptian, or Hittite written forms on the other. Nor is it likely that writing had emerged in China as early as it had done in Mesopotamia (Boltz 1999:108; Keightley 1989:187–99; Xueqin Li et al. 2003:31; Qiu Xigui 2000:29). But the Chinese writing system, once it had developed, was to reign supreme in China right down to the present and was to play a similarly paramount role in the neighboring states of Vietnam, Korea, and Japan.

Turning to the origins of the script, it is possible to identify two major impulses in Neolithic sign making, the naturalistic or realistic (Figure 9.1A) and the diagrammatic or schematic (Figure 9.1B) (cf. Qiu Xigui 2000:30; Yang Xiaoneng 2000:101, 204), and it is, I believe, from the latter tradition, which I associate in particular with the Liangzhu 良渚 (Jiangsu) and Dawenkou 大汶口 (Shandong and northern Jiangsu) cultures of eastern China, that, during the fourth to third millennia B.C., the earliest "characters" started to emerge (Keightley 1989:195–8). How such signs actually functioned is hard to tell. Many were placed on pots, often before firing, that were used as food vessels, and it has generally been supposed that they represented social markers that, when placed in burials, also served some ritual function (Yang Xiaoneng 2000:71, 80). For the naturalistic tradition, for example, it has been proposed that "the image of the white heron" painted on the urn from Yancun 閻村 in Henan (ca. 3500–3000 B.C.) (Figure 9.1A), "signified a place name or the name of a clan associated with it. The axe likely served

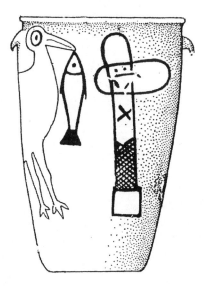

Figure 9.1A Naturalistic heron, fish, and axe design painted on a *gang* urn from Yancun, Henan (ca. 3500–3000 B.C.) (*Zhongyuan wenwu* 中原文物 1981.1:4, Fig. 1.1.)

as an honorific attribute, indicating rank or status" (Fitzgerald-Huber 1999:64, 66). (Others, however, have proposed that what they see as the *yue* 鉞 axe form was equivalent to *sui* 歲, the word for "year" (Lu Sixian and Li Di 2000:132, 169).) And for the diagrammatic tradition, Wu Hung (1985:34–6; 1995:40–4; see also Keightley 1996:76–87) has proposed that, for example, the sun and bird pictographs found on a small number of Liangzhu jades (ca. 3000 B.C.) should be treated as "emblems" of the *yang niao* 陽鳥 "Sun Bird," the name of a people thought, on the basis of later texts, to have been living in this eastern area between the Yellow River and the Yangzi.

But these pictographs were not necessarily writing, not necessarily characters. As William Boltz has noted, "there is no evidence that these or any other graphs at this time stood for words of any kind, *yang niao* or other" (Boltz 1994:46). That is to say, they have meaning, but it cannot be said with certainty that they are "characterized by a conventionally associated pronunciation" (Boltz 1994:48; 45, Figure 12). Since, moreover, it is not yet certain what language was being spoken in this part of Neolithic China—it has been proposed, for example, that one group would not have spoken "a form of Chinese" but "very likely an Austroasiatic language related to Vietnamese" (Pulleyblank 1996:2–6; cf. Boltz 1999:81–3)—or what it would have sounded like, even if it were Proto-Chinese (Boltz 1999:100–3; Takashima 2000:xxii, n. 6)—the difficulty involved in assigning phonetic values to these pictographs is considerable. Nevertheless, one may note that the Liangzhu and Dawenkou peoples, in different parts of China, were already sharing some signs (Cheung Kwong-yue 1983:372–3, Table 12.4; Yang Xiaoneng 1999:102; 2000:73, 197; Xueqin Li et al. 2003:40), an indication

Figure 9.1B Schematic sun, fire, mountain(?), axe, and adze designs incised on pots from the Dawenkou culture (*Dawenkou: Xinshiqi shidai muzang fajue baogao* 大汶口：新石器時代墓葬發掘報告. Beijing: Wenwu chubanshe 1974: p. 118, Fig. 94.1–4.)

of their widespread use. And it may also be noted that a significant number of the Neolithic signs represented ritual implements, such as axes, adzes (Figure 9.1B), and scepters, and that such images may have been ancestral to the pictographic emblems, often taken to be clan-name insignia, distinct from the regular Shang script, inscribed on early Shang bronze vessels (Figure 9.2B). To the extent that one can separate the two functions, such emblems seem to have served as both ornaments and symbols (Boltz 1994:48–50, Figures 14, 15; Fitzgerald-Huber 1999:66; Yang Xiaoneng 2000:71, 81, 84–102, 112, 117, 144).

Whether, given the inability to attach specific names and phonetic values to such Neolithic marks or signs, one is willing to identify them as proto-writing, on the grounds that they still communicated information if not words, is a matter of theoretical taste (Harris 2000:64–90; Salomon 2001; Sampson 1985:26–30). And, as Sampson (1985:29, 49, 50), commenting on the "ambiguous middle ground between clear semasiography"—involving "systems of visible communication ... which indicate ideas directly"—and "clear glottography"—systems "which provide visible representation of spoken-language utterances"—has noted, given that pre-writing seems to have developed into writing by a slow process of gradual evolution, it may be a rather artificial exercise to decide that the transition to writing has definitely occurred by any particular stage. This point is reinforced by the fact that, when inscriptions are limited to abbreviated jottings rather than full sentences, the distinction between semasiography and logographic writing tends to dissolve.

That some Neolithic signs (Figure 9.2A), however, involving the depiction of a human-and-animal figure, carved into high-status jade axes and *cong* 琮 tubes from

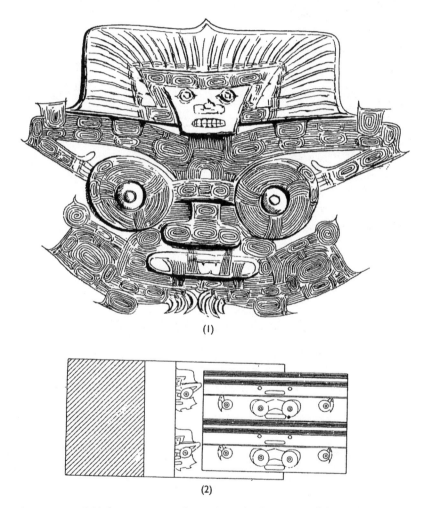

(1)

(2)

Figure 9.2A (1) The more naturalistic, "In Clear" version of the human-and-animal figure incised on a Liangzhu culture jade *cong* (M12:98 from Fanshan); figure is ca. 3 cm high (*Wenwu* 文物 1988.1:12, Fig. 20.). (2) The "In Clear" version in the central track (left), the "Coded," schematic version (opened up, on right) (*Wenwu* 1988.1:12, Fig. 19.)

Figure 9.2B Shang lineage insigne or emblem involving two human silhouettes, back to back, and a dagger-axe, on a bronze *gui* 簋 tureen (early Anyang 安陽 (*Henan Chutu Shang Zhou Qingtonqi*) 河南出土商青銅器 (l). Beijing: Wenwu chubanshe 1981: p. 219, Fig. 274.)

elite Liangzhu burials in the Yangzi delta area, seem to have been written both "in clear" (naturalistic; Figure 9.2A, left) and "in code" (schematic: Figure 9.2A, right) suggests that even at this stage the readability of certain signs on ritual objects was to be limited to the initiated, those who could read the "code." The enduring impulse to replace pictures (more naturalistic) with graphs (more schematic, more stylized) was already present (Keightley 1996:76–85; Qiu Xigui 2000:45–8, 64), and this preference for the graph over the picture, for the coded sign over the naturalistic picture, may also have been encouraged by the consideration that the more naturalistic form, although more easily "read" by the uninitiated, would have been more difficult to cut into jade than the more schematic motif, with its simpler lines and circles. If so, it may be that "the schematic version would have been more attractive to artisans, being easier to produce, and more attractive to elites, because it embodied a more esoteric code" (Keightley 1996:81). One needs to consider the role of the craftsmen, the "writers," in addition to the role of the consumers, the "readers," even at this early stage.

The Bronze Age: Shang and Western Zhou

Several signs have been found at the so-called "Early Shang" site of Erlitou 二里頭 (ca. 16th century B.C.) in north Central Henan, generally incised on various pots (Yang Xiaoneng 2000:84–7), but there is, once again, no way to "read" their meaning. A few more symbols and graphs have been found on "Middle Shang" artifacts, from sites like Erligang 二里崗 (16th and 15th centuries B.C.); some of them may have been precursors of oracle-bone graph forms—inscriptions have been found on three bone fragments—but different systems of signs appear to have been involved at different sites (Kwang-chih Chang 1980:268–9, 305–6). And few if any Erligang ritual bronzes—the new symbols of prestige—were being cast with inscriptions (Bagley 1999:182, n. 92). As Qiu Xigui (2000:42) has concluded, "all the written material from the early Shang discovered thus far is both scant and fragmentary … and is of minor value to our study of the formative process of Chinese writing."

Chinese writing, as we see it in its fully developed form in the oracle-bone and bronze inscriptions of the Late Shang, was logographic: it used graphs to record words (Boltz 1994:52–9; DeFrancis 2002; Sampson 1985:148–9; Unger 2004). It was not ideographic, using graphs to record ideas or things without the mediation of language, although a number of Western scholars and commentators have argued that it was (e.g., Hansen 1993; Vandermeersch 1980:473–88). By the time of the oracle-bone inscriptions, moreover, the Shang were not generally writing pictographs; the graphs "show the effects of graphic conventionalization and are not readily recognizable as realistic depictions of anything specific" (Boltz 1994:56; see also Boltz 2000–2001:4–6). The oracle-bone inscriptions thus represent the first large corpus of texts written in a well-developed system whose principles, combining phonetic and semantic elements, we can identify as those of the later script (Boltz 1994:68–9; 1999:110). And it is generally assumed that the writing system came into existence in the previous centuries, probably around the middle of the second millennium B.C. or a little earlier (Boltz 1994:39; Qiu Xigui 2000:44).

The rubbings and drawings of some 41,956 oracle bones (many bearing numerous individual inscriptions) have been reproduced in the *Heji*-合集 corpus; several thousand more have been published in other collections. The oracle-bone inscriptions—modern scholars use the term to refer to inscriptions on both bone (mainly cattle scapulas) and shell (turtle plastrons and carapaces)—employed a vocabulary of some 4,500 to 5,000 individual graphs, about half of which can be deciphered with certainty (Boltz 1999:88–9; Qiu Xigui 2000:49–50). The inscriptions provide much information about the Late Shang world as the kings saw it or, more precisely, as they divined it. The twenty-first Shang king, Wu Ding 武丁 (ca. 1200–1189 B.C.), in particular, divined a wide range of royal topics: sacrifices, military campaigns, hunting expeditions, other excursions, the good fortune of the coming ten-day Shang week, the good fortune of the coming night or day, the weather, agriculture, sickness, childbirth, distress or trouble, dreams, settlement building, the issuing of orders, tribute payments, divine assistance or approval, and requests addressed to ancestral or natural Powers (Keightley 1978:33–5; Keightley [2000] provides translations of 157 oracle-bone inscriptions in context).

It is striking, however, that, with the exception of the generally terse bronze inscriptions, few other Shang documents exist, and that even a majority of the pre-Eastern Zhou 東周 texts (770–256 B.C.) that have come down to us exist only in later redactions. Writing in early China—at least as it has been preserved in the archaeological record—thus appears at first glance to have played a rather different role than it did in early Mesopotamia. We have few if any Bronze-Age Chinese equivalents to, for example, the "inventories of all types and sizes, promissory notes and receipts, deeds of sale, marriage contracts, wills, and court decisions" from Lagash and Nippur (dating from the last half of the third millennium B.C. to the last centuries of the first) (Kramer 1963:23–4; see also pp. 109, 229). Why this should be so is well worth exploring.

Does this comparative scarcity of primary sources mean, as many have supposed, that writing in early China was primarily used in religious or divinatory contexts (e.g., Vandermeersch 1980:289–90, 473–88)? Or does it mean that the "archival fallacy" must be avoided and that the resolutely non-secular nature of the sources that have been preserved on shell and bone reflects primarily, if not only, the perishability of the materials, such as bamboo, wood, and silk, on which other kinds of texts might have been written?

There are reasons to think, for example, that the oracle-bone inscriptions represent a secondary, rather than a primary, record of the rituals performed by the dynasty's diviners and kings. The diviners must, in a significant number of cases, have kept an initial record—presumably written with a brush, on perishable materials such as bamboo strips—of the divinations. The engravers (who were not the diviners) then digested the primary information that had been recorded in these "diviners' notebooks" and carved the final record into the bones and shells, days, if not months, after the pyromantic events they recorded (Keightley 2001). Such primary documents might not have been used in every case, but some inscriptions do indeed suggest that they were copies of texts that have now been lost to us (Venture 2002:303–7).

It is known, furthermore, from traces of writing left on the oracle bones and on pots, that the writing brush already existed and was used for writing characters (Liu Yiman 1991:546–54, 572; Qiu Xigui 2000:60, 63; Venture 2002:52–3). And the oracle-bone inscriptions alone show that the Shang kept numerical records of military conscriptions, casualties suffered by the Qiang or other enemies, animals offered in sacrifice, animals caught in the hunt, tribute offerings of turtle shells, numbers of days, strings of cowries, measures of wine, and other miscellaneous data (Chen Mengjia 1956:111–13; Keightley 1999c:287). It is probable, therefore, that these records kept by the diviners would have been matched by, and based upon, comparable accounts in the non-oracular sphere where some system of record-keeping would have been needed to coordinate the complex dynastic economy. Given the theocratic nature of the Shang state, the distinction between secular and religious writings is not easy to draw, but it seems likely that a considerable amount of Shang writing would not have been focused primarily on ritual and cult. A small number of non-oracular Shang writings have indeed survived on bone, stone, ceramic, human and animal skull, and jade. These records evidently served as tribute notations, exercises in engraving, labels for ancestral tablets, sacrifice records, genealogies, and potter's or other marks (Venture 2002:136–69). That the marks found on Late Shang pots rarely exceeded one or two in number (Zheng Zhenxiang 1994:248–55) accords with the view that their function was to label the pot in some way; lengthy texts would not have been required.

In later periods, texts such as ritual manuals, calendars, official regulations or lists of funerary goods are mostly written on wooden or bamboo slips. So it is reasonable to suspect that the Shang people may also have had some sort of documents written on wooden slips, and that they may not have survived, due to the perishable nature of the materials used for such writing. Indeed, actual bamboo or wood strips are attested as early as the fifth century B.C. and support the conclusion that these were probably the materials used for writing everyday documents in earlier times as well. (Postgate et al. 1995:475)

If such perishable materials have not survived (see also Bagley 1999:182; Boltz 1999:108; Postgate et al. 1995:459, 463, 464), then it would seem, on the basis of the records' durability, that the Shang valued ritual, or ritualized, records more than they did secular records. And we can, perhaps, be more specific about the nature of the valuation. It would only have been when the society had become sufficiently differentiated for the ruler to employ specialist engravers who were working with expensive, durable artifacts that long inscriptions on non-perishable materials are found; putting these inscriptions into jade, bronze, or bone, for example, would have required considerable effort on somebody's part.

But more was involved than just value. Early inscriptions in China—whether on bone, bronze, or ceramic—are characterized by the close link between the inscribed object itself and the text, so that the text itself refers to the object (Venture 2002:162, 245–6, 255). Thus, an oracle-bone inscription may be regarded as a "label" informing us that "This is the bone that such-and-such a diviner cracked on such-and-such a day about such-and-such a topic." A bronze inscription is a "label" informing us that "This is the ritual vessel that So-and-so made for (and uses in rituals offered to) his Ancestor Such-and-such" (on this inscription type see von Falkenhausen 1993:153). A pictographic clan insignia cast into a ritual bronze vessel (Figure 9.2B) or other artifact such as a weapon or musical instrument (Yang Xiaoneng 2000:91) would have served a similar function. And even the marks found on Neolithic pots (Figure 9.1A and B), whatever their precise meaning, presumably indicated: "This is the pot belonging to, made by, to be used for, So-and-so or such-and-such." These inscriptions were all self-referential; they were not independent texts that had an existence of their own. And once again, it seems unlikely that a culture able to label objects in this way with considerable frequency, would have limited itself to writing labels and nothing else. It is hard to believe, in short, that a label-writing culture would not at the same time have produced non-label writings, documents on bamboo or wood, for example, which could have referred to events that had occurred independently of the act and object of inscription. In this view, for example, the numerous divinations about when and where the dependent laborers, mobilized in their thousands, should be conscripted and employed (Keightley 1999c:284–5) would have represented only a fraction of the written orders required to muster and supply the armies and labor gangs. Cultures, such as the Inca, have certainly constructed major works without writing to assist them. But the Shang already had a developed writing system; it is hard to believe that they would not have used it in many non-oracular aspects of their daily lives.

The Oracle-Bone Inscriptions: Who Read Them?

Scapulimancy (divination that uses animal shoulder bones) and plastromancy (divination that uses turtle shells) had undoubtedly been associated with the rise of ritual experts and the increasing specialization and stratification of Late Neolithic society. Such forms of pyromancy would have been one of the techniques by which chieftains and their supporters laid claim to the special knowledge that validated their status. Scapulimancy, which evidently appeared in north China some two millennia earlier than did plastromancy (Li Ling 2000:294, 302–4), may have developed when leaders, making burnt meat offerings of sheep, pig, or cattle to the spirits, claimed that the cracking of the bones in the fire represented the voices or responses of those spirits and, in particular, their acceptance or rejection of the sacrifice (Itô 1962:255, 256; Vandermeersch 1994:249). If offerings were made to the dead—and the richness of the mortuary cult in Neolithic China suggests that early forms of ancestor worship were emerging—then one can see that the practice of divination, even at this early date, could have been associated with sacrifices and an emerging ancestral cult.

The oracle-bone inscriptions of the Late Shang were heirs to this tradition, but they raise a number of questions. Why, for example, did the Shang kings have the divination record incised into the bones? Who incised it? Who was the audience? Were Shang kings (and their ancestors) literate? And why were these records stored?

There is no doubt that, in some cases, the inscriptional record served to legitimate the king's status as an accurate forecaster; the engravers did not generally record his erroneous forecasts (Keightley 1988:372–3; 1999a:208–10). But why did the Shang engravers bother to carve their inscriptions into the bone? Why did the original notes, the primary documents (see above), not suffice? Why could the king's prognosticatory triumphs not have been written on the bone with a brush, as a few divination records indeed were (Keightley 2001:23–5)? Many aspects of Shang practice will probably never be recoverable, and I suspect that, had they been pressed, different diviners might have provided their own varying rationales for what they did, particularly when it is considered that more than 30 of the 120 diviners whose names are recorded in the divinatory prefaces came from regions that lay beyond the Shang cult center at Xiaotun 小屯 (on the northwest outskirts of Anyang 安陽 in northern Henan) and may well have been influenced by local divinatory traditions (Takashima and Yue 2000:21–3). Nevertheless, the following nine features are worth consideration.

First, it should be noted that the carving of the record was labor intensive. It would have required a special staff of engravers. The "value added" nature of the inscribed bones presumably conferred prestige on their sponsor, the king, quite apart from whether anybody read the inscriptions or not. Uninscribed divination bones—and many have been found (Djamouri 1999:14, 16; Keightley 1978:166; Qiu Xigui 2000:62, n. 3)—might have been cracked by anybody, but only the elites could sponsor the production of divination inscriptions (which is not to say, of course, that they could read them). It is worth recalling that many fine Shang and Western Zhou ritual bronzes carry no inscriptions whatever (von Falkenhausen 1993:167; Venture 2002:277); like the uninscribed divination bones, these bronzes had presumably served an important ritual function, but a function that would have been less evident, less dedicated, than if their makers had labeled them with an inscription. And one may even speculate that many of the Shang bones may have remained uninscribed because the "diviners' notebooks" or the bones to which they referred were never passed on to the engravers; these cases may represent "bureaucratic slippage," perhaps because as an overworked staff might have complained, "Too many bones, too few engravers!"

Second, on occasion, the engravers for some diviner groups also carved out and deepened the *bu* ⌐-shaped pyromantic cracks in the bones themselves (Keightley 1978:53; Venture 2002:48). (The word written with the Shang graph *bu* which appears with great frequency in the divinatory prefaces—14 *bu* graphs are present in Figure 9.3—still has the meaning of "to divine.") One may assume, accordingly, that in Shang divinatory theology a homology would have been thought to exist between the cracking and carving of the bone and the carving of the graphs (Lewis 1999:14). That the engravers had cut into the bone both the cracks and the message to which the cracks had responded would have assured that the divinatory results achieved through the making of those cracks would also not lose their visibility, their efficacy (Keightley 1978:22, n. 93). If, as Venture (2002:267) has argued, the principal function of inscriptions on Shang and Western Zhou artifacts was to give a ritual act the possibility of durable existence, in the hope that the makers of the inscription would long benefit from its anticipated blessings, this would again suggest that the creation of the inscription was intended to obtain these benefits; it was not required that a human audience read it.

For the oracle-bone "record," I believe, was meant to mark or label as much as it was meant to document. Nylan (2000:246, n. 90), citing Rosalind Thomas (1992, chapter 3, esp. p. 94) has noted "the crucial distinction between making records [i.e., the oracle-bone inscriptions] and making documents, where [unlike records] there is the expectation that documents will be consulted later." The graphs were a permanent record, a permanent register, placed into the bone like the cracks, that amplified and confirmed what the bone, the cracks, and the ancestors working through those cracks, had already done or were about to do. The graphs were, as suggested earlier, labels, and they were labels that formed part of the particular medium that they labeled. As Harris (2000:87) has reminded us about the reading of books,

> It seems rather obvious that people do not write on paper as they write on soft clay or on wax. But it would be a mistake to conclude that the material is no more than an adventitious or "external" factor ... in the birth of a writing system. In other words, it is implausible to suppose that the written sign exists from the beginning at a level of abstraction that is independent of its biomechanical realization.

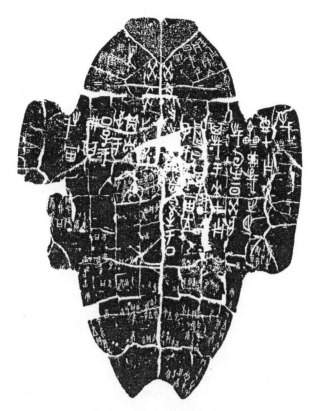

Figure 9.3 Rubbing of a turtle plastron inscribed with Late Shang divination inscriptions that may have spanned a period of fifteen days; their calligraphy varied in size and they were inscribed at different times. Satisfying the requirements of a "display inscription," King Wu Ding forecast in one inscription that the Shang would harm the enemy on the day *jiazi* 甲子; the verification confirms that they did indeed do so (bold inscription, center-right). (*Heji* 6834f; plastron is 30cm long.)

Whoever may have read the oracle-bone inscriptions, they had to, needed to, wanted to, read them in the bone.

Anything written on a bamboo slip, by contrast, would have been merely a written document of no particular efficacy. So far as divinatory texts were concerned, in fact, I would not argue that the Shang court was text-centered; it was "bone-sign"- or "bone-mark"-centered, with the signs or marks sometimes represented by the *bu* ト-shaped cracks, sometimes by the graphs. The link between bone, crack, and graph is also demonstrated by the way in which the right–left orientation of the graph forms might be linked to an inscriptions' placement on the bone, particularly on the plastrons from the reign of Wu Ding 武丁 (?–ca. 1189 B.C.), where the engravers, as in Figure 9.3, often balanced the positive and negative divination "charges" (the term modern scholars use to refer to the divinatory propositions that the diviners submitted to the bone or shell), as they had also balanced the cracks, symmetrically (see below). This provides additional support for the view that the cracks and the graphs were homologous.

Third, there is some tantalizing evidence that a magico-religious impulse may have been involved in the act of inscribing (as opposed to mere "writing"). A small number of scapulas—which were probably not divined by the usual court diviners—were excavated near Xiaotun in 1971. The eight charges on the front of one bone involved offerings, mainly of various kinds of pigs, and exorcisms to various ancestors and ancestresses. Strikingly, the engravers had erased the heads of virtually all (it is hard to be certain in two cases) the various "pig" graphs on the bone, together with the head of the one "dog" graph (also offered in sacrifice), a practice that must have had some significance, possibly magical (Keightley 1999b:184). Perhaps the "erasure" of the head confirmed that the sacrifice had indeed been offered; perhaps it indicated that the animal's head had been removed and offered separately. If the consistent "de-engraving" of the graphs in this way had some symbolic meaning for the Shang, one may suppose that the regular engraving of the graphs would also have done so. And, once again, one notes a lack of interest in making the graphs readable. The erasing of the heads would, in fact, have made the graphs harder to read.

Fourth, some of the inscribing appears to have been performed on a mass-production basis. "In these cases, the engraver first cut all the vertical and sloping strokes for every graph on the bone and then rotated the bone to carve all the horizontal strokes" (Keightley 1978:49). This too suggests that, at least in some cases (see too Yan Yiping 1978:943), the act of "writing *onto*" bone was less important than the act of writing "*into*" bone. The incising of the graphs mattered more than the writing of them. Such mass-produced inscriptions, in fact, can hardly be said to have been "written" at all, but they evidently served a purpose. It is likely, to be sure, that the great majority of the inscriptions were not mass produced in this way (Venture 2002:51 and the scholarship cited there), but the fact that some were does suggest, at the least, that not all inscriptions were created equal, and that different engravers took different approaches to their work.

Occasional evidence of inscriptional insouciance, in fact, can be found in all periods, and by Period V (see Table 9.1) some of the incised records were increasingly perfunctory. (For the five oracle-one periods employed by modern scholars, see Table 9.1 and Keightley 1978:92–4; Shaughnessy 1982–83). That the incising mattered more than the writing is also once again indicated by the fact that strokes were sometimes missing, or graphs were written upside down (see, e.g., Keightley 1978:49, n. 111; Yan Yiping 1978:943–7). This again suggests that the presence of the incised graph may have been more important than its accuracy. Of particular interest are two Period III inscriptions (*Heji* 27382), in which the engraver had twice written the oracle-bone character 夨 (for *wang*) 王, ("king") upside down; he had also written the *xin* character upside down in the prefatory day-date, *xinyou* 辛酉. It is hard to assess the significance of these inversions. That the king had twice been inverted on the same bone suggests either that the

Table 9.1. Oracle-bone periods (Sources: Keightley 1978:203; Loewe and Shaughnessy 1999:25)

Period	Approximate B.C. date	Shang kings
I	1200–1189	Wu Ding
II	1189–1158	Zu Geng, Zu Jia
III	1157–1132	Lin Xin, Kang Ding
IV	1131–1106	Wu Yi, Wen Wu Ding
V	1105–1045	Di Yi, Di Xin

inversion was intentional or that the engraver was badly trained (the calligraphy is certainly crude). That the oracle-bone *xin* form 辛, was similar in shape to an inverted *wang* form 天, and that the engraver inverted them both, lends support to the view that he might have been having trouble distinguishing certain graph shapes. I doubt, accordingly, that the inverting of the "king" graphic indicates a malcontented engraver, hoping to dishonor the king in this way. The inversion, in any event, whether its origins lay in ignorance or animus, suggests once again that, for the elites who commissioned such work, the value of the inscriptions may have lain primarily in their existence; the engraver might have been confident that his audience would not notice—or, if they were not literate, would not even have known—that the king had been stood on his head. As Venture (2002:270–1) has noted, when Western Zhou elites commissioned artisans to make copies of bronze inscriptions, some of these copies contained numerous wrong characters; he calls the artisans "illiterate" and he likewise concludes that in these cases the integrity of the text mattered little to the elites.

Given the scale of the inscriptional enterprise, such cases in which the incising of inscriptions was perfunctory to one degree or another are hardly surprising. Generally speaking, however, the inscriptions contain remarkably few "typographic" errors of this sort. The engravers appear on the whole to have performed their task conscientiously; presumably, they and their colleagues scrutinized their product and took professional pride in what they produced. At the same time, however, the practice of incising the most routine of divinatory topics into the bone for a period of a century and a half would not only have led to its routinization—as in the "assembly-line" production referred to above—but might well have led to questions about its necessity. The shrinkage in the scope of divinatory concerns notable in the Period V inscriptions (Keightley 1988:379, 382) could certainly be explained in this way. And it may well be that by the end of the dynasty, the practice of cutting the graphs into the bones was increasingly continued out of traditional inertia rather than deep religious conviction or the need to satisfy a readership.

Fifth, on a good number of the bones—though not all (see, e.g., the discussion of "display inscriptions" below)—the "page design" (as in Figure 9.3) would have given readers no guidance where to begin or what to read next. To be sure, there were certain conventions that would have guided the initiate's eye (Keightley

1978:52; Venture 2001; Yan Yiping 1978:960–1085). But these conventions were often ignored, so that once again, one is left with the impression that many of the oracle-bone inscriptions on plastrons were not designed for easy or consistent reading. The potential Shang reader—and especially the casual uninformed reader, if such existed—would have been confronted with a jumble of notations that would have required, as it has required of modern scholars, considerable effort to negotiate. The inscriptions appear to have been inscribed to leave a record rather than a document; they had not been inscribed for routine reading.

Sixth, I would suggest that the inscribed characters represented, so to speak, the engravers' "rice bowl." That the number of characters would not have been overly large—I estimate, crudely, that the engravers would have carved some 45 to 90 characters per day—may have made it all the more to the engravers' advantage to persuade the king that "The Spirits need these inscriptions. This is hard, creative work, in Your Majesty's service." Part of the impulse to carve the characters may thus have come from the self-interest of the engravers themselves. This possibility again bears on the extent to which the inscriptions actually were read, on why they were needed to be read, after the engravers had done their work.

Seventh, these considerations also bear on the oracle-bone sets, which in Period I consisted of five "carbon copies" of the same inscriptions, with cracks numbered "1" to "5," often on five separate plastrons. It is worth considering why anybody would want to write—let alone read—the same pedestrian charge, 隹父甲" (His Majesty's sick tooth) is due to Father Jia," five different times on the back of the five different plastrons in the same set (as discussed in Keightley 1978:76–90). Any viewers with the plastron in hand could read the inscription once; he or she did not have to read it five times over—unless, of course, the repetitive incising and reading had been part of the ritual. One has the sense in these cases that, from the point of view of both the engravers and the king, it was a matter of "the more ritual writings the better," and that the inscriptions, once again, were not there to be read but to be present. Although the use of such sets declined after Period II (Peng Yushang 1995; Venture 2002:57–9), their prevalence in Period I again strongly supports the view that the Wu Ding inscriptions did not primarily function as documents to be read.

An eighth consideration, already alluded to, suggests the same conclusion. Much of the inscriptional record seems so banal or routine—"In the next ten days there will be no disasters," "The king hunts at X, going and coming back there will be no disasters," et cetera—that the interest of the "reading public" would hardly have been intense or sustained. There would seem to have been little need for most of the court to actually read each routine inscription day after day, week after week. Seeing it on the bone, or, more precisely, knowing it was in the bone, might have been enough. Many of the inscriptions can probably be compared to the "legal notices" that appear in our own newspapers; they are there for the record, there to protect their writers, but only occasionally consulted or invoked by a few interested parties on a "need to know" basis. Once again, I would suggest that the importance of the inscriptions was that they were there, that they existed, not that they were read.

Ninth, the placement of many Shang bronze inscriptions, inside and not infrequently at the dark bottom of tall ritual vessels, would have rendered them virtually invisible and hence unreadable (Venture 2002:282). The placing of the inscriptions *inside* the vessels may have been to provide symbolic contact between the inscription and the sacrificial offering placed in the vessel (Kane 1982–83:14). These considerations, however, again suggest that many Shang bronze inscriptions were not primarily designed to be read, or not, at least, by everybody: it is probable that "the intended recipients of the texts were the ancestral spirits in heaven" (von Falken-hausen 1993:147). It is likely, therefore, that the inscriptions on bone, like the inscriptions on bronze, also participated in a system of symbolic communication that functioned as much through its presence as its readability.

Readers and Reading

The above features—involving the prestige attached to the labor invested, the homology of crack and inscription, the presence of inscribing errors and the mass-production of the graphs, the confusion of the page design, the engravers' vested interest in the engraving, the existence of "carbon-copy" sets of inscriptions, the banality of much of the record, and the way in which Shang bronze inscriptions were not placed for readability—all bear to varying degree on the question of audience. Any conclusions are bound to be speculative, because as Connery (1998:27) reminds us, "Reading leaves no residue of its existence." My sense is that the early inscriptions were intended both for (1) the ancestors or other Powers, whose intentions the divinations were intended to ascertain, confirm, certify, and record, and (2) the king's immediate supporters at court—at least in the case of the "display inscriptions" of Period I (e.g., Figures 9.3 and 9.4), defined by their bold calligraphy, by the prognostication and verification being written as a single, continuous unit, and by the verification confirming the accuracy of the king's prognostication (Keightley 1978:46, n. 90). But even in these cases it is worth reflecting that the incised version would only have been available some time after the divinatory episode it recorded, when the engravers, working from the primary records of the diviners' notebooks (Keightley 2001; see also Djamouri 1999:16), had finished their task of incision. The inscriptions, in other words, would have been "old news" by the time they "went to print." The time lag suggests once again that many of the inscriptions were not designed to be read, at least for new or current information; they were designed to be present, designed to record, in a religiously charged medium and mode, what had transpired. This does not mean, accordingly, that the king's supporters were necessarily literate; some probably were, some probably were not. For it is possible that the value of the characters lay less in the audience's ability to read them, more in the king's ability to have the inscriptions carved into the bone, causing them to appear just as he had caused the cracks to appear in the bone—cracks that were, like the inscriptions, sometimes cut into the bone themselves. Had the supporters been literate, a brush-written account might have sufficed. But the inscriptions were not just characters; they were characters that the king had caused to appear in the bone!

The engravers of Periods I and II had commonly carved boundary lines (two are visible in Figure 9.4) into the bone to separate one inscription from another (Keightley 1978:53–4). That these readers' aids were virtually never used by Period V (Keightley 1978:112; Venture 2002:64–5) appears to have been related to the increasing order and regularity of the late period inscriptions:

> The order which was introduced into the sacrificial schedule in Period IIb … was also reflected in the more systematic placement of the inscriptions on bone and shell. Similarly, the scrambled mix of topics generally found on the Period I bones and shells … became less common in Period II, when divinations about just one topic, such as the hunt or the sacrificial cycle, might be clustered on a particular bone or shell over a series of days. Such pure clusters had become the norm by Period V. (Keightley 1978:112)

The conventions for inscribing and placing the oracle-bone inscriptions, in short, evolved over time. A different aesthetic had come into play: bold, assertive display

Figure 9.4 Cattle scapula inscribed with series of "display inscriptions." On three occasions Wu Ding forecast that somebody would bring alarming news; on three occasions the verification records that was what had happened (*Heji* 6057f; scapula fragment is 22cm long.)

had been replaced by good, routine order. Venture, in fact, has suggested that later diviners, noting the difficulty involved in reading some of the earlier pieces, had resorted to more precision in their work. Whether, however, such good order was achieved in the interests of "readability and intelligibility" (Venture 2002:272), or was simply a result of greater bureaucratic routinization, is hard to determine.

It would appear, in any event, that different diviner groups and their engravers may have had different conceptions of their task in mind. The Bin 賓-group diviners of Period I (on the diviner groups see, e.g., Shaughnessy 1982–83), for example, tended to record many of their divination charges as positive and negative charge-pairs (Keightley 1978:37–8, 43, 78–80; 1988:367–8, 373–5), as in "We will receive millet harvest," the positive charge on the right side of a plastron, and "We might not receive millet harvest," the negative charge on the left (*Heji* 9950f). The right–left placement of the inscriptions on plastrons evidently mattered a great deal, with the right side of the shell (both front and back) generally being reserved for the charges, prognostications, and outcomes that the Shang desired. Where the Bin-group diviners had used two complementary charges, however, the approximately contemporary Li 歷-group diviners limited themselves to a single, unpaired charge that focused on the desired or intended consequence; they did not employ a matching charge to address the result that was undesired or unintended. The materiality of the record appears to have played a role here, for the Li-group preference for single charges can be related to their preference for scapulas over plastrons—scapulas lack the central median line and right–left symmetry of plastrons—and to features that were suited to the Bin-diviners' balanced placement of positive-negative charge-pairs. The medium in which the Shang were to make their pyromantic cracks and engrave their inscriptions, in other words, appears to have been influenced by the way they formulated the divinatory charges.

The "one-unit" solution of the Li-group diviners—as in "If (we) pray for harvest to the River Power, we will receive harvest" (*Heji* 33271)—was to be the model that survived. Not only were the divination inscriptions more "efficient" in Period V than they had been in Period I, but the accompanying reduction in the size of the calligraphy suggests that the nature of the intended audience had also changed by the end of the dynasty. The minuscule calligraphy of the Period V inscriptions, no longer for "display," would have made them harder to read—and certainly harder for a large audience to have seen. I find, in a crude test, that I can read the large-calligraphy *ganzhi* 干支 day-dates on the rubbing of a Period I inscription (Figure 9.3) from a distance of 8 feet; I have to be 2 feet 6 inches way from the rubbing of a Period V inscription. And even in the case of the Period I plastron the graphs, engraved at different times, might be large or small (Keightley 1978:85, n. 113, 105, n. 48, 211, Table 19). Even under Wu Ding, not all inscriptions had been rendered equally readable. (These conclusions should also be considered in the context of Rawson's conclusion [1999:44] that the "intricate decoration" on Shang ritual bronzes "implies handling and appreciation from close quarters.")

That the inscriptions were not intended to be read by a wide audience is also indicated by the engravers' frequent "failure" to carve any prognostication and,

even more strikingly, any verification into the bone. "Tedious and crude calculations … suggest that the Bin-group diviners recorded only one prognostication
for every 83 divinations for a prognostication-per-episode rate of 1.2 percent"
(Keightley 1999a:223, n. 30.) As with many other aspects of the divination
inscriptions, practice varied here too; some diviner groups recorded prognostications and verifications far less frequently than others. I am in agreement, accordingly, with Venture's conclusion (2002:231,247) that the desire to register the
divinatory ritual was basic to the practice of inscribing the divination records and
that that is why the divination charge was recorded far more frequently than the
verifications were. The main thing, he concludes, was to make the point that the
divinatory act had taken place.

It may seem counter-intuitive to argue that the Shang engravers were
recording inscriptions that they did not expect many others to read. Yet such a
situation was evidently not unknown in other early cultures. At a 1999 symposium on the origins of writing held at the University of Pennsylvania, "scholars
noted that the early rulers could not write or read; they relied on scribes for their
messages, record keeping and storytelling" (Wilford 1999:2). In the Shang case,
I conceive of the inscriptions as a form of conspicuous cultural capital, in which
the Shang elites invested considerable labor resources to produce artifacts whose
overwhelming value was ritual. And I would suggest that, with the possible exception of the "display inscriptions" discussed above—and even they may have been
"displayed" for the spirits not for humans—the only regular, human audience
that eventually read the graphs on a regular basis, and then only as they produced
them, is likely to have been the engravers themselves, and, presumably, the officers
whose job it was to make sure that the records written in the diviners' notebooks
were faithfully incised into the bones.

This view of the matter is supported by the consideration that the concept
of unread divination records was not entirely foreign to the political mythology
of the Zhou. The record of the Duke of Zhou's divination about the health of
King Wu 武 was, according to the "Jin teng 金縢" chapter of the Shangshu
尚書, locked away in the metal-bound coffer, and was not apparently known to
the young king Cheng 成 until the coffer was unlocked some two years after his
accession. The historicity of this tale is of course problematic; but the impulse to
limit the reading of divinatory records was not, evidently, thought to be unusual.
That no Zhou text refers to writing an oracle-bone inscription, let alone reading
one, also suggests that the writing and reading of these inscriptions was highly
esoteric, not widely practiced, or both. The word did not get out.

An Archive? For Posterity?

The tendency to refer to the corpus of oracle-bone inscriptions that has come
down to modern times as an "archive" (e.g., Djamouri 1999:20; Postgate et al.
1995:471) should, I think, be resisted. The diviners or their assistants certainly
appear to have used some form of filing system for storing and retrieving at least

certain shells or bones during the relatively brief period when they were being divined. Thus five plastrons from the reign of Wu Ding were used for one set of charges and were then reused, eleven days later, in precisely the same sequence, for a different set of charges (Keightley 1978:39, n. 54). Other examples reveal the cracking of single bones over periods as long as, in one case, nine months (Keightley 2001:6–7). I think it is likely, however, that, on the death of a king, his old oracle-bones—which might have been stored above ground, in a temple, perhaps, during the course of his reign—were consigned to underground pits (see also Venture 2002:232, 272).

The Western Han historian Sima Qian 司馬遷 (d. ca. 85 B.C.) had heard that the Xia 夏 and Shang threw away their divining stalks and shells after use because they felt that stored plastrons were not spiritually efficacious (1959:3223). It would appear that he was correctly informed about the Shang. The Shang attached little spiritual or historical significance to their divination records after they had served their primary function—to label the divination bone while it was still, as it were, "in play." The bones and shells, after whatever temporary exaltation they may have enjoyed as they were sanctified for divination, cracked, prognosticated, and inscribed, eventually became once again mere bones and shells. The oracle bones come to us from the cellars and refuse pits of the Shang, not from the temple archives. (Venture [2002:222] also rejects an archival function for the inscribed bones.) The variety that we find in the pit contents—some inscriptions of one period, some of several; some all shell or bone, some mixed; some all of one-diviner group, others mixed; one group of plastrons buried with a human skeleton (pit YH 127); some bones dumped in, others arranged more carefully; some plastrons whole, some broken and incomplete; some bones inscribed, some not—all suggests that historical circumstance, such as haste, accident, the need to make room above ground, the need to store reusable bone and shell material, rather than any religio-bureaucratic, or archival principle, dictated the way in which the Shang disposed of their divination bones. I would also note that the bones, by their very nature, would have been difficult to "archive," and particularly in Period I, when the "scratch-paper" approach to recording the inscriptions meant that any plastron or scapula might contain a mix of dates, topics, and diviners. Finding a particular bone five years, or even five months, after the event would have been difficult. (The problem of classification, in fact, has remained to trouble the editors of modern collections of oracle-bone rubbings; see, e.g., Keightley 1990:45–6.) The oracle-bone inscriptions, not much read before they were put into the ground, were not intended to be read after the Shang buried them. And for some 3,000-plus years, until their discovery around 1899, they were not.

Conclusion

The making of oracle-bone inscriptions virtually ceased with the fall of the Shang in 1045 B.C. This suggests that the defeat itself may have discredited such pyro-mantic practices. Nevertheless, it is worth reflecting that the Shang king, by appealing to the authority of the written word, would also have been ceding some of his own authority to those who were, perhaps, more literate than he was. To the extent that writing would have tended to demystify the mysterious (cf. Djamouri 1999:23, 24), its routine use would have tended to promote the diviners and engravers at the expense of the king, who, in the pre-writing stage, would have embodied the paramount divinatory authority (based on his ability to read the cracks), an authority that he now increasingly shared with his staff.

The association of the script with religious communication, in any event, undoubtedly conferred value on the graph forms—see Sampson (1985:16) on the theme, "script follows religion"—which, by the Bronze Age, were already providing one of the characteristic ways in which the elites ordered and made their mark on Chinese society. The status of the elites, who were to be increasingly associated with literacy, encouraged a general respect for literature and for texts. But the close association between writing and authority that scholars (e.g., Connery 1998; Lewis 1999) have found in the Eastern Zhou and Han was not yet, I suspect, fully developed in Shang and Western Zhou. As Trigger (1998:40) has noted, in early societies such as China's,

> even specialized knowledge remained closely linked to oral traditions, and distinctive literary forms and devices for organizing and conveying knowledge did not develop to any considerable degree until a much later period. For that reason writing's impact on thought in the early civilizations was … limited.

Those who were mastering the new skills of writing and reading were no doubt promoting the links between writing and authority as literacy itself was becoming more widespread. But it may not have been until the first century A.D. that written texts were to achieve their paramount cultural role (Nylan 2000:252). The Shang writing that has survived played a powerful role in labeling and recording various ritual activities, including divination, but since most of the writing that I believe existed in the Shang has not survived, the larger extent of its influence is not yet easy to assess.

The written graph forms were to evolve and become standardized over time. And the basic principles and the character forms that the Shang had employed were to endure over the next three-plus millennia. The origins and functions of the first Chinese script, as they may be discerned in the continually expanding archaeological record, are well worth study.

Acknowledgments

The editor extends special thanks to Tianlong Jiao for technical assistance in preparing this manuscript for publication.

References

Bagley, Robert W. 1999 Shang Archaeology. *In* The Cambridge History of Ancient China: From the Origins of Civilization to 221 B.C. Michael Loewe and Edward L. Shaughnessy, eds. pp. 124–231. Cambridge: Cambridge University Press.

Boltz, William G. 1994 The Origin and Early Development of the Chinese Writing System. American Oriental Series 78. New Haven: American Oriental Society.

— 1999 Language and Writing. *In* The Cambridge History of Ancient China: From the Origins of Civilization to 221 B.C. Michael Loewe and Edward L. Shaughnessy, eds. pp. 74–123. Cambridge: Cambridge University Press.

— 2000–01 The Invention of Writing in China. Oriens Extremus 42:1–17.

Chang, Kwang-chih 1980 Shang Civilization. New Haven: Yale University Press.

Chen Mengjia 陳夢家 1956 Yinxu buci zongshu 殷墟卜辭綜述. Beijing: Kexue chubanshe.

Cheung Kwong-yue 1983 Recent Archaeological Evidence Relating to the Origin of Chinese Characters. *In* The Origins of Chinese Civilization. David N. Keightley, ed. pp. 323–91. Berkeley: University of California Press.

Connery, Christopher Leigh 1998 The Empire of the Text: Writing and Authority in Early Imperial China. Lanham MD: Rowman and Littlefield.

DeFrancis, John 2002 The Ideographic Myth. *In* Difficult Characters: Interdisciplinary Studies of Chinese and Japanese Writing. Mary S. Erbaugh, ed. pp. 1–20. Pathways to Advanced Skills Series, 6. Columbus: National East Asian Language Resource Center, Ohio State University.

Djamouri, Redouane 1999 Ècriture et divination sous les Shang. *In* Extrème-Orient, Extrème-Occident (Divination et rationalité, en Chine ancienne) 21. Karine Chemla, Donald Harper, and Marc Kalinowski, eds. pp. 11–35. Paris.

Falkenhausen, Lothar von 1993 Issues in Western Zhou Studies: A Review Article. Early China 18:139–226.

Fitzgerald-Huber, Louisa G. 1999 The Yangshao Culture: Banpo. *In* The Golden Age of Archaeology: Celebrated Discoveries from the People's Republic of China. Xiaoneng Yang, ed. pp. 54–77. Washington: National Gallery of Art; Kansas City: Nelson-Atkins Museum; New Haven: Yale University Press.

Hansen, Chad 1993 Chinese Ideographs and Western Ideas. Journal of Asian Studies 52:373–99.

Harris, Roy 2000 Rethinking Writing. London: Athlone.

Heji. Guo Moruo 郭沫若 ed., Hu Houxuan 胡厚宣 ed. in chief *Jiaguwen heji* 甲骨文合集 13 vols. N.p.: Zhonghua shuju, 1978–82.

Itô Michiharu 伊藤道治 1962 In izen no ketsuen soshiki to shûkyô 殷以前血緣組織宗教 hô gakuhuô 東洋學報 32:225–70.

Kane, Virginia C. 1982–83 Aspects of Western Zhou Appointment Inscriptions: The Charge, The Gifts, and The Response. Early China 8:14–28.

Keightley, David N. 1978 Sources of Shang History: The Oracle-Bone Inscriptions of Bronze Age China. Berkeley: University of California Press.

— 1988 Shang Divination and Metaphysics. Philosophy East and West 38.4:367–97.

— 1989 The Origins of Writing in China: Scripts and Cultural Contexts. *In* The Origins of Writing. Wayne M. Senner, ed. pp. 171–202. Lincoln: University of Nebraska Press.

— 1996 Art, Ancestors, and the Origins of Writing in China. Representations 56:68–95.

— 1999a Theology and the Writing of History: Truth and the Ancestors in the Wu Ding Divination Records. Journal of East Asian Archaeology 1:207–30.

— 1999b Shang Oracle Bone Inscriptions from Anyang, Henan Province. *In* The Golden Age of Archaeology: Celebrated Discoveries from the People's Republic of China. Xiaoneng Yang, ed. pp. 182–86. Washington: National Gallery of Art; Kansas City: Nelson-Atkins Museum; New Haven: Yale University Press.

— 1999c The Shang: China's First Historical Dynasty. *In* The Cambridge History of Ancient China: From the Origins of Civilization to 221 B.C. Michael Loewe and Edward L. Shaughnessy, eds. pp. 232–91. New York: Cambridge University Press.

— 2000 The Ancestral Landscape: Time, Space, and Community in Late Shang China (ca. 1200–1045 B.C.). Berkeley: Institute of East Asian Studies. China Research Monograph 53.

— 2001 The Diviners' Notebooks: Shang Oracle-Bone Inscriptions as Secondary Sources. *In* Actes du colloque international commémorant le centenaire de la découverte des inscriptions sur os et carapaces (Proceedings of the International Symposium in commemoration of the oracle-bone inscriptions discovery). Yau Shun-chiu and Chrystelle Maréchal, eds. pp. 11–25. Paris: Èditions Langages Croisés.

Kramer, Samuel Noah 1963 The Sumerians: Their History, Culture, and Character. Chicago: University of Chicago Press.

Lewis, Mark Edward 1999 Writing and Authority in Early China. Albany: State University of New York Press.

Li Ling 李零 2000 Zhongguo fangshu xukao 中國方術續考 Beijing: Dongfang chubanshe.

Li, Xueqin, Garman Harbottle, Juzhong Zhang, and Changsui Wang 2003 The Earliest Writing? Sign Use in the Seventh Millennium B.C. at Jiahu, Henan Province, China. Antiquity 77:31–44.

Liu Yiman 劉一曼 1991 Shilun Yinxu jiagu shuci 試論殷墟甲骨書辭 Kaogu 考古 1991.6: 546–54,572.

Loewe, Michael, and Edward L. Shaughnessy, eds. 1999 The Cambridge History of Ancient China: From the Origins of Civilization to 221 B.C. Cambridge: Cambridge University Press.

Lu Sixian 陸思賢, and Li Di 李迪 2000 Tianwen kaogu tonglun 天文考古通論. Beijing: Zijin cheng chubanshe.

Nylan, Michael 2000 Textual Authority in Pre-Han and Han. Early China 25:205–58.

Peng Yushang 彭裕商 1995. Yindai bufa chutan 殷代卜法初探 *In* Xia Shang wenming yanjiu 夏商文明研究. Luoyang shi dier wenwu gongzuodui 洛陽市第二文物工作隊 ed. pp. 229–30. Zhengzhou: Zhongzhou guji chubanshe.

Postgate, Nicholas, Wang Tao, and Toby Wilkinson 1995 The Evidence for Early Writing: Utilitarian or Ceremonial? Antiquity 69:459–80.

Pulleyblank, Edwin G. 1996 Early Contacts Between Indo-Europeans and Chinese. International Review of Chinese Linguistics 1.1:1–25.

Qiu Xigui 2000 Chinese Writing. Gilbert L. Mattos and Jerry Norman, trans. Berkeley: The Society for the Study of Early China and The Institute of East Asian Studies, University of California, Berkeley.

Rawson, Jessica 1999 Ancient Chinese Ritual as seen in the Material Record. *In* State and Court Ritual in China. Joseph P. McDermott, ed. pp. 20–49. Cambridge: Cambridge University Press.

Salomon, Frank 2001. How an Andean "Writing Without Words" Works. Current Anthropology 42:1–27.

Sampson, Geoffrey 1985 Writing Systems: A Linguistic Introduction. Stanford: Stanford University Press.

Shaughnessy, Edward L. 1982–83 Recent Approaches to Oracle-Bone Periodization. Early China 8:1–13.

Sima Qian 司馬遷 1959 Shiji 史記. 10 vols. Beijing: Zhonghua.

Takashima, Ken-ichi 2000 Foreword. *In* Chinese Writing, by Qiu Xigui. pp. xix–xxv. Gilbert L. Mattos and Jerry Norman, trans. Berkeley: The Society for the Study of Early China and The Institute of East Asian Studies, University of California, Berkeley.

Takashima, Ken-ichi, and Anne O. Yue 2000 Evidence of Possible Dialect Mixture in Oracle-Bone Inscriptions. *In* Yuyan bianhua yu Hanyu fangyan: Li Fanggui xiansheng jinian lunwenji 語言變化與漢語方言：李方桂先生紀念論文集. Ting Pang-hsin and Anne O. Yue, eds. pp. 1–52. Taibei, Seattle: Zhongyang yanjiuyuan Yuyanxue yanjiusuo, Academia Sinica; University of Washington.

Thomas, Rosalind 1992 Literacy and Orality in Ancient Greece. Cambridge and New York: Cambridge University Press.

Trigger, Bruce 1998 Writing Systems: A Case Study in Cultural Evolution. Norwegian Archaeological Review 31:39–62.

Unger, J. Marshall 2004 Ideogram: Chinese Characters and the Myth of Disembodied Meaning. Honolulu: University of Hawaii Press.

Vandermeersch, Léon 1980 Wangdao ou la voie royale: Recherches sur l'esprit des institutions de la Chine archaique. Tome II: Structures politiques, les rites. Paris: École Francaise d'Extrème-Orient.

— 1994 Ètudes sinologiques. Paris: Presses Universitaires de France.

Venture, Olivier 2001 Quelques observations au sujet de la mise en page des textes de divination sur plastron. *In* Actes du colloque international commémorant le centenaire de la découverte des inscriptions sur os et carapaces (Proceedings of the International Symposium in commemoration of the oracle-bone inscriptions discovery). Yau Shun-chiu and Chrystelle Maréchal, eds. pp. 71–90. Paris: Èditions Langages Croisés.

— 2002 Ètude d'un emploi rituel de l'écrit dans la Chine archaique (xiiie–viiie siècle avant notre ère): Réflexion sur les matériaux, épigraphiques des Shang et de Zhou Occidentaux. Ph.D. dissertation, Université, Paris 7/Denis Diderot.

Wilford, John Noble 1999 When No One Read, Who Started to Write? New York Times, 6 April, sec. F:1–2.

Wu Hung 1985 Bird Motifs in Eastern Yi Art. Orientations 6.10:30–41.

— 1995 Monumentality in Early Chinese Art and Architecture. Stanford: Stanford University Press.

Yang Xiaoneng 1999 Pottery *Zun* Urn With Incised Pictograph. *In* The Golden Age of Archaeology: Celebrated Discoveries from the People's Republic of China. Xiaoneng Yang, ed. pp. 102–3. Washington: National Gallery of Art; Kansas City: Nelson-Atkins Museum; New Haven: Yale University Press.

— 2000 Reflections of Early China: Decor, Pictographs, and Pictorial Inscriptions. Kansas City: Nelson-Atkins Museum of Art.

Yan Yiping 嚴一萍 1978 Jiaguxue 甲骨學 2 vols. Taibei, Yiwen.

Zheng Zhenxiang 鄭振香 1994 Taowen yu fuhao 陶文與符號 *In* Yinxu de faxian yu yanjiu 殷墟的發現與研究. Zhongguo shehui kexueyuan Kaogu yanjiusuo 中國社會科學院考古研究 所 ed. pp. 248–55. Beijing: Kexue chubanshe.

Further Reading

Bagley, Robert W. 1987 Shang Ritual Bronzes in the Arthur M. Sackler Collections. Washington DC and Cambridge MA: Arthur M. Sackler Foundation and Arthur M. Sackler Museum.

— In press Anyang Writing and the Origins of the Chinese Writing System. *In* The First Writing: Script Invention in Early Civilizations. Stephen D. Houston, ed. Cambridge: Cambridge University Press.

Barnard, Noel 1986 A New Approach to the Study of Clan-Sign Inscriptions of Shang. *In* Studies of Shang Archaeology: Selected Papers From the International Conference on Shang Civilization. K. C. Chang, ed. pp. 141–206. New Haven: Yale University Press.

DeFrancis, John 1991 Chinese Prehistorical Symbols and American Proofreader's Marks. Journal of Chinese Linguistics 19.1:116–21.

Djamouri, Redouane 1997 Écriture et langue dans les inscriptions chinoises archaiques (xive–xie siècle avant notre ère). *In* Paroles à dire, Paroles à écrire. pp. 209–40. Paris: Ed. de l'EHESS.

Dorofeeva-Lichtmann, Véra 2001 Spatiality of the Media for Writing in Ancient China and Spatial Organization of Ancient Chinese Texts. Göttinger Beiträge zur Asienforschung 1:87–135.

Keightley, David N. 1990 Sources of Shang History: Two Major Oracle-Bone Collections Published in the People's Republic of China. Journal of the American Oriental Society 110.1:39–59.

Lefeuvre, J. A. 1975 Les inscriptions des Shang sur carapaces de tortue et sur os; aperçu historique et bibliographique de la découverte et des premières études. *T'oung Pao* 61:1–82.

Porter, David 2001 Ideographia: The Chinese Cipher in Early Modern Europe. Stanford: Stanford University Press.

Pulleyblank, Edwin G. 1996 Zou and Lu and the Sinification of Shandong. *In* Chinese Language, Thought, and Culture: Nivison and His Critics. Philip J. Ivanhoe, ed. pp. 39–57. Chicago: Open Court.

Schuessler, Alex 1987 A Dictionary of Early Zhou Chinese. Honolulu: University of Hawaii Press.

Shaughnessy, Edward L. 1991 Sources of Western Zhou History: Inscribed Bronze Vessels. Berkeley: University of California Press.

Takashima, Ken-ichi 2001 A Cosmography of Shang Oracle-Bone Graphs. *In* Actes du colloque international commémorant le centenaire de la découverte des inscriptions sur os et carapaces (Proceedings of the International Symposium in commemoration of the oracle-bone inscriptions discovery). Yau Shun-chiu and Chrystelle Maréchal, eds. pp. 37–62. Paris: Èditions Langages Croisés.

Tsien, Tsuen-hsuin 1962 Written on Bamboo and Silk: The Beginnings of Chinese Books and Inscriptions. Chicago: University of Chicago Press.

Tung Tso-pin 1964 Fifty Years of Studies in Oracle Inscriptions. Tokyo: Center for East Asian Cultural Studies.

Wang Yunzhi 王蘊智 1994 Shiqian taoqi fuhao de faxian yu Hanzi qiyuan de tansuo 史前陶器 符號的發現與漢字起源的探索. Huaxia kaogu 華夏考古 3:95–105.

Wang Yuxin 王宇信 1981 Jianguo yilai jiaguwen yanjiu 建國以來甲骨文研究. Beijing: Zhongguo shehui kexue chubanshe.

10

CLEAN HANDS AND SHINING HELMETS: HEROIC ACTION IN EARLY CHINESE AND GREEK CULTURE

David N. Keightley

For large periods of time in both the West and China the authority of a "classical" past had a paramount importance in shaping the conception of what it was to be human. It is true that between the fall of the Roman Empire and the fall of Constantinople, knowledge of Greece had been lost to Christendom for the better part of a millennium,[1] but a renewed interest in the traditions of Greece and Rome was a central feature of the great cultural and humanistic revolution that we call the Renaissance. It is evident, furthermore, as Frank M. Turner has written, that "extensive ... concern with ancient Greece" became an important and "novel factor in modern European intellectual life" as "the values, ideas, and institutions inherited from the Roman and Christian past became problematical." Europeans turned to the Greeks, accordingly, "for new cultural roots and alternative cultural patterns ... in the wake of the Enlightenment and of revolution." This led to a situation in which "to no small extent knowledge of the classical world and acquaintance with the values communicated through the vehicle of classical education informed the mind and provided much of the intellectual confidence of the ruling political classes of Europe."[2]

What had become true of England and late modern Europe had, more or less, been true of China for a period of some two thousand years. The degree to which Chinese elites, down to the intellectual and political revolutions of the late nineteenth and the twentieth centuries, found their power in the authority of tradition is well known. This tradition had been institutionalized in a system of education and recruitment based on an orthodox classical curriculum that took as its core a series of so-called Confucian texts, some of which dated to the first part of the first millennium B.C. Just as late modern Europe had accepted "the centuries-old belief that a man had only to know Greek and Latin to be educated—to be a cut above humanity,"[3] so had the Chinese accepted the millennia-old belief that knowledge of the Classics and the rather arcane language in which those hallowed texts were written gave a man the right, as well as the duty, to rule his fellow men.

Certain early texts served in Greece and China, at roughly comparable stages of development, to exemplify what it was to be human in terms of past heroic action. In what follows, I shall look primarily at epics and histories, not at philosophical or other texts, though I suspect that many of the distinctions I identify could be found in those materials as well. For Greece, 1 rely primarily upon the epic traditions, represented by Homer's *Iliad* (and to a lesser extent, his *Odyssey*) and by Hesiod's *Theogony*: these texts were compiled and recorded, give or take a century, around 700 B.C. but had their roots in the oral compositions of the previous centuries. For China, I rely primarily upon the closest equivalents we have: the *Book of Songs* (*Shi*), the pronouncements of the *Book of Documents* (*Shu*), and the extensive historical anecdotes recorded in *Zuozhuan*; the material in these texts is of varying date, running from the early part of the first millennium to about the fourth century B.C.[4]

These Chinese and Greek materials are not, strictly speaking, comparable documents. Indeed, if I wanted to reduce the burden of my essay to one idea, it would be that the early Chinese did not produce—or at least did not preserve—the kind of epics that the early Greeks did.[5] This does not mean that we cannot compare the two cultures in a fruitful way. It means, rather, that we need to consider what kinds of representations of the human condition the Chinese did produce and preserve in the place of such epics, why they produced and preserved them, and what kinds of humanity were portrayed and venerated in those representations. If the works of Homer and Hesiod helped to define what it was to be Greek, the *Songs, Documents,* and *Zuozhuan* played a similar role in China, particularly in the long imperial period that followed the Han dynasty (206 B.C.-A.D. 220).

The traditional Chinese, in fact, invested so much philosophical and literary effort in their classical tradition that when China was faced with the onslaught of the West and with the social upheavals accompanying the end of the Qing dynasty (1644–1911), it did not—unlike the Europeans of the eighteenth century—have its own Greece to turn to for *fresh* inspiration. The attempt was certainly made, in the forced and even tragic exertions of the *jinwen* ("modern text") thinkers and late Qing political reformers, but China had already, as it were, exhausted that inspiration. It could not be made fresh and new. Whether in the Marxism of Mao Zedong or the yearnings for democracy of student dissidents after him, the West has, for better or worse, now become, to a significant degree, China's Greece and Rome.

The Asian Games, recently held in Beijing, like the Olympics that the Chinese hope to host in the year 2000, can thus be seen as the descendants of the games that Achilles held for Patroclus's funeral, games that the Greeks felt lay at the origin of their own Olympic and other pan-Hellenic competitions. They serve as one example of China's attempt to appropriate part of the West's classical and now international heritage into China's modern culture. The modernization of China—including the modernization of its artistic as well as its political culture—will inevitably involve a reconsideration of classical representations of the human condition, whether in China or the West.

Representations of the Hero

I define the hero in broad terms as a protagonist of exceptional courage and fortitude who engages in bold and significant actions. I do not insist in a comparative essay of this sort on the hero's most fundamental Homeric aspect, "that the hero must experience death" and be associated with religious cult.[6] The nature of religious belief and practice has a fundamental influence in such matters (see the discussion of ritual and worship below), but here I would simply note that my instinctive preference for using, in an essay about humanity, a basic analytical category derived from the Greek *heros* suggests the degree to which my concerns are shaped—even misshaped—by Western assumptions. I shall return to this point in my conclusion.

Let me start with a specific example: the legendary theme of Achilles and Penthesileia, the Amazon queen. The theme, which was popular in both Greek and Roman culture, expresses significant views about the individual and society that would have been entirely foreign to Chinese contemporaries. It provides an excellent example of the way in which Chinese and Greek conceptions of man and hero may be distinguished.

If we consider the theme as treated by the Attic black-figure potter and painter Exekias on an amphora from around 540 B.C. (fig. 1), we can note a variety of characteristic features. The two protagonists are heroic in size, seeming to burst the confines of the bowl. Achilles is naked from the waist down. His face is concealed by his helmet so that only his eye glares forth; his victim's face, by contrast, is exposed and vulnerable.[7]

The painting is characterized by the particularity of both its subject and author. We can identify the two figures, Achilles and Penthesileia, and we can identify the individual, Exekias, who made the vase; all three names are actually painted on the vase. And, most importantly, there is the irony of the tale itself. At the moment when Achilles plunges his sword into the breast of his swooning victim, their eyes meet and he desires her! The artist has captured precisely this moment of dramatic and fatal pathos. The painting and the legend express in powerful, individual, and supposedly historical terms one of the major assumptions of the heroic tradition in the West, namely, that man's condition is tragic and poignant, that the best and most valorous deeds may lead to undesired consequences, and that heroic virtue must be its own reward. Man lives in a quirky, unpredictable, and ironic world that is, by its very nature, unresponsive to human values and desires.

The gods of the *Iliad* are unpredictable in precisely this way and they are frequently hostile to certain men. "Hera, the wife of Zeus, and Athena, his daughter," for example, "hate Troy and the Trojans with a bitter, merciless hatred."[8] As Apollo says in Book 24 of the *Iliad*, "Hard-hearted are you, you gods. You live for cruelty" (24:39).[9] Like Homer, Hesiod in his *Theogony* and *Works and Days* portrays the gods as "changeable, irresponsible, and frequently hostile to individuals or groups of men."[10]

Figure 1 Detail from black-figure amphora by Exekias, ca. 540. B.C., depicting Achilles fighting Penthesileia at Troy. London: British Museum B210. Photo: Max Hirmer.

We may consider, by contrast, the decoration found on an Eastern Zhou bronze *hu*-vase (fig. 2), probably about one hundred years later in date.[11] The differences are striking: the Chinese artisans depicted stereotypical silhouettes rather than individuals (see note 7). We know the names of none of the people represented or of the master craftsmen and artisans who cast the vessel. Whatever is being represented, the viewer receives a strong impression of regimented mass activity. An anonymous master-designer has subordinated the small and anonymous individuals to a larger, impersonal order. Indeed, they cannot really be called "individuals" at all. Such art expresses the bureaucratic ideals of impersonal

Figure 2 Decor on an Eastern Zhou *hu*. From *Wenwu* 1977.11:86. Among the scenes depicted are a battle (bottom); archers, a banquet, and an orchestra (middle); and more archery and the plucking of branches (top).

administration that Chinese social theorists and ministers were applying during the Warring States period (453–221 B.C.).

To be sure, one can see superficial similarities between these orderly soldiers who fought in the Eastern Zhou ranks and the Greek hoplites who, from around 700 to 550 B.C. "fought in close-packed phalanxes, their round, emblazoned shields interlocked, their safety depending on the steadfastness of the next man in line, their individual prowess less important than the integrity of the whole."[12] But major differences separate the two experiences. In terms of artistic representation, the painting on the Late Protocorinthian *olpe* (ca. 640 B.C.; fig. 3) depicts the ranged bodies of the hoplites with a perceptual

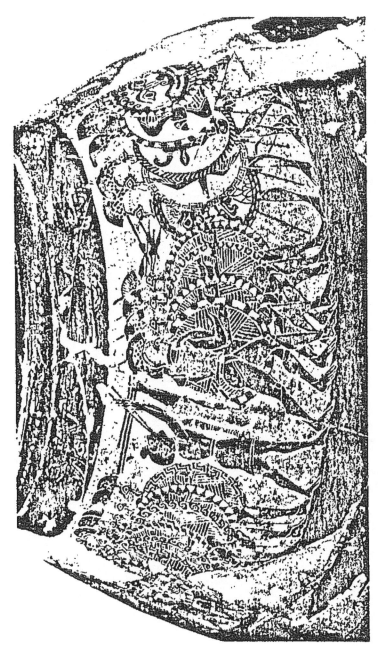

Figure 3 Detail from the Late Protocorinthian *olpe* known as the Chigi vase. Rome, Villa Giulia. Photo: Max Hirmer.

realism and individual detail (including the attention lavished on the shield emblems) lacking in the Chinese case.[13] That realism, it should be noted, is also not emphasized in the Eastern Zhou battle literature, which in fourth and third century B.C. texts like *Zuozhuan* and *Discourses of the States* (*Guoyu*) tends to minimize the actual details of the shock and blood of combat in favor of moralizing speeches and stratagems.[14]

Several points, in fact, distinguish the accounts of fighting in Homer and in *Zuozhuan*. First, the Chinese accounts are of battle, in that they usually involve the fate of armies; the protagonist is not alone, but is fighting in the company of, and talking to, companions; Homer's accounts are more frequently of individual combat as hero meets hero. Second, the *Zuozhuan* accounts provide little or no reference to the immediate adversary. Chinese protagonists suffer wounds but we often do not know who administered them. Third, there is no reference in the Chinese accounts to the presence of gods on the field of battle who stimulate the warriors or who influence the outcome; no goddess like Pallas Athena feeds nectar and ambrosia, the food of the gods, to a Chinese Achilles to take the field with his energy refreshed; no goddess like Pallas Athena dons mortal form to trick a Chinese Hector into fatal combat (as happens in the *Iliad*, Book 22). Fourth, the Chinese concern is less with the fighting than with the morale and willpower of the fighters, less with the details of the combat and more with the larger issues of strategy and morality.

In short, early Chinese representations of conflict reveal no interest in depicting hands-on experience with all its harsh and disorderly detail (see 261). The Chinese representations, to anticipate the argument to come, were more concerned with conception than perception, for the hero was increasingly not the fighter, as Achilles had been, but the statesman and general who planned and directed the fighting of others. This "bureaucratization" of action, moreover, is implicit both in the decor of our Chinese bronze (fig. 2)—for somebody was presumably overseeing these stereotypical soldiers and orchestra players—and in its manufacture—for somebody had surely directed the numerous artisans involved in the industrial-scale casting that such a vessel required. Once again, we see reinforcement and similarities: the manufacturing process contrasts sharply with the practices of the early Greeks, who both admired the individual and who tended to organize their workshops, like their battle accounts, around a series of acts performed by a small number of protagonists.[15]

Turning to representations of the human figure, military or otherwise, it is significant that we have no large, identifiable human figures from Shang or Zhou bronzes or vases, and certainly not from statuary, comparable to those made in contemporary Greece. Geometric Greek art, like the designs found on Shang and Western Zhou bronzes, had been "overwhelmingly abstract," but the human figure had begun to emerge in the last half of the ninth century. A historian of Greek art refers to "a mighty confrontation between the pictorial and the abstract" during the Middle Geometric period (ca. 800 B.C.), a confrontation that was eventually won by the advocates of pictorial representation who placed man and the human figure at the center of classical art.[16] No such "confrontation"

can be discerned in the art found on Shang or Zhou bronzes; the figures on the
Eastern Zhou *hu* (fig. 2), for example, evolved from and continued to express
older conceptions of linear and symmetrical order. In this respect, accordingly,
Zhou culture remained closer to the culture of the Greek Geometric than to that
of the Greek classical age.

Heroic Types—A Choice

It is difficult to generalize about early Greek views of heroism because the subsequent elite culture appears to have been more pluralistic, more given to the preservation and transmission of conflicting views than the elite culture of early China
was (at least as that culture has been represented and transmitted to us). Homer's
quintessential hero presented in the *Iliad* is Achilles, "best of the Achæans," who
will sacrifice his life for *kleos* ("glory"). Homer and Hesiod both lay great stress
on *eris* ("strife") as an essential theme. It is significant, however, that even at this
early stage, other visions of the hero were present. Hector, the defender of the civilized, urban Troy, is—to use the terms of this account—represented as far more
"Chinese" than the dreadful Achilles. He is, to be sure, a great warrior:

> "War—I know it well, and the butchery of men ...
> I know it all,
> How to charge in the rush of plunging horses—
> I know how to stand and fight to the finish,
> twist and lunge in the War-god's deadly dance."
>
> (7:275–81)

But Hector is also presented as a domestic figure with wife and child; he is a filial
son, a defender not just of his selfish honor but of his people.[17] Homer's other
epic, the *Odyssey*, also qualifies Achilles' "all-or-nothing" view of heroic action
quite radically. In the *Iliad*. Achilles had taken "unfailing glory" as compensation
for his impending, deliberately chosen, death. In the *Odyssey* (Book 11), by contrast, his shade tells Odysseus in a famous passage that he, Achilles, "would rather
be another's hired hand,/ working for some poor man who owns no land ... / than
to rule over all whom death has crushed."[18] The Achilles of the *Odyssey*, in short,
had found glory less attractive than the Achilles of the *Iliad* had hoped. Indeed,
the disruption of good order portrayed by the *Iliad* is challenged by the restoration
of order that forms the main theme of the *Odyssey*.

It is striking to find this tension between martial glory and destruction,
on the one hand, and well-ordered domesticity and governance, on the other,
in Homer's two epics, the works that were, for Late Geometric Greeks, not just
artistic masterpieces, but also, as one modern Western historian has called them,
"storehouses of values and ethics and textbooks of conduct ... full of information
detailing what it was to be Greek."[19] The Zhou Chinese, by contrast, appear to
have resolved the tension between martial heroism and administrative domesticity
unambiguously in favor of civilian rule—in favor, one might say, of the cities

rather than the marauders—so that the texts that have been transmitted to us give little attention to matters of glory, killing, and, as we shall see, death. There were at least two Greek views of the heroic enshrined in the major tradition, that represented by Achilles and that represented by Ulysses or Hector. For the Chinese of much of the Eastern Zhou, as we see them in the transmitted record that was to form the Classics, there was only one view. The pluralism of the Greek views and the greater unanimity of the Chinese view is itself significant. This is not to say that alternate models of action, excluded from the orthodox classical canon, were not available in early China. By the late Eastern Zhou and Han dynasties, the eremitic ideal—best exemplified in the Taoist teachings of the *Zhuangzi* (ca. 300 B.C.)—had become increasingly attractive.[20] Characteristically, however, the contemplative recluse rejected most forms of cultural engagement, removing himself from the arena of action; he did not, in contrast with, say, Odysseus, provide an alternate model for social, political, and military action in the world. His ideal, rather, was that of *wuwei*, spontaneous action through "nonpurposive action."[21]

Hands—Dirty and Clean

The role of hero and protagonist was represented, as I have suggested, in radically different ways in Greece and China. Achilles, whether in the *Iliad* of the late eighth century, or on the painted vases of the sixth and fifth centuries, acts and speaks for himself. He feels the thrust of the blade as it pierces Penthesileia's breast (fig. 1); he is directly responsible; he has "dirty hands." The "terrible, man-killing hands" of Achilles are, in fact, one of the standard tropes that identify him.[22] (When, one wonders, does an early Chinese text, transmitted to us, ever emphasize any part of the anatomy in this way?) Hector too, who, as we have seen, knows "how to charge in the rush of plunging horses," admits to dirty hands when his mother urges him, fresh from the field of battle, to make an offering to Zeus:

> "I'd be ashamed to pour a glistening cup to Zeus with unwashed hands. I'm splattered with blood and filth."
>
> (6:315–16)

Zeus, too, speaks of his power to subdue Poseidon in struggle in terms of "my mighty hands" (15:270). Such bodily engagement and physical prowess were part of the Greek hero's qualities. The valiant and wise Nestor in Book 23 of the *Iliad* can reminisce in detail about his athletic feats—in running, boxing, wrestling, the javelin throw, and charioteering—and can give the names of the particular individuals he defeated: Klytomedes, Angkaios, Phyleus, Polydorus. In the classical age, too, the tragic heroes (and heroines) of Athenian drama, such as Oedipus, Antigone, and Cleon, continued to act for themselves and to take personal responsibility for their deeds.

One assumes that the Bronze Age Shang kings may have done the same, though our sources provide little direct representation of the royal emotions and perceptions. By the late Eastern Zhou, there were stories of notable feats of strength performed by political leaders. King Wu of Qin (310–307 B.C.), for example, loved to lift heavy tripods; the incident has given rise to a cautionary phrase, *ju ding jue bin* ("lift the tripod and wrench the knee"), which cautions against overestimating one's strength. The dynastic claimant Xiang Yu lifted tripods too, but such feats do not seem to have been regarded with favor; the strong men who joined with King Wu in tripod-lifting, for instance, were put to death after he died.[23] Feats of strength, it is worth remarking—along with prodigies, disorders, and spirits—was one of the four topics about which Confucius (ca. 551–479 B.C.) chose not to speak (*Lunyu*, 7:20; *Zi bu yu guai li luan shen*). Homer, by contrast, sang of them all.

In Zhou China, heroic action, at least as it is reflected in our elite texts, increasingly involved delegation and planning. The hero was the clean-handed leader, the exhorter, the strategist; he was not the doer. The *Zuozhuan* contains numerous accounts of moral judgment, moral prophecy, and discussions of statecraft, but, as we have already seen in the case of accounts of battle, the focus tends to be on strategies and justifications, on deciding how other people should act, rather than on the leader's personal action.

Sima Qian, in his early first century B.C. history *Records of the Grand Historian* (*Shiji*), presents a series of biographies of Eastern Zhou figures that confirm this emphasis. One may discern in his account of Wu Zixu of the fifth century B.C. some remnants of direct, hands-on action, but these appear to have been increasingly edited out of the later texts. At the start of the story, for example, Wu Zixu "drew his bow, snatched an arrow, and stood facing" those who had come to arrest him.[24] He does not actually shoot the arrow. The rest of the tale involves his wanderings, stratagems, and counsels, but it is only when he eventually cuts his own throat—as a loyal servitor and bureaucrat must do when the king requests it—that he puts his hands on a weapon again.

Sima Qian's biography of the general Tian Dan (first half of the third century B.C.), who saved the state of Qi after Yan had occupied most of its territory, is equally "clean-handed." At one point, Tian Dan "took up trowel and mortarboard and personally joined [his officers and men] in their work on the fortifications," but at no point is he described as having fought in the ranks; he is the director, the coordinator, devising such stratagems as the flaming torches tied to the tails of a thousand-plus oxen. His role was to furnish, as Sima Qian remarks, "an inexhaustible supply of surprise moves."[25] There is little doubt that the Zhou Chinese tradition had chosen to emphasize the Odysseus-like rather than the Achilles-like hero and to emphasize the hero's intellectual and moral, rather than martial, qualities.

Sima Qian also presents five Zhou and Qin case histories in his chapter, "Biographies of the Assassin-Retainers."[26] Unlike most Greek heroes, these protagonists act at the behest of a lord, not for monetary gain but to repay the tremendous honor conferred by the lord's request that they perform the deed on his behalf. "The lord in these accounts delegates what, in the Greek case, would have been the heroic, the personal, and thus the tragic, task. His hand is clean; it is not on the sword; he is not even near when the deed is undertaken."[27] A bureaucratic chain of command protects the initiator—who, in the Greek view, would have been no hero, but merely an administrator—from the shock and consequences of his deeds. The true hero in these accounts is the delegate, the subordinate, who does his lord's bidding.

Representations of Death

The early Chinese interest in conceived pattern and general order rather than in perceived, particular detail (see 259), may also be seen in representations of death. No early Chinese text provides vivid, unflinching details like the description of brains bursting and covering a spearhead that is found in Book 17 of the *Iliad*. No Chinese text follows the *Iliad* in presenting "the harsh realities of the work of killing ..., the pain and degradation of death."[28] Consider how the demise of one minor combatant, Harpalion, is vividly and precisely—even anatomically—described:

> with a bronze-tipped arrow, hitting his right buttock up under the pelvic bone
> so the lance pierced the bladder. He sank on the spot, hunched in his dear
> companion's arms, gasping out his life as he writhed along the ground like
> an earthworm stretched out in death, blood pooling, soaking the earth dark
> red....
>
> (13:749–55)

No early Chinese text portrays a mortal blow in this realistic way; no early Chinese text *sees* the physical details with such precision. In terms of the visual arts, there is no early Chinese representation of death or dying to match the numerous mourners and mortal thrusts portrayed on Geometric and Archaic Greek vases or to match the late sixth-century B.C. vase painting of Sarpedon's corpse, its wounds gushing blood (fig. 4).

Achilles' lament over the body of Patroclus in Book 19 of the *Iliad* is particularly informative about death and heroism. He says to his departed friend:

> There is no more shattering blow that I could suffer.
> Not even if I should learn of my own father's death ...
> or the death of my dear son ...
> if Prince Neoptolemus is still among the living.
>
> (19:382–89)

The degree of Achilles' anguish and alienation, as well as the distinctly non-Chinese quality of his response, is to be found in his willingness to put his love for his friend Patroclus above his love for his nearest kin, his father. The hero's kin ties have been displaced by his personal and transcendingly selfish emotions.

One finds a similar displacement of normal—or should I say, of Chinese?—familial and political relationships in Book 24 of the *Iliad*, when Priam, whose

Figure 4 Attic red-figured kalyx-crater by Euxitheos and Euphronios, ca. 515 B.C. Death and Sleep carry away the corpse of Sarpedon as Hermes presides. New York, Metropolitan Museum of Art, 1972. 11.10.

son, Hector—the filial, Chinese-style son—has just been killed by Achilles, comes
to Achilles' camp by night and begs for his son's body:

> Pity me in my own right,
> remember your own father! I deserve more pity …
> I have endured what no one on earth has ever done before—
> I put to my lips the hands of the man who killed my son.
>
> (24:588–91)

As Schein notes, the two enemies, Trojan and Achæan, "virtually adopt one
another as father and son."[29] No early Chinese text plays on such fundamental
themes of death and kinship and with such paradoxical, ironic complexity.

Not only is the *Iliad* filled with accounts of death, but it seems likely that the
earliest forms of Geometric pictorial art in Greece were created precisely "to exalt
the dead and preserve ritual."[30] Given the importance of death ritual and ancestor
worship in Neolithic and Bronze Age China, the virtual absence of representations
of death in Chinese art and text is all the more striking. It is true that some of the
falling figures in the battle depicted on the Eastern Zhou *hu* (fig. 2) may be dead,
but they are given no emphasis, and their silhouettes differ in no way from those
of the living. It would be interesting to determine, in fact, when the first Chinese
representation of a dead or dying person appeared. Death was evidently reserved for
the ritual texts, such as the *Book of Etiquette and Ceremonial* (*Yili*; ca. third to first
centuries B.C.), which contain remarkably detailed recipes for dealing not so much
with a particular death but with the dead in general.[31] We are told much about how
to mourn, little about what it was like to mourn.[32] The ritualists, like the artists,
were ordering, controlling, and impersonalizing experience, rather than describing
or dramatizing it. Death in Zhou China was not represented as a cathartic experience. It was a subject for ritual, not a subject for art. Or, to put the matter another
way, what art was to the early Greeks, ritual was to the early Chinese.

Shining Helmets

This Chinese concern with essential generalizations or standard recipes for
behavior, whether about death or other topics, stands in sharp contrast to the passionate Archaic Greek attention to individual detail, the joy in existential reality.
Auerbach has identified the "Homeric need for an externalization of phenomena
in terms perceptible to the senses."[33] Finley has referred to this Archaic Greek
attitude as that of "the heroic mind," arguing for "a natural bond between the
heroic temper and a gaze that sees the world with sharp and bright particularity."[34]
He refers in particular to a passage so striking that I would like to consider it
in full. A series of conversations in Book 6 of the *Iliad* first shows us Hector
approaching his family. Paris speaks with him, but "Hector, helmet flashing,
answered nothing." Helen speaks to him, and "turning to go,/ his helmet flashing,
tall Hector answered." And then, "a flash of his helmet/ and off he strode and
quickly reached his sturdy/ well-built house." He then finds his wife and child

on the ramparts, where she urges caution upon him; "and tall Hector nodded, his helmet flashing." And, after all this preparation—on my part, and Homer's—we come to the passage that Finley refers to:

> In the same breath, shining Hector reached down
> for his son—but the boy recoiled,
> cringing against his nurse's full breast,
> screaming out at the sight of his own father,
> terrified by the flashing bronze, the horsehair crest,
> the great ridge of the helmet nodding, bristling terror—
> so it struck his eyes. And his loving father laughed,
> his mother laughed as well, and glorious Hector,
> quickly lifting the helmet from his head,
> set it down on the ground, fiery in the sunlight,
> and raising his son he kissed him, tossed him in his arms,
> lifting a prayer to Zeus and the other deathless gods.
>
> (6:556–67)

Hector's prayer is the famous one that the child will one day return from battle himself, "a better man than his father," having killed a mortal enemy in war, and thus be "a joy to his mother's heart."

The shining helmet serves a complex rhetorical and dramatic function. As Fagles notes, it

> not only makes Hector's own career appear meteoric and abruptly snuffed out, but it also supports a chain of tragic ironies throughout the epic. For the flashing helmet—Hector's own at first—is soon replaced by the one he strips from Patroclus when he kills him: the helmet of Achilles. Thus ... when Achilles destroys Hector in revenge he must destroy himself.[35]

I would also note the ominous foreshadowing with which Hector's child (who will presumably be killed or enslaved when Troy falls) reacts to the helmet in terror—just as other Achæan warriors, who fell before the shining Hector, must have reacted as they died. The child will become one with the warriors in this. I would note too that the child is perceiving the helmet—"so it struck his eyes," says Homer. But above all, I would agree with Finley that the flashing helmet—which has been so frequently referred to in the preceding passages—takes on a life of its own in this scene. From a mere formulaic epithet used to identify Hector it becomes a presence, "the flashing bronze, the horsehair crest,/ the great ridge of the helmet nodding, bristling terror" and "fiery in the sunlight."

Its presence is powerful precisely because of the way that, at this critical point in the story, Homer particularizes and vivifies it. As Finley has said,

> In so deeply felt a scene surely no one but Homer would have paused to note that helmet still shining beside the human figures. It is as if in whatever circumstances it too keeps its particular being, which does not change because people are sad or happy but remains what it is, one of the innumerable fixed entities that comprise the world.[36]

There are no comparable "shining helmets" in early Chinese literature. In no text do we find this sustained interest in a thing, perceived in itself, that reappears in its own right in different situations and contexts. Even in the *Book of Songs*, where early Chinese lyricism is most prominent, the general supersedes the particular and natural objects are present because they are pregnant with allegorical or symbolic meaning, usually moral. Nature in the *Songs* does change, to use Finley's words, "because people are sad or happy"; it takes its meaning from the humans for whom it serves as background. The opening lines of Mao 1 do not call attention to the bird for its own sake—for it disappears, in fact, from the rest of the song:

> "Guan-guan" calls the osprey
> residing on a river isle.

The next two lines imply by their proximity some symbolic connection between the bird and a maid:

> A pure maid, so alluring,
> a good mate for a Lord.[37]

The general result of this allusive, generalized, symbolic approach is that there are love poems in the *Book of Songs*, but these poems express metaphorical connections; they do not portray great or famous lovers. There are heroic actions and emotions, but there are no personalized heroes who, in their particularity and "shiningness" would have been recognizable as heroes to the early Greeks. There are "things" in the *Songs*, but they have come to be appreciated because they mean something else.

To put the matter another way, Zhou texts, like Shang and Western Zhou bronze designs, reveal evidence of what to a Geometric Greek poet or artist would have seemed like severe "editing" (see note 24), in which the particular—the shining helmets and the brains covering spearheads—no matter how formulaically expressed, had been sacrificed to the general, to a concern with rules and order—as in the Chinese case. Either there was no Chinese equivalent of Finley's "heroic mind," or it left no reflection; in either case, its absence in China constitutes one of the important contrasts between the transmitted cultures of classical China and classical Greece. Early Greek art, as we have seen, was one of percepts; early Chinese art was one of concepts.

Homeric and Zhou Passages Compared

The different artistic and cultural approaches to heroism can be seen in a consideration of two passages from Homer and some Chinese analogs. The first passage, from the *Iliad*, describes the last moments of the chariot race that formed part of Patroclus's funeral games:

> In the same breath
> Diomedes came on storming toward them—closer, look,
> closing—lashing his team nonstop, full-shoulder strokes,
> making them kick high as they hurtled toward the goal.

Constant sprays of dust kept pelting back on the driver,
the chariot sheathed in gold and tin careering on
in the plunging stallions' wake, its spinning rims
hardly leaving a rut behind in the thin dust
as the team thundered in—a whirlwind finish!
He reined them back in the ring with drenching sweat,
lather streaming down to the ground from necks and chests.
Their master leapt down from the bright burnished car,
propped his whip on the yoke.

(23:555–67)

There is to my knowledge no comparable Chinese text of Zhou date that appre-
hends with such vividness the experience of chariot riding—the laying on of the
whip, the high-kicking horses, the shallowness of the ruts, the dust pelting back
on the charioteer, the drenching sweat and lather. This was evidently a passage
composed by somebody who knew what it was to race a chariot, who took joy in
recapturing the experience, and who assumed that his audience would do so too. I
am particularly struck by Homer's noting the absence of deep wheel marks; such a
perception has the effect of telling the audience, "this event was even more special,
more particular, than you might have conceived; there were no deep wheel marks,
even though there generally would have been." The long whip propped against the
yoke is another "shining helmet"—a small, insignificant detail, recorded primarily,
it would seem, to enhance the sense of reality, the sense of perception, the sense of
having been there.

What follows is an account of chariots from the Chinese *Book of Songs*
written at roughly the same time:

Our chariots are strong,
Our horses well matched.
Teams of stallions lusty
We yoke and go to the east.

Our hunting chariots are splendid,
Our teams very sturdy.
In the east are wide grasslands;
We yoke, and a-hunting we go.

My lord follows the chase
With picked footmen so noisy,
Sets up his banners, his standards,
Far afield he hunts in Ao.[38]

Five more stanzas follow. Certainly some visual details are presented:
mention is made of "the tortoise-and-snake banner and the oxtail flag" and the
"red knee-covers and gold-adorned slippers" of the riders. There is even a note of
something deficient:

If footmen and riders are not orderly
The great kitchen will not be filled.

But that deficiency is prospective, and it is one of behavior, of disorder, not of perception, of keen observation; it derives from the expectations of administrators and diviners, of people responsible for filling kitchens, not from the expectations of chariot riders. Indeed, the poem—with its account of the size, color, and condition of the horses, the direction and geography of travel, the banners displayed, the amount of the catch, the need for proper order—suggests the report of a groom or steward. The intent and the perception of reality are radically different in the Chinese and Greek texts. The tradition of Homer attempts to particularize and to vivify; the composers of the *Songs* tend to generalize and to catalog.

Similar distinctions hold for a second passage from Homer. Book 24, the moving climax of the *Iliad*, describes Priam's night-time visit to Achilles' camp to redeem the corpse of his slain son, Hector. The scene shifts from 1) Achilles' quarters, to 2) Mount Olympus, the home of the gods, to 3) Troy, as Priam is emboldened to undertake the perilous journey and instructs his still living sons (whom he despises for still being alive, now that Hector is dead) to ready a conveyance. Homer then shifts from Priam's viewpoint to 4) that of his sons, of whom he says:

> Terrified by their father's rough commands
> the sons trundled a mule-wagon out at once,
> a good smooth-running one,
> newly finished, balanced and bolted tight,
> and strapped a big wicker cradle across its frame.
> They lifted off its hook a boxwood yoke for the mules,
> its bulging pommel fitted with rings for guide-reins,
> brought out with the yoke its yoke-strap nine arms long
> and wedged the yoke down firm on the sanded, tapered pole,
> on the front peg, and slipped the yoke-ring onto its pin,
> strapped the pommel with three good twists, both sides,
> then lashed the assembly round and down the shaft
> and under the clamp they made the lashing fast.
>
> (24.313–325)

Coming as it does at a moment of great emotion, as the grieving father, lamenting the death of his favorite son and the now-certain destruction of Troy, faces the dangers of a night visit behind enemy lines, such a technical digression is puzzling, for it impedes the development of the story. The delay, of course, may have heightened the suspense,[39] but it is the nature of the delay that concerns me. One supposes that both Homer and his audience knew a lot about the activity being described—in this case the harnessing of mules to carts—and took pleasure in hearing such details. I know of no comparably detailed Zhou passages about carts or indeed about any aspect of secular activity. The only texts that display such a passion for technical minutiæ are the ritual texts like the *Book of Etiquette and Ceremonial* (see 265) and the third-century B.C. legal texts like the coroner's reports from Shuihudi.[40] In both cases the details had their particular religious or administrative, but not artistic, function. The authors of most Zhou texts that have survived were not interested in descriptions of manual labor and artisan skill.

Several conclusions can be drawn from these two examples from Homer. First, I should like to propose as a suggestive generalization that realistic details—such as the sweat from horses and the equipage of a cart—are regarded as uninteresting, even as threatening, by nonheroic (and here I am still using "heroic" in its Western sense) elites. In the Greek world men of action—such as the heroes about whom, and the audiences for whom, the Homeric bards performed—presumably take pleasure in descriptions of things they can do for themselves. In the Chinese world civilian, literati elites who do not get their hands dirty find such accounts of sweat, horses, carts, and fighting uninteresting and, because they cannot or do not do these things for themselves, threatening and delegitimizing. If early Chinese texts and art have been "edited" in the ways that I have been implying in this essay (see 267), one may associate this "editing" with the hierarchical nature of Zhou society. It is precisely what one would expect of authors and transmitters who conceive of a world divided, as *Mencius* puts it, between the rulers (who keep their hands clean) and the ruled (who get their hands dirty): "Hence it said, 'Some labor with their minds and some labor with their muscles. Those who labor with their minds rule others; those who labor with their muscles are ruled by others (*Gu yue: 'huo lao xin, huo lao li. Lao xin zhe zhi ren, lao li zhe zhi yu ren*)" (3.A.4.6).

Second, I would suggest that oral story-telling—as entertainment—encourages realistic detail. The kind of perceptual description that we have encountered above brings tales alive for listeners who know horses, harness, dust, sweat, and carts. It attracts and entertains by enhancing the familiar, making it fresh and wonderful, and giving it structure. The conceptual, expository tradition in the Zhou texts that have been preserved is less one of entertainment, and more one of instruction and exhortation. Their authors or transmitters were interested in stories about protagonists who promoted concepts of moral and religious order, concepts that they, as authors and transmitters, would like to promote themselves. They were less interested in recapturing the existential detail and perception. The difference is that between drama—which must attract its audience—and sermon—to which the audience has, as it were, already committed itself in advance.

Points of View

The absence of critical and dramatic tension—or, to put it positively, the emphasis on nonadversarial harmony—in early Chinese art and literary expression may also be contrasted with one of the characteristic and non-Chinese features of the *Iliad*, namely, that the audience hears various sides of the story. It is taken within the walls of Troy as well as without, seeing Priam's visit to Achilles from the viewpoints of Zeus, other gods, Achilles, the old man himself, and his sons. Early Greek art, by this pluralism of viewpoint, encourages the audience to sympathize with and to understand the motivations of both victor and vanquished. Achilles and Penthesileia are presented with equal force in the vase paintings. By the classical age, neither Creon in *Antigone*, nor Oedipus in Sophocles' tragedies are presented as unsympathetic or unremittingly evil figures. This ambiguity about what and who is right, about what and who is important, already present in Homer's *Iliad*, lies at the essence of the tragic view of the hero; our sympathies are not, should not be, and cannot be all on one side.[41]

Greek epics also derive much of their complexity and dramatic tension from the frank recognition that unresolvable conflicts exist in the world. This fundamental assumption is symbolized in the conflict between the values and wills of men and gods. It underlies the recognition that choices are frequently made not between good and evil but between one good and another. Early Chinese writings, by contrast, adopt a less detached, less complex view of the human condition. The vanquished in early China, from the San Miao of the South, who troubled Yao. Shun, and Yu, to Jie of the Xia and Di Xin of the Shang, who led their dynasties to destruction, were categorized as immoral. Their points of view were not presented. From the *Documents* down through *Mencius* and beyond, the last rulers of dynasties were by definition bad, and those who overthrew them, whom the ruled should unquestioningly trust, were by definition good; no "loyal opposition" was conceivable, let alone desirable or human. There are few admirable and vanquished "Trojans" in early Chinese literature; there are generally only admirable and virtuous victors and misguided and defeated villains. This lack of pluralism in politics and artistic representation (and also, as we shall see, in mythology), must have been reinforced by the Chinese cult of ancestor worship (see 272), in which only one viewpoint—that of the fathers and grandfathers—was conceived, both in this life and the next.

Death, Morality, and the Absence of Theodicy

As I have discussed elsewhere, the themes that attracted early Chinese mythologists were social order and social morality; stories of dying and death were not emphasized. The general harmony that pervades the relations of the Chinese to their gods contrasts strongly with the heroic and adversarial universe of early Greece, in which warrior gods and goddesses like Apollo, Artemis, and Pallas Athena involve themselves in the lives of mortals like Achilles or Hector. Early Chinese society was dominated by kinship ties, the royal ancestors representing the most senior members of the kinship unit in heaven. There was little discord between gods and men.[42] Obedience and filiality ruled on earth as they did in Heaven.

There was little expectation, accordingly, that in such a benevolent world, virtue would not be rewarded. Early Chinese thinking, like early Chinese mythology, showed little interest in theodicy; a fundamental optimism seemed to render any explanations for the presence of evil unnecessary.[43] The main function of the Chinese flood myth, for example, however rich its original narrative details might once have been, was to serve as a background for the sage emperor Yu as he laid out the political geography of ancient China.[44] No extant version of the myth addresses the moral significance of the flood.[45] Early Chinese mythology thus does not present malevolent gods who resented human success or conspired to destroy man. The Chinese knew neither a Prometheus nor a Zeus. Reflecting this lack of divine hostility, death in China was not regarded, to the degree that it was in Greece, as an affront to the living; it was, rather, regarded as part of the inevitable and harmonious order, as a subject for ritual rather than tragedy.

Art and Ancestor Worship

The impersonal unselfishness of the early Chinese hero was encouraged and validated by an ancestor worship that stressed the continuity of the lineage and defined the individual in terms of his generational role and status in a highly ritualized system of sacrifice, descent, and unequal distribution of power. The Chinese hero derived his authority from operating within formal boundaries rather than by overstepping them, from emulating previous heroes, who were now ancestors, so that he might be emulated and become an ancestor in his turn.

The early Chinese lack of æsthetic and even philosophical interest in particular detail is entirely congruent with the assumptions underlying ancestor worship. "The ancient Greeks," as Meyer Fortes has noted, "appear to have had elaborate cults concerned with beliefs about ghosts and shades, but no true ancestor cult." He has proposed that ancestor worship be regarded as "a representation or extension of the authority component in the jural relations of successive generations: it is not a duplication, in a supernatural idiom, of the total complex" of kin or other relationships.[46] Ancestor worship, in this view, does not merely involve belief in the dead; it involves beliefs about the dead, who are in turn conceived in a certain way. It does not involve the perceptual commemoration of the total personality of the deceased; it involves an appeal to certain powers that the deceased is conceived as possessing.

The spirit of Achilles, when he appears to Odysseus in Book 11 of the *Odyssey* (see 260), is thus not an ancestor. As when alive, he still has no knowledge of his descendants: "But tell me something of my worthy son:/ Has he, a lord of men, gone off to war,/ become a chieftain?"[47] Above all, Achilles has no power. Whereas our early Chinese texts contain many accounts of ghosts who return to wreak moral vengeance on the living,[48] the powerlessness of the dead in Homer is well known.[49] Greek ghosts were powerless precisely because they were shades of their former personalities; their powers had not been abstracted and formalized; they were still truly personalities but they were also truly dead. The Archaic Greeks, one might also observe, were not afraid of ghosts because, in a culture ridden with a sense of tragedy, ghosts could do nothing worse to man than man and the gods had already done to himself.

Three instances of the empowerment and "ritualization" of the dead in the early Chinese evidence will demonstrate the contrast with Greek religious conceptions. First, the Shang practice of conferring temple names on their dead kings and other elites, so that the dynasty founder, who, according to later texts, had been called Cheng Tang, was instead worshiped under the name of Da Yi,[50] indicates the loss of individual personality that was involved in becoming an ancestor. These impersonal temple names were typological and jural; taken from the names of the ten days of the Shang week, they were used primarily for scheduling the ancestral sacrifices on appropriate days. Da Yi, for example, received cult on *yi* days, Wu Ding on *ding* days, and so on.[51] The Shang ritualists used the temple names to place the depersonalized dead in their ritual slots.

Second, the "Pan Geng" chapter (probably written during the Western Zhou) of the *Documents* provides a clear instance of a Shang ruler using his ancestors as authority figures to legitimate his decision, which was evidently unpopular with his people, to remove the capital to Yin. Not only did Pan Geng appeal to the wise and benevolent government of the former kings when they had been alive, but he spoke of the continuing relationship—entirely jural and impersonal—among the dead ascendants:

> Now when I offer the great sacrifices to my predecessors, your forefathers are present to share in them.
>
> (pt. 1, para. 14)

> Were I to err in my government, and remain long here, my High sovereign (the founder of our House), would send down great punishment for my crime, and say, "Why do you oppress my people?" If you, the myriads of the people, do not attend to the perpetuation of your lives, and cherish one mind with me, the one man, in my plans, my predecessors will send down on you great punishment for your crime, and say, "Why do you not agree with our young grandson, but so go on to forfeit your virtue?" When they punish you from above, you will have no way of escape.... Whereas my royal predecessors made happy your ancestors and fathers, your ancestors and fathers will cut you off and abandon you, and not save you from death.... Your ancestors and fathers urgently represent to my High sovereign, saying, "Execute great punishments on our descendants." So they intimate to my High sovereign that he should send down great calamities.
>
> (pt. 2, paras. 11–14)[52]

Thus was the Shang king thought to have assigned functions to the dead, both royal and nonroyal, legitimating his needs and imposing sanctions on those who would oppose him.[53] Although these dead have power, they have no personality.

Third, the *Zuozhuan* relates the following story for the year 554 B.C.:

> Xun Yan (a victorious general from the state of Jin who commanded the army of the center) was now suffering from an ulcer, which grew upon his head; and after crossing the Yellow River [on his way back from campaigning in Lu to return to his state] and getting as far as Zhuyong, he was quite ill, and his eyes protruded. The great officers who had returned (to Jin) before him all came back, and Shi Gai (his deputy commander) begged an interview with him which he did not grant. (Shi Gai) then begged to know who would succeed [Xun Yan as commander], and Yan said. "My son by the daughter of Zheng can do it." In the second month, on the day *jiayin*, he died with his eyes staring, and (his teeth so firmly closed that) nothing (such as a ritual Jade) could be put into his mouth. Xuan Zi (= Shi Gai) washed (the corpse's

face), and stroked it, saying. "Shall I not serve Wu (Yan's son) as I have served
you?" But still (Yan) stared. Luan Huaizi said, "Is it because he did not complete his campaign against Qi?" And he also stroked (Yan's face), saying, "If
you are indeed dead, it would have to be something like the Yellow River that
would prevent me from carrying on your work (i.e., the campaign) against
Qi." The eyes of the corpse then closed, and the (customary jade] was put
between his teeth. When Xuan Zi (= Shi Gai) left the room, he said. "As a
man of valor how shallow I am (when I compare what I said to what Luan
said to the corpse)."[54]

This remarkable story of necrodivination, in which the corpse itself was used,
rather like an oracle bone, to determine the wishes of the deceased, dramatizes
the first step on the path from corpse to ancestor. Xun Yan is still conceived as
having wishes, but they are precisely wishes involving official appointments and
succession; just as Pan Geng was using the ancestors to validate his policies, so
too were Xun Yan's survivors using his recently dead body to legitimate their
own decisions. In accounts such as these, the dead are not grieved; they are put
to work.

There is no doubt that the Greeks of the Geometric and Archaic Ages com-
memorated their dead, and that by the second half of the eighth century various
hero cults proliferated, frequently centered on Late Bronze Age or Mycenæan
graves. The demonstrable genealogical link, so central to early Chinese ancestor
worship, however, appears to have been lacking, as does the systematic articulation
and instrumentality of the cult. Furthermore, the Greek hero cult was associated
with a decline in the importance of the family and the increasing strength of the
polis, so that its role in early Greece increasingly diverged in significant ways from
the role of the ancestral progenitors in early China.[55]

Following these lines of thought I would speculate that heroic cultures (such
as that represented in Homer's universe) are unlikely—at the time the heroes are
conceived as having been active—to produce a strong ancestral cult. We have seen
the way in which Achilles was ready to devalue his family ties when his friend
Patroclus died (see 263); martial heroes, filled with their own sense of individual
glory, are not likely to venerate, and may even be at odds with, their kin group.
Ancestor worship, by contrast, is created and nurtured by civilian elites anxious
to stabilize the good order and hierarchy that strong lineage units both encourage
and replicate.

I would further speculate that an inverse relationship exists between the
degree to which an ancestor cult is articulated and the degree of attention paid
to the actual circumstances of the soul in the afterlife. In this view, cultures such
as early Greece that provide imaginative, perceptual depictions of the afterworld,
and also of this one, may not need a well-structured ancestral cult. Indeed, they
may well depict postmortem existence in detail precisely because the ancestors
are missing. The presence of an impersonalized ancestral cult in early China,
by contrast, would help explain the classical texts' general lack of interest in the
particulars of death and the afterlife. It would also explain the well-known fact
that, although many mythic personages appear very briefly in ancient Chinese

texts, they do not participate in a sustained, anecdotal mythology.[56] In this view, early Chinese elites would have felt less need for the precision of event and personality and for the existential details that are such notable features of the art and mythology of early Greece precisely because they did not conceive their ancestors in these ways. The problems, including that of theodicy, that the Greeks had treated as "mythological issues," had been resolved by the Chinese creation of ancestors, who, following Fortes's definition, were ancestors precisely because they were *not* comprehensive or detailed representations of personality and social role.[57] The concern with unstructured and potentially adversarial personality—in both religion and art—had been displaced by harmonious order and design. Chinese ancestors, like Chinese heroes, were valued for the good order of what they did, as in the "Pan Geng," not for the uncertain individuality of what they were. They were, once again, conceived rather than perceived.

The Chinese Hero

Although I have more than once suggested that early China "lacked" certain features of representation and content present in the culture of early Greece, this does not necessarily imply that such features ought to have been present. I find nothing admirable, for example, in having gods who, like Zeus, assume the form of a swan to rape a woman, or who, like Kronos, devour their own children. I find nothing attractive in what has been called the Greek "lust to annihilate."[58] That the martial heroism of the Greeks has found its emulators in later Western history is as much a cause for concern as for pride. It has indeed been argued that Greek models of warfare and diplomacy have had a disastrous impact on western history. "The Classics, it is the Classics!" said William Blake, referring to Homer, "that Desolate Europe with wars."[59] For Eric Havelock, the classics helped explain the outbreak and continuation of World War I (and the Vietnam War), most of the statesmen and officers of the early twentieth century having been educated in the Greek classical tradition.[60]

In answer to the question, "Where have all your heroes gone?" the Zhou—or later—Chinese answer might well be, "Who needs them?" And the answer to that, presumably, is that certain kinds of civilizations, like Western civilization, do. All great civilizations have their costs as well as benefits. It would be instructive, accordingly—and I encourage the readers of this essay to make the attempt—to rewrite it from the Chinese point of view, stressing and seeking to explain all the features that early Greek culture "lacked."

Such an essay would begin by defining the hero differently, presumably offering various types: the hero as inventor of culture, as dynasty founder, as sage, as patriarch, as plebeian or recluse raised, on the base of merit, like Yi Yin or Tai Gong Wang, to great status and administrative influence.[61] The Chinese hero would be older, more mature. He would be literate. All Chinese heroes, moreover, would be socially engaged. Rather than employing the alien concept of "hero," the essay would, I suspect, base its categories of comparison upon the radically different Chinese term, *Junzi*, originally a lord's son but, by the time of the Eastern Zhou, a moral "noble man."[62] Great stress would be laid on the *Junzi's* respectful treatment of his parents and on his numerous male progeny. He would primarily be a man of peace not war, an administrator, a harmonizer, a man whose own personal desires were downplayed. There would be little evidence of dramatic conflict, of ironic or tragic incapacities, and there would be little interest in particular detail. The hero's role would be a generalized one.

Using this Chinese definition of "hero," the essay would then note the way in which these traits had been deemphasized in favor of the more particularistic, combative, blood-thirsty, juvenile features of the Greek heroic tradition. Major questions would be asked or implied. Why do the early Greeks and the heroes whom they admire place so little emphasis on kindness, benevolence, a concern for the people, and social harmony? Why does early Greek art lay such unsettling and, in a way, parochial, egotistical, and youthful stress on individual detail and the human form? Why did the Greek city-states, despite, or perhaps because of, their curious conception of heroism, virtually commit suicide?[63] Why, in the Greek case, had something displaced the good sense of order and abstraction with which the Zhou Chinese had come to represent their own society and its leaders and ancestors? An understanding of that "something" would be, and should be, the focus of the discourse. The essay might well conclude with the suggestion that in the perspective of world history, Greece and its heroes and its art were an unusual case. Sima Qian, in any event, would have relegated the Greeks, had he known of them, to a monograph, along with the Xiongnu, Hu, and other barbarian tribes.

Our Western conceptions of man and art, of the individual and the body, of the epic and heroic in both life and literature, and of man's place in the cosmos, still resonate, whether we like it or not, in sympathy with the powerful, imaginative creations of the early Greeks. For their creations have the power to move us still, to be beautiful for us, in ways that defy easy explanation because they are so central to our conception of ourselves. Early Chinese conceptions of man and art have stirred, with equal profundity, the elites of traditional China for a period of some two millennia. If we would understand China and what it means to be Chinese, we must understand its early art and its early protagonists as the Chinese themselves have chosen to see them. And if Westerners would more fully understand themselves, understand the authority of their own past and how its religious conceptions have shaped their views of the individual protagonist and his responsibilities, an understanding of China and its cultural imperatives provides a valuable perspective.

Notes

1. Bernard Knox, "Introduction" to *The Iliad*, trans. Robert Fagles (New York: Viking, 1990) 5–6.
2. Frank M. Turner, *The Greek Heritage in Victorian Britain* (New Haven: Yale, 1981) 1–2, 5.

3. Ved Mehta, "Personal History: The Classics at Oxford. A Lasting impression," *The New Yorker*, 11 November 1991, 92. Mehta's fascinating memoir is an account of Jasper Griffin's education and career as a classicist in the mid-twentieth century.

4. A useful introduction to these and related texts is provided by Burton Watson, *Early Chinese Literature* (New York: Columbia University Press, 1962). For a more technical introduction to the dating and authenticity of the Chinese texts referred to in this essay, see Michael Loewe, ed., *Early Chinese Texts: A Bibliographical Guide* (Berkeley: Society for the Study of Early China, 1993).

5. The point is well argued by C. H. Wang, "Towards Defining a Chinese Heroism," *Journal of the American Oriental Society* 95, 1 (January-March 1975): 25–35.

6. Gregory Nagy, *The Best of the Achæans: Concepts of the Hero in Archaic Greek Poetry* (Baltimore: Johns Hopkins University Press, 1979) 9.

7. My discussion of the Greek vase and the of the *hu* below is largely taken from Ch. 2 in the volume.

8. Knox, "Introduction" 41.

9. All translations of the *Iliad* are from Fagles; the line citations are those of his English text.

10. Robert Lamberton, *Hesiod* (New Haven: Yale University Press, 1988) 90–91: see also 113. 115. 120.

11. Similar scenes have been found on at least three other bronze *hu*. See Jenny F. So. "The Inlaid Bronzes of the Warring States Period," in *The Great Bronze Age of China*, ed. Wen Fong (New York: Metropolitan Museum and Knopf, 1980) 316, and Esther Jacobson, "The Structure of Narrative on Early Chinese Pictorial Vessels," Representations 8 (Fall 1984): 77–80.

12. Jeffrey M. Hurwit, *The Art and Culture of Early Greece, 1100–480* B.C. (Ithaca: Cornell University Press, 1985) 143, 160; fig. 67.

13. For an introduction to the Chigi vase, see Tom Rasmussen. "Corinth and the Orientalising Phenomenon," in *Looking at Greek Vases*, ed. Tom Rasmussen and Nigel Spivey (Cambridge: Cambridge University Press, 1991) 57–62.

14. See, in particular, Wang, "Towards Defining a Chinese Heroism."

15. "Typically, Greek [pottery] workshops employed between ten and fifty potters and painters"; see John Onlans. "Idea and Product: Potter and Philosopher in Classical Athens." *Journal of Design History* 4. 2 (1991): 66. According to Andrew Stewart, sculpture workshops employed no more than a dozen workers; see *Greek Sculpture: An Exploration* (New Haven: Yale University Press, 1990) 33–34. For the industrial scale of Chinese bronze production, see Ursula Martius Franklin, "On Bronze and Other Metals in Early China," in *The Origins of Chinese Civilization*, ed. Keightley (Berkeley: University of California Press, 1983) 279–96; "The Beginnings of Metallurgy in China: A Comparative Approach," in *The Great Bronze Age of China: A Symposium*, ed. George Kuwayama (Seattle: University of Washington Press, 1983) 94–99. As Robert J. Poor notes, a typical set of molds for making a Shang *gu* beaker, a relatively simple shape, "might consist of twelve interlocking parts"; see "The Master of the 'Metropolis'-Emblem Ku." *Archives of Asian Art* 41 (1988): 74. There was, as he notes, no "eccentric" Shang notion of "personal or individual style" (77).

16. Hurwit, *Art and Culture* 61–70, 94–95.

17. Knox, "Introduction" 56.

18. *The Odyssey of Homer: A New Verse Translation*, trans. Allen Mandelbaum (Berkeley: University of California Press, 1990) 234.

19. Hurwit. *Art and Culture* 83, 85, citing Eric A. Havelock. *The Greek Concept of Justice* (Cambridge: Harvard University Press, 1978) 106–14.

20. Aat Vervoorn, *Men of the Cliffs and Caves: The Development of the Chinese Eremitic Tradition to the End of the Han Dynasty* (Hong Kong: Chinese University Press, 1990).

21. For an introduction to this complex idea, see Herrlee G. Creel. *What is Taoism? And Other Studies in Chinese Cultural History* (Chicago: University of Chicago Press, 1970).

22. For example, *Iliad* 24:561. Achilles' hands, ominous but now gentle, play a large role in his meeting with Priam: see 24:591. 593. 602, 789, 790.

23. Edouard Chavannes. *Les mémoires historiques de Se-ma Ts'ien*, vol. 2 (Parts: Adrlen-Maisonneuve. 1967) 76. Burton Watson, trans., *Records of the Grand Historian of China: Translated from the Shi chi of Ssu-ma Ch'ien*, vol. 1 (New York: Columbia University Press, 1961) 38.

24. Burton Watson, trans., *Records of the Historian: Chapters from the Shi Chi of Ssu-ma Ch'ien* (New York: Columbia University Press, 1969) 18, 26. David Johnson, "Epic and History in Early China: The Matter of Wu Tzu-hsü,." *Journal of Asian Studies* 40, 2 (February 1981): 265, deduces the existence of a longer Wu Zixu narrative from which the didactic anecdotes that now form its core were extracted. The *Zuozhuan*, he concludes is "highly processed…. its subject matter is 'epic,' but nothing else in it is" (268). And he discerns a general Confucianizing trend in which "narrative drive was subordinated to generic classification and intense focus on a few great heroes was replaced by a multitude of short biographies of the merely eminent or exemplary" (271).

25. Watson, trans., *Records of the Historian* 32, 33.

26. Watson, trans., *Records of the Historian* 45–67.

27. Keightley, "Early Civilization in China" 41.

28. Knox, "Introduction" 26.

29. Seth L. Scheln, *The Mortal Hero: an Introduction to Homer's* Iliad (Berkeley: University of California Press, 1984) 159.

30. Hurwit, *Art and Culture* 64, 66; figs. 29, 30.

31. John Steele, trans., The *I-Li or Book of Etiquette and Ceremonial* (1917; reprint, Taipei: Ch'eng-wen. 1966).

32. As Marcel Granet noted, the gestures of grief stipulated in early Chinese ritual texts could not be simple and spontaneous physiological and psychological reflexes. They were regulated, ceremonial acts that used the words and formulas of a systemic language. See "Le language de la douleur d'après le rituel funeraire de la Chine classique," In Granet, *Etudes sociologiques sur la Chine* (Paris: Presses Universitaires de France, 1953) 235.

33. Erich Auerbach, *Mimesis: The Representation of Reality in Western Literature* (Princeton: Princeton University Press, 1953) 3–4.

34. John H. Finley, Jr., *Four Stages of Greek Thought* (Stanford: Stanford University Press, 1966) 28.

35. Fagles, trans., "Translator's Preface" x.

36. Finley, *Four Stages* 4.

37. Jeffrey K. Riegel. "*Shih:* A Translation and Interpretation of the Ancient Chinese Book of Songs" (unpublished manuscript) "Song 1." As Riegel notes, "the osprey … symbolized both ferocious tenacity and chastity…. Having the osprey rest upon an island in a river serves to emphasize not only its isolation but perhaps its chasteness as well." On how Chinese commentators have understood such metaphorical allusions, see Pauline Yu, "Imagery in the Classic of Poetry," in her *The Reading*

of Imagery in the Chinese Poetic Tradition (Princeton: Princeton University Press, 1987) 44–83, which includes a discussion of this song.

38. Mao no. 179; Arthur Waley, trans., *The Book of Songs* (New York: Grove, 1960) 287.

39. For the dramatic function of Nestor's various hortatory and apologetic digressions, see Norman Austin, "The Function of Digressions in the *Iliad.*" *Greek, Roman, and Byzantine Studies* 7 (1966): 301–3.

40. Derke Bodde, "Forensic Medicine in Pre-Imperial China," *Journal of the American Oriental Society* 102. 1 (January-March 1982): 1–16, translates four such legal texts. The degree of detail is remarkable. Here is an example from the section "Death by Hanging": "C's corpse, facing south, was hanging from the rafter at the northern wall within the bedroom on the east side of the house. The neck was encircled by a hemp rope as thick as one's thumb, which came together (i.e., was knotted) at the nape of the neck…. Upon releasing the rope, the breath issued with a gasp from the mouth and nose. The rope left a compression bruise mark (around the neck), except for an untouched two-inch space at the nape of the neck." This and other cases have also been translated by Katrina C. D. McLeod and Robin D. S. Yates. "Forms of Ch'in Law: An Annotated Translation of the *Feng-chen shih,*" *Harvard Journal of Astatic Studies* 41 (1981): 111–63.

41. "Before Greece and outside the Greco-Western tradition, societies are instituted on a principle of strict closure: our view of the world is the only meaningful one, the 'others' are bizarre, inferior, perverse, evil, or unfaithful. As Hannah Arendt has said, impartiality enters this world with Homer…. Not only can one not find in the Homeric poems a disparagement of the 'enemy,' the Trojans, for example, but the truly central figure in the *Iliad* is Hector, not Achilles, and the most moving characters are Hector and Andromache." See Cornelius Castoriadis. *Philosophy, Politics, Autonomy* (New York: Oxford University Press, 1991) 82, 118: he cites Arendt "The Concept of History" in her *Between Past and Future* (New York: Viking. 1968) 51.

42. Keightley, "Early Civilization in China" 34.

43. On the question of philosophical optimism in early Chinese culture, see Thomas A. Metzger, "Some Ancient Roots of Modern Chinese Thought: This Worldliness, Epistemological Optimism, Doctrinality, and the Emergence of Reflexivity in the Eastern Chou," *Early China* 11–12 (1985–1987) especially 64, 66–76. Metzer's discussion of the imperfect distribution of sanctions in this world, a concern that was much on the mind of Confucius, provides additional grounds for remarking the unexpected lack of theodicy in early Chinese thought (98–99).

44. For an introduction to the flood story, see William G. Boltz, "Kung Kung and the Flood: Reverse Euhemerism in the *Yao Tien,*" *T'oung Pao* 67, 3–5 (1981): 141–53.

45. Keightley. "Early Civilization in China" 68.

46. Meyer Fortes, "Some Reflections on Ancestor Worship in Africa," in M. Fortes and G. Dieterlen, eds., *African Systems of Thought* (London: Oxford University Press, 1965) 125, 133.

47. *The Odyssey of Homer* 234.

48. See, for example, Alvin P. Cohen, "Avenging Ghosts and Moral Judgment in Ancient Chinese Historiography: Three Examples from *Shih-chi,*" in Sarah Allan and Alvin P. Cohen, eds., *Legend, Lore, and Religion in China: Essays in Honor of Wolfram Eberhard on His Seventieth Birthday* (San Francisco: Chinese Materials Center, 1979) 97–108.

49. See, for example, Erwin Rohde, *Psyche: The Cult of Souls and Belief in Immortality Among the Greeks*, trans. W. B. Hillis (London: Kegan. Paul. 1925) 24; Christiane Sourvinou-Inwood. "To Die and Enter the House of Hades: Homer, Before and After," in Joachim Whaley, ed., *Mirrors of Mortality: Studies to the Social History of Death* (London: Europa, 1981) 22.

50. Keightley. *Sources of Shang History: The Oracle-Bone Inscriptions of Bronze Age China* (1978; reprint Berkeley: University of California Press, 1985) 204, 207, n. a.

51. For a detailed analysis of the system of temple names and the way they were awarded after death, see Keightley, "Lucky Days, Temple Names, and the Ritual Calendar in Ancient China: An Alternative Hypothesis" (unpublished manuscript, 1987); for an earlier version (but published later) see Ji Dewel (David Keightley), "Zhongguo gudai de jiri yu miaohao (Lucky Days and Temple Names in Ancient China)." *Yinxu bowuyuan yuankan* (1989): 20–32.

52. Based on James Legge, trans., *The Chinese Classics: Volume III, The Shoo King or the Book of Historical Documents* (London: Frowde, 1865) 230, 238–40.

53. For another instance of this use of the dead, see Keightley, *Sources of Shang History*. "Preamble" 1–2.

54. Based on Legge, trans., *The Chinese Classics: Volume V, The Ch'un Ts'ew with the Tso Chuen* (London: Trübner, 1872) 482–83, and Séraphin Couvreur, trans., *La Chronique de la principauté de Lou: Tch'ouen ts'lou et Tso tehouan.* vol. 2 (1914: reprint, Paris: Cathasia. 1951) 345–46.

55. See Walter Burkert, *Greek Religion*, trans. John Raffan (Cambridge, Mass.: Harvard University Press, 1985) 204; he concludes that "the hero cult, in fact, is not an ancestor cult at all"; Hurwit, *Art and Culture* 121.

56. Derk Bodde, "Myths of Ancient China," in Samuel Noah Kramer, ed., *Mythologies of the Ancient World* (New York: Doubleday Anchor. 1961) 369–370; he notes that "the gods of ancient China ... appear very rarely or not at all in art, and are commonly described so vaguely or briefly in the texts that their personality, and sometimes even their sex, remains uncertain,"

57. Keightley, "Early Civilization in China" 53–54.

58. Eli Sagan, *The Lust to Annihilate: A Psychoanalytic Study of Violence in Ancient Greek Culture* (New York: Psychohistory Press, 1979).

59. Cited by Fagles, "Translator's Preface" xiv.

60. Eric A. Havelock, "War as a Way of Life in Classical Greece" and "War and the Politics of Power," Georges P. Vanier Memorial Lectures, University of Ottawa, 21 and 28 October 1970.

61. For Yi Yin, see, for example, Chang Kwang-chih. "*Tien kan:* A Key to the History of the Shang," in *Ancient China: Studies in Early Civilization*, ed. David D. Roy and Tsuen-hsuin Tsien (Hong Kong: Chinese University Press, 1978) 15. 38–40: *Shang Civilization* (New Haven: Yale University Press, 1980) 177. 192. For Tai Gong Wang, see Sarah Allan. "The Identities of Taigong Wang in Zhou and Han Literature," *Monumenta Serica* 20 (1972–1973): 57–99.

62. On the way this term evolved, see Cho-yun Hsu. *Ancient China in Transition: An Analysis of Social Mobility, 722–222 B.C.* (Stanford: Stanford University Press, 1965) 158–74.

63. For one instructive answer to this question, see W. G. Runciman, "Doomed to Extinction: The *Polis* as an Evolutionary Dead-End." in *The Greek City from Homer*

to Alexander, ed., Oswyn Murray and Simon Price (Oxford: Clarendon Press, 1991) 347–67. He argues in part that within the polis there was never "internal consensus on a value-system entitling either the rich or the well-born to deference from their superiors," nor was there ever "any doctrine or legitimate accretion of power at the expense of fellow-Greeks" (354). The contrast with most Eastern Zhou religious, social, and political assumptions is palpable.

11

EPISTEMOLOGY IN CULTURAL CONTEXT: DISGUISE AND DECEPTION IN EARLY CHINA AND EARLY GREECE

David N. Keightley

This chapter originates with the simple observation that disguise (i.e., the transformation of external appearance that makes recognizing a living person's identity difficult) played, as scholars have long noted, a significant role in early Greek literature, most notably in Homer, and that it played no significant role in early Chinese literature. The chapter then argues that the interest in disguise, manifested in early Greek literature, may be correlated with the uncertainties about the nature of reality and about man's ability to know reality with confidence present in early Greek philosophy and that the lack of interest in disguise in early Chinese narratives may be correlated equally well with the metaphysical and epistemological optimism that underlies much early Chinese philosophy. This chapter attempts to document and compare the ways in which philosophical concerns share and express strategic concerns and assumptions found in other areas of a culture. Early Chinese authors and thinkers were certainly aware of the difference between appearance and reality but, unlike a significant number of their early Greek counterparts—and with the possible exception of Zhuangzi (see p. 298 following)—they did not regard that difference as a significant concern of either narrative or philosophy.

Disguise in Homer

The degree to which disguise, deception, and recognition play a role in the plot of the *Odyssey* is well known.[1] As Sheila Murnaghan writes, "Odysseus' assumption of a disguise" on his return to his homeland of Ithaca, in Book 13, "initiates an extended narrative in which a widespread and traditional plot type, the hero's return in disguise, is used to describe the highest achievement possible within the specific values of the Homeric epics."[2] She argues, in fact, that "Odysseus' distinguishing capacity for disguise marks him out as a hero" of a kind different from other Homeric heroes, notably those in the *Iliad*. Odysseus is "a hero who not only endures but also embraces the obscurity that comes when either misfortunes or the challenges of rivals deprive him of the outer marks of heroic status"

(*Il.* 13.8). Moreover, the contrast with Achilles is very strong. "It is no accident," Murnaghan notes, "that the *Iliad's* greatest hero is noted for his quickness to anger" (*Il.* 13.8). And it is entirely consistent that: Achilles expresses his hostility to the duplicity inherent in disguise at *Il.* 9.312—13.[3] His own attempt to employ a disguise, when he allows Patroclus to enter the battle wearing his armor, is a complete failure. Virtually no one is deceived, and Achilles' impossible aim of gaining glory while avoiding risk (cf. *Il.* 16.80-86) is thwarted as he is drawn back into battle to avenge Patroclus' death."[4]

Murnaghan also notes the link between disguise and divinity among the Greeks, a point that is critical for the argument of this essay: "The superiority over circumstances allowed by Odysseus' disguise can be related to the fact that disguise is typically not a human but a divine strategy. As has been increasingly noted, the *Odyssey's* account of Odysseus' homecoming is cast in the form of a kind of story that is regularly told about the gods. Greek mythology provides many examples of gods who disguise themselves as mortals, go among men, usually for the purpose of testing them, and ultimately disclose themselves."[5] In Homer, such impersonation by gods or goddesses was common. In the *Iliad,* for example, Aeneas and Pandarus, discussing the onslaught of Diomedes, must consider if he really is Diomedes or a god masquerading as Diomedes. Aeneas cries out to his comrade, Pandarus:

> "you whip an arrow against that man, whoever he is
> who routs us, wreaking havoc against us, cutting the legs
> from under squads of good brave men. Unless it's a god
> who smoulders at our troops, enraged at a rite we failed—
> when a god's enraged there's thunder at our heads."

To which Pandarus replies:

> "he looks like Tydeus' son to me in every way—
> I know his shield, the hollow eyes of his visor,
> his team, I've watched them closely.
> And still I could never swear he's not a god . . .
> but if he's the man I think he is, Tydeus' gallant son,
> he rages so with a god beside him—not alone, no—
> a god with his shoulders shrouded round in cloud
> who deflects my shaft to a less mortal spot.
> I had already whipped an arrow into him . . .
> and I thought I'd sent him down to the House of Death
> but I've still not laid him low. So it *is* some god rampaging!"

> (*Il.* 5.194–214)

Similarly, Athena assumes "the build and vibrant voice" of Hector's brother, Deiphobus, to trick Hector, fatally, into standing his ground against Achilles (*Il.* 22.271). So too, in the *Odyssey,* Athena assumes "the build and voice" of Odysseus' old comrade Mentor to assist him in his struggle with the suitors.[6] And the "climactic moment" of the second half of the epic "is Odysseus' imitation of a divine epiphany when, having strung the bow, he reveals himself to the suitors with bewildering suddenness and proceeds to punish them for their transgressions against him":[7]

> Horror swept through the suitors, faces blanching white,
> and Zeus cracked the sky with a bolt, his blazing sign,
> and the great man who had borne so much rejoiced at last
> that the son of cunning Cronus flung that omen down for *him*.
>
> (*Od.* 21.459–62)

The narrative in Books 21 and 22 of the *Odyssey*, in fact, throws much light on the theme of disguise and recognition. First, Odysseus, on his return, in disguise, to Ithaca, tests or is tested in turn by those who had not recognized who he was or who doubted who he claimed to be. He even tells Penelope, his wife, who has not recognized him, that

> "My own name is Aethon. . . .
> Now, it was there in Cnossos that I saw him . . .
> Odysseus—and we traded gifts of friendship. . . .
> So I took Odysseus back to my own house,
> gave him a hero's welcome, treated him in style. . . ."
>   Falsehoods all,
> but he gave his falsehoods all the ring of truth.
>
> (*Od.* 19.208–36)

And in this epic world where gods and goddesses walk as men and women, where Odysseus, "the great master of subtlety" (*Od.* 19.255) roamed, it is no wonder that Penelope was reluctant to accept the old nurse's account of Odysseus' return and his slaughter of the suitors:

> "You know how welcome the sight of him would be
> to all in the house, and to me most of all
> and the son we bore together.
> But the story can't be true, not as you tell it,
> no, it must be a god who's killed our brazen friends. . . ."
>
> (*Od.* 23.66–70)

The nurse, Eurycleia, appeals to a vivifying detail, a particular mark, that had identified Odysseus for her:[8]

> "I'll give you a sign, a proof that's plain as day.
> That scar, made years ago by a boar's white tusk—
> I spotted the scar myself, when I washed his feet."
>
> (*Od* 23.82–84)

But Penelope remains uncertain. Reality seems to shift before her eyes:

> One moment he seemed . . . Odysseus, to the life—
> the next, no, he was not the man she knew,
> a huddled mass of rags was all she saw.
>
> (*Od.* 23.108–10)

Her husband accordingly responds to his son

> . . .with pointed, winging words:
> "Leave your mother here in the hall to test me
> as she will. She soon will know me better.
> Now because I am filthy, wear such grimy rags,
> she spurns me—your mother still can't bring herself
> to believe I am her husband. . . ."

(Od. 23.127–32)

It is the externals of his appearance, Odysseus believes, that continue to mislead his wife.[9]

Once the suitors have been killed, Homer extends the theme of disguise and deception, still involving dress and appearance, by introducing Odysseus' stratagem to forestall a counterattack by the suitor's allies. Speaking to his son, Odysseus says:

> "First go and wash, and pull fresh tunics on,
> and tell the maids in the hall to dress well too.
> And let the inspired bard take up his ringing lyre
> and lead off for us all a dance so full of heart
> that whoever hears the strains outside the gates—
> a passerby on the road, a neighbor round about—
> will think it's a wedding-feast that's under way."

(Od. 23.147—53)

The success of this stratagem permits the poet several ironic observations that, as irony frequently does, depend on a misunderstanding by the audience in the poem of the true situation, that depend on that audience's 'blindness':

> And whoever heard the strains outside would say,
> "A miracle—someone's married the queen at last!"
>   "One of her hundred suitors."
>   "That callous woman,
> too faithless to keep her lord and master's house
> to the bitter end—"
>   "Till he came sailing home."
> So they'd say, blind to what had happened:
> the great-hearted Odysseus was home again at last.

(Od. 23.165–71)

Athena then "undisguises" Odysseus but, at the same time, "overdoes" it by making the human godlike:[10]

> The maid Eurynome bathed him, rubbed him down with oil
> and drew around him a royal cape and choice tunic too.
> And Athena crowned the man with beauty, head to foot,
> made him taller to all eyes, his build more massive,
> yes, and down from his brow the great goddess
> ran his curls like thick hyacinth clusters

full of blooms. As a master craftsman washes
gold over beaten silver—a man the god of fire
and Queen Athena trained in every fine technique—
and finishes off his latest effort, handsome work . . .
so she lavished splendor over his head and shoulders now.
He stepped from his bath, glistening like a god. . . .

(Od. 23.172–83)[11]

One may also note that Athena here reverses the "debeautification" she had performed on Odysseus when he first returned to Ithaca:

"First I will transform you—no one must know you.
I will shrivel the supple skin on your lithe limbs,
strip the russet curls from your head and deck you out
in rags you'd hate to see some other mortal wear;
I'll dim the fire in your eyes, so shining once—
until you seem appalling to all those suitors,
even your wife and son you left behind at home."

She shriveled the supple skin on his lithe limbs,
stripped the russet curls from his head, covered his body
top to toe with the wrinkled hide of an old man
and dimmed the fire in his eyes, so shining once.

(Od. 13.454–60,493–96)

Penelope, still not persuaded by the transformation, proceeds to test her
husband by asking Eurycleia to move the bed that "the master built with his
own hands," and that, as she and Odysseus well know, would be an impossible
task (*Od.* 23:197–203). Interestingly it is the stranger's knowledge of the way the
bed had been constructed—"I know, I built it myself—no one else . . . ," he says
(*Od.* 23.213)—rather than his godlike external appearance, that provides Penelope
with her "living proof" (*Od.* 23.230). Knowledge was what counted, not external
reality.[12] But, then persuaded, she remarks, not unreasonably,

"But don't fault me, angry with me now because I failed,
at the first glimpse, to greet you, hold you, so. . . .
In my heart of hearts I always cringed with fear
some fraud might come, beguile me with his talk;
the world is full of the sort,
cunning ones who plot their own dark ends."

(Od. 23.240–45)

Given the extravagant way Athena has "lavished splendor" on Odysseus' head,
one may wonder if some degree of "fraud" were not still involved, even if it were
Penelope's husband who had at last come home. The episode is rich with degrees
of deception. "The world" was indeed "full of the sort."

So, the *Odyssey* in particular builds on a series of incidents involving the disguise of humans and of gods and the consequent uncertainty of identification that
leads to epiphanies as the true identity of the protagonist is revealed—by physical

evidence, in the case of the maid; by knowledge in the case of Penelope.[13] Surface appearance, at critical moments, is often not what it seems.

Jean-Pierre Vernant has analyzed the themes of heroic disguise in Homer in ways that stimulate further reflection about the topic's wider cultural significance. He demonstrates, in particular, the way in which various Homeric gods and goddesses bring about changes in appearance, so that things "seem" to be something else. "What does it mean," he asks:

> to change one's identity in "the world of Odysseus," that face-to-face society, that culture of shame and honor where each person is subjected to the other's gaze and recognizes himself only in the mirror of the image presented to him by others. . . . An individual's social and private status, both in the eyes of others and in his own eyes, cannot be separated from his appearance—or perhaps I should say rather from his "appearing": the way in which he is seen, known, and recognized, in both senses of the word. . . . In order to falsify your identity, it is not enough to change your title and give yourself a different origin, a false fatherland, and fake genealogy; or to invent an illusory past and dress up in strange clothing. It is the thing that you yourself immediately offer to view, your visage, your face—this *prosôpon,* which literally means what is presented for viewing from the front—that you must render unrecognizable.[14]

And Vernant notes a number of key moments in the *Odyssey* in which the protagonists, confronting some form of disguise, marvel at the difference between appearance and reality:

> The restoration of Odysseus' form to a full brilliance which makes him appear "like to the gods" is repeated—thanks, as always, to Athena—before the Phaeacians (8.18–23); before Telemachos (16.172–76); and before Penelope (23.156–63): likewise Athena restores Penelope's form while she sleeps (18.189–96) and that of Laertes after bathing (24.365–75). . . . Telemachos does not believe his eyes: right under his nose he has seen a tattered old beggar, whose base appearance told a pitiful tale, instantly transform himself into a completely different (*alloios,* 16.181) being, whose presence is such that the young prince can only say to him: "An instant ago you were an old man, covered in filthy (*aeikea*) rags, but now you resemble the gods (*nun de theoisi eoikas*)" (16.199).[15]

Vernant's study is of particular relevance because of the light he throws on the nature and mechanisms of disguise, transformation, and recognition. Homer was evidently concerned to convey an existential sense of how these mysteries of "appearing" worked. And indeed, the epic's "hands on" interest in disguise, with its accounts of Odysseus as "an old man, covered in filthy rags," or of his spy mission inside Troy, "bruising himself with disfiguring blows, having cast a rag over his shoulders, like a slave,"[16] well accords with what I have elsewhere referred to as the "dirty-handed" representations of protagonists in the *Iliad* of the late eighth century or on the painted vases of the sixth and fifth centuries.[17] In that earlier analysis I had proposed, drawing comparisons with analogous Chinese forms of representation, that

> realistic details—such as the sweat from horses and the equippage of a cart—are regarded as uninteresting, even as threatening, by non-heroic . . . elites. Men

of action—such as the heroes about whom, and the audiences for whom, the Homeric bards performed—presumably take pleasure in descriptions of things they can do for themselves. Civilian, literati elites who do not get their hands dirty find such accounts of sweat, horses, carts, and fighting uninteresting and, because they cannot or do not do these things for themselves, threatening and delegitimizing. If early Chinese texts and art have been edited in the ways that I have been implying . . . , one may associate this editing with the hierarchical nature of Zhou society. It is precisely what one would expect of editors who conceive of a world divided, as Mencius puts it, between the rulers (who keep their hands clean) and the ruled (who get their hands dirty): "Hence it is said, 'Some labor with their minds and some labor with their muscles. Those who labor with their minds rule others; those who labor with their muscles are ruled by others (*Gu yue: huo lao xin, huo lao li. Lao xin zhe zhi ren, lao li zhe zhi yu ren* 故 日：或 勞 心，或 勞 力 • 勞 心 者 治 人；勞 力 者 治 於 人*)*." (3A:4.6)

"Clean-handed" elites, in other words, like "clean-handed" stories. I had also suggested that:

> oral story-telling—as entertainment—encourages realistic detail. The kind of perceptual description that we have encountered above brings tales alive for listeners who know horses, harness, dust, sweat, and carts. It attracts and entertains by enhancing the familiar, making it fresh and wonderful, and giving it structure. The conceptual, expository tradition in the Zhou texts that have been preserved is less one of entertainment, more one of instruction and exhortation. Their authors or transmitters were interested in stories about protagonists who promoted concepts of moral and religious order, concepts that they, as authors and transmitters, would like to promote themselves. They were less interested in recapturing the existential detail and perception. The difference is that between drama—which must attract its audience—and sermon—to which the audience has, as it were, already committed itself in advance.[18]

I am proposing in this chapter that the representational preferences in early Chinese and Greek narratives also reflected, as they were reflected in, the existential assumptions and similes of their philosophical texts, and that one may also think of these matters in terms of "clean-handed" (i.e., optimistic, nonprobing; see the following) and "dirty-handed" (i.e., pessimistic, probing) epistemologies.

Epistemological Optimism and Pessimism: Greece and China

I am seeking to establish links between the treatment of disguise on the one hand and the understanding of reality on the other. Thomas Metzger's reference to the "epistemological optimism." of early Chinese thought proves valuable at this point.[19] By epistemological optimism he means an approach to the reliability of knowledge that confidently uses looser standards than those found in much classical Western philosophy "to accept a larger range of ideas as reliable, such as roughly clear ideas defining morality as universal and objective, describing the ultimate nature of the human, physical, or divine realms, or indicating the path to eternal salvation."[20] I maintain that early Chinese art and narrative—like early Chinese philosophy—manifested its own qualities of epistemological optimism, qualities that, for the human or physical realms, we might refer to as "representational optimism." 1 also maintain that the optimism about the general reliability of ideas that Metzger discerns was consonant with an optimism about the general reliability of appearances and about man's ability to take reality for granted.

There is no doubt that much of Homer has been characterized as epistemologically optimistic. To Bruno Snell, "Homeric man is sheltered by a world without blemish, which speaks to him in unambiguous terms, and to which he replies in the same manner. His deity is transcendent, for it is greater than man; but its nature is fixed and its existence permanent since it is independent of man's understanding."[21] John H. Finley Jr. writes of the "unfaltering confidence in outer reality" displayed by what he calls "the heroic mind"; he discerns in Homer "an outgazing bent of mind that sees things exactly, each for itself, and seems innocent of the idea that thought discerps and colors reality. . . . It has no doubt that what it sees is real," and "acts abruptly on that unquestioned assumption."[22] And Edward Hussey notes that "Homer and his characters take the structural and determining features of the world to be absolutely beyond doubt: in particular, the existence of the gods, their separate individualities and powers, and their general relationship to human beings."[23] It is only about the time of the fifth century that the mythological began to evolve into the conceptual. "Aeschylus and Sophocles spoke for the older outlook that saw things through shape; Socrates and Thucydides for the nascent mind that saw them through idea."[24]

But the heroic mind was a naive mind, and it was subject to deceit. My point is that although the Homeric heroes and heroines did not question the existence of the gods and the world, they nevertheless had good reason to distrust what they saw in the world. The problem, in fact, was sufficiently common for the participants to comment on it, but without particular emphasis. Thus, the Ithacan Noëmon, explaining to the suitors why he had let Telemachus have a ship, explained:

> "And Mentor took command—I saw him climb aboard—
> or a god who looked like Mentor head to foot,
> and that's what I find strange. I saw good Mentor
> yesterday, just at sunup, here. But clearly
> he boarded ship for Pylos days ago."

> (*Od.* 4.734–38)

The "Mentor" he had seen, of course, had been Pallas Athena, who had, not for the last time, impersonated Mentor to lull the suitors to sleep and to summon Telemachus to the ship (*Od.* 2.434–47).

Not only the gods could disguise themselves; so could other humans. There was no reason to question the truth of experience; but there was reason to question its good faith. And many critical moments in the epics and dramas turn, as we have seen, precisely on such deceptions and their unmasking, often with consequences fatal to the deceived. "For human beings, the contrast between divine and human knowledge, and the possibility of deception by the gods, is obviously discouraging. It stimulates some of the Homeric characters not to take all appearances at face value, and to remind themselves and others that about many things they cannot 'know for certain.'"[25]

For the Greeks of the fifth century, the classic account of epistemological pessimism, where the world of the senses is concerned, is Plato's "famous simile" of the cave in Book 7 of *The Republic*, in which, in Bertrand Russell's account,

> those who are destitute of philosophy may be compared to prisoners in a cave, who are only able to look in one direction because they are bound, and who have a fire behind them and a wall in front. . . . All that they see are shadows of themselves, and of objects behind them, cast on the wall by the light of the fire. Inevitably they regard these shadows as real, and have no notion of the object to which they are due. . . .

"From Heraclitus," Russell continued, Plato

> derived the negative doctrine that there is nothing permanent in the sensible world. This, combined with the doctrine of Parmenides, led to the conclusion that knowledge is not to be derived from the senses, but is only to be achieved by the intellect. This, in turn, fitted in well with Pythagoreanism.[26]

Penelope, we may consider, had found herself very much "in the cave" as reality "shimmered" (see note 19) before her—"One moment he seemed . . . Odysseus, to the life— / the next, no, he was not the man she knew." But, in ways that Plato would have approved, it had been knowledge of how their bed had been constructed, an "achievement of the intellect" rather than of the senses, that had led her to recognize her husband without doubt.

"The Cave," as Julia Annas writes, may be seen as "Plato's most optimistic and beautiful picture of the power of philosophy to free and enlighten. Abstract thinking, which leads to philosophical insight, is boldly portrayed as something liberating." But this is an optimism reserved only for the philosophers.

> In the imagery of the Cave Plato presses so far his antipathy to the passive and acquiescent state of the unreflective that the unenlightened state is presented as being totally substandard. . . . It is clear that to liken all our ordinary beliefs to the seeing of shadows creates a sharp cut-off between the state of the enlightened and that of the unenlightened. They do not inhabit the same cognitive world
>   . . . . The whole tenor of the Cave is to downgrade our ordinary beliefs, to urge us to regard them as being no better than looking at shadows. The Cave is more pessimistic than the Line [a reference to *Republic*, 509d] about even the best of our everyday beliefs. . . .
>   . . . Everything but the studies that lead one out of the Cave are mere rubbish.[27]

Not even Zhuangzi (see p. 298) regards the indeterminacy of knowledge and experience in terms as pessimistic as these.

Russell quotes a striking passage from Book 6 of *The Republic,* which also bears on the theme of this essay:

> The soul is like an eye: when resting upon that on which truth and being shine, the soul perceives and understands, and is radiant with intelligence; but when turned towards the twilight of becoming and perishing, then she has opinion only, and goes blinking about, and is first of one opinion and then of another, and seems to have no intelligence. . . . Now what imparts truth to the known and the power of knowing to the knower is what I would have you term the idea of good, and this you will deem to be the cause of science.[28]

The passage correlates well with the accounts of appearing and seeming in the *Odyssey.* In the *Odyssey,* as Vernant has noted of an episode at the start of Book 7 where Athena has rendered Odysseus invisible and advised him not to look any human in the face, "there is such a strict reciprocity between seeing and being seen that the best way to escape the view of others is to cease from trying to stare at them yourself, lest an alien eye pierce the cloud of obscurity that envelops you."[29] To Plato the act of seeing and of understanding the real nature of things depends on an active eye as well as on an intelligent, morally educated soul.

Knowing, the piercing of disguises, required a critical intelligence—whether Penelope's or Plato's—and not mere opinion.[30] Medon, Odysseus' herald, when speaking to the dead suitors' angry supporters, reported:

> "Hear me, men of Ithaca. Not without the hand
> of the deathless gods did Odysseus do these things!
> Myself, I saw an immortal fighting at his side—
> like Mentor to the life. I saw the same god,
> now in front of Odysseus, spurring him on,
> now stampeding the suitors through the hall,
> crazed with fear, and down they went in droves!"
>
> (*Od.* 24.490–96)

Like Noëmon (p. 290 above), Medon had detected or suspected the presence of a god, or he at least wished the suitors to think he had. But he does not claim that he had been able to identify the god (actually, a goddess), and it was evidently not expected that he could. The suitors, by contrast, had not recognized the presence of an immortal by Odysseus' side; they had not even been able to penetrate his disguise—Amphimedon's ghost laments that "none of us, not even the older ones / could spot that tramp for the man he really was" (*Od.* 24.175–76). Similarly, Hector, locked in fatal combat with Achilles outside the walls of Troy, had not recognized Athena's deception until it was too late: "Athena's tricked me blind" (*Il.* 22.353).

The situation in early China was quite different. Disguise—especially disguise practiced or created by gods and spirits—plays no major role in the narratives of the Zhou and Han.[31] We do find occasional stories of self-inflicted disguises, the most notable of which is probably that of the "assassin-retainer" Yu Rang 豫讓, who, having changed his name and become a convict laborer, painted his body with lacquer to induce sores like those of a leper, destroyed his voice by drinking lye, and completely changed his appearance until no one could recognize him [使 形 狀 不 可 知]. When he went begging in the market place, even his wife did not know him. But, as he was going along, he met a friend who recognized him [其 友 識 之] and asked, "Aren't you Yu Rang?"

Not only is the disguise self-inflicted, and not only does it not deceive a friend, but it does not even deceive Xiangzi 襄 子, the man he was trying to kill:

Sometime later, word got about that Xiangzi was going out on an excursion, and Yu Rang accordingly went and hid under the bridge he was to pass over. When Xiangzi came to the bridge, his horse suddenly shied. "This must be Yu Rang!" he said, and sent one of his men to investigate. It was indeed Yu Rang.[32]

We find neither a sense of any divine transformation of reality, no sense of epistemological magic nor a description of what he actually looked or sounded like; we merely find a report of what he did not look like ("until no one could recognize him"); there is only the (not-entirely-successful) application of lacquer and lye, as one human seeks to deceive another.

More unusual, perhaps, is the story of a second assassin-retainer, Nie Zheng 聶 政 who, after he had killed Xialei 俠 累, the prime minister of Han 韓, "flayed the skin of his face, gouged out his eyes, and, butchering himself as he had once done animals, spilled out his bowels and in this way he died." For a long time, no one could identify the corpse (久 之 莫 知 也), but his elder sister, Nie Rong 聶 榮 eventually did so, saying:

"A gentleman will always be willing to die for someone who recognizes his true worth (士 固 爲 知 己 者 死). And now, because I am still alive, he has inflicted this terrible mutilation upon himself so as to wipe out all his traces. But how could I, out of fear that I might be put to death, allow so worthy a brother's name to be lost forever?"

Having astounded the people of the market place with these words, she cried three times in a loud voice to Heaven and then died of grief and anguish by the dead man's side.[33]

Once again, the disguise is self-inflicted, not god-conferred; and once again, it does not deceive one who was close to the protagonist. There is, to be sure, an epiphany of sorts when Nie Rong recognizes her brother's corpse.[34] But the issues are entirely those of human action and deception, worked out through the normal workings of the human body. The nature of reality and of man's ability to know it is not at issue. Nor, it seems, was disguise a practice in which elites engaged; it was the "dirty-handed" men of action, a onetime convict laborer such as Yu Rang, a former butcher such as Nie Zheng, who disguised their physical identities in this way. No Chinese elite of Odysseus' status resorts to such a stratagem.

Considering these matters in terms of the distinction between appearance and reality is also instructive. G. E. R. Lloyd has observed that, in the case of the Greeks, "Although it would be an exaggeration to say that the *whole* of subsequent Greek philosophy and science is articulated round the contrast between appearance and reality, a very great deal of it is." And although noting that, in the case of the Chinese, there is, "in a variety of contexts, . . . awareness that things may not be what they seem, or that there may be more to events than meets the eye," he concludes that:

> while *yin yang* and the five phases may, in some weak sense, be termed theories, they do not depend on anything like the sharp contrast between reality and appearance that is so often found in Greek physical and cosmological specu- lation. . . . There is no sense of a *gulf* between the two, no sense of the *gap* between the mere appearances and the inferred structure of the hidden, under- lining reality. . . . The Chinese thinker can and does move smoothly along a seamless continuum, from the apparent to the hidden, from the particular to the universal. . . . But [*yin yang, qi,* and the five phases] do not postulate a hidden structure of reality that is quite unlike the appearance of things.[35]

The contrast, in this regard, between the treatment of appearance in the narratives and philosophies of the two cultures is particularly striking. Sima Qian tells us that when Yu Rang "went begging in the market place, even his wife did not know him." But he gives us none of the vivifying, psychological, ironic detail about the encounter that we find in Book 19 of the *Odyssey* where Penelope engages her disguised husband, whom she does not recognize, in lengthy conversation. Did Yu Rang's wife speak to him, and if so, why? We are not told. It is not important.

For a further example of the relative lack of interest in appearance shown by the Chinese texts, consider the following story from the *Zuozhuan* in which two notables of the state of Zheng 鄭 were competing for the hand of a young woman of status:

子晳盛飾人，布幣而出，子南成服人，左右射，超乘而出，
女自房觀之，田：子晳信美矣，抑子南，夫也。

> Zi Xi, splendidly arrayed, entered the house, set forth his offerings, and went out. Zi Nan entered in his military dress, shot an arrow to the left and another to the right, sprang into his chariot, and went out. The lady saw them from a chamber, and said, "Zi Xi is indeed handsome but Zi Nan is my husband."[36]

The chronicle gives us none of the detail of the finery or the weapons or the mar- tial skills displayed; these features are merely digested and itemized. And, indeed, the story is not really about the appearance that the two suitors displayed. The young woman had already been betrothed to Zi Nan. Her choice, accordingly, is less a reaction to the physical attractiveness of the two suitors than an acceptance of her duty. As she continues, 夫 夫 婦 婦 , 所 謂 順 也 , "For the husband to be the husband and the wife to be the wife, is what is called the natural course."[37] And the rest of the story, after a fight between the suitors, involves questions of seniority and deference that the officers of the state decide, at least temporarily, in favor of Zi Xi, the older of the two suitors and, as Zi Chan 子 產 notes, "a great officer of the first degree" (*shang dafu* 上 大 夫).[38] The contrast with Hom- er's detailed reporting on the way Athena had beautified Odysseus and Penelope (as discussed above) is stark. Once again, the Chinese interest was not in drama-tizing the existential impact of a situation, but in abstracting the message.

Early Chinese writers—quite apart from Zhuangzi 莊子, to whom I will turn shortly—were indeed well aware of the appearance/reality distinction, but they preferred to intellectualize it rather than vivify it. A story related in the *Xunzi* is typical:

> South of the mouth of the Xia 夏 river there was a man named Juan Shuliang 涓梁. He was a foolish man who was prone to fright. One evening when the moon was bright, he was out walking when he looked down and saw his own shadow, which he took to be a crouching ghost. Raising his head, he caught sight of his own hair and took it to be an ogre standing over him. He turned his back on the shadow and raced away. Just when he reached his house, he lost his *qi* 氣 ("vital breath") and died. Alas, what a shame![39]

The issue is not the nature of reality—clearly the man had seen his shadow and his hair—but the tendency of the mind to misapprehend it. As Xunzi comments:

> As a general rule, when men think there are ghosts, the confirmation of it is certain to be an occasion when they are startled or confused. There are occasions when these men take what does not exist for what does and what does exist for what does not, and they settle the matter on the basis of their own experience.[40]

But there is no doubt about "what does not exist" and "what does." There is no question of intervention by the gods. The general principle is:

> As a general rule, when examining things about which there are doubts, if the mind is not inwardly settled, then external things will not be clear. . . .
> Someone walking along a road in the dark may see a fallen stone and think it a tiger crouching in ambush, or he may see an upright tree and think it a standing man. The darkness has beclouded the clarity of his vision. . . . Pressing against the eye while looking at an object will make it appear double; covering the ears when listening will make silence seem like a clamor. The force applied to the sense organs has disordered them. . . .[41]

And Xunzi concludes, in a striking proclamation of epistemological optimism:

> As a general principle, the faculty of knowing belongs to the inborn nature of man [凡以 (=可) 知, 人之性也]. That things are knowable is a part of the natural principle of order of things [可以知, 物之理也]. Men use their innate faculty of knowing to seek the natural principles of order, which allow things to be known.[42]

The knowing of things, in short, is natural and unproblematic. "The means of knowing which is within man is called 'awareness' [所以知之在人者謂之知]. Awareness tallying with the facts is called 'knowledge' [知有所合謂之智]."[43] Xunzi's anecdotes were not about the uncertain nature of reality, but only about the obtuseness of the protagonist. An intelligent "knower" was not expected to have difficulties in determining the reality behind the appearance. As Zi Pi 子皮,

an officer of the state of Zheng 鄭, is said to have remarked, "It is not the knowing that is difficult. It is the acting that is difficult" （非 知 之 實 難 , 將 在 行 之）.44

　　Knowing, in the view of Confucius, in fact, seems to have been almost a matter of will and determination:

子 田 ： 由, 誨 女 知 之 乎, 知 之 爲 知 之, 弗 知 爲 弗 知, 是 知 也。The Master said, You, shall I teach you about knowing? To regard knowing it as knowing it; to regard not knowing it as not knowing it—this is knowing."45

The passage has been seen as a warning "against overconfidence in knowledge,"46 but the issue does not appear to have been one that greatly troubled Confucius or other persuaders of the time. Lloyd reaches similar conclusions: "More attention is paid to epistemology as such in our Greek sources than in our Chinese ones," but he cautions that "we should bear in mind that some of the classical Chinese philosophers who were most interested in such issues are particularly badly served in our extant sources: that is true especially of the Mohists."47 The point is well taken, but the conclusion remains that we are not dealing with a tradition that gave priority to the preservation and transmission of such concerns.48

　　Indeed, problems of knowledge, problems involving appearance and reality, were frequently treated as involving the general acceptability of the names that could be applied to reality, rather than the nature of the reality itself. This strain of argument is strong in the *Han Fei Zi* 韓 非 子, a late Eastern Zhou text (Han Fei died in 233 B.C.E.):

> (Pang Gong [龐 恭]) said: "Suppose one person maintains there is a tiger in the market. Would you believe it?" (The King [of Wei 魏]) replied "No." "Suppose two people maintained that there is a tiger in the market. Would you believe it?" "No!" "Suppose three people maintained there is a tiger in the market. Would you believe it?" "Yes I would." Pang Gong continued: "It is perfectly clear that there is no tiger in the market, but when three maintain that there is one, that makes a tiger [然 而 三 人 信 而 成 虎]!"
>
> It is in the nature of words that they are taken to be trustworthy (*xin* 信) when many people advocate them. Take a thing that is not so (*bu ran zhi wu* 不 然 之 物). When ten people maintain it, one has one's doubts. When one hundred people maintain it, one thinks it is probably so (*ran* 然). When one thousand people maintain it, it is incontrovertible.49

As Harbsmeier concludes, "discursive knowing in ancient China (as in ancient Greece and in the modern West) was just familiarity with things and knowing how to apply names to things."50 But the important distinction lies in the willingness of most early Chinese thinkers to rely upon discursive knowledge in their philosophical discussions:

> There is little room in traditional Chinese culture for knowledge for its own sake. There was little enthusiasm for "academic knowledge" as cultivated by philosophers such as Plato and Aristotle, who continued the heritage of Socrates. For the ancient Chinese it was action that was primary, personal action and political action.

When ancient Confucian and Legalist texts address the problem of *zhi* (knowledgeable, intellectual excellence), they do not address a problem of epistemology at all. Often they address a problem of public administration. . . .[51]

Not surprisimgly, there are no epistemological and metaphysical epiphanies in the early Chinese narratives comparable to those we have seen among the Greeks. There is, for the mainstream philosophies, no cave; there are no shadows. There is no metaphysics of ideal forms. The early Chinese concern was primarily with a unitary moral metaphysics rather than with a problematic, bifurcated one. The verb "to know" (*zhi* 知) served a variety of functions—"to perceive, to recognize, to appreciate, to discern, to grasp, to pierce through disguises"[52]—and the "disguises," when present among the elites, were not produced by the gods or by the deliberate intent of the "disguised"; they were, instead, the product of the viewer's, the knower's, obtuseness, of his failure to recognize the true moral worth of the knowee.

Eric Henry has referred to "the disguise-piercing insight" that begins to appear in the *Shijing,* as in Mao 65 ("Shuli 黍 離"):

> I go on my way, bowed down
> By the cares that shake my heart.
> 知 我 者
> 謂 我 心 憂
> 不 知 我 者
> 謂 我 何 求
> Those who know me
> Say, "It is because his heart is so sad."
> Those who do not know me
> Say, "What is he looking for?"[53]

The speaker laments not being "known." But there is no disguise in the Homeric sense here, no magical or divine distortion of reality. Rather, "this poem," as Henry notes, "lightly foreshadows the 'no one knows me' themes—the motif of recognition in tragic reversal—that was later to be so extravagantly developed in 'Li sao [離 騷].'"[54] In the early texts, such as the *Shangshu* 尚 書 and *Shijing* 詩 經,

> To know people is in a ruler a sign of virtue (*de* [德]), in a friend a sign of regard, and in a diviner a sign of perspicacity; *but we do not yet feel . . . that any great or unusual obstacles lie in the path of the knower. . . .* The great knowers of the Warring States era, on the other hand, employ people because their virtues are known to none but themselves; their virtues, that is, are too great to be visible to people of ordinary discernment.
>
> This intensification in the concept of knowing is reflected in a series of stories concerning the seeking of sage ministers that began to appear and proliferate some time after the closing decades of the Spring and Autumn era . . . [with the] tales of dynastic founders and leaders of dynastic revival seeking out menials and recluses of various kinds to be their ministers.[55]

Henry notes that "interviews with rulers that last for three days are a regularly recurring motif in recognition stories indicating that the ruler finds he can talk easily with a man he is considering for use."[56] Three-day interviews, I should note, are not the stuff of which epiphanies—which depend on rapid and dramatic rec-ognitions—are made. Knowing another person, in these early Chinese texts, was a major activity of the evaluative judgmental community, as moralists and rulers strove to recognize the worth of those they were observing.[57] It required moral insight into the *xin* 心 "heartmind" (as suggested by Mao no. 65, quoted earlier), but it did not require the penetration of physical disguises created by the gods.

Not surprisimgly, the only early Chinese thinkers who play with the inde-terminacy of reality were the Daoists. Their treatment of the matter, however, as seen in the famous passage from *Zhuangzi* 莊 子, is again quite different from the treatments we have seen in early Greece.

> Last night Zhuang Zhou dreamed he was a butterfly, spirits soaring he was a butterfly (is it that in showing what he was he suited his own fancy?), and did not know about Zhou. When all of a sudden he awoke, he was Zhou with all his wits about him. He does not know [不 知] whether he is Zhou who dreams he is a butterfly or a butterfly who dreams he is Zhou. Between Zhou and the butterfly there was necessarily a dividing [必 有 分 矣]; just this is what is meant by the transformations of things [此 之 謂 物 化].[58]

Homer thought in terms of a reality that the gods could manipulate with a view to displacing or dominating ordinary forms of reality with other forms, "lavished [with] splendor," that were still more real or efficacious. Plato conceived of a world in which some forms of reality were better than others, in which the ideal forms did indeed represent the true and superior reality. Zhuangzi, by contrast, suggested that all forms of reality were relative and uncertain; that one form was not to be privileged over the other. Zhuangzi, one might say, was less an epistemological pessimist than an epistemological indeterminist. Neither, to use Plato's terms, the shadows on the wall of the cave nor the objects that throw the shadows are privi-leged; they are of equal value. And Zhuangzi was cheerful about the human pre-dicament; the "transformation of things" was not a philosophical problem; it was a philosophical insight.[59] The Chinese had no sense, in other words, as Homer had, that reality could be manipulated to suit the purposes of gods; the Chinese had no sense, as Plato had, that some realities were better than others and that it was of paramount importance to distinguish between them. And such epistemological indeterminacy, which Zhuangzi had apprehended while dreaming, was presented only in exemplary fables; other myths and historical anecdotes did not echo it. It was instead the optimistic epistemology of legend and historical anecdote that was to be canonized in the Confucian classics.

Modes of Representation

The epistemological optimism of much of early Chinese "knowing" may be related, as I have suggested, to the concern with "clean-handed" *schemata* rather than with "dirty-handed" mimetic representation of nature (and all the problems of accuracy and indeterminacy that involves). An early interest in *schemata*, I suggest, had emerged as early as the third millennium B.C.E. in the eastern part of China.[60] And the preference for *schemata* characterizes, I argue, both the ancestor worship of the Late Shang kings, which treated the royal dead as abstract, juridical powers,[61] and the general philosophical concerns of the Eastern Zhou, reflected in the focus on abstract, status-related rules and regulations. In aesthetic terms, too, there appears to have been a reluctance to represent reality for reality's sake, a lack of interest in which I have called "shining helmets."[62] This may be demonstrated, for example, by an anecdote in the *Han Fei Zi*, in which an artist responded to the king of Qi's 齊 question about what was the hardest thing to draw: "Dogs and horses are the hardest. . . . Devils and demons are the easiest. Indeed, dogs and horses are what people know [人 所 知 也] and see at dawn and dusk in front of them. To draw them no distortion is permissible. Therefore they are the hardest [不 可 類 之, 故 難]. On the contrary, devils and demons have no shapes and are not seen in front of anybody, therefore it is easy to draw them."[63] The result of such concerns was a series of stylistic choices that led to forms of representation— whether visual or literary—that were essential and "iconic," in the sense that a conventional, stylized resemblance between the image and the object was enough; precise verisimilitude was not required.

Early Chinese art and narrative were, as I have suggested, not designed to change opinions, to stimulate new emotions, to create epiphanies. They were, rather, like the ritual observances that were central to elite culture, designed to confirm received opinions, to legitimate old emotions. And they did so by employing general schemas of symbols and concepts, rather than precise representations of individuals and percepts.[64] They did not challenge or dissect reality; they categorized and ordered it.

Magical Disguise in Art

In origin, and for certain viewers, the schematic forms of representation in Early China may also have been magical, manifesting spiritual or ultra-human efficacy. The images found on ritual jades and bronzes in the Neolithic and Bronze Ages, by their very shape and nature, were potent representations of force and status. But they may also have been capable of magical transformation.[65] Another anecdote in *Han Fei Zi* may, in fact, record a faint memory of the potency of the earlier art:

> Once a traveller, who painted the whip for the ruler of Zhou, spent three years to complete it. When the Ruler saw it, it looked exactly like a plainly varnished whip. Thereby the Ruler of Zhou was enraged. Then the painter of the whip said, "Build a wall twenty feet high and a window eight feet long. Place the whip upon it at sunrise and then look at it." The Ruler of Zhou, accordingly, looked at the features of the whip in the way he had been instructed and found them all turning into dragons, serpents, birds, beasts, carriages, and horses, and the forms of myriad other things all present [成 龍 蛇 禽 車 馬, 萬 物 之 狀 備 具]. Thereat he was greatly pleased.[66]

I am struck that, in this story, the art took three years to create, and that it had to be placed in a proper context and viewed at a proper time (i.e., sunrise) before it could become efficacious. Some members of Han Fei's world evidently believed that art could transform itself in this way. And one may speculate that the decor on the Shang bronzes, when the bronzes were placed in the right context, may have come alive in this way for those who practiced the ancestral cult. Who knows what the Shang elites saw when their bronzes were touched by the rising sun?[67] We have no way to test such speculations, but the argument implies that those who knew the code could read messages denied to those who did not.

Those speculations aside, however, I am struck by the almost encyclopedic or generic nature of the transformation described in this anecdote. There was nothing personal about it. The features of the whip turned into so many things— "the forms of myriad other things"—that there was no specificity, no particularity, no narrative meaning in the episode. Han Fei Zi employed it, rather, to make a philosophical point, not to dramatize or provide an epiphany. "The work done to this whip certainly was delicate and difficult. Yet its utility was the same as that of any plainly varnished whip [然 其 用 與 素 髹 荚 同]";[68] embellishment, even of this high sort, had no practical utility. It is a "clean-handed" anecdote and the myriad things "disguised" in the whip deceived nobody; they had simply been present but hidden until—rather like the sage ministers discovered in obscurity— they were seen in the right light. The transformation was in the knower; there was no existential change in the object, which, as Han Fei—anxious to provide examples of thinkers who, "like the painter of the whip," provided theories that were "roundabout, profound, magnificent . . . exaggerating, [and] not practical [論 有 迂 深 閎 大 非 用 也]"[69]—notes, retained only the utility "of any plainly varnished whip." Once again, it was the viewer's responsibility to know and to recognize what was there.

Conclusions

The stories that people tell themselves, the way that they view the world, conceive of personal identity, and think about the nature of reality—particularly when, as in the case of the early Chinese, most of the evidence comes from a group of texts that created the core values of an elite, literati class—are not isolated or independent cultural elements. They cohere with and reinforce one another.

The links between the "pre-philosophical" assumptions of the Homeric epics, the concerns of the sceptics, and the dualistic metaphysics of Plato have certainly been noted before. Thus, Von Fritz, considering the episodes of deception in Homer, concluded that such cases frequently "have in common the fact that the first recognition or classification turns out to be deceptive and has to be replaced by another and truer recognition which, so to speak, penetrates below the visible surface to the real essence of the contemplated object."[70] It is true that, as J. H. Lesher has noted, the Homeric epics are thought to "lack those features which usually mark off the beginning of distinctly philosophical thought: a critical attitude toward earlier views, the detection of inconsistencies, and the reduction of various phenomena to a single unifying principle." But, as he continues: "The prominence in the *Odyssey* of the gap between perception and knowledge (or recognition, realization, understanding) should lead us to wonder whether 'pre-philosophical' is really a fair description. If, as is sometimes the case, philosophical thinking takes the form of reflection on the nature of our cognitive faculties . . . the *Odyssey* merits reconsideration."[71] Parmenides' poetic account "of the nature of the real is modeled extensively on the epic, borrowing a whole family of Homeric epithets and phrases, still operating under the acoustic cues of the epic." And

> Heraclitus observed that although sense perception . . . may be useful for knowing . . . , perception may be deceptive . . . and does not ensure understanding, . . . for people may see and not recognize and hear but not understand. . . . In these remarks, Heraclitus stated a view of perception and knowledge that was not entirely without precedent.[72]

The Homeric interest in disguise and deception appears to have contributed to the idealistic metaphysics of Plato, a metaphysics that seems, paradoxically, at odds with that "unfaltering confidence in outer reality," that "outgazing bent of mind that sees things exactly, each for itself, and seems innocent of the idea that thought discerps and colors reality" that Finley (as discussed earlier) had found in Homer. But the transformation is due precisely to the injection of "thought" into the apprehension of reality. Homer's heroes did not generally "think" about "outer reality"; they marvelled at it. Hussey has written about

> the ever-renewed flight from subjectivity, the repeated effort to distance oneself from one's own experience, and to examine it with critical detachment; and, consequently, scepticism about how it is related to truth. The first stage of the process is already observable in Homer: criticism of claims to know certain things which fall outside the range of immediate human experience. While Homer takes a generous view about what falls within it, some further erosion of confidence, particularly about claims of privileged access to knowledge, can be traced in the *Odyssey* and in Hesiod.[73]

For Plato, as Annas has written, "The form of Good is not in the world of our experience, since it is not the same as anything we call good. But," she asks: "is it not then odd, that when people seek what is good they are looking for something which is *ex hypothesi* different from anything to be found in people and actions? Aristotle criticizes Plato sharply, clearly with this passage in mind, at *Nicomachean Ethics* I, 6: it is absurd, he says, for the object of people's strivings to be something unattainable in the world of particular actions, a Form separate from particular good things."[74] Chinese accounts of reality and their lack of interest in the kinds of deception in which the Homeric Greeks delighted were to encourage a metaphysical vision strikingly different from that of Plato.

The Chinese narratives, when compared with the Greek, are remarkable for the lack of dramatic complexity. They generally provide the essence of the action;

they are parables, sermons, lacking the kind of existential irony and ambiguity that flows through critical scenes, such as the slaughter of the suitors in Book 22 of the *Odyssey*.[75] At the same time, of course, the Chinese narratives lack the interest and delight in slaughter, vividly described. Instead, these are texts that are frequently concerned with how men should act, or how, ideally, they did act. The concern is not with appearances but with significance. The early Chinese, I think, would have found it strange that highly individualized gods could disguise themselves as highly individualized humans and disrupt the normal workings of reality. This was not the way the world worked—or should work.

It might be instructive, in closing, to indulge in a moment of counterfactual history, imagining how the story of Odysseus' return to Ithaca would have been represented by the authors of the *Zuozhuan* 左 傳. The return of Chonger 重 耳, the future Jin Wen Gong 晉 文 公, to his state of Jin in 636 B.C.E. affords an instructive comparison; he had, after all, like Odysseus, wandered through much of the known world for, in his case, nineteen years. But at no point in the story is there any question of *who* is returning. The interest lies entirely elsewhere: how the new ruler will reward and punish those who had supported or opposed him during his years of trouble, and how he will comport himself as one who would heal old political wounds. There is no Chinese Penelope. There is no idiosyncratic, individualized Chonger to match the sharply etched portrait of Odysseus. Indeed, the only hint of the distortion of self in the entire story came years earlier when his wife, distressed that Chonger appeared to be settling down to the easy life in her home state of Qi 齊, "plotted with Zi Fan 子 犯 and together they contrived to get him drunk and send him off in a carriage. When he sobered up, he chased after Zi Fan with a halberd." Chonger, drunk, may not have known who or where he was for a brief period; but everybody else would have done so. There was little doubt, indeed, of how the story was to end. Moral stature—demonstrated by the worthiness of his wife and by the worth of the supporters he had gathered about him—would be recognized and rewarded. For when he had been in Cao 曹, the wife of a minister there had remarked to her husband, "I have observed the followers of the prince of Jin [i.e., Chonger], and all are worthy to serve as chief minister of a state. If they continue to assist him, he is bound in time to return to his own state. . . ."[76] It is worth noting that she observed his followers, rather than the prince himself. Once again, the interest was in function and social role rather than identity.

These emphases—which portray Chonger as a stereotypical leader in the making and which place all the drama on the political and bureaucratic questions of how a ruler wins, maintains, and rewards the allegiance of his followers—no doubt reflect a process of editorial selection at the hands of the elites who formed and transmitted the *Zuozhuan* that we know. For it is possible to posit the existence of a longer, pre-*Zuozhuan* narrative that had provided considerably more existential detail. Consider for example, the clues that remain. Attacked in the city of Pu 蒲 in an event recorded for 655 B.C.E., "Chonger himself climbed over the wall and fled. Pi 披 sliced off the cuff of his robe, but in the end he escaped and fled to the territory of the Di 翟 tribes."[77] One could hardly call that sleeve a "shining helmet," but it is nevertheless a gritty, nonmoral, non-didactic detail that suggests the existence of a fuller account. This seems confirmed by the anecdote recorded in Xi 24 (636 B.C.E.) as Chonger, returned from his wanderings, berates Pi (the same man who had attacked his city of Pu in Xi 5); he says, "At the time you attacked me at the city of Pu, my father gave you orders to attack on the following day, but you launched your attack immediately! . . . The sleeve [of which you cut off a part at Pu] is still in my possession. Go away!"[78] I find it far more plausible that a narrative story would span nineteen years, keeping the sleeve as a trope (which had no evident moral dimension), than that a didactic anecdote would preserve the sleeve in this way.[79] The *Zuozhuan* compilers record it, I assume, because it was in their sources, and because it provides a telling detail about Chonger's memory. Particularly telling, I suggest, is the comment, "my father gave you orders to attack on the following day, but you launched your attack immediately." That anecdote had *not* been given at Xi 5 at the time of the attack; its appearance in Xi 24, therefore, can serve no "artistic" function. It seems to be prime evidence for the existence of an original, more detailed narrative or romance of Chonger's escapades, a narrative whose interest in existential events might have shared more in common with the *Odyssey* than the present *Zuozhuan* does.

A similar remnant detail may be discerned in the story of Chonger's ribs: "When the prince visited the state of Cao 曹, Duke Gong 共 of Cao, having heard that the prince's ribs were all grown together, wanted to catch a glimpse of him naked. When the prince took a bath, therefore, he peered in through the curtain."[80] It is a story entirely without sequel. We are not told what the Duke saw; we are not told if Chonger knew he had been spied on; no further reference is made to the episode, which serves no evident narrative, characterological, or narrative purpose.[81] I presume it was left over from a fuller account of Chonger's adventures. The incident, furthermore, reminds us of how Homer had, by contrast, woven such a precise physical detail into the denouement of Odysseus's return. It had been the scar on his body that had proved his identity to his nurse: "I spotted the scar myself, when I washed his feet" (as noted earlier). For Homer, physical detail established identity; for the compilers of the *Zuozhuan* it did not.

As a closing speculation, one might wonder if, in early China, as in Greece, the putative "full" epics had originally been oral. Writing them down, however, assumes a writer and an audience committed to the massive task of recording that would have been involved. At a time when, on the basis of texts such as the *Lunyu* and *Mengzi,* one can see that expository narrative was only gradually developing as a prose style, we can suppose that the writers would have been interested in recording the "essence" of the epics, that is, those parts that were of most-interest to the *shi* 士 and *dafu* 大夫 readers involved in moral arguments that bore on their political careers. These more "useful, interesting" parts of the epics—useful and interesting, that is, from the viewpoint of the recorders and readers—would have "bobbed to the surface" and been given pride of place on the bamboo strips and silk documents. Indeed, the "didactification" or "essentialization" of these tales might have been a condition of their recording as the writer assumed that a good, entertaining, oral story was just that, but that a good moral point was worth writing down.[82] The prestige and dedication associated with mastering the logographic script may also have encouraged these tendencies. This model would also explain why we find no reference to the epics in the pre-Han or Han texts that remain to us. Not being written down, they would have left no bibliographic footprints. And being originally oral they may well have had no titles to record. The comparative newness of recording such texts might also have encouraged a preference for recording "essences" rather than "existences." The *Lunyu,* after all, sticks to the message; it tells us virtually nothing of the existential, as opposed to exemplary, details—of the protagonist's "massive build," of "his curls like thick hyacinth clusters," of "the fire in his eyes," of his "vibrant voice," to employ some of the terms found in the Homeric accounts. The Socratic dialogues, like the Homeric epics before them, take place in a world that is more fully described—and more duplicitous.

In the texts that have been handed down to us, Odysseus and Chonger thus live in entirely different worlds. The Greek account focused on who Odysseus was, or, in Vernant's words, "Odysseus in Person." The Chinese account focused on what Chonger did, on Chonger as a process rather than an identity, an exemplar of what should be done rather than a portrait of who was doing it. Each account expressed the story that their cultures—or, more precisely, certain audiences within those cultures—wanted to hear; each dramatized the epistemological interests that their audiences valued. A roughly contemporary Chinese version of Odysseus' return to Ithaca, modeled on that of Chonger, would have been, by Homeric standards, undramatic, even unrealistic. By omitting the Homeric trope of disguise and deception, the putative *Zuozhuan* version would, by Greek standards, have transformed and thus disguised the hero and his story, rendering him less interesting and less dramatic, and, finally, unrecognizable as a Homeric hero at all. The protean and shimmering protagonist of the Odyssey, accompanied by the equally protean Athena, would have struck the readers of the *Zuozhuan* as unsocial, unrealistic, and disruptive. Those readers would, in Xunzi's words (p. 133 herein), have concluded that the *Odyssey,* and also perhaps Plato's ideal Forms, was the product of a "mind . . . not inwardly settled."

Notes

1. For other examples not presented in this chapter, see for example K. von Fritz, "*Noos* and *Noein* in the Homeric Poems," *Classical Philology* 38 (1943): 79–93; J. H. Lesher, "Perceiving and Knowing in the *Iliad* and *Odyssey,*" *Phronesis 26* (1981): 2–24. As Lesher (p. 14) notes, "Aristotle in fact described the *Odyssey* as characterized throughout by the theme of disguise and recognition (*anagnōrisis, Poetics,* 1459b)."

2. Sheila Murnaghan, *Disguise and Recognition in the Odyssey* (Princeton, N.J.: Princeton University Press, 1987), p. 5. Lesher ("Perceiving and Knowing," p. 19) makes a similar point: "*mêtis* and *noos* play a central role in the story of Odysseus' return and . . . , in contrast with the *Iliad,* they typically involve the creation and penetration of deceptive appearance and utterance. When coupled with the roles played by

noein and *gignôskein,* they reflect an interest in sense perception, knowledge, and intelligence that was absent in the *Iliad.* "

3. "I hate that man like the very Gates of Death / who says one thing but hides another in his heart" (Robert Fagles, trans., *The Iliad* [New York: Viking, 1990], 9. 378—79). All the following translations of Homer, given below, unless quoted in the writings of other scholars, are from Fagles' translations, cited by book and by his line number(s).

4. Murnaghan, *Disguise and Recognition,* p. 4, n. 2

5. Murnaghan, *Disguise and Recognition,* pp. 11—12; she cites the relevant scholarship at n. 16.

6. Robert Fagles, trans., *The Odyssey* [New York: Viking, 1997], 22.214–15.

7. Murnaghan, *Disguise and Recognition,* p. 20.

8. Odysseus later uses the scar to persuade Laertes ("Give me a sign, some proof—I must be sure") that he is his son (*Od.* 24.367).

9. For the way those externals had misled the suitors, see the words of Amphimedon's ghost (*Od.* 24.172–76.)

10. Cf. Jean-Pierre Vernant, "Odysseus in Person," *Representations* 67 (Summer 1999): 4: "Odysseus' sojourn in Phaeacia provides examples of the two ways in which a person can maximally diverge from his own usual guise. It is as if beyond the ordinary, average form of his 'appearing,' *there existed in both directions a margin of variation . . .*" (italics added). Vernant also notes (p. 5) the power of Athena "to 'unfold' over a man a cloud of obscurity now concealing him from view, now shrouding his eyes in the night of sleep," the same power that "also allows Athena to 'unfold' over the person she chooses a flood of light whose radiation makes him taller, more beautiful, and more brilliant." Athena's power to exalt her favorites in this way was not limited to men. Upon Penelope too "she lavished immortal gifts . . . to make her suitors lose themselves in wonder. . . . She made her taller, fuller in form to all men's eyes" (*Od.* 18.216–23).

11. Homer employs an almost identical passage in *Od.* 6.253–60, when Odysseus is about to be entertained by Nausicaa.

12. As Lisa Raphals (*Knowing Words: Wisdom and Cunning in the Classical Traditions of China and Greece* [Ithaca, N.Y.: Cornell University Press, 1992], p. 211) notes, "The reunion of Odysseus and Penelope ends not with faithful and rejoicing Penelope falling into the arms of triumphant Odysseus but with her final and unassailable test of his identity. Odysseus comes to the surprising and happy realization that Penelope's *mêtis* exceeds even his own and that his own attainment is not quite what he thought it was."

13. The story of Oedipus, as told by Sophocles in *Oedipus Rex* with its tragic epiphany as Oedipus and Jocasta "recognize" their true identities that have until that point been disguised even from themselves, shares many of these elements.

14. Vernant, "Odysseus in Person," pp. 3–4.

15. Vernant, "Odysseus in Person," p. 25, n. 6.

16. Vernant, "Odysseus in Person," p. 6. The passage may be found in *Od.* 4.274–78.

17. David N. Keightley, "Clean Hands and Shining Helmets: ch. 10, pp. 261–63.

18. Keightley, "Clean Hands and Shining Helmets," ch 10, p. 270.

19. Other treatments of these issues are, of course, possible. The arguments presented in this chapter can certainly be correlated with those made about the varying emphases placed upon *mêtis* or "cunning intelligence" in the two cultures. Marcel Detienne and Jean-Pierre Vernant (*Cunning Intelligence in Greek Culture and Society* [Chicago: University of Chicago Press, 1991], pp. 11, 19, 21), for

example, note how *mêtis* might involve magic tricks, frauds, and deceits, that "shimmering sheen and shifting movement are so much a part of the nature of *mêtis* that when the epithet *poikilos* is applied to an individual it is enough to indicate that he is a wiley one, a man of cunning, full of inventive ploys (*poikiloboulos*) and tricks of every kind," and that "The many-coloured, shimmering nature of *mêtis* is a mark of its kinship with the divided, shifting world of multiplicity in the midst of which it operates." Raphals (*Knowing Words*) demonstrates the ambivalence toward cunning intelligence shown by both the early Chinese and early Greeks. At page 129 she proposes "two approaches to the relationship between knowledge and language, approaches that I shall venture to call 'face facts' and 'distrust appearances.'" (The terms were suggested to her by Angus C. Graham, *Reason and Spontaneity* [London: Curzon, 1985].) Similarly, Geoffrey Lloyd ("Appearance versus Reality: Greek and Chinese Comparisons and Contrasts," in *Beiträge zur antiken Philosophic: Festschrift für Wolfgang Kullmann,* ed. Hans-Christian Günther and Antonios Rengakos [Stuttgart: Franz Steiner, 1997], p. 306) has spoken of a rationalist versus an empirical epistemology: "The first suggests that the appearances have to be rejected, dismissed or discounted, to get to the underlying reality by means of abstract reasoning or argument. The second uses the appearances at least as a starting-point to infer the realities, while acknowledging that the two are distinct." These analyses are all useful when considering the topic of disguise and deception.

20. Thomas A. Metzger, "Some Ancient Roots of Modern Chinese Thought: This Worldliness, Epistemological Optimism, Doctrinality, and the Emergence of Reflexivity in the Eastern Chou," *Early China* 11–12 (1985–1987): 64; see too, 66–76.

21. Bruno Snell, *The Discovery of the Mind: The Greek Origins of European Thought* (Cambridge, Mass.: Harvard University Press, 1953; New York: Harper and Row, 1960), p. 108.

22. John H. Finley Jr., *Four Stages of Greek Thought* (Stanford, Calif.: Stanford University Press, 1966), pp. 8, 3.

23. Edward Hussey, "The Beginnings of Epistemology: From Homer to Philolaus," in *Epistemology,* ed. Stephen Everson (Cambridge: Cambridge University Press, 1990), p. 12.

24. Finley, *Four Stages of Greek Thought,* p. 35.

25. Hussey, "The Beginnings of Epistemology," p. 12.

26. Bertrand Russell, *A History of Western Philosophy and Its Connection with Political and Social Circumstances from the Earliest Times to the Present Day* (New York: Simon and Schuster, 1945), pp. 125, 105–6. Russell noted that the origins of this epistemological vision, "anticipated by Empedocles," were "in the teachings of the Orphics." On this point, see Peter Kingsley, *Ancient Philosophy, Mystery, and Magic* (New York: Oxford University Press, 1995), pp. 112–32.

27. Julia Annas, *An Introduction to Plato's Republic* (Oxford: Clarendon Press, 1982), pp. 253, 255, 264.

28. Russell, *A History of Western Philosophy,* p. 125. His translation comes from B. Jowett, trans. *The Works of Plato: Four Volumes Complete in One* (New York: Tudor, n.d.), p. 260. For a critical analysis of the metaphor of the Cave and its philosophical implications and problems, see too Annas, *An Introduction to Plato's Republic,* pp. 242–64.

29. Vernant, "Odysseus in Person," p. 2.

30. Note too that Odysseus had not been fooled when Athena appeared in the guise of Mentor to assist him in his fight with the suitors. Odysseus had cried out to this

Mentor, "'Remember your old comrade. . . . / . . . We were boys together'! . . . / yet knew in his bones it was Athena, Driver of Armies" (*Od.* 22.218–20).

31. I do not deal with postmortem transformations or metamorphoses in which, for example, "a person who feels wronged and injured after death appears as a ghost in the shape of some wild animal to take revenge" (Bernhard Karlgren, "Legends and Cults in Early China," *Bulletin of the Museum of Far Eastern Antiquities* 18 [1946]: 251). Karlgren cites the case of Gun 鯀, whose spirit, in some accounts, turned into a bear or other animal, and the case of Peng Sheng 彭生 who returned in the form of a wild pig to seek vengeance on the ruler who had executed him (*Zuozhuan,* Zhuang 8; Burton Watson, trans., *The Tso Chuan: Selections from China's Oldest Narrative History* [New York: Columbia University Press, 1989], pp. 17–19). It is instructive in this connection to consult the "Index of Concepts" in Anne Birrell, *Chinese Mythology: An Introduction* (Baltimore, Md.: Johns Hopkins University Press, 1993); on page 319, under "Metamorphosis," she lists many entries, but these involve only entries for animal, bird, insect, mythical beast, star, stone, tree, and universe. She has no entry for disguise.

32. Burton Watson, trans., *Records of the Historian: Chapters from the* Shih Chi *of Ssu-ma Ch'ien* (New York: Columbia University Press, 1958, 1969), p. 49; Sima Qian 司馬遷, *Shiji* 史記 (Beijing: Zhonghua, 1959), *j.* 86, "Cike liezhuan 刺客列傳" pp. 2520, 2521. (Here, as I do later, I convert all romanizations in quoted passages to pinyin.) The *Zhangguo ce,* which contains an earlier version of this story, refers to the assassin as Bi Yurang 畢豫讓 (J. L. Crump Jr., trans., *Chan-kuo ts'e* [London: Clarendon Press, 1970], pp. 285–87).

33. Based on Watson, trans., *Records of the Historian,* pp. 53, 54; Sima Qian, *Shiji* 86, "Cike liezhuan," p. 2525.

34. Similarly, Helen, in telling the story of how Odysseus disguised himself to infiltrate Troy, remarks, "and no one knew him at all . . . / I alone, I spotted him for the man he was" (*Od.* 4.280–81). But in this case, Odysseus had been practicing what one might call a "Chinese disguise"; he had not been subjected to a transformation produced by the gods.

35. Lloyd, "Appearance versus Reality," pp. 306, 311, 312, 313.

36. *Zuozhuan,* Zhao 1. Translation based on James Legge, trans., *The Chinese Classics: Vol. V, The Ch'un Ts'ew with The Tso Chuen* (London: Trübner, 1872), p. 578; Yang Bojun 楊伯峻, ed., *Chunqiu Zuozhuan zhu* 春秋左傳注 (Beijing: Zhonghua, 1981), p. 1212.

37. The allusion is to Confucius' definition of government found at *Lunyu* 論語 12.11.

38. Legge, trans., *The Ch'un Ts'ew with the Tso Chuen,* Vol. 5 of *The Chinese Classics,* p. 578.

39. John Knoblock, trans., *Xunzi: A Translation and Study of the Complete Works: Vol. III, Books 17–32* (Stanford, Calif.: Stanford University Press, 1994); "Dispelling Blindness," p. 109; Zhang Shitong 章詩同, ed., *Xunzi jianzhu* 荀子簡注 (Shanghai: Renmin, 1974), *j.* 21, "Jie bi 解蔽," p. 240. The passage is also translated by Christoph Harbsmeier, "Conceptions of Knowledge in Ancient China," in *Epistemological Issues in Classical Chinese Philosophy,* ed. Hans Lenk and Gregor Paul (Albany: State University of New York Press, 1993), p. 11; the article is reprinted with characters added, minor revisions, and different romanization in Christoph Harbsmeier's volume in the Joseph Needham series, *Science and Civilization in China, Vol. 7 Part 1, Language and Logic* (Cambridge: Cambridge University Press, 1998), pp. 247–60.

40. Knoblock, trans., *Xunzi. Vol. III,* p. 109; Zhang Shitong, ed.. *Xunzi jianzhu,* p. 240.

41. Knoblock, trans., *Xunzi. Vol. III,* pp. 108–9; Zhang Shitong, ed., *Xunzi jianzhu,* p. 239.

42. Knoblock, trans., *Xunzi. Vol. III,* p. no; Zhang Shitong, ed., *Xunzi jianzhu,* p. 240.

43. Knoblock, trans., *Xunzi. Vol. III,* "On the Correct Use of Names," p. 127; Zhang Shitong, ed., *Xunzi jianzhu, j.* 22, "Zheng ming 正 名," p. 244.

44. Harbsmeier, "Conceptions of Knowledge," p. 14, citing *Zuozhuan,* Zhao 10; Yang Bojun, ed., *Chunqiu Zuozhuan zhu,* p. 1319.

45. *Lunyu* 2.17; E. Bruce Brooks and A. Taeko Brooks, trans., *The Original Analects: Sayings of Confucius and His Successors. A New Translation and Commentary* (New York: Columbia University Press, 1998), p. 112. They follow the Lu 魯 text, which twice reads *fu zhi* 弗 知 rather than the transmitted *bu zhi* 不 知 (see Hebei sheng wenwu yanjiusuo Dingzhou Han mu zhujian zhengli xiaozu, "Dingzhou Xihan Zhongshan Huaiwang mu zhujian 'Lun yu' shiwen xuan 定 州 西 漢 中 山 懷 王 基 竹 簡 '論 語' 釋 文 選," *Wenwu* 文 物 1997.5:50 [strip 1378]).

46. Brooks and Brooks, trans., *The Original Analects,* p. 112.

47. G E. R. Lloyd, "Techniques and Dialectic: Method in Greek and Chinese Mathematics and Medicine," in *Method in Ancient Philosophy,* ed. Jyl Gentzler (Oxford: Clarendon Press, 1998), p. 373. He refers to A. C. Graham, trans., *Later Mohist Logic, Ethics and Science* (Hong Kong: Chinese University Press and School of Oriental and African Studies, 1978), esp. pp. 30 ff.

48. The concerns expressed by Jane N. Geaney, moreover ("A Critique of A. C. Graham's Reconstruction of the 'Neo-Mohist Canons,'" *Journal of the American Oriental Society* 119, no. 1 [1999]: 1–11), suggest the degree to which our modern understanding of Mohist logic may be defective. Of particular interest for the subject of this chapter is Geaney's questioning (p. 1) of "Graham's contention (fundamental to his restructuring of the Canons) that the Mohist divides the world into an eternally necessary realm and a transient, non-necessary realm. . . . This separation of a necessary, atemporal realm from a non-necessary, temporal realm does not seem grounded in the thought of ancient China. And the intelligibility of Graham's reconstruction is not compelling enough to justify his theorizing that the Neo-Mohists invented such a world-view."

49. Translated by Harbsmeier, "Conceptions of Knowledge," p. 13. Chen Qiyou 陳 奇 猷, ed., *Han Fei Zi jishi* 韓 非 子 集 釋 (Taibei: Shijie, 1963), *j.* 30, "Nei chushuo shang qi shu 内 儲 説 上 七 術," p. 537; *j.* 48, "Ba jing 八 經," p. 1029.

50. Harbsmeier, "Conceptions of Knowledge," p. 18.

51. Harbsmeier, "Conceptions of Knowledge," pp. 14, 22.

52. Eric Henry, "The Motif of Recognition in Early China," *Harvard Journal of Asiatic Studies* 47, no. 1 (1987): 8. On *zhi* 知, see too Thomas A. Metzger, "Some Ancient Roots," p. 94: "'Know' could connote or even mean 'morally evaluate' or 'morally evaluate and give the esteem due.'" Harbsmeier ("Conceptions of Knowledge," p. 14) writes that "when it comes to 'knowing the Way' (*zhi dao* [知 道]), this is not cerebral knowing that something is the case. It is mainly understood as a moral and prudential skill." Raphals (*Knowing Words,* pp. 16–17) discusses the etymology of *zhi* and its semantic field. For Knoblock (trans., *Xunzi,* Vol. III, p. 333, 11. 79), *zhi* as used by Xunzi "means both awareness and the knowledge that derives from sensory awareness."

53. Henry, "Motif of Recognition," p. 15, citing the translation of Arthur Waley, *The Book of Songs* (New York: Grove, 1960), p. 306.

54. Henry, "Motif of Recognition," p. 15. For a study of this theme, "the disgruntlement of authors at the failure of the world to recognize and make use of their matchless talents" (p. 434), as it was worked out in the *fu* 賦 of the Han dynasty, see David W. Pankenier, "The Scholar's Frustration Reconsidered: Melancholia or Credo? *"Journal of the American Oriental Society* 110, no. 3 (1990): 434–59.

55. Henry, "Motif of Recognition," p. 18 (italics added). He cites (p. 18, n. 26) recognition stories involving the employment of Yi Yin 伊尹 and Fu Yue 傅說. On this important motif, see too Sarah Allan, "The Identities of Taigong Wang 太公望 in Zhou and Han Literature," *Monumenta Serica* 30 (1972–73): 57–99; Raphals, *Knowing Words,* pp. 11, 224–25.

56. Henry, "Motif of Recognition," p. 19.

57. "A great proportion of the [*Lunyu*] is given over to comments concerning the habits and motivations of others, a type of discussion of which the Confucian circle seems never to tire" (Henry, "Motif of Recognition," p. 20). "Confucius and Mozi agreed on the goal of having a polity that perfectly evaluated people and then perfectly distributed sanctions" (Metzger, "Some Ancient Roots," p. 65; see too pp. 89–110).

58. A. C. Graham, trans., *Chuang Tzu: The Seven Inner Chapters and Other Writings from the Book Chuang-tzu* (London: Allen and Unwin, 1981), p. 61. In Graham's view, ". . . the point is that the Taoist does not permanently deem himself a man or a butterfly but moves spontaneously from fitting one name to fitting another"; Guo Qingfan 郭慶藩, ed., *Jiaozheng Zhuangzi jishi* 校正莊子集釋 (Taibei: Shijie, 1962), *j.* 1 *xia*, "Qiwu lun 齊物論," p. 112.

59. As Harbsmeier ("Conceptions of Knowledge," p. 25) writes: "Zhuangzi nowhere directly and dogmatically states that we cannot know. He only persists in asking, 'How do we know?' He is not an adherent of the dogma that we cannot know anything."

60. David N. Keightley, "Art, Ancestors, and the Origins of Writing in China," *Representations* 56 (Fall 1996): 68–95.

61. Keightley, "Clean Hands and Shining Helmets," pp. 272–75.

62. Keightley, "Clean Hands and Shining Helmets," pp. 265–67.

63. W.K. Liao, trans., "Outer Congeries of Sayings, The Upper Left Series," Vol. 2 of *The Complete Works of Han Fei Zi* (London: Probsthaim, 1959), p. 40: Chen Qiyou, ed., *Han Fei Zi jishi, j.* 11, "Wai chushuo zuoshang 外儲說左上," p. 633.

64. For a fuller account of this argument in the texts and visual art of the Eastern Zhou, see Keightley, "Clean Hands and Shining Helmets," pp. 255–60, 265–70.

65. For the view that the *taotie* animal mask was involved in metamorphosis, see Elizabeth Childs-Johnson, "The Ghost Head Mask and Metamorphic Shang Imagery," *Early China* 20 (1995): 79–92.

66. Liao, trans., "Outer Congeries of Sayings," pp. 39–40; Chen Qiyou, ed., *Han Fei Zi jishi, j.* 11, "Wai chushuo zuoshang," p. 632.

67. For the view that Shang divination (and thus other Shang rituals?) took place at daybreak, see David N. Keightley, *Sources of Shang History: The Oracle-Bone Inscriptions of Bronze Age China* (Berkeley: University of California Press, 1978), p. 2, n. 1.

68. Liao, trans., "Outer Congeries of Sayings," p. 40; Chen Qiyou, ed., *Han Fei Zi jishi, j.* 11, "Wai chushuo zuoshang," p. 632.

69. Liao, trans., "Outer Congeries of Sayings," p. 27; Chen Qiyou, ed., *Han Fei Zi jishi, j.* 11, "Wai chushuo zuoshang," p. 612.

70. Von Fritz, "*Noos* and *Noein* in the Homeric Poems," p. 89.

71. Lesher, "Perceiving and Knowing," p. 2.

72. Lesher, "Perceiving and Knowing," pp. 7, 20.

73. Hussey, "The Beginnings of Epistemology," pp. 34–35.

74. Annas, *An Introduction to Plato's Republic,* p. 244.

75. Lesher, "Perceiving and Knowing," pp. 14–15: "The lengthy account of Odysseus' return and destruction of the suitors continually contrasts those who fail to comprehend the true identity of the disguised guest, with those who sense the ominous

meaning of his actions and words. What is obvious and apparent to the suitors is in fact furthest from the truth."

76. *Zuo zhuan,* Xi 23; Watson, trans., *The Tso chuan,* p. 42, trans, adjusted; Yang Bojun, ed., *Chunqiu Zuozhuan zhu,* p. 407.

77. *Zuo zhuan,* Xi 5. My translation is based on Legge, trans., *The Ch'un Ts'ew with the Tso Chuen,* p. 145; Watson, trans. *The Tso Chuan,* p. 25, trans. adjusted. For the Chinese text, see Yang Bojun, ed., *Chunqiu Zuozhuan zhu,* p. 305.

78. *Zuo zhuan,* Xi 24. My translation is based on Legge, trans., *The Ch'un Ts'ew with the Tso Chuen,* p. 191; Watson, trans., *The Tso Chuan,* pp. 25, 46. For the Chinese text, see Yang Bojung, ed., *Chunqiu Zuozhuan zhu,* p. 414. The story, with the detail of the sleeve preserved, was also repeated in Sima Qian, *Shiji, j.* 39, "Jin shijia 晉 世 家," p. 1661.

79. I am responding here to the argument of Ronald Egan ("Narratives in *Tso Chuan,*" *Harvard Journal of Asiatic Studies* 37, no. 2 [1977]: 323–52), who has conjectured that the *Zuozhuan* "may have developed, in large part, out of a tradition of didactic historical anecdote" (p. 350). In this case, at least, Maspero's view that much of the *Zuo* "comes from a rich corpus of historical romance" (p. 352) receives some support. See too n. 82.

80. *Zuo zhuan,* Xi 23; Watson, trans. *The Tso chuan,* p. 42, who notes the textual difficulties; Yang Bojun, ed., *Chunqiu Zuozhuan zhu,* p. 407. The anecdote also appears in the *Guoyu* (Wu Shaolie 吳 紹 烈 et al., eds., *Guoyu* 國 語 [Shanghai: Guji, 1988], "Jin yu 晉 語," p. 346), and *Shiji* (Sima Qian, *Shiji, j.* 39, "Jin shijia," p. 1658).

81. Even if it be allowed that the incident tells us something about Duke Gong of Cao's character—in both the *Guoyu* and *Shiji* references cited in note 80 the Duke's behavior is characterized as "not in accordance with the rites" (*bu li* 不 禮)—Chonger makes no reference to the incident when, in 632 B.C.E. (Xi 28), his army takes Cao, but blames the Duke for quite another matter (Legge, trans., *The Ch'un Ts'ew with the Tso Chuen,* p. 208; Yang Bojun, ed., *Chunqiu Zuozhuan zhu,* p. 453).

82. For an analysis that would generally support such a model, see David Johnson, "Epic and History in Early China: The Matter of Wu Tzu-hsü," *Journal of Asian Studies* 40 (1981): 255–71. He suggests (p. 271) that there was a loss of epic in Han as "narrative drive was subordinated to generic classification and intense focus on a few great heroes was replaced by a multitude of short biographies of the merely eminent or exemplary."

12
NOTES AND COMMENTS

"There Was an Old Man of Chang'an....":
Limericks and the Teaching of Early Chinese History

DAVID N. KEIGHTLEY

"UNABATED WAS HIS DELIGHT IN LIMERICKS," wrote W. Perceval Yetts of L. C. Hopkins (1854–1952) when Yetts visited him a few months before his death.[1] That Hopkins, one of the pioneer collectors and scholars of oracle-bone inscriptions, was thus committed to the joy of the limerick encourages this small communication as a minor aid to the teaching of early Chinese history.[2]

Over the years I have invited students in my lecture courses to submit limericks about the events and persons of early China they encounter. The students submit their verses anonymously;[3] I select the best (many are mere doggerel, some can be truly awful: "I broke up my dear mother's *zong,*/It fell with a bing, bang, and bong....") and read them aloud to the class; there is a mix of laughter and groans. I do this for two reasons. First, in the hope that some of the phrasing may help fix a particular Chinese name or episode in the mind of the writer and the audience. Second, because it encourages precision in the use of language and attention to form ("His mind was alert and his memory vivid," wrote Yetts of Hopkins in his ninety-seventh year). Not the least of the virtues of using limerick-writing in this way is that it teaches many of the students precisely what a limerick is. A few even find the form addicting.

There is little more to be said except to offer a sampling of some of the more promising submissions. (Since the introductory lecture course runs from Yao to Mao, I include one limerick that derived from a reading of Jonathan Spence's, *The Death of Woman Wang.*) I observe the request frequently attached, "If you should read this out, please don't use my name."

Then out of the West came the Zhou:
"All dissolute drunkards must go!"
    We were strong in the West
    In the East not our best,
But Heaven's command made it so.

There once was an old man named Lao
Who preached the great way of the Tao.
    When butterflies zoomed
    Or peach blossoms bloomed,
He'd peacefully say a soft "Wow!"

Young Mencius, due back home at seven,
Got through the front door at eleven.
    He explained to his mother
    While running for cover,
"But Ma, it's the Mandate of Heaven."

A naturalist coming from Qin
Had no money to sleep at the inn,
    So he bellowed, quite bold,
    While out in the cold,
"I've got to get yang, let me yin!"

There once was an Emperor of Qin
Who vowed to eliminate sin
    By setting up rules
    And punishments cruel,
Which only made Qin a has-been.

At Pingyuanjin fishing so well,
Into illness the First Emperor fell.
    The truth's hard to hide,
    When he finally died,
The First Emperor started to smell.

Gao Zu was both virtuous and wise
While Xiang Yu was cruel and told lies.
    Xiang Yu once was strong
    But he didn't last long
For evil *must* bring its demise.

Sima Qian out of bitter frustration
Over suicide chose his castration.
    I think as time flew
    There was no cause for rue,
But his wife surely felt the negation.

Woman Wang met her maker one night,
As any adulteress might.
    Her spouse his fuse blew,
    Nearly broke her in two,
But two Wangs just don't make a right.

I would not wish to overstate the pedagogic virtues of this approach, but any device that encourages a student to write a sentence containing the place name Pingyuanjin has something to recommend it. A sampling of some other promising first (and second) lines will suggest the range of students' imagination and their engagement with the material: "There once was a sage king named Yu,/Whom the problem of floods made quite blue...," "The Black Pottery people did not...," "The Zhou kings gave lands to their own...," "Like the Beatles, Mo Zi had a creed...," "Said Lao Zi, 'The Tao can't be told'...," "There once was a man named Sun Pin,/Who taught all his armies to win...," "The Junzi were noble scholastics...," and so on.

I have occasionally found it helpful to suggest a first line to the class, and encourage students to finish the limerick for themselves. Hence the old man of Chang'an in my title. And for the modern period, there is always, "How delightful to know Mao Zedong,/A Hunanese son of a gun...." If readers would care to accept the challenge....

Notes

1. Yetts, "A Memoir of the Translator," in L. C. Hopkins, tr., *The Six Scripts or the Principles of Chinese Writing by Tai T'ung* (Cambridge, England: Cambridge University Press, 1954), p. xviii.

2. For a more massive application of limericks to pedagogy, see Richard E. Aquila, *Rhyme or Reason: A Limerick History of Philosophy* (Washington DC: University Press of America, 1981); the verses were apparently written by Aquila, rather than by his students. See, too, Richard Severo, "Wisdom of Ancient Egypt Comes to Life as Limericks," *New York Times,* 27 August 1981, for Dr. Carol R. Fontaine's use of limericks to "make the task of learning the old symbols easier."

3. Since the limericks were the work of students whose location, and even, in some cases, identity (the limericks were submitted anonymously) is unknown to me, they are reproduced here without any guarantee that "I am the sole owner of this work and have the full power and authority" to publish it.—D.N.K.

BIBLIOGRAPHY OF THE WRITINGS OF
DAVID N. KEIGHTLEY

Books

Sources of Shang History: The Oracle-Bone Inscriptions of Bronze Age China.
Berkeley: University of California Press, 1978; 2d ed. and paperback, 1985.

[Editor]. *The Origins of Chinese Civilization.* Berkeley: University of California
Press, 1983.

*The Ancestral Landscape: Time, Space, and Community in Late Shang China
(ca. 1200–1045 B.C.).* Berkeley: Institute of East Asian Studies, 2000.
China Research Monograph 53.

*Working For His Majesty: Labor Mobilization in Late Shang China (ca. 1200–1045
B.C.), as Seen in the Oracle-bone Inscriptions (With Particular Attention to
Handicraft Industries, Agriculture, Warfare, Hunting, Construction and Its
Legacies).* Berkeley: Institute of East Asian Studies, 2012.

Review Articles and Reviews

"[Review of] Shima Kunio 鳥邦男, *Inkyo bokuji sôrui* 殷墟卜辭綜類."
Monumenta Serica 28 (1969):467–471

"[Review of] *The Origins of Statecraft in China: Volume One: The Western
Chou Empire.* By Herrlee G. Creel." *Journal of Asian Studies* (1971)
30.3:655–658

"'Benefit of Water': The Approach of Joseph Needham." *Journal of Asian Studies*
31 (1972):367–371

"Religion and the Rise of Urbanism." *Journal of the American Oriental Society* 93
(1973):527–538

"Where Have All the Swords Gone?: Reflections on the Unification of China."
Early China 2 (Fall 1976):31–34

"Ping-ti Ho and the Origins of Chinese Civilization." *Harvard Journal of Asiatic
Studies* 37 (1977):381–411

"*The Cradle of the East:* Supplementary Comments." *Early China* 3 (1977):55–61.

"Akatsuka Kiyoshi and the Culture of Early China: A Study in Historical Method."
Harvard Journal of Asiatic Studies 42 (1982):267–320. (Review of Akatsuka
Kiyoshi 赤塚忠, *Chûgoku kodai no shûkyô to bunka: in ôchô no saishi* .)

"Shang China is Coming of Age: A Review Article." *Journal of Asian Studies* 41 (1982):549–557

"[Review of] Wang Yü-hsin 王宇信, *Chien-kuo yi-lai chia-ku-wen yen-chiu* 建國以來甲骨文研究*.*" *Harvard Journal of Asiatic Studies* 42 (1982): 331–34. (Chinese translation published in *Lishi jiaoxue* 歷史教學 1981.11:62–63.)

"[Review of] Jean A. Lefeuvre, *Fa-kuo so-ts' ang chia-ku lu (Collections d'inscriptions oraculaires en France; Collections of Oracular Inscripitons in France.*" *Journal of the American Oriental Society* 109.3 (1989):482–484. (Chinese translation in *Zhongguo shi yanjiu dongtai* 中國史研究動態 1990.11:16–18.)

"Oracle-Bone Collections in Great Britain: A Review Article," *Early China* 14 (1989):173–82 (Chinese translation in *Zhongguo shi yanjiu dongtai* 中國史研究励態 1991.7:20–24.)

"[Review of] *Kôkotsu moji: Hito mono kokoro,*" *Harvard Journal of Asiatic Studies* 50.1 (1990):378–83.

"Sources of Shang History: Two Major Oracle-Bone Collections from the People's Republic of China," *Journal of the American Oriental Society* 110.1 (1990):39–59.

"Interactions, Weak and Strong (Commentary on Pulleyblank, 'Early Contacts Between Indo-Europeans and Chinese')." *International Review of Chinese Linguistics* 1.1 (1996):27–29.

"Graphs, Words, and Meanings: Three Reference Works for Shang Oracle-Bone Studies, With an Excursus into the Religious Role of the Day or Sun." [Review Article of: Matsumaru Michio 松凡道雄 and Takashima Kenichi 高嶋謙一. *Kôkotsumoji Jishaku Sôran* 甲骨文字字釋綜覽; Yao Xiaosui 姚孝遂 and Xiao Ding 肖丁 eds., *Yin xu jiagu keci moshi zongji* 殷墟甲骨刻辭蔡釋總欒; Yao Xiaosui and Xiao Ding, eds., *Yinxu Jiagu keci leizuan* 殷墟甲骨刻辭類經]. *Journal of the American Oriental Society* 117.3 (1997):507–24.

"Comment on Cecilia F. Klein, et al., 'The Role of Shamanism in Mesoamerican Art." *Current Anthropology* 43.3 (June 2002):408–09.

Articles

"Archaeology and History in Chinese Society." In W.W. Howells and Patricia Tuschitani, eds., *Paleoanthropology in the People's Republic of China.* Washington, D.C.: National Academy of Sciences, 1977:123–129.

"On the Misuse of Ancient Chinese Inscriptions: An Astronomical Fantasy." *History of Science* 15 (1977):267–272.

"Space Travel in Bronze Age China?" *The Skeptical Inquirer* 3.2 (Winter 1978):58–63

"The Religious Commitment: Shang Theology and the Genesis of Chinese Political Culture." *History of Religions* 17 (1978):211–224

"The *Bamboo Annals* and Shang-Chou Chronology." *Harvard Journal of Asiatic Studies* 38 (1978):423–438

"The Shang State as Seen in the Oracle-Bone Inscriptions." *Early China* 5 (1979–80):25–34

"The State," "Divination," "Religion," "The Economy," "Bronze Working," in Brian Hook, ed., *The Cambridge Encyclopedia of China.* Cambridge: Cambridge University Press, 1982. pp. 163–65.

"The Late Shang State: When, Where, and What?" in Keightley, ed., *The Origins of Chinese Civilization* (1983):523–564

"Late Shang Divination: The Magico-Religious Legacy." In Henry Rosemont, Jr., ed., *Explorations in Early Chinese Cosmology.* Journal of the American Academy of Religion Studies 50.2 (1984):11–34

"Reports from the Shang: A Correction and Some Speculations." *Early China* 9–10 (1983–1985):20–39, 47–54

"Main Trends in American Studies of Chinese History: Neolithic to Imperial Times," *The History Teacher* 19.4 (August 1986):527–543

"Zhongguo zhi zhengshi zhi yuanyuan: Shang wang zhanbu shifou yiguan zhengchue? 中國正史之淵源:商王占卜是否一貫正確 (The Origins of Orthodox Historiography in China: Were the Shang Kings Always Right?)." *Guwenzi yanjiu* 古文字研究 13 (1986):117–128

"Archaeology and Mentality: The Making of China." *Representations* 18 (Spring 1987):91–128. (Chinese version published as "Cong kaogu qiwu kan Zhongguo siwei shijie de xingcheng 從考古器物看中國思維世界的形成," *Zhongguo wenhua yu Zhongguo zhexue* 中國文化與中國哲學 1988: 466–500. A second Chinese version, tr. by Chen Xingcan 陳星燦, published as "Kaoguxue yu sixiang zhuangtai—Zhongguo de chuangjian 考古學與思想奘態—中國的創建," *Huaxia kaogu* 華夏考古 1993.1:97–108.

"Prehistory" and "The First Historical Dynasty: The Shang." *The New Encyclopedia Britannica: Macropaedia* (Chicago 1987) 16:62–67

"Astrology and Cosmology in the Shang Oracle-Bone Inscriptions." *Cosmos* 3 (1987):36–40

"Shang Dynasty," in Ainslee T. Embree, ed., *Encyclopedia of Asian History* (New York, Scribner's: 1988) 3:426–429

[Translator] Wang Ningsheng, "Yangshao Burial Customs and Social Organization: A Comment on the Theory of Yangshao Matrilineal Society and Its Methodology," *Early China* 11–12 (1985–87):6–32

"Shang Divination and Metaphysics," *Philosophy East and West* 38.4 (October 1988):367–397

[Translator, with Igarashi Yoshikuni] Toyoda Hidashi and Inoo Hideyuki, "*Shigaku zasshi*: Summary of Japanese Scholarship," *Early China* 13 (1988): 297–327

"The Origins of Writing in China: Scripts and Cultural Contexts," in Wayne M. Senner, ed., *The Origins of Writing* (University of Nebraska Press, 1989):171–202

"Comment" (in the *Early China* Forum on Qiu Xigui, "An Examination of Whether the Charges in Shang Oracle-Bone Inscriptions Are Questions"), *Early China* 14 (1989):138–46

"'There Was an Old Man of Changan. . .': Limericks and the Teaching of Early Chinese History," *The History Teacher* 22.3 (May 1989):325–28.

"Zhongguoren shi zenmeyang chengwei zhongguoren de? 中國人是怎麼樣成為中國人 (How Did the Chinese Become Chinese?)." *Zhongguo wenhua yu Zhongguo zhexue* 中國文化與中國哲學 (1988) (Beijing).

"Craft and Culture: Metaphors of Governance in Early China." *Proceedings of the 2nd International Conference on Sinology. Section on History and Archaeology* (Taibei, 1989):31–70

"Zhongguo gudai di jiri yu miaohao 中國古代吉日與廟號 (Lucky Days and Temple Names in Ancient China)." *Yinxu bowuyuan yuankan (chuangkan hao)* 殷墟博物苑苑刊 (創刊號) 1989:20–32

"Early Civilization in China: Reflections on How It Became Chinese." In Paul S. Ropp, ed., *Heritage of China: Contemporary Perspectives on Chinese Civilization* (University of California Press, 1990):15–54. (Translated: [1] as "L'antica civilta della Cina: riflessioni su come divenne 'cinese.'" In Paul S. Ropp, ed., *L'eredità della cina* [Turino: Fondazione Giovanni Agnelli, 1994]:33-68; [2] "Fansi zaoqi Zhonguo wenhua zhi chengyin 反思早期中國文化之成因." In Luo Puluo 羅溥洛 (Paul Ropp), ed., *Meiguo xuezhe lun Zhongguo wenhua* 美國學者論中國文化. [Beijing: Zhongguo Guangbo dianshi chubanshe, 1994]:17–52.)

"Ancient Chinese Art: Contexts, Constraints, and Pleasures," *Asian Art* 3.2 (Spring 1990):2–6

"The Quest for Eternity in Ancient China: The Dead, Their Gifts, Their Names." In George Kuwayama, ed., *Ancient Mortuary Traditions of China: Papers on Chinese Ceramic Funerary Sculptures.* (Los Angeles County Museum of Art, 1991):2–12

"Clean Hands and Shining Helmets: Heroic Action in Early Chinese and Greek Culture." In Tobin Siebers, ed., *Religion and the Authority of the Past.* (Ann Arbor: University of Michigan Press, 1993):13–51

"A Late Shang Divination Record." *The Columbia Anthology of Traditional Chinese Literature.* Ed. Victor H. Mair. New York: Columbia University Press, 1994. pp. 3–4.

"Sacred Characters." In Robert E. Murowchick, ed., *China: Ancient Culture, Modern Land* (North Sydney: Weldon Russell), 70–79. (Distributed by University of Oklahoma Press.)

"Early Jades in China: Some Cultural Contexts, Social Implications." *Collecting Chinese Jade.* 16–19. Bernstein, S. ed. San Francisco: S. Bernstein & Co., 1995.

"Bibliography" (72 annotated and indexed items) for American Historical Association's *Guide to Historical Literature.* Ed. Mary Beth Norton. Oxford University Press, March 1995

"Chinese Religions—The State of the Field: Part I, Early Religious Traditions: The Neolithic Period Through the Han Dynasty (ca. 4000 B.C.E.–220 C.E.): Neolithic and Shang Periods." *Journal of Asian Studies* 54.1 (1995): 128–45.

"A Measure of Man in Early China: In Search of the Neolithic Inch." *Chinese Science* 12 (1994–95): 16–38

"Art, Ancestors, and the Origins of Writing in China." *Representations* 56 (Fall 1996): 68–95.

"Shang Oracle-Bone Inscriptions." In Edward L. Shaughnessy, ed., *New Sources of Early Chinese History: An Introduction to the Reading of Inscriptions and Manuscripts.* Berkeley: Society for the Study of Early China, Special Monography series, 1997: 15–56.

"Shamanism, Death, and the Ancestors: Religious Mediation in Neolithic and Shang China (ca. 5000–1000 B.C.)." *Asiatische Studien* 52.3 (1998):763–831.

"The Environment of Ancient China." In Michael Loewe and Edward L. Shaughnessy, eds., *The Cambridge History of Ancient China: From the Origins of Civilization to 221 B.C.* New York: Cambridge University Press, 1999, 30–36.

"The Shang: China's First Historical Dynasty." In Michael Loewe and Edward L. Shaughnessy, eds., *The Cambridge History of Ancient China: From the Origins of Civilization to 221 B.C.* New York: Cambridge University Press, 1999, 232–91.

"At the Beginning: The Status of Women in Neolilthic and Shang China." *Nannü: Men, Women and Gender in Early and Imperial China* 1 (1999): 1–62.

"The Oracle-Bone Inscriptions of the Late Shang Dynasty." In Wm. Theodore de Bary and Irene Bloom, eds., *Sources of Chinese Tradition.* New York: Columbia University Press, 1999, pp. 3–23.

"Theology and the Writing of History: Truth and the Ancestors in the Wu Ding Divination Records." *Journal of East Asian Archaeology* 1.1–4 (1999):207–30.

"Lun taiyang zai Yindai de zongjiao yiyi 論太陽在殷代的宗教意義" (The Religious Significance of the Sun in Shang Times). *Yindu xuekan* 殷都學刊 1999.1:16–21. Tr. by Liu Xueshun.

"Shang Oracle Bone Inscriptions from Anyang, Henan Province." In *The Golden Age of Archaeology: Celebrated Discoveries from the People's Republic of China,* ed. Xiaoneng Yang. Washington: National Gallery of Art, 1999. pp. 182–86.

"Die chinesischen Orakelnochen." In *Orakel: Der Blick in die Zukunft,.* eds. Axel Langer, and Albert Lutz. Zurich: Museum Rietberg, 1999. pp. 18–33.

"What Did Make the Chinese 'Chinese'?: Musings of a Would-be Geographical Determinist." *Lotus Leaves* 3.2 (Summer 2000): 1–3.

"The Diviners' Notebooks: Shang Oracle-Bone Inscriptions as Secondary Sources." In *Actes du Collogue International Commémorant le Centenaire de la Découverte des Inscriptions sur Os et Carapaces; Proceedings of the International Symposium in Commemoration of the Oracle-Bone Inscriptions Discovery.* Eds. Yau Shun-chiu and Chrystelle Maréchal. Paris: Editions Langages Croisés, 2001. pp. 11–25.

"Kwang-chih Chang (1931–2001)." *Journal of Asian Studies* 60.2 (2001):619–21.

"Epistemology in Cultural Context: Disguise and Deception in Early China and Early Greece." In *Early China, Ancient Greece: Thinking Through Comparisons,* eds. Steven Shankman and Stephen Durrant. Albany: State University of New York Press, 2001. pp. 119–53.

"Shang Dynasty." *Microsoft Encarta Reference Library 2002.*

"Comment on Cecilia F. Klein, et al., 'The Role of Shamanism in Mesoamerican Art." *Current Anthropology* 43.3 (June 2002):408–09.

Ji, Dewei. "Si er bu wang: Zhang Guangzhi de gongxian 死而不亡：張光直的貢獻." *Sihai Wei Jia: Zhuinian kaogu xuejia Zhang Guangzhi* 四海為家：追念考古學家張光直. Li Ling, ed. in chief. Beijing: Sanlian, 2002. pp. 195–98.

"The Making of the Ancestors: Late Shang Religion and Its Legacy." In John Lagerwey, ed., *Chinese Religion and Society: The Transformation of a Field. Vol. 1.* Hong Kong: École Française d'Extrême-orient and the Chinese University of Hong Kong Press, 2004. pp. 3–63.

"Marks and Labels: Early Writing in Neolithic and Shang China." Miriam T. Stark, ed., *Archaeology of Asia.* Blackwell, 2006. pp. 177–201.

"Sacred Waste: Theirs or Ours." In Christoph Anderl and Halvor Eifring, eds., *Studies in Chinese Language and Culture: Festschift in Honour of Christoph Harbsmeier on the Occasion of the 60th Birthday.* Oslo: Hermes. pp. 3–12.

David N. Keightley, "The Period V Ritual Postface: Prospective or Retrospective," *Early China* 35–36 (2012–2013), 57–68.

INDEX

45, *45*; conceived in terms
of employment, reward, and
recognition rather than suffering,
54; construction of coffin
chambers, 44–45; continuity
and, 52; distinction between
funeral rites and grave rites in,
187; divination during burial
process, 191*n15*; early treatment,
21; effect of delay between death
and burial on lords and slaves,
85*n19*; effects of geography
on, 78, 79; egalitarianism and,
43; farewell rituals, 31*n56*;
grave goods in, 22, 43–48;
impersonalization of the dead
and, 174–176, 181, 182,
184, 185; individuals and the
supernatural, 54–55; Neolithic,
43, 44, *44*; nihilistic view of, 55;
positionality, 44, *49*; rammed
earth tombs, 49; representations
of, 263–265; royal tombs, *50*;
rules for mourning rites, 184;
seen as form of promotion, 91;
sex ratios in cemeteries, 21, 22;
as social problem, 71*n10*; status
differentiation and, 43; taxes
on, 50; ties of obligation and
servitude persisting after, 48;
treatment of children at, 22; as
unproblematic, 52–53
DeFrancis, John, 234
Depew, Michael, 85*n19*
Descartes, Rene, 42
Diamond, Jared, 80
Di (High God), 157, 158, 159
Discourses of the States, 259
Disguise: in ancient Greece, 283–289;
in art, 299–300; clean hands/dirty
hands and, 288, 289, 293; by
gods, 290; link to divinity, 284;
magical, 299–300; mechanisms
of, 288; no role in narratives of
Chou and Han dynasties, 292;

not practiced by elites, 293;
piercing of, 292; role in literature,
283; self-inflicted, 293
Divination: action-oriented form
of charges, 113; alternatives
in charges, 105; ambiguous
pronostications in, 117*n11,*
210, 211; assertive mode of,
105, 111; during burial process,
191*n15*; cause-and-effect
dependent on spiritual approval,
105; changes in procedures,
133–138; charges expressed in
results desired, 128; charges
recorded as complementary
charge pairs in positive/
negative mode, 102, 103, 218,
219, 220; climate and, 216;
compensations for inaccuracies
in, 212; complementary
charges' implications,
129–132, 147*n28*; concern
with dynamics of decision-
making in, 133; concern with
momentary balance and, 131;
concern with rightness of, 103;
confirmation of prognostications,
126; contrasting charges
in, 124; disappearance of
complementarity in, 139;
"disaster," 138; display
inscriptions, 239, 244; display
inscriptions in, 117*n18,*
128–129; editorial manipulation
of verifications, 214, 215;
evolution of practice and belief
in Shang dynasty, 133–138;
evolution of prognostications,
133–138; exclusion of negative
alternatives from charges, 105;
on five major rituals, 134;
flexibility of timeliness of,
106–108; as form of learning,
145*n15*; function of ritual of,
xiii; function to encourage

of economic incentives for development of strong merchant class, 82; tribute, 65

Trigger, Bruce, 248

Tso-chuan, 41, 64, 114

Tsu Chia, 134, 147*n38,* 148*n39*

Tsu Keng, 97*n41,* 123, 144*n3*

Tung Tso-pin, 151*n75*

Turner, Frank, 253

Unger, J. Marshall, 234

Vandermeersch, Léon, 234, 235, 237

Vase, Chigi, 248

Venture, Olivier, 235, 236, 238, 241, 242, 243, 245, 246, 247

Vernant, Jean-Pierre, 288, 305*n10*

Waley, Arthur, 113, 117*n22,* 120*n52*

Wang Hai (High Ancestor), 157, 191*n23,* 193*n25,* 193*n26,* 194*n41*

Wang Hui, 205*n149*

Wang Mang, 114

Watson, Rubie, 186

Weber, Max, 89, 90, 96*n21*

Wenwu Ding, 166

"What Did Make the Chinese 'Chinese'?" (Keightley), xv

Wilford, John, 246

Willey, Gordon, 81

Wittfogel, Karl, xvii*n7,* 66, 78

Wolf, Arthur, 159, 160, 187, 204*n135*

Works and Days (Hesiod)

Writing. *See also* Sign making, early: componential in construction of, 20; continuities in, xv; distinction between secular and religious, 235; earliest "characters" in, 229; early marks and signs, 229–233; function of, 229; graphic conventionalization and, 234; logographic system, 1, 234; Neolithic and Shang,

229–248; oracle bones as early form of, xiv, xv; in overcoming problems of mensuration, 20; perishability of materials for, 235, 236; phonetic and semantic elements of, 20; prototype, 24; scarcity of primary sources on, 235

Wu Ding, 160, 161, 164, 166, 177–181, 186, 190, 194*n10,* 194*n41,* 207, 234, 239, 241

Wu (Emperor), 54

Wu Hong, 34*n82*

Wu Hung, 230

Wu Ting, xv, 96*n30,* 97*n41,* 102, 103, 104, 106, 107, 118*n23,* 123–127, 130, 132, 133, 134, 139, 141, 144*n3,* 147*n35,* 148*n39,* 148*n45,* 151*n76*

Wu Yi, 164, 165, 205*n150*

Wu Zixu, 262, 278*n24*

Xiao Jia, 163, 165, 170, 173, 180

Xiao Shi, 167, 168

Xiao Yi, 161, 164, 165, 194*n39,* 194*n40*

Xiong Geng, 199*n82*

Xiong Ji, 199*n82*

Xunzi, 25

Yang Jia, 164, 165, 170, 180, 194*n39*

Yang (Mountain Power), 157, 194*n41*

Yang Xiaoneng, 229, 230, 231

Yan Yiping, 242

Yetts, W. Perceval, 311

Yi-ching (The Book of Changes), 107, 108, 114, 120*n52,* 130, 143

Yin-yang: complementaty alternations of, 79; impersonal cycles of, 54; metaphysics of, 132; union resulting in organized totality, 133

Yue, Anne, 237

Yu Rang, 292

Yu (Sage Emperor), 79